'*Critical Humanities from India* opens up new avenues for comparative research in the human sciences. The prospect that it uncovers is a daunting one, exciting and important. This volume is destined to become a forerunner in a burgeoning scholarly field.'

Jürgen Pieters, Professor, Ghent University, Belgium

'Seventy years after Indian political independence, a contemporary academic generation still faces the problems of radical intellectual emancipation. Not just consolidating versions of a post- or anti-colonial problematic or combating a still pervasive orientalism. But risking the recognition that the most difficult tasks of thinking disturbingly arise when the very concepts and terms with which one tries to think are themselves the problem. Whether questioning definitions of 'discipline', rethinking 'community', challenging the notion of 'caste', shifting 'geo-graphical' categories, or reconceptualising 'religion', this collection of essays contributes to the construction of an emerging 'critical humanities' for an Indian university terrain now potentially shaped as much by its pan-Asian student intake as by still dominant 'European' paradigms of how to think at all. A demanding but exhilarating collaborative undertaking by an impressive array of actively critical practitioners.'

Bernard Sharratt, Honorary Senior Research Fellow, University of Kent, UK

CRITICAL HUMANITIES FROM INDIA

The field of humanities generates a discourse that traditionally addressed the questions of what is proper to man, rights of man, crimes against humanity, human creativity and action, human reflection and performance, human utterance and artefact. The university as a philosophical-political institution transmits this humanist account. This European humanistic legacy, which is little more than Christian anthropology, barely received any questioning from cultures that faced colonialism. In such a context, this volume attempts to unravel the 'barely secularized heritage' of Europe (Derrida's phrase) and its fatal consequences in other cultures. The task of Critical Humanities is to explore the ways in which the question of being human (along with non-human others) today from heterogeneous cultural 'backgrounds' can be undertaken. The future of the humanities teaching and research is contingent upon the risky task of configuring cultural difference from non-European locations. Such a task is inescapable and urgently needed when tectonic cultural upheavals have begun to show devastating effect on planetary coexistence today. It is precisely in such a context that this collection of essays on critical humanities affirms, 'without alibi', the urgency of collective reflection and innovative research across the traditional disciplinary and institutional borders and communication systems on the one hand and Asian, African and European cultural formations on the other. Critical Humanities are at one level little more than communities on the verge (critical) but whose centuries long survival and resilient creations of cultural (and /as natural) habitats are of deeply enduring significance to affirm the biocultural diversities of living that compose the planet.

Topical and timely, this book will be useful to scholars, researchers and teachers of cultural theory, literary studies, philosophy, cultural geography, legal studies, sociology, history, performance studies, environmental studies, caste and communalism studies, postcolonial theory, India studies, and education.

D. Venkat Rao is Professor of English Literature, School of English Literary Studies, The English and Foreign Languages University, Hyderabad, India. In addition to books in English and Telugu, he has published several articles in national and international journals. His recent work is *Cultures of Memory in South Asia* (2014). His other publications include *In Citations: Readings in Area Studies of Culture* (1999), a translation of Ashis Nandy's *The Intimate Enemy* into Telugu. He has also translated into English, a Telugu intellectual autobiography entitled *The Last Brahmin* (2012). He has co-edited *Reflections on Literature, Criticism and Theory* (2004) and an anthology of essays on U. R. Ananthamurthy's *Samskara*. His interests include literary and cultural studies, image studies, comparative thought, translation, and mnemocultures. He has designed several courses interfacing culture, technology, and literary studies.

CRITICAL HUMANITIES FROM INDIA

Contexts, Issues, Futures

Edited by D. Venkat Rao

LONDON AND NEW YORK

First published 2018
by Routledge
2 Park Square, Milton Park, Abingdon, Oxon OX14 4RN

and by Routledge
711 Third Avenue, New York, NY 10017

Routledge is an imprint of the Taylor & Francis Group, an informa business

© 2018 selection and editorial matter, D. Venkat Rao individual chapters, the contributors

The right of D. Venkat Rao to be identified as the author of the editorial material, and of the authors for their individual chapters, has been asserted in accordance with sections 77 and 78 of the Copyright, Designs and Patents Act 1988.

All rights reserved. No part of this book may be reprinted or reproduced or utilised in any form or by any electronic, mechanical, or other means, now known or hereafter invented, including photocopying and recording, or in any information storage or retrieval system, without permission in writing from the publishers.

The essays (except that of Kailash Baral) included in this book were first published in a Special Issue of the *Journal of Contemporary Thought*, Summer 41, 2015.

Trademark notice: Product or corporate names may be trademarks or registered trademarks, and are used only for identification and explanation without intent to infringe.

British Library Cataloguing-in-Publication Data
A catalogue record for this book is available from the British Library

Library of Congress Cataloging-in-Publication Data
A catalog record for this book has been requested

ISBN: 978-1-138-74304-5 (hbk)
ISBN: 978-1-351-23494-8 (ebk)

Typeset in Sabon
by Apex CoVantage, LLC

CONTENTS

List of figures	ix
Notes on contributors	xi
Foreword	xiv
VELCHERU NARAYANA RAO	
Acknowledgements	xvii

Introduction: crossing (the) legacies   1
D. VENKAT RAO

1 Education and structures of moral formation: the limits of liberal education in India   26
SHASHIKALA SRINIVASAN

2 In-discipline(s): diversity, disciplinarity and the humanities   57
KAILASH BARAL

3 Sites of learning and intellectual parasitism: the case for new humanities   72
VIVEK DHARESHWAR

4 Why communalism is an *Indian* problem: the relationship between communalism and Hinduism in colonial discourse   95
SUFIYA PATHAN

CONTENTS

5 Sacerdotal violence and the caste system: the long shadow of Christian-Orientalism   117
PRAKASH SHAH

6 Caste as an impediment in the journey of a Bhakta: Lingayat Vachanas, jati and aadhyatma   149
DUNKIN JALKI

7 River literacy and the challenge of a rain terrain   177
DILIP DA CUNHA

8 Accents of memory: critical humanities and the question of inheritance   205
D. VENKAT RAO

9 Indian culture and its social security system   233
S. N. BALAGANGADHARA

10 The politics of knowledge, here and now: a conversation with Ashis Nandy   274
ASHIS NANDY AND ANANYA VAJPEYI

Glossary   292
Index   296

FIGURES

7.1	Achilles' shield in Alexander Pope's *The Iliad of Homer*, Vol. 5. London, 1736.	180
7.2	Achilles' shield in Malcolm M. Willcock's *A Companion to the Iliad*. Chicago: The University of Chicago Press, 1976, 210.	181
7.3	There is no record of Anaximander's map. But it likely resembled a map by Hecataeus which scholars have been able to reconstruct from fragments of writings. Edward Herbert Bunbury, *A History of Ancient Geography among the Greeks and Romans from the Earliest Ages till the Fall of the Roman Empire*, Vol. 1. London: John Murray, 1883.	182
7.4	A section cut through Achilles' shield shows an artefact crafted with layers. Oceanus in this crafting is not circumfluent; it is foundational, a first presence. The shield is by Quatremere de Quincy from *The Penny Magazine of the Society for the Diffusion of Useful Knowledge*, September 22, 1832.	185
7.5	Anaximander's and Hecataeus's maps may well have been two-tiered artefacts: a tier of Oceanus performing by the cycles and transformations of hydrology, terms that are familiar today in the hydrological cycle; and a tier of earth performing by the points and lines of geography. Water here has no edge.	186
7.6	G. W. Colton, 'Mountains & Rivers', in *Colton's Atlas of the World, Illustrating Physical and Political Geography*. New York: J. H. Colton and Company, 1856.	188

FIGURES

7.7 A section through the centre of the earth showing rivers descending from the sea to reservoirs near the fiery centre of the earth presumably before rising to *hydrophylacia* in mountains where they began their flow on the surface.   193

7.8 Robert E. Horton's 'The Hydrologic Cycle' in Robert E. Horton, 'The Field, Scope, and Status of the Science of Hydrology', *Transactions of the Geophysical Union*, Vol. 12, 1931.   195

7.9 The River Ganges in Jean Baptiste Bourguignon d'Anville's *Carte de l'Inde*, November 1752.   199

7.10 Rain does not flow; it rather holds before overflowing, extending like a stain across a blotting paper. With saturation and nearer the level of the sea, these overflows get deeper and move faster, appearing to the uninitiated to flow.   200

CONTRIBUTORS

S. N. Balagangadhara is Professor at the Ghent University, Belgium, and the Director of the India Platform and the Research Centre *Vergelijkende Cutuurwetenschap* (Comparative Science of Cultures). He focuses on the analysis of Western culture through its representations of other cultures, with a particular emphasis on Western representations of India and translates the knowledge embodied by Indian traditions into the language of the 21st century. He is the author of multiple books and articles. His first book *"The Heathen in His Blindness . . .": Asia, the West, and the Dynamic of Religion* (1994) develops a theory of religion that shows that religion is not a cultural universal.

Kailash Baral is Senior Professor of English and Pro-Vice Chancellor (HAG) at the English and Foreign Languages University at Hyderabad, India. He has ten books to his credit. His last edited volume *Theory after Derrida* was published in 2009. Many of his articles have been a part of anthologies. His areas of expertise include critical theory, pedagogy and northeast studies.

Dilip da Cunha is an architect and planner. He teaches at the School of Design, University of Pennsylvania, USA, and is a visiting faculty member at Sristhi School of Art, Design, and Technology, Bengaluru, India. He is co-author of *Mississippi Floods: Designing a Shifting Landscape* (2001), *Deccan Traverses: The Making of Bangalore's Terrain* (2006) and *Soak: Mumbai in an Estuary* (2009), and co-editor of *Design in the Terrain of Water* (2014).

Vivek Dhareshwar is Scholar-in-Residence at Srishti Institute of Art, Design & Technology, Bengaluru, India. He is at present working on the idea of ethical action in Indian thought and on the link between normativity and experience. His recent work has revolved around reconceptualizing the human sciences through the resources of Indian intellectual traditions.

Dunkin Jalki is Director of SDM Center for Interdisciplinary Research in Humanities and Social Sciences (CIRHS), Ujire, India. He has previously written about the caste system, Indian traditions and colonialism, both in English and Kannada. He has co-edited the book *Western Foundations of the Caste System* (2017). He is currently working on the way European story of Shaivism developed and crystalized between 16th and 18th centuries, and the way it influenced the late 19th century anti-Brahmin movements in Tamil Nadu and Karnataka. He is a member of the India-Platform.org.

Ashis Nandy is a renowned social theorist and public intellectual. He is former Director and currently Senior Honorary Fellow of the Centre for the Study of Developing Societies, New Delhi, India. His recent work is *Regimes of Narcissism, Regimes of Despair* (2013).

Sufiya Pathan is Assistant Professor at the Centre for Interdisciplinary Research in the Humanities and Social Sciences (CIRHS), Shri Dharmasthala Manjunatheshwara College (SDMPG) College, Ujire, India and a Research Collaborator with the India Platform. She works within the research programme of the Comparative Science of Cultures and has mainly addressed research questions within the domains of communalism and caste studies.

Prakash Shah is Reader in Culture and Law at Queen Mary University of London, UK. He is co-editor of the book, *Western Foundations of the Caste System* (2017, with Martin Farek, Dunkin Jalki, and Sufiya Pathan). His other recent publications include *Against Caste in British Law: A Critical Perspective on the Caste Discrimination Provision in the Equality Act 2010* (2015) and *Family, Religion and Law: Cultural Encounters in Europe* (2014, co-editor). He is also editor of the Routledge series on Cultural Diversity and Law.

Shashikala Srinivasan is an independent research scholar based in Bengaluru, India. A Fulbright–Nehru Scholar (2012–2013) and formerly a senior faculty member of the English Department in Mount Carmel College, Bengaluru, she pursued her doctoral study at the Centre for Study of Culture and Society (CSCS), Bengaluru in the field of education and culture. She is currently working on a book that is based on her doctoral thesis. She is also a visiting faculty member at Srishti Institute of Art, Design and Technology, Bengaluru.

CONTRIBUTORS

Ananya Vajpeyi is Fellow and Associate Professor at the Centre for the Study of Developing Societies, New Delhi, India, and a Global Ethics Fellow with the Carnegie Council for Ethics in International Affairs, New York, USA. She is the author of *Righteous Republic: The Political Foundations of Modern India* (2012).

FOREWORD

Of all the evils of colonialism, the most insidious one is that the evils appear as benefits. A colonized mind cannot by itself see that it is colonized. Some inner disturbance or feeling of inadequacy should provoke it to go deeper into itself and search. Such a search does not immediately yield the necessary results. The search itself unfortunately follows the known habits of thinking colonially inevitably. But the search slowly, by trial and error, begins to break the hard shell of habit.

I used to tell my friends that English as a language is not innocent – no language is; but English has erased our languages, instead of existing alongside as a new language in any multilingual mind. That's when we began translating everything. We could only see anything through this translated view, which has become our worldview. Without English, which gave us our worldview, we were afraid, we lose our world.

Imagine a person whose head is covered by a large pot, with two holes in it. The pot has become inseparable from his head, and therefore it is his head. The two holes in it through which he has got used to see the world are his eyes. If you tell him that you would break the pot so he can see better, he vehemently objects, because he fears he loses his eyes.

That's where the colonized minds are: seeing everything through translation, seeing everything through the two holes in the pot which we know/think are our eyes.

The mother tongues we speak are themselves translations; they are no more the languages of our own. 'Mother tongue' itself is a borrowed word. We live in a world given to us through translation.

To see a world our own languages created for us, we have to break the epistemological pot that envelops us. We cannot break it from inside, because there is no outside we can see from there. Is there anybody out there who could help crack this pot?

FOREWORD

I am saying 'language', which is itself a translated word. Does Dandin intend this when he said,

Idamandham tamah krutsnam jayate bhuvanatrayam
Yadi sabdahvayamjyothi rasamsaram na deepyate

[If the light named sabda (resonance) has not shone from the beginning of the universe, all the three lokas would have remained in darkness]

Over the last few decades, a wave of brilliant flashes of light have kept appearing giving us hope that the darkness that this translation has enveloped us may be dispelled, may be. And this anthology of essays edited by D. Venkat Rao is one such flash, or a collection of flashes.

S. N. Balagangadhara, Ashis Nandy, Vivek Dhareshwar and Venkat Rao, who leads the path, have generated a trail of new thinking about colonial impact on Indian psyche. Each in a different way, they have brought up the need to uncover what lies hidden under the thick layer of colonized consciousness. It is not an easy task when everything attractively called modern in India is inevitably the product of colonized mind. One runs the risk of appearing anti-modern, and backward looking – two damaging labels in contemporary intellectual culture. It might sound shocking if I say that Gandhi, Tagore and Ambedkar are products of colonial thinking. The BJP and the *sanatanadharma* it promotes is the brainchild of Max Mueller.

There is the perennial question: is precolonial culture recoverable at all? For scholars like Gayatri Spivak think it is not. It is so far gone from our memory that we can only think along the hybrid world that produced us. We cannot avoid the route given to us by Plato, Hegel, Heidegger and, especially, Foucault and Derrida. Even Shankara, Abhinavagupta, Manu, the Mahabharata and the Ramayana do not escape colonial footprints. We read them through linear critical editions which the Western knowledge of the text has given to us. Time and space has been linearized for us, so we have no problem in asking questions like when was the Mahabharata war fought and when did Valmiki write his Ramayana.

The awareness of an epistemic violence done by colonialism is healthy, but to locate and recover the episteme that was subjected to violation is not going to be easy. There is always the risk of inventing a precolonial past that sounds plausible, but one that leads to an undesirable future.

FOREWORD

There is a very thin line to tread or we would fall into the abyss of regression. One way to go beyond the distortions of translation is to attend to precolonial literatures of India's languages, both oral and written. A few writers during colonial and postcolonial period moved through the epistemological crisis. Viswanatha Satyanarayana is one such writer in Telugu with a clear awareness of the colonial impact.

Venkat Rao has presented substantial summaries of all the papers of the volume in his Introduction, much better than I can. Still, I would not refrain from expressing my wonder (*adbhuta*), at the pathway to new knowledge in Indian thinking which I experience in reading the essays in the book.

Velcheru Narayana Rao
Visweswara Rao and Sita Koppaka
Professor in Telugu Culture, Literature and History
Middle Eastern and South Asian Studies
Emory University, Atlanta, USA

ACKNOWLEDGEMENTS

No work is just an individual's alone; a work emerges as an instant of converged efforts of many in an inexhaustible duration that precedes and follows the convergence. This particular volume is the result of the efforts of several people, and I wish to express my gratitude to them.

First of all, I wish to thank P. C. Kar who invited me to edit a special number of the *Journal of Contemporary Thought* on *Critical Humanities*. This volume is the result of the special number. I am grateful to P. C. Kar for permitting me to bring out the special number in a book form.

Despite his very busy schedule, Velcheru Narayana Rao kindly agreed to write the foreword to the volume. I deeply appreciate his gracious support despite my frantic mails.

It is always a pleasure when one receives critical and informed response about one's work. I was lucky to get such response from both Bernard Sharratt and Jürgen Pieters. I gratefully acknowledge their extended comments and views on the volume.

I wish to take this opportunity to thank the two anonymous reviewers of the proposal and the manuscript for their insights and suggestions.

No work can see the light of day without the tireless efforts of an invisible team that shapes the work into a book. I wish to thank such a significant team working at Routledge (India) for their extended support. Dr Shashank Sinha, Antara Ray Chaudhury and Avneet Kaur have taken care of the work from the initial correspondence to the final review.

I greatly appreciate Kate Fornadel and the editorial team for the meticulous attention and care with which they processed the manuscript for publication. I am grateful to Shreesha Udupa for compiling the index.

Finally I wish to thank my wife Shobha for her patience and support.

INTRODUCTION
Crossing (the) legacies

D. Venkat Rao

The double bind

India's largest student population in tertiary sector goes to study the humanities and social sciences; perhaps this is the largest in the world pursuing such studies. The classroom composition in India has changed significantly in the last few years. Students from Africa, Iraq, Iran, Yemen, the Central Asian Republics, Afghanistan, Indonesia, Vietnam and many other countries and cultures commingle in the humanities classroom in India today. But the Indian classroom that receives the members of these other diverse cultures itself is composed of a (restive) dynamic assemblage of students from varied cultural backgrounds from within India. Yet, this remarkable factor of divergent cultural backgrounds plays no role at all in the teaching and research in the humanities in the country. The university and the college – on both sides of the table – are yet to address the question of cultural background in the context of what we do on a daily basis in the classroom. In the absence of inquiry into such a critical issue, other set of related questions – pertaining to the necessity and purpose (why?), nature and substance (what?), the mode and manner (how?) and above all, and in a word, the context and location (where?) – does not find any place in what we do in the classroom or in the university. Consequently, the field of humanities as a European cultural and historical legacy, an epistemically and epistemologically violent transplant gets reinforced by the very illegitimate addressee (the native subject) that was brought forth by colonial violence. Illegitimate because the implied reader of the discourses of humanities was not the native, but by default the European (or North American).

The discourse and the institution (university) of the humanities are a part of European adventure – an adventure in elevating itself as the vanguard of mankind and the leader of the planet. It is also a protracted adventure culminating into the creation of what can be called the European (or Western) episteme. This episteme gets forged on the basis of appropriating the pre-European pagan (Greek and Roman) cultures on the one hand and suturing the flayed bonds of the children of Abraham on the other. Now it is this episteme that crusaded its path to ascendancy and institutionalized itself as the paradigm for thinking in general. To parody Derrida, there *is* nothing outside this Euro-Western episteme. Every concept one deals with (such as politics, literature, ethics, law, aesthetics, history and others), and every institution one works in (such as the university, judiciary, parliament and economy) is rooted in the European genus. The penetration of this genus is much more lethal, but more effective than any territorial and coercive colonialism or imperialism. For, it perpetuates an 'enabling violence' in its dissemination – the 'double solicitation' – of Europeanization and critique of its legacy (Derrida 2004b: 178).

The European episteme in its manifold forms tears apart the native from his or her long cherished epistemic and epistemological, affective-praxial experience. One gets wrenched apart from the reflective-imaginative sphere of one's existence. In a word, one loses one's language which birthed and succoured the fibres and tissues, flows and ways of one's life. Two centuries of such sustained violence has resulted in cognitive-imaginative destitution in cultures that faced colonialism. Figuring one's thought, one begins to learn, is yet to begin.

This state of being out-of-joint with the enduring inheritances cannot be simply smoothened over, and the past cannot be triumphantly exhibited at will in our contexts. History and anthropology as cognitive discursive channels to retrieve and represent the past are the very mechanics that perpetrate the epistemic fracture. Nor one can hastily, at least in the context of cultures of India (by extension, if one can hazard, Asia and Africa), proceed to write obituaries and mourn the dead. But the dead won't simply cease to exist; for, the dead too are not free from their enemies, when the latter become victorious (Benjamin 1992b: 247). Above all, without the 'dead' 'ancestors' living with/in us, Derrida contends, there can be no inheritance at all (Derrida 1996: 35–36). Language, for instance, is a 'deadly' living force that can throw us out of joint; for, it can, as recounted in Sanskrit poetic traditions, reawaken memories deeply submerged in the folds of our mnemoscapes (Sriramachandrudu 2002: 375). How to communicate such a language remains a haunting and interminable question, especially in cultures that faced colonialism.

Approaches

The locution 'reawaken submerged memories' may sound ominous to the sceptical. But such an expedient response can be more a symptom of the disjuncture – a destitute response to a cultural learning that configured transgenerational memory as an effective deterrent against the impulse for asserting agentive supremacy; intractable but transmissible, such memory disallows self-aggrandizing agencies. Whereas the discourse of humanities evolved from a culture that conditioned the possibility of foregrounding and privileging the agentive potential of man – man made in the image of god – the humanities represent human accounts of human actions, creations, reflections, habitat and relations in the world. The world as a purposive creation of a supremely intelligent and intentional creator – and man in it endowed with the same attributes and powers in a minor key – are the generative sources of the humanities. Since the world has a reason to come into being – as the effect of an intention – everything in the world can be probed and explained as the effect of reason. 'Nothing is without reason,' said Leibnitz in an epochal utterance (Derrida 2004b: 135); the import of that utterance was seen as the provocation or invitation for inquiring into and rendering account for everything that exists. Without this 'principle of reason' at work, neither the university nor science could come into existence, said Heidegger (Derrida 2004b: fn. 11. 293). The principle of reason as a humanistic concept constitutes the university and its discourses. The university is a theo-philosopheme.

The discourses and the institution of the humanities represent the human in the humanities as conceived by a particular culture. This culture appropriating the pre-European pagan and wading through the sibling battles culminates into a Greco–Judeo–Christian–Protestant form in German thought and sublimates into a philosophical nationalism in the last two centuries. This culture dexterously unites reason and faith by configuring conscience as the immanent rational spirit and elevates it as the highest moral and scientific authority. It is this faith in the accounting of conscience that alone enables a discovery of truth by means of the labour of conscience. That is, truth no longer was contingent upon an external authority either of dogma or doxa on the one hand and on an external institution (the Catholic church) on the other. Such a conscientious spirit of inquiry unleashed interpretative wars and multiplied hermeneutic institutions in Europe. This Lutheran spirit, as Derrida analyses it, was at once anti(Catholic)-institutional, but also at the same time, archi-institutional phenomenon (Derrida 2002c: 160–161). Challenging the institutional authority resulted in the advent of multiple conscientious interpretative institutions.

The Lutheran spirit universalizes what is a cultural particularity, a theologically derived relationship between man and god – as a bond of piety, by means of faith and knowledge, reason and science. The modern university in principle is driven essentially by this Lutheran spirit; the discourses of the humanities are the conscientious human inquiries. This university implanted itself everywhere forcefully. Where/how does the non-European pagan (especially Asian) find himself or herself in this genealogical theatre of Europe? Well, like Kafka's Nature Theatre of Oklahoma (Benjamin 1992a: 121), this theatre can absorb and appropriate anyone and everyone – Plato, Buddha, Nambikwara, and the Warli and Warlpiri. It can turn them into conscience-driven beings expanding faith and knowledge. Given that Europe always demarcated and distinguished itself as endowed with logos from the muthos-engrossed pagan Asia, how should the pagan Asian respond to this apparatus fabricating semblables?

Are the conscientious acts of othering of the self or teleporting and assimilationism of selves of the other mutually exclusive alternatives? Isn't empathizing quite proximate to the fraternal embrace of absorptive affective-intimacy? Isn't the faculty of imagination in all these acts essentially in the service of a unifying, totalizing and harmonizing mechanism – a universalizing drive? Should the pagan-Asian experience subsume itself under this grand planetary Abrahamic kinship? Can there be an outside for the Pagan from – to use Derrida's formulation describing Levinas's rebellion against the Greek heritage – this 'metaphysical [or theological] oppression?' (Derrida 1981b: 82–83).

Writing in memory of Bimal Krishna Matilal, Gayatri Spivak once said, one must learn to philosophize in general from the Indian sources today (Spivak [2007] 1993: 372). But, she warned, if one simply indulges in ferreting out an Indian episteme in opposition to a European one, one will be still doing old-type anthropology (Spivak 2012: 12). One must philosophize without anthropologizing. But does philosophizing free us from the European spirit of conceptualizing and universalizing? We are pushed toward the deeply sedimented problematic of the relation between the universal and the singular. Universality is the destination of conceptual reflection and such reflection abstracts from the singular and erases or suppresses its difference or its idiom. For the premise of the singular is the presumed substratum of the (abstract) universal. Any letter of the alphabet presupposes the system of alphabet and makes sense only in the context of that system; a singular life form presupposes the species of which it is an example. For such a universalizing reflection, comparison is essential; comparison appears to be a means but comparison itself presupposes the universal – the abstractable identity from the divergent comparables.

It is the premise of the universal, observes Rodolphe Gasche in a related context, that makes possible 'any relation to the non-identical . . . that is the irreducible marks proper of a singularity' (Gasche 2007: 184). It is precisely this a priori universalist thrust that determined the Romantic idea of comparative study of poetry. The task of comparison is to unite the *letter* of singularity (individual work or national literature) with the universality of its *spirit*. It is precisely with this credo that F. Schlegel 'could devote himself to the study of the non-European spiritual culture of India. *In principle*, the universal allows for a relation with the Other, even with what is inassimilable' (Gasche 2007: fn. 26 385 italics original). But with such overarching and overwhelming presence of the universal can any singular ever remain inassimilable? Isn't comparison the violent means of effacing the singular unleashed by this logic of relating ends (premises) and means? Two centuries of European thought embraced the radical singularities of the planet precisely with this imperial empathic logic of incorporating the other. The entire universalizing conceptual grid (among them the concept of religion as a cultural universal reigns supreme) of European episteme disseminated this logic of ends and means, universal and the singular – where the 'end' is presupposed as the *archia* or *telos* of reflection.

Legacies – crossings

What if the universal is little more than a reflective fiction – a particularity peculiar to a particular culture which plots reflective modes and means into divided, hierarchical opposites? Thus, what if the privileged identity of European episteme in the name of its capacity for the universal is little more than a particular cultural bias? What if the universal itself is only a variety of the singular? After all, aren't all alphabetic systems just individuated singular, particular, systems of different languages? This path of inquiry leaves us only with heterogeneity of singularities. It is indeed such singularities that proliferate and people what we call the planet. It is only the European episteme which castigates such heterogeneity as chaos in need of an originary ordering leader or a structuring architecton. What if we see the leaders and architectons also as only singular species of a genus that appears to lend itself to categorizations (singular as well as universal as singular) but defies all categorizations interminably? Or, to turn to the classical problematic: doesn't the poetic or the literary confound the division between the singular and universal? It is indeed, to take yet another pregnant example, such 'scandalous' confounding that Levi-Strauss was exposed to when he approached the Brazilian Indians with the opposed hierarchy of nature and culture or universal and particular. What he presumed to be a natural universal phenomenon – prohibition of incest – Levi-Strauss found to be deeply conditioned by cultural interdictions (Derrida 1981a: 282–284. It must be mentioned here, however, that Derrida's critique of Levi-Strauss too deploys the opposed binary between a priori propositions on the one hand and empirical deduction on the other).

Theoretical thinking, we being to learn, is only a species of thinking in immeasurable dispersals of infinite modes and articulations of being in existence. But when such a particular species of thinking arrogates to itself the power to lay claim over the divergent species of the planet in the name of humankind, it tends to appropriate the other into the same and thus effaces the distinction of the other as the other. The logic of sameness erases the difference of the other.

'But in comparing', wrote Heidegger, 'it is almost as if the sameness in question would only serve as the background against which to emphasize the differences' (Gasche 2007: 187). Sameness of the background becomes the condition of translation in dealing with singularities of existence in this logic. In a related context Derrida wrote:

> To address oneself to the other in the language of the other is both the condition of all possible justice, it seems, but, in all rigor, it appears not only impossible (since I cannot speak the language of the other except to the extent that I appropriate it and assimilate it according to the law of an implicit third) but even excluded by justice as law, inasmuch as justice as law seems to imply an element of universality, the appeal to a third party who suspends singularity of the idioms.
>
> (Derrida 2002b: 245)

Even if one agrees to the structure of this aporetic relation between the other and the language of the self(same), one cannot disavow the fact that a particular cultural response to (decision or resolution of, if there is one) this aporia and the idiom particular to the language (law, justice, politics, ethics, religion) of this particular culture continue to be disseminated as the universal model today. The double bind of this idiom is that recognition by that *particular* language is contingent upon the visibility of *its* idiom. But you cannot use this idiom without confirming your complicity with (and at once your effacement by) that language and its heritage. It is difficult to see how deconstruction – so deeply immersed in the Judeo-Christian heritage even when it devotes itself scrupulously to unravel and countersign it – can be seen as an exception to the logic of the double bind that turns the other complicitous with the programme of the same. Derrida is certainly not unaware of this.

In the context of speaking unequivocally against all kinds of injustices perpetrated historically in the present, Derrida enunciates an 'invincible desire for justice', and links it to the yearning of the 'messianic' – to the to-come. Such a yearning, declares Derrida, 'alone allows the hope . . . of a universalizable culture of singularities, a culture in which the abstract possibility of the impossible translation,' (of the other) 'could nevertheless be announced' (Derrida 2002a: 56). As can be seen here, the entire idiom of the relation to the other is pervasively Abrahamic. But the 'desire' here without any doubt is to yearn for an atheological 'religion' (Derrida's words) which will be 'effectively universal' (Derrida 2002a: 53). Even such a religion is also conceived in terms of a fiduciary relationship to the other – the other with whom one is closely fastened in a profound bond of piety.

Justice is inscribed in this act of faith in the other. That faith and pact universally constitute all singularities; everyone, in other words, is fastened in such a bond a priori. But the basis of such a pact (between self and the other) and its 'invincible desire' for universalizing such a faith are absolutes of a theological culture at once avowed and unavowed (in the attempts to salvage the heritage) in Derrida's programme of deconstruction: 'The universalizable culture of this faith, and not of another or before all others, alone permits a "rational" and universal discourse on the subject of "religion"' (Derrida 2002a: 56). How can this idiom from such a powerful and violent religious background promise the translatability of the idiom of the other (where the very concepts of translation and comparison are quintessentially derivative of this theological provenance)? Doesn't the kind of 'expectation' of the 'promise' or the 'messianic justice' it avows already convert us to the faith – which presupposes the cultural universality of religion (with or without quotation marks) and hierarchizes 'religions' – and privilege one 'before all others'?

Whereas, in contrast, the praxial modes of being and reflection that evince no use for the hierarchic idioms of universal/singular, letter/

spirit, law/justice proliferate multiplicity of idioms in heterogeneity of languages – in play and in delight. Neither of these experiential acts (play and delight) and effects can be measured in translation, nor can they be advanced as deferred promises of an infinite future. The efficacy of their auto-affective generative impulse releases immeasurable and infinite genos and genres, and these genos as cultural formations and genres as cultural forms traverse across centuries without projecting either a sovereign leader or a universal faith. Further, this pagan multiplicity, in its radial proliferation, senses the (insecure) urge to indulge in comparing singularities from the vantage of the same; but they remain indifferent to such indulgences.

One of the most significant implications of the lively praxial phenomenon is that it implicitly ('unconsciously') embodies the reflective practice of living on along with the completely other, radically different, with the wholly unlikely. It carries on clusters and constellations of non-semblables. Above all, these multitudes of singularities have remained impervious (even vehemently resist) any ideal of philosophical nationalism; in the same breath one can also say that, perhaps as a consequence, they have not surrendered to any genos-exterminating (or genocidal) drive in their millennia of cohabiting shared topo-temporalities.

The singularities of these hetero-genos neither compare nor translate and therefore do not succumb to the template of privileging theorization exclusively. But they do indeed receive and respond to the inheritance of idioms (of genos and genres) and consequently multiply and infinitize idioms in response. The idioms have no use for normativized binaries (such as the sensible/intelligible, transcendent/empirical, theoretical/practical, religious/ secular, universal/particular etc.) What such lively mnemopraxial non-semblable clusters and constellations of genos and genres can communicate in a world, dominated by the violent ipsocratic structure and the conceptual grid it unleashed globally, is the most urgent question: and it concerns everyone who is enveloped by the fraternal embrace of the Abrahamic episteme of Europe. Critical humanities reflect more an impulse drawn to respond to the urgency of the question.

The critical humanities initiative has a double task: (1) it reiterates the need to unravel the particularity of the (theological) cultural background that conceived and institutionalized discourses of the humanities and the social sciences on the one hand and the very institution called the university on the other; (2) simultaneously initiating an irredentist affirmation of pre- and non-European pagan hitherto coiled into the fatal hospitality of Europe. The risk of critical humanities is, while receiving and responding to the mnemopraxial tradition outside Europe, to explore the possibility of reconfiguring the tasks of being human in constellations composed of differentiated singularities of modes of being and their articulations.

It may look hopelessly naive to entertain such tasks in institutions, discourses and above all in a language that are through and through the legitimate heirs of the European episteme. But that is precisely the point. It is indeed the non-European locations and genos – the unintended hence illegitimate addressees and recipients of European psyche (in the sense of a mirror reflecting self-talk of Europe) – that perhaps can affirm *and* indicate the limits of Europe's invested rhetoric about mankind. It is indeed through the illegitimate non-European pagan's responsive reception of the universally legitimated European heritage that an unforeseen post-European pagan or indeed a new 'Indo-European' might, perhaps, come forth. But even for the minimal realization of any such possibility, the primary task is to sense the critical (in the sense of culturally on the edge – vanishing point) humanities (hetero-genos of singularities) that throb the classrooms of our universities.

We are yet to prepare ourselves to receive and respond to these cultural genos and their genres: that shows the measure of our responsibility and tasks in relation to our inheritances.

Experiments

This volume first appeared as a special number of the *Journal of Contemporary Thought* in 2015. The original Call for Papers formulated the theme for the special number in the following statement:

> The field of humanities as a discourse addressing the questions of what is proper to man, rights of man, crimes against humanity has come under critical scrutiny in recent years. Derrida devoted over two decades to unravel the philosophy-covered ('low') faculties constituting the humanistic institution called the university, their grounding in the 'principle of reason' (nihil est sine ratione), and went on to propose a New Humanities. The New Humanities must confront the aporia of arche (the foundational resources/heritage of reason, profession, professing, and faith) and an-archy (moving beyond or suspending the guardrail of arche through invention and the coming of arrivant), he professed. Spivak affirmed the need for a 'matricial humanities' which would

non-coercively rearrange desire. The two powerful manipulators of human desire are religion and politics – and they can be coercive in their claims over desire. In such a context through a tending of the imagination (to sense the self as the other), which only a dynamic humanities programme can impart, such a rearranging of desire can be achieved, urges Spivak.

The matrix of Derrida's meditations on the humanities and the university in particular (and his decades of oeuvre in general) remained rooted within the heritage of 'metaphysics of the West' which he characterized as 'our heritage of barely secularized theology'. His early work on the mythogram and the unity of gesture and speech of pre-agricultural modes of being, which was displaced by the millennia of writing and sedentary forms of living did not seem to initiate inquiries into the humanities from outside the heritage of the West. Similarly, Spivak emphasises that the tending of the imagination can be achieved also by attending to the most ancient traditions where myth and history are imbricated and draws attention to 'ethnicities'. Yet such affirmations are yet to open up, especially in countries that faced colonialism, any new inquiries into humanities beyond their humanistic provenance (sovereignty, agency) in the West.

No such reorientation of the discourses (of the human sciences) is likely to happen unless we undertake the task of thinking from our 'backgrounds', contends S. N. Balagangadhara. Countries that survived the colonial devastations are yet to draw on their millennial cultural resources and configure their cultural difference. Philosophical anthropology continues to be dominated by the heritage of the West; ventures of comparative thought continue to appropriate the other in the image of the self. If there were to be a future to/of the humanities, it is contingent upon the risky task of configuring cultural difference from the singularity of cultural provenance of heterogeneous communities (without community – without ecclesia) that compose our planetary existence. Such a task is inescapable and urgently needed among the cultures of the South that survived colonialism.

The experience of the South should contribute to reorienting teaching and research in the humanities. A South–South dialogue can be seen as a platform for articulating the tasks of Critical Humanities.

INTRODUCTION

Critical Humanities initiatives move in the double bind of the Western heritage. While being vigilant of the theological-humanist arche of the humanities (discourse and institution), the Southern experience will inquire into the question of being human in a given habitat along with (non-human) others. Critical Humanities initiate a series of questions of common concern such as:

1. How to teach and research in the humanities in cultures that are heterogeneous to the heritage of the West?
2. What is the place and relation of the so-called human among other life (and non-life) forms in the surviving experience of our (non-) European locations?
3. What is the place of the objectifying (constative) discourses among cultural formations which lived on for millennia by means of reflexive-praxial modes?
4. Is there any epistemic space for the filiation of logos and anthropos among the cultures of the South? Does the theological principle of reason make any cognitive sense in such cultural formations?
5. How to reconfigure the role and space of heterogeneous cultural singularities (such as jatis) within a Southern culture (like India) in the Critical Humanities?
6. If the disciplinary grid (composed of concepts such as sovereignty, agency, humankind, the world, democracy, art, philosophy, university, life, health, etc. – and the list is endless) that universalizes the particular experience of a theological culture through political power (and through cognitive ruptures – epistemic violence) what are the ways and forms through which other cultural formations can articulate commonly shareable experience?
7. How to rethink and reorient (after the epistemic rupture) cultural forms (verbal-acoustic, visual-performative, poetic-reflective, narrative-non-narrative) beyond the (constative) disciplinary appropriations of them in the discourses of anthropology and history?
8. In what ways can we learn to suture ('without alibi') the millennial relationships between cultural formations (communities, ethnicities, jatis, 'tribes') and their cultural forms – a relationship that was tore apart by the colonial violence?

9 Can we begin to conceive teaching and research activities drawing on the centripetal clusters of cultures within a geopolitical region (say Africa) and their centrifugal links to other cultural constellations (say, of Asia, Latin America, Gondwana) which lived on for millennia?

Critical Humanities are at one level little more than communities (without community) on the verge (critical) but whose centuries-long survival and resilient creations of cultural (and/as natural) habitats are of deeply critical significance to affirm the biocultural diversities that compose the planet.

It is from these heterogeneous millennial resources which are covered over by the hegemonic theological-humanist-ipsocratic discursive heritage of the West – that the South–South dialogue may forge the impulse of Critical Humanities to reorient the teaching and research in the humanities (in general) from the context of our locations.

It is from this critical context of South–South dialogue that the *Journal of Contemporary Thought* invites contributions from concerned scholars. The Critical Humanities themes for the special issue can draw on the questions and concerns indicated above. Contributions can focus on (and move beyond) themes such as:

1 Cultural singularities
2 Cultural difference
3 Conceptions of being human in a habitat
4 Clusters of cultural formations and cultural forms
5 Epistemic comparisons
6 Transcultural Critical Humanities
7 Conceptions of life and living
8 Cultures of memory and cultural technologies (from oral to digital).

From a whole range of enthusiastic responses to the call, this volume brings together a collection which intimately but critically grapples with the consequences of European intellectual and institutional legacy in/from the Indian context. Each contribution thematizes in different ways the disjuncture between cognitive and experiential domains resulting from the irruption of European legacy. All the contributions indicate (and some even demonstrate) the possibility

INTRODUCTION

of alternative ways of thinking and thematizing the problematic of being in and going about in the world along with others. It may be worth noting that this volume is not the result of any conference with a shared thematic or of a common academic project. The contributors to this volume come from different disciplinary backgrounds such as philosophy, social theory, political psychology, geography and design, law and cultural theory and literary studies. This is a clear indication that there is a deep-seated unease or disturbance among thinking individuals from cultures that faced colonialism. Some of these intellectuals like Ashis Nandy, Gayatri Spivak and S.N. Balagangadhara have over decades restlessly, publicly expounded their challenging positions through their critical work. The impact of their work is palpable in this collection. While grappling with the rupturing European legacy in the Indian context, the contributors clearly thematize, critique and distance themselves from prevailing academic approaches to colonial legacy (such as postcolonial and cultural studies.)

In her contribution, Shashikala Srinivasan confronts the oft discussed question of 'crisis' in liberal-humanities education in the Indian context. But her historical-theoretical approach to the problem sets her contribution apart from the other approaches which reduce the crisis to mere 'external', instrumental factors (such as dearth of funding, infrastructure, faculty etc.). Srinivasan traces the aetiology of the problem to the failure to understand the very concept of (humanities) education and the theoretical cultural foundations that birthed such a concept. She locates the concept in deeply nurtured Christian theological ideas of moral self-formation (*Bildung*).

In her critical account, she shows that colonialism dissimulates this theologically rooted idea of learning as knowledge-making (against the native learning) essentially aimed at moral transformation of the native. The crisis in (humanities) higher education, she contends, is mainly due to our failure to understand the conception of man that is deeply enshrined in the discourses of the humanities that we continue (instrumentally) to service. It is, however, in the work of Gandhi and Tagore she sees an acute sense of the deep cultural difference between the modern European and Indian civilizations with regard to the notion of self and its relation to human learning. Srinivasan sees the possibility of reorienting humanities education in the Indian context by drawing on Gandhi and Tagore's non-theological cultural resources.

In a way, K.C. Baral's chapter extends the arguments developed in Srinivasan's chapter and emphasizes the consequences of a failed or thwarted understanding of the humanities in the Indian context today. For Baral, the old humanities grew out of our creative engagement with the idea of utopia having immense human possibilities, with the core that underwrites human well-being. He contends that a misplaced understanding of 'diversity' has spawned indiscipline among the universities in India today. He differentiates indiscipline from 'in-discipline' – a hyphenated entry which contributed significantly to the development of the humanities. 'In-discipline' here is not an antonym to discipline as such, but it would imply a 'third position'. The 'concept' of 'in-discipline' operates with 'the logic of disciplining a discipline that ascertains its boundary' and thus puts the disciplinary formation to tests. It would provide internal critique of the discipline which would contribute to the growth of the discipline; thus, 'in-discipline' is internal to and at the same time exceeds the discipline. 'In-discipline' here would be some kind of 'anarchy' that Derrida affirmed as a necessity to question the limits of the 'arche' (foundation). Whereas, indiscipline (without hyphen) disregards and defies the disciplinary logic; in all such cases indiscipline invades as an external force on the work of the university; it becomes a corollary, say, to the 'politics of representation'. Baral contends that in the context of Indian universities, indiscipline has decisively replaced 'in-discipline'. Due to certain kind of policy decisions taken in the universities, which breed indiscipline, the 'epistemic inwardness' of the discipline declines – the internal critique of the discipline which would advance and transform the discipline through dialogue suffers; for, the decisions are taken in the name of accommodating diversity.

A glaring consequence of this is the demand for more universities and demand for 'new' but ill-thought courses. 'Mass has replaced merit, and the voice of the enlightened minority is silenced,' contends Baral. 'The outside has been the force of indiscipline on university campuses.' Without addressing this crucial problem of disciplinary decay, he argues, any amount of mushrooming of the universities is going to be only an expedient and futile exercise. Debates on re-energizing the humanities in a 'post-human era', observes Baral, have resulted in a widespread cynicism and negation. And how to find proper mooring within the humanistic disciplines in the face of 'post-tradition' and 'post-method' scenario wherein humanities are constantly interrogated by race, gender, caste, religion and so on? In the din, notes Baral, the democratic impulse of humanistic education is somewhere lost.

But can something be done? Pedagogy as a stirring force, affirms Baral, in the context of making education inclusive and productive needs to be rethought in teaching of humanities today. Like Srinivasan, he too thinks of Gandhi's Nayee Taleem as an important model in this rethinking. He concludes by pointing to the possibilities of changing humanities education in a context where the 'liberal-humanistic' model has failed in addressing the question of diversity.

In an incisive analysis of the prevailing discursive and institutional domains, extending Baral's arguments, Vivek Dhareshwar offers a focused critique of colonial legacy. This legacy has resulted either in making the long-standing Indian 'sites of learning' (in the domains of politics, art and the sciences) disappear or turned them 'parasitic' on Western models of learning. A framework from Christian European self-understanding has colonially programmed this parasitism; and such programmed model is at work in making sense of Indian intellectual traditions and cultural world resulting in the epistemic disjuncture between learning and experience, contends Dhareshwar. In a cogently and lucidly developed argument, Dhareshwar demonstrates how parasitism works in the domains of history and philosophy today. If history with its fetishism of facts destroys the past (as it was generationally imparted through the *itihasic* learning), philosophy occludes our access to experience and programmatically converts the intense reflection in Indian traditions on experience (nurtured over millennia as *aadhyatma*) into 'philosophy'.

As in the case of the previous contribution, Dhareshwar's argument too throws up a serious challenge to the way these disciplines are practiced today. Given the rupture between parasitical learning and reflective experience that the displaced sites of learning embody, it is necessary to inquire into ways of reconnecting reflection and experience by focusing on Indian sites of learning. Such inquiries, Dhareshwar contends, will open up 'new humanities' and reconfigure the university as a new site of learning freed from parasitism.

It might look counter-intuitive to many when one points out that several terms that have become commonplace parlance of the educated public today have deep roots in Christian theological culture. Some such terms that appear 'desirable' are *fraternity*, *neighbour*, *responsibility* and *freedom*. Another important term of the same set is *community* or *communality*. The term or concept already implies a certain kind of unity among the group of people it designates. In certain contemporary discussions, the term communality has acquired pejorative connotations, especially when it is ascribed to an aggressive drive to unify a group of people. But describing groups of people as communities itself is of a recent colonial origin in the Indian context.

Colonialism can be said to have initiated communalization of disparate groups of people. As a consequence, conflicts among people cohabiting a common area are labelled as 'communal conflicts'.

This tendency is historically specifiable, argues Sufiya Pathan in her nuanced critique of communalism problematic. Conflicts and tensions among groups living together get enframed, contends Pathan, from the late 18th century in terms of communalized categories such as Hindu and Muslim. It is such a tendency that designates communalism as a peculiar problem of Indian society. Despite significant historical evidence that different groups of people lived in rather relative harmony and peace – evidence recorded by colonial accounts – colonial discourse perceived and characterized only communalist conflict among such groups.

What comes out most interestingly from Pathan's argument is that the 'solution' to what colonialism designated as communal conflict was *not* what Europe invented when facing protracted communal violence in its territories. From the extended religious violence perpetrated by different Christian communities in Europe, the idea of 'tolerance' was invented as a solution. But in the Indian case, it is not the virtue of tolerance that was recommended, but a wholesale 'reform' or eradication of 'religion' itself was advanced as a solution. For the Christian Europe, the solution is toleration but for Indian 'religion' – a 'different system of religion' (not a 'religiously purged' secularism) – a solution 'that will overhaul their [Indian] thought and practice' was recommended, contends Pathan. Pathan also exposes the forked nature of the colonial 'solution'. While recommending eradication of religion in the context of Hindu communalism, administrator-scholars advanced political economic manipulation of Muslim communalism. Underlying this apparently divisive solution is the deeper theological root model of Christianity ('proselytization' as the essence of 'world religions'), which communalism discourse fails to comprehend, contends Pathan.

Clearly, as in the case of education discussed by Srinivasan earlier, where 'moral reform' was recommended, in the case of conflict religious reform (abandoning of native religion) was offered as a solution. Pathan's argument critically demonstrates the double take of religious paradigm of thought which on the one hand configures the native practices as a part of a religion and then recommends its abandonment; and, disregarding of the native modes of living along with others was blatantly at work.

If there is one single thematic about which most of the educated and many leading intellectuals of India and almost all European intellectuals (say, from Marx to Clifford Geertz) have universal consensus, it is the thematic which the Portuguese dubbed as 'caste'. What is most amazing about this consensus is that it precedes any serious inquiry by these consenting individuals; it appears to be more the result of a moralistic position than the result of any research. Such a position emerges from a Christian-Orientalist episteme, argues Prakash Shah in his contribution. This episteme, Shah adds, holds disciplinary power in designating caste as a *system*. The idea of caste as a system of oppression in this episteme, argues Shah, emerges from the presumed constitutive force of the sacerdotal or priestly violence of India.

Imposition of a religion and a priestly class on Indian cultural formations itself is the work of Christian-theological reflections on Indian culture and society. The most important aspect of this contribution is Shah's incisive critique of the legislation of the Equality Act of 2010 in the United Kingdom. This act provides a provision against caste discrimination in United Kingdom. The UK legislation is the first of its kind to emerge in the entire Western hemisphere. Shah's contribution gives a detailed account of the factors and forces behind the enactment of such legislation. But what is foregrounded in Shah's analysis is the 'disciplinary power' that regulates the legislation.

The idea of the caste system that was at work in the discussions was entirely drawn from the Christian-Orientalist theorization. What is more intriguing here is that the legislation itself preceded any adequate conceptualization of the problem – for the legislation presupposed tacitly (or moralistically) caste system as a problem – argues Shah. In the absence of any coherent theory of caste as a system and as the continuing hegemony of the disciplinary power, there is a need, argues Shah, for newer ground-level inquiries into this challenging phenomenon. His contribution points to the beginnings of such inquiries in the Indian context today.

The 'caste system' emerges as a much maligned monster of Indian culture in colonial discourse. Such a discourse generates a reactive response which, shamed by the European accounts of this cultural phenomenon, strives to fabricate a narrative of reform and seeks to legitimize it by selectively projecting it into Indian cultural past. The telos of such a narrative is to purge Indian culture of this singular cultural phenomenon as an abomination. Given the *idée fixe* of Brahmins as the originators, custodians and beneficiaries of the caste *system* an attack on this system comes out as an attack on Brahmins (or 'Brahminism'). Forged in the 19th century, this anti-caste as anti-Brahmin template motivated revisionary cultural histories in many parts of India; such histories unify disparate cultural creative figures and their enduring melopoeiac and performative compositions into an anti-caste, anti-Brahmin reformist work. What is labelled as the 'Bhakti movement' is appropriated to bolster this narrative. Dunkin

Jalki's contribution challenges this narrative with vigour and precision. Although his essay focuses closely on the cultural tradition of Karnataka known in the name of Vachana, his thesis has significant consequences for the colonial modern understanding of the Bhakti traditions of India.

Jalki demonstrates that the concerted effort to read the Vachana tradition as an anti-caste discourse is an untenable enterprise in modern Karnataka. His approach to the problem is direct and his analysis unsparing. In order to check the veracity of the claim that Vachana compositions were anti-caste enunciations, he puts the alleged anti-caste expletives to statistical analysis. His research shows that from thousands of Vachana compositions, only a miniscule proportion can be identified as alluding to *jati* nomenclatures. But his analysis further reveals that even this tiny proportion is barely unequivocal in making any statement against caste as such. The Vachana reflective compositions worked from within the cultural imagination that lives on with jati differences without coding them into some escalated communal antagonisms pitted against some putative Brahmanism.

In critiquing the colonial narrative template, Jalki does not take recourse to portraying jatis as a harmonious lot coexisting in total peace and tranquillity. On the contrary, his piece significantly demonstrates that *polemos* (in the sense of 'setting apart' or polemical differentiation) is a non-trivial critical ingredient of cultural communication and reflection among heterogeneous groups cohabiting a common sphere. *Polemos* provokes thought and response, and *polemos* enables differentiated articulations of a commonly received inheritance. Jalki shows how *polemos* worked across Buddhist, Jain and Vaidika groups traditionally and sees the spirit of *polemos* at work in the Vachana rendering of jatis. While differentiating the cultural *polemos* from the anti-caste rhetoric, Jalki's essay offers a compelling reading of Vachanas that demonstrates an alternative approach to understanding the Bhakti traditions of India.

In a substantial work of lasting significance in the first half of 20th century, the French archaeologist-palaeontologist Andre Leroi-Gourhan had argued that linearization of human thought can be related to sedentary forms of existence and to the emergence of agricultural cultivation. Leroi-Gourhan has had decisive impact on Derrida's early major work – *Of Grammatology*. In his contribution that reminds one of Leroi-Gourhan's thought, Dilip da Cunha advances the view that it is the oculocentric imagination manifesting in cartographic demarcations of the earth that led to linearization of thought. It is such a cartographic visual literacy that dominates our contemporary administrative, planning, agendas aimed at designing spatial management of human habitats and nature's rhythms.

In order to show the fatal alliance between visual literacy and 'line-thinking', da Cunha focuses on a most counter-intuitive trope: *river*. The rivers, he contends, from Thales of Miletus to the menacing master plan to network rivers of India, has emerged as a product of visual literacy and cartographic manoeuvring. All the discourses and disciplines of mythology, geography and hydrology are deeply determined by line-thinking in their repeated conceptualization of river as the flows between clearly demarcated lines (banks or boundaries).

In a gripping narrativization of this line-river thinking from European antiquity, da Cunha turns our attention to the violence of this design-engineering cartographic thought. The colossal casualty of this sedimented violence is the suppression or erasure of what da Cunha calls the 'rain terrain': 'Have rivers been imposed upon "rain terrain" that refuse to conform to the line of rivers?' Rains are ubiquitous and trans-local. They regard no borders as sacrosanct. The sheer heterogeneity of names in Indian languages to allude to the flows of precipitous waters of rain defies the dominant river-line thinking. Compared to the quanta of dispersed rain waters the bordered and regulated water flow of river is miniscule, contends da Cunha.

In the Indian context, da Cunha argues, it is the imperial Alexander rushing to invade India who seeded a 'river landscape in a rain terrain', and transformed the heaven-descending Ganga into a cartographed Ganges that flows between the engineered lines. What if the descending Ganga – due to the magnific effort of Bhageeratha – was let out by Shiva not as a line of water as is often represented, but through the multiple strands of his hair? – asks da Cunha. Although he misrecognized it and distorted its name, what in fact daunted and prevented the emperor Alexander and his army was not the water flowing between the lines (as he thought), but the immeasurably powerful downpour of rain waters of Indian monsoon. These precipitous waters aborted the emperor's ambition, contends da Cunha in his fascinating reading.

Da Cunha's critical intervention affirms the possibility of resisting the violence of river–flow–line paradigm that strides with boundaries and territorial proprietorial demarcations ('riverfront' real estate). An alternative to 'river thinking' can emerge when we learn to move with 'precipitating waters' of rain thinking. This is an unfamiliar representation, points out da Cunha, that would initiate an imagination of 'the past and future as yet unimagined'. Given the existential difference 'between river and rain thinking, Ganga and Ganges', we need a transdisciplinary imagination to return and respond to Ganga suggests da Cunha.

It should be transparent from the contributions discussed so far, though emerging from different contexts and interests, all the contributors in their own ways grapple with the European intellectual legacy and its institutional impact. They all underline the cultural specificity of European episteme – and reiterate the necessity of engaging with the question of cultural difference for reconfiguring the practices and presentations of our practices. In his contribution D. Venkat Rao focuses attention on the Indian classroom as a strategic point to engage with the European legacy and explores the possibility of reorienting this legacy from the (epistemically and epistemologically disregarded) locations of its reception. In a word, he confronts the question of teaching and researching in the humanities today *from* (and *in*) the Indian context.

If the human addressee implied in the humanities is not the non-European pagan what is his or her epistemic and epistemological space in this alienating abode that we ('pagans') continue to inhabit, asks Rao. But who is this apparently unified plural 'we' in the first place? The Indian classroom with an assemblage of hetero-genos provides a challenging context to explore these questions, contends Rao. For each of the students comes from a millennial cultural legacy proliferated in terms of differentiated cultural forms; and these cultural forms are deeply shaped by differing communicational systems.

The Indian classroom provides an immense opportunity to engage with the interfaces between cultural formations (as jatis), their cultural forms (in image, music, text and performative formats) and communicational systems. More importantly, exploration of this interface is absolutely needed in the contexts of cultures where colonialism fractured the relationship between cultural formations (jatis) and cultural forms. Without such an enduring intimate relationship, one cannot think of Indian culture in the first place, argues Rao. In order to explore these interfaces and their expansive extensions, Rao outlines a transcultural experimental critical humanities project that can be tested from any of the nodes and clusters sketched out in the experiment. Such an experimental teaching and research, contends Rao, which is sensitive to cultural resources (that is, ruptured inheritances) for the purposes of theorizing in general, may provide the possibility of thinking otherwise than the ways institutionalized by the European legacy.

Destinies

Over the years, the provocative work of S. N. Balagangadhara has begun to throw up new challenges to reflective minds. Emerging from outside the folds of continental phenomenological tradition, Balagangadhara insists upon inquiring into the cultural basis of European conceptual-theoretical claims as universally valid accounts of human experience. He advances this inquiry with uncompromising logical rigour and offers a productive hypothesis to theorizing cultural difference.

In his contribution, taking off from the major crisis of 2008 economic meltdown, Balagangadhara probes into the fundamental question: what is the place of culture in the development of a social security system? In this context, a social security system is a set of salient measures that a culture evolves to safeguard and sustain a society in times of crisis. Any such set presupposes a conception of the human being. Balagangadhara contends that the conception of human that dominates disciplines like economics, management and psychology is deeply rooted in the Christian worldview. In this conception, Balagangadhara observes, the human being is a need-based organism where needs are hierarchically (pyramidally) organized ranging from 'basic needs' to needs of 'self-actualization'. Since needs and desires are insatiable, this worldview recommends that the desire be constrained and needs be curtailed ascetically.

Implicit in this account of worldly experience is the view that the circle of objects/needs/desires will never provide true happiness on earth. Such true happiness can be attained only in seeking god. But on the earth, such a view privileges the position of a desire-constraining agency, which is none other than the state (or the church). The state manages the social security system by imposing austerity measures and dismantles welfare measures, especially when they are deeply in need for human survival. It is this theologically derivative conception of human being, Balagangadhara contends, that is at work in the so-called secular disciplines of psychology and economics.

In contrast to this dominant conception of the human, Balagangadhara develops a conception of the human from the Indian context as a being oriented toward happiness. 'Everyone can attain happiness' can be said to be the maxim of Indian culture. The happiness in question, it must be noted, is unqualified (in terms of 'true' or 'false') and it is non-competitive. Indian 'social security system' is deeply shaped by such a maxim. But happiness can be sought only when one knows what it is. But there is the rub. Ignorance – not-knowing – comes in the way as an active force in seeking happiness. Ignorance is like Desire in Indian traditions. They both are objectless but can cathect on any object or issue. Ignorance and desire perennially try to dissimulate the dualities of pleasure and pain as real happiness. Indian traditions advance a conception of the human who can seek happiness by enduring the transient dualities of pain and pleasure, suffering and joy *and* experience happiness that is irreducible to such dualities. Happiness here is not a discursive but experiential knowledge which each individual can attain by seeking it through, but beyond, desire and ignorance. Happiness (*eudaimonia*) is not a need or desire, but something that can be sought and which is open to everyone, contends Balagangadhara.

Such a conception of human happiness has no use for the sovereign state (or all powerful god) as the supreme agent of social security. In countering the theologically determined conception of the 'human nature' (as corrupt) Balagangadhara's inquiries into cultural difference (in the context of the hegemonic conceptual corpus mentioned earlier) have radical consequences for thinking about the humanities and the social sciences from the Indian context.

The question of inheritances has profoundly preoccupied all the major European thinkers since at least the 18th century. 'We are only', declared Derrida, 'what we inherit' (Derrida 2002a: 111; Derrida 2004a: 1–19). All thinking takes place, observed Heidegger, only within the bounds sketched out by the tradition (J.L. Mehta 1970: 307). But in both these affirmations, the concepts of inheritance and tradition are seen primarily as tasks and not as some retrievable cultural capital for celebrating cultural supremacy (though, ironically, philosophical nationalism is one blatant outcome in European rendering of the tasks). Where are affirmations of such tasks in the Indian contexts today, asks the work of Ashis Nandy.

This volume concludes with a conversation with the indefatigable Nandy challenging yet again the politics of knowledge in the institutional pursuits of knowledge production. It is no exaggeration to say that in the Indian context, Ashis Nandy is the only thinker who identified professionalized discourses of knowledge production and the regulated shelters that institutionalize such productions – the university and other (social science) institutions – as part of the problem of colonized mind. Over the last three decades, he challenged the university and its progeny to reflect on their professionalized modes of production, their objectifying shenanigans of knowledge. He did not throw this critical gauntlet from some invisible self-marginalizing periphery. Almost all of his work has been for decades imploded in the hallowed precincts of some of the best universities of the world. Despite venomous polemics against him from the academy and outside, Nandy's challenge continues vigorously to unravel attempts at professionalist governance of everyday life.

The colonized mind perpetuates two kinds of politics of knowledge, suggests Nandy: (1) one that maintains an asymmetric and

INTRODUCTION

hierarchical relation between European-Western knowledge forms and idioms and the Indian or 'native' ones; and (2) the other replicates a similar hierarchy in representing Indian knowledge forms – with a hierarchy between the elite Sanskrit-textual culture on the one hand and the discredited multiple little cultures of India on the other. Nandy is intolerant of both these kinds of politics. In this conversation, what comes out most eloquently is the persistent strain of thought which demands that intellectual inquiries in India must demonstrate continuities – if they claim to be any – between ancient or classical knowledge forms and contemporary ones. In other words, culture must be experienced as a lively current and not as the vivisectable object of a cold laboratory table or dusty archive. Nor can it be projected as some precious colossus enshrined in the past for veneration. Nandy is outspoken against such claims of cultural capital. Instead of reinvigorating cultural currents, such approaches actively destroy inheritances, contends Nandy.

Nandy's work moves with the force of the weak. Only if you are sensitive to the weak force you can see its silent and almost impalpable but inescapable pull. The 'weak' referred to here are not some self-marginalizing or state-bestowed, 'statist' marginal groups. The weak here refers to the life currents of immemorially nurtured creative sources – but which barely receive attention from the colonized professional gaze. These currents and their resources certainly are the elements of 'critical humanities' that seek liveable locations on this planet. The 'colonized mind' disregards and discards such live currents. Once again, one is exposed to the intimations of these currents in Nandy's indefatigable voice in this conversation.

Nandy's critical reflections raise fundamental questions with regard to the efficacy of the discourses and institutions implanted in non-European cultures by the European episteme. Can these institutions, their methods of inquiry and the telos of their knowledge production ever open up the possibility of suturing the torn threads of cultural fabric? As is clear from his discussion of Indian classical musical and dance traditions, Nandy is sceptical of the efficacy of these discourses and institutions in advancing the tasks of inheritance indicated earlier. Nandy calls for a daring and risky reflective imagination that defies the politics of knowledge prevailing today – here and now. Ananya Vajpeyi, herself an accomplished political-cultural critic in contemporary India, adds vigour to the conversation with her concerned questions.

The European West mostly speaks with itself; this is so even when it claims to talk about/with the other. The passion, rigour, concern, and confidence and assurance with which European thinkers (and writers) engage with the question of European inheritance are difficult to find in the contexts of cultures that faced colonialism. For, the latter's cultural inheritances have been fatally ruptured by the very 'enabling violence' of European legacy. It is from this double bind (enabling rupture) that these *critical humanities* (must) learn to forge their strategies without finality and tasks without alibi through their enduring backgrounds. As can be witnessed from the contributions for this volume many voices and varied reflective idioms are deeply concerned about a common problematic: how to rethink and reimagine our pasts for bringing forth different forms of liveable learning and thinkable futures – in a word: *what do you do with what you have!?*

References

Benjamin, Walter. 1992a. 'Franz Kafka', in *Illuminations*. Trans. Harry Zohn. London: Fontana.

———. 1992b. 'Thesis on the Philosophy of History', in *Illuminations*. Trans. Harry Zohn. London: Fontana.

Derrida, Jacques. 1981a. 'Structure, Sign and Play in the Discourse of the Human Sciences', in *Writing and Difference*. Trans. Alan Bass. London: Routledge & Kegan Paul.

———. 1981b. 'Violence and Metaphysics: An Essay on the Thought of Emmanuel Levinas', in *Writing and Difference*. Trans. Alan Bass. London: Routledge & Kegan Paul.

———. 1996. *Archive Fever: A Freudian Impression*. Trans. Eric Prenowitz. Chicago: Chicago University Press.

———. 2002a. 'Faith and Knowledge: The Two Sources of "Religion" at the Limits of Reason Alone', in Gil Anidjar (ed.), *Acts of Religion*. Trans. Samuel Weber. New York: Routledge.

———. 2002b. 'Force of Law: The "*Mystical Foundations of Authority*"', in Gil Anidjar (ed.), *Acts of Religion*. Trans. Mary Quaintance. New York: Routledge.

———. 2002c. 'Interpretations at War', in Gil Anidjar (ed.), *Acts of Religion*. Trans. Moshe Ron. New York: Routledge.

———. 2002d. *Negotiations: Interventions and Interviews 1971–2001*. Trans. Elizabeth Rottenberg. Stanford: Stanford University Press.

———. 2004a. 'Choosing One's Heritage', in *For What Tomorrow . . . A Dialogue*. Trans. Jeff Fort. Stanford: Stanford University Press.

———. 2004b. 'In Praise of Psychoanalysis', in *For What Tomorrow . . . A Dialogue*. Trans. Jeff Fort. Stanford: Stanford University Press.

———. 2004c. 'The Principle of Reason: The University in the Eyes of Its Pupils', in *Eyes of the University: Right to Philosophy 2*. Trans. Jan Plug and others. Stanford: Stanford University Press.

Gasche, Rodolphe. 2007. 'Comparatively Theoretical', in *The Honor of Thinking: Critique, Theory, Philosophy*. Stanford: Stanford University Press.

Mehta, J. L. 1970. 'Heidegger and the Comparison of Indian and Western Philosophy', *Philosophy East and West*, 20 (3): 303–317. JSTOR website (accessed on 28th July 2008).

Spivak, Gayatri Chakravorty. [1997] 2003. 'A Memoir', in P. Bilimoria and J. N. Mohanty (eds.), *Relativism, Suffering and Beyond: Essays in Memory of Bimal K. Matilal*, pp. 372–375. New Delhi: Oxford University Press.

———. 2012. *An Aesthetic Education in the Era of Globalization*. Cambridge, MA: Harvard University Press.

Sriramachandrudu, Pullela. 2002. *Alamkarashastracharitra*. (Telugu). Hyderabad: Nandanam.

1
EDUCATION AND STRUCTURES OF MORAL FORMATION
The limits of liberal education in India[1]

Shashikala Srinivasan

When we examine the narrative of crisis in the institution of the university as articulated in the West and non-West, we find a striking difference. The story told of the university in the West is often one of decline of liberal education. The anxiety is that the university of culture, central to which is the idea of humanities, has fallen prey to the global market and given way to the university of administration. The typical response to such a crisis has taken the form of a recognition that yet another moment has emerged when the conception of education has to be clarified, the original arguments recovered and reasserted.[2] In contrast, in postcolonial Asian contexts such as India, the story told is one of the university of culture and the corresponding idea of liberal education and learning *never having taken root*. It is this conviction that underlies the more recent response of a few scholars who have proposed that the solution to the current crisis in the university is the introduction of liberal (arts) education.[3] While one may readily accede to this solution, on reflection, the solution is stranger than it first appears. The 19th century university has always been tied to the idea of liberal education. If despite the university being around for more than one and half centuries in India, liberal education has not taken root, then it is unclear as to what it means to introduce liberal (arts) education as a solution to the current crisis.

Has the scholarship on the university in India been driven by a search for an answer to the question of institutional crisis and the idea of liberal education not having taken root? In the first section, I examine the dominant diagnoses forwarded to understand the crisis in the university in India. I extract a peculiar feature of the contemporary debate on the university: though the scholarship is keen on understanding the crisis in higher education, it does not talk about *the core concepts of education* at all. It instead sees external reasons – institutional, social, political and managerial issues – as causes for the crisis. Why is this so? This silence, as I show in the second section, is not because there is something deficient with our social fabric, but because the concept of education as *Bildung* (self-formation) or the realization of the moral agent as a self-determining individual that undergirds the modern university derives from a theological frame and is not easily accessible to us. When this normative model of education comes to us with British colonization, far from being neutral as the 'sciences of man' may expected to be, it is evaluative and detects a 'moral lack' in the natives. Liberal education in India is therefore *aimed at the moral transformation of an entire people*. I trace the debate on the effects of liberal education and the distortions that manifest as a crisis in the late 19th century in the third section. In the last section, I show how Tagore and Gandhi respond to the late 19th century debate and reopen the question of education and formation. They offer a diagnosis that is as relevant today as it was then and which the contemporary scholars on education entirely miss: the crisis in education is a crisis in *education*. I analyze Tagore and Gandhi on education in order to show that underlying their problematisation of liberal education is another conception of education involving different structures of moral formation that we have barely begun to conceptualise.

Contemporary diagnoses and proposed solutions

Contemporary scholarship on the university in India is replete with the rhetoric of crisis. However, till date, we have no systematic analysis of the crisis or an assessment of the various explanations forwarded to explain the phenomenon. With some effort, we can extract four basic explanations in the scholarship that attempt to understand the problem.

The first strand of scholarship locates the problem in the *structural limitations* of our institutions which are said to bear the imprint of colonial times. Given the formulation of the problem, the solutions are structural in nature: the creation of more deemed universities and autonomous colleges, the restructuring of the system of affiliation, the creation of research academies within the ambit of the university, and so on.[4] However, institutions are always more than just the physical structure. They are formalizations of already existing organized patterns of actions and traditions of learning in a particular community. Without having an adequate understanding of these underlying conceptual and learning structures, we can mistake effects for causes. After all, it is possible to say that what are identified as causes, such as unplanned expansion of affiliated colleges and the decoupling of research from the universities, are more *an effect* of incomprehension or a lack of self-understanding of the nature of modern institutions than being the cause of the crisis.

The second response locates the problem in *a systemic collapse* of our institutions of higher learning and emphasizes quality with a managerial focus on governance and measurement as solutions.[5] Often, the lack of quality in higher education is correlated to the lack of quantity. The National Knowledge Commission, for instance, followed this route and recommended an increase in the number of colleges, universities, infrastructure, funding and doctoral students. This is despite the fact that in many state and central universities, enrolment is way below the expected levels (Tilak 2007: 630). Moreover, the paucity of good research proposals in recent times has been a greater area of concern than lack of funds per se, at least in certain disciplines (Deshpande 2008: 26–27; Vaidyanathan 2008: 21). Further, the concept of quality remains fuzzy and mostly of rhetorical value. Rather than focus on any core aspects of education, it restricts itself to an instrumentalist approach to education and a narrow understanding of learning as 'something that can be planned, predicted and accurately measured when it has occurred' (Kumar 2010: 10). While the concept of quality may help *indicate* the problem, it does not help us conceptualize the *nature* of the problem which clearly lies outside the ambit of a managerial gaze.

For the third strand of scholarship, the crisis is one of *inherited intellectual frameworks*. Postcolonial studies, for instance, argues that the crisis of our institutions is the result of the imposition of alien frameworks of categories and thoughts produced in another culture. When these sets of ideas and institutions are transplanted into the non-Western contexts through British colonization, they not only limit our understanding of these cultures, but have unforeseen and complex consequences, the effects of which are still to be investigated (Joseph 2006).

While the mismatch between concepts and 'lived experience' is a common theme that runs through much of postcolonial writing, the emphasis of each is different. At the risk of sounding reductive, one could say that while Ashis Nandy focuses on the imperialism and alienness of European categories which violently fit the people of a different culture into certain given normative European categories, Partha Chatterjee focuses on the different trajectories these concepts take in our context making a case for 'our modernity', Chakrabarthy calls for 'provincializing Europe' and Kaviraj on the limited penetration and externality of these concepts and institutions in India.[6]

It is unclear, however, why ideas, concepts and institutions cannot be imported from one culture to another. For instance, if we take the example of natural sciences, we find that nobody would dispute the universality of concepts such as gravity, mass or force, despite the fact that natural sciences originated in the West. What determines the mobility of a concept? What kind of concepts lose their cognitive value in a different cultural context, and why? These questions remain unanswered. Although the postcolonial theorists draw attention to the disjunction between experience and inherited intellectual frameworks, a generalized understanding of the problem is insufficient for our purposes and the space of higher education continues to be opaque to us.

The fourth response, mostly from a section of humanities scholars and social scientists, *questions the very perception of crisis*. It attempts to nuance the generalized understanding of the problem in two ways: by showing through empirical analysis that the crisis story does not hold for all of South Asia equally and its extent also varies across institutions and disciplines (Chatterjee 2002a), or by arguing that the motif of 'decline and crisis' is a reflection of changes in the social context (Deshpande 2008: 25–28). Here, it is not the crisis as much as its perception or *the crisis discourse* itself that is seen as requiring investigation. Chatterjee's attempt is to draw attention to the fact that the crisis is not a *macro* phenomenon as it is often thought to be but a result of *micro, region-specific* or perhaps even *institution-specific* problems which cannot be generalized. He observes that where institutions have indeed declined, it is due to varied reasons: in some cases, the foundations for research were not properly laid out, in some political reasons played a role and, in certain other cases, it was due to the withdrawal of government funding and the changing nature of research. Deshpande sees the changing place of academia, the entry of new castes and classes into higher education into spaces hitherto occupied by the elite and the later generations having to share intellectual and institutional space with much larger numbers as the reasons behind this perception. Implicit in Deshpande's formulation is the idea that the crisis discourse itself is an expression of interest groups in the society.

While one can agree that we need to take into account the changing social composition at various levels, it is not clear why this change should result in the growing but 'false' perception that there is a crisis in the Indian higher education. Even if this is the reason for the perception, it should be possible to counter it through other means such as garnering statistical data to show that it is a faulty perception, without any basis in evidence.[7] Besides, if we assume that 'good' institutions should be able to produce creative, independent thinkers irrespective of the social background of the students, then their failure to do so is reason enough to think about the vitality of our institutions. After all, strong, vibrant institutions are likely to have the ability to initiate students (irrespective of their social background) into the tradition of learning they embody rather than themselves be transformed by the interests of varying groups who come into these institutions (which is more often the case in our context).

While sociological factors are indeed extremely important to nuance our understanding of the crisis, as an *explanation* of the crisis, it remains unconvincing: rather than explain why people perceive a crisis if there is none, it merely 'explains away'. To use an example, if a pencil appears bent in water when it actually is not, a good explanation must be able to tell us why it *appears* bent without questioning the integrity of the perceiver's experience. This should also be the case when we seek to explain the perception of a crisis in higher education. Instead, the perception of the crisis itself is seen to be generated by one's location and therefore an immoral act driven by interests. If all accounts can be reduced to interests of groups, then each explanatory account, including the one under discussion can be charged of furthering specific interests, *ad infinitum*. If our arguments, perceptions and use of concepts are, as Mehta puts it, mere 'ruses of power', primarily structured by our identity and class/caste interests, then why bother to have a discussion at all? (Mehta 2006: 2425)

The various diagnoses considered above, despite their differences, share a puzzling feature. Although each strand of the scholarship is an attempt to understand the crisis in the sphere of higher education (directly or indirectly), they do not talk about *the conception of education* at all. The debate on the crisis in higher education quickly becomes a crisis in institutional structure, a governance issue, a reflection of crisis in politics or an expression of interest groups indicative of the divided nature of the Indian social fabric. This is true even of postcolonial scholarship which deals *specifically with the domain of education*. Influenced largely by Said's Orientalism, this strand of scholarship sees education as a reflection of politics: as a site for either manufacturing consent for those in power or one of resistance by the oppressed.[8] Why is this so? What is the specific conception of education underlying the modern university, and why is it not easily accessible to us? For an answer to this question, we have to turn to the emergence of Bildung or education as self-formation that emerged as the highest good (*summum bonum*) in late 18th century Prussia (Beiser 2003), leading to the rise of the Humboldtian ideal of the university, the model that is still with us today. Grasping the concept of Bildung will not only make us appreciate the depth of the debate on education in the West, but will also allow us to identify the line of thinking, the 'category habit',[9] that governs this model of education.

The idea of Bildung (education as self-formation)

The concept of education encompassed by the term Bildung emerged as central to the European cultural-intellectual landscape in the late 18th century. The term, however, has its origins in 14th century mysticism and is based on the biblical doctrine that man is created in the image of God.[10] The idea of Bildung as seeking self-perfection derives from the theological model of learning where one moves towards God by means of self-fashioning, where the soul (the copy) models itself after the original that God has imprinted in each of us. In its religious form, the model was related to the monastic order and involved spiritual practices, central to which were (a) *absolute obedience* to the master of the monastic order and (b) *contemplation of one's thoughts* (involving introspection of one's conscience *which was anterior to all actions, will and desires*) to separate those 'true' thoughts that led towards God from 'false' thoughts that were implanted by Satan (Foucault 1999: 174–176). In this process, the authority of the texts and the master played a crucial role. By disclosing one's impurities to God or the larger monastic community and bearing witness against oneself, one purified one's soul, a necessary condition for access to truth or God. It was through this verbalization and continuous disclosure of the self that one moved towards the renunciation of one's own self: 'We have to sacrifice the self in order to discover the truth about ourself, and we have to discover the truth about oneself in order to sacrifice ourself' (Ibid. 179).

The theological model, however, is secularized by the Pietist[11] thinkers of late 18th century Germany. The concept gets divested of its explicit theological content and emerges as a rallying point around which the idea of education and self-formation are debated. While Bildung earlier acquired its meaning within the framework of salvation, the idea of self-sacrifice to an *external, sovereign* agency now gets reconfigured by *pushing God (and divine attributes) within oneself*. The process of active self-fashioning that the copy is engaged in, in order to approach the archetype, becomes in the hands of Pietist thinkers like Herder, 'rising up to humanity through culture' (Gadamer 2004: 9). The technique of disclosure which was earlier related to the renunciation of one's self in monastic practices gets linked to the constitution of a new, positive, expressive self (Foucault 2000: 249).

In the process, the Aristotelian legacy is completely transformed. In *Nichomachean Ethics*, Aristotle (2004) had identified the highest good for human beings as *eudaimonia* (happiness) which could be attained by leading a life of excellence. Such a life involved *exercising reason (arête* or the virtue of a human being), developing the *potentia* or *capacity to discern and contemplate the order underlying the world*. In the German thinkers, we find the notion of 'reason' still resonating; however, it gets mediated through secularized Christian theology[12] to mean *the ability to set ends and be self-defining*.[13] Human potential now gets understood as the cultivation of self-determination, setting one's ends to realize one's unique, individual personality and, above all, cultivation of one's will as that of God's (the archetype) intent. Thus, conceptually *freedom* supplants Aristotle's *eudaimonia*: the end strived for is moral and intellectual autonomy, that is, imparting purpose to one's life by following the law one gives oneself and realizing one's true self. It is by transcending the limits set by nature, traditions and other forms of authority, by *committing ourselves to values/ends that we set ourselves by choice* that we become really human. Only then do our actions have moral worth and *are our own*. Further, in Aristotle, virtues actualized are ideals in human nature, that is they are available as exemplars *within* the culture. In contrast, the ideal for the Romantic Bildung is modelled on God who is perfect and *transcends* the world. Even with secularization when the overt emphasis on God is removed, the idea of a normative ideal that goads us *from beyond and against nature* remains. The human 'form' now involves an inner force within oneself struggling against an external world to reveal the unique form of life that one is called to realize.

We see here that secularization is not hostile to Christianity, but religious ideals are reformulated such that *they could be realized in this world*. The transcendent becomes immanent, with the unity of reason and will to be realized as a universal duty, in the form of the categorical imperative. One can recall here the Kantian exhortation to use *one's own understanding* (Kant [1784] 1996: 58) and the categorical imperative where one ought to act in accordance with 'that maxim through which you can at the same time will that it become a universal law' (Kant [1785] 2002: 37).

While all thinkers agreed that Bildung or education was the highest good, they inflected the theological model in specific ways. Kant emphasized ([1785] 2002, [1803] 2003) the cultivation of reason as the autonomous willing of moral law to guide action (as theoretical knowledge regulating practical actions) in the process of Bildung.[14] Herder (2002), Schiller ([1794] 2005), Hamann ([1784] 1996) and Humboldt ([1809] 1970, [1793] 2000) objected to the Kantian understanding of reason as an autonomous, a-historical faculty and the *singling out* of reason as the *only* potential worth cultivating. They instead highlighted the salience of the 'expressive' being articulating nature and man as a harmonious unity and underlined the importance of cultural inheritance – religion, history, literature, art and sensibility – as a means for cultivating Bildung.[15] For Hegel, Bildung is the development of conceptual thought through 'the *education* of consciousness itself to the standpoint of Science' (Hegel [1807] 1998: 50). Here, consciousness (the divine imprint) moves away from objects of nature towards itself as the source of categories of understanding, leading further to self-consciousness where *the self emerges as an object* for further reflection.

Secularization, we see, universalizes the religious model by privileging the self as an entity, the source of relating mind and the world, subject and object through the process of education or Bildung. In this process, the overtly religious emphasis on God is removed. However, God is now transmuted into concrete forces of history. Divine attributes are transferred to man and reason and morality are combined within the individual self, now to be cultivated as human capacity. The theological origins of these attributes become invisible over time and emerge as self-evident truths.[16]

The 'universal man' and *cultivation of humanity through culture* emerge as separated from the logic of practices in and through which one is constituted, and education emerges as a distinct, separate domain. It is through education that one becomes autonomous where *one actualizes one's will/self* by establishing independence from nature, traditions and other forms of authority and emerges as *a rational and moral agent*. In this scheme, *beliefs and theoretical justifications based on principled reasoning are seen to be prior to actions,* and actions themselves are *subject-expressive*. These assumptions and the notion of moral agent, as is evident by now, cut across several disciplines – both humanities and social sciences.

However, the development of one's capacities to emerge as autonomous and the unfolding of it was a process which took place in history – both as an individual and *as a species*. Bildung then becomes the development of given capacities of individuals and the human race to be realized in history, with the theory of education and self-formation firmly placed within the philosophy of history, where 'less-advanced', 'inferior', civilizations progress towards their species-end of *moral autonomy*, thereby actualizing their species-essence through education. History, then, is the education of the human race, with people and nations struggling towards the development of their humanity, towards reason and freedom.

Colonial education: a solution to 'moral lack'

The debate on Bildung in Europe, despite internal differences, aimed at the harmonious self-development of the individual in varied and open-ended ways. However, when this normative model of education with its deep cultural roots and evaluative force comes to us with British colonization, the anthropological 'picture of man' central to it breaks down. The background conditions that exist in a religious culture like Europe, such as notions of man modelled in God's image, God's plan, the world and the actions in it as an expression of His will, God's imprint in each of us, introspection of one's conscience to separate out actions that are 'true' from those that are 'false', obedience to God's moral laws and the medieval monastic practices are all absent in the Indian context. Secondly, there are myriad, alternative forms of knowledge and learning with a focus on 'actions', 'application' and 'practice' that are present and transmitted. However, rather than probe into this difference and inquire into forms of understanding of another culture, the normative ideal of education that the Europeans possess, only makes them detect a 'moral lack' in the natives. They find the natives violating a fundamental norm of truth that regulates their own lives in Europe which they consider as universal. Therefore, they consider the natives as immoral and as having lapsed from an approved normative standard of morality. As a result, colonial education focused on a moral transformation of natives at the expense of knowledge generation, discovery and understanding.

The problem of truth and moral lack surfaced in two significant ways in the cultural encounter between the Europeans and the natives: (a) the natives, according to the Europeans, had no respect for truth and their actions did not correspond with what they 'genuinely believed' or held to be true. They were 'insincere', 'unprincipled', 'liars', 'deceitful', 'dishonest' and 'hypocritical'.[17] (b) They did not make truth claims about the realm of practices. In other words, they were insensitive to the truth claims of doctrines of Christianity or any other religion.[18]

The British located the cause for this 'lack' in Hinduism, the 'false' religion which was the source of immoral practices and cognitively false claims. This is true of the Orientalists, Anglicists and the missionaries, all of whom shared a common description of the problem.[19] All factions agreed that the natives and their society were degenerate and that Western education was required for 'the moral, intellectual and spiritual improvement' of the natives. There were, no doubt, internal differences. The Orientalists believed that India was once morally and intellectually excellent, based on the sound principles embodied in its ancient texts. However, subsequently, the natives had become ignorant of this scriptural knowledge and the laws embodied in them, resulting in their current degenerate and immoral state. The task therefore was now to cleanse the native texts which had been corrupted by the priestcraft and the accretions of tradition, and give the natives their own laws back. The means to improve the society and reform the traditions of the land was therefore through a renewal of its ancient textual heritage in Sanskrit, Arabic and Persian.

The Anglicists and Utilitarians on the other hand believed that the ancient texts of the land were riddled with errors and that Hinduism was always a false religion with false gods and a corrupt priestly class. Forming the natives through initiation into their own classical texts was to be indifferent to truth and worse, encourage the cultivation of falsehood. These traditions and texts *could not be reformed and purified*, but must be *rejected as false*. Instead, the natives should be formed through their education in English literature and sciences and introduced to 'useful' knowledge. The missionaries emphasized education in the vernaculars, which would make the natives capable of reading these texts on their own without any mediation from the priestly class.

Thus, a Judeo-Christian conception of a true, monotheistic natural religion based on universal reason which subsequently degenerated to heathen polytheism due to the machinations of the corrupt priestly class structured the European conception of non-Western societies like India.[20] The colonial framework to understand other cultures did not emerge in a vacuum or purely out of interaction with the colonized and the need to consolidate colonial rule, but was shaped by the larger history of religion in Europe (Balagangadhara 1994: 31–64).[21] Liberal education was therefore envisaged as a solution to native immorality. It was advanced on moral and intellectual grounds where it would teach the natives to subject their traditions to the cognitive test of truth and falsity and inquire into their traditions as objects of historical analysis for verifiable and demonstrable truth claims. It would thereby perform the double task of liberating the natives from false religion and orienting them towards the true religion, thereby making possible moral reform. Contrary to our expectation, introduction to secular arts and sciences was not seen by the colonial participants to be in opposition to the true religion but as leading to the same goal.

The colonial truth regime therefore sought theoretical and rational grounds for the various practices of the land. This cognitive compulsion of liberal education set about a process where natives were compelled to represent their traditions and practices as expressions of underlying belief system grounded in doctrines of Hinduism. We see the emergence of a new attitude towards practices in native accounts which is best characterized as *hermeneutic*.[22] Colonial education thereby introduced new structures of reflexivity: seeking prior theoretical justifications for practices through historical analysis, subjecting the practical domain of everyday life that now comes to be overwhelmingly looked upon as a domain of beliefs to the norm of truth, involving an appraisal of them as true or false and the 'training of conscience,' which induced a form of self-examination where one evaluates one's actions against prior moral norms, a form of self-consciousness where *one's self emerges as an object* for further reflection. The emphasis on the textualization of the Indian past and the very process of social reform was the result of introducing this theological scheme through colonial education.

However, by the end of the 19th century, there emerged an overwhelming consensus that there was a failure in the dissemination of modern knowledge. Even if the expectation that liberal education would orient the natives to the 'true' religion was by the end of the century almost given up, the optimism that liberal education would result in an intellectual and moral transformation of the natives and cultivate their taste in science and arts was slowly replaced by the anxiety that Indian students did not understand the value, purpose and principles of modern knowledge and instead largely learnt it by rote. While nobody disputed the growing popularity of Western education among the natives, it was noted that Indian students pursued knowledge for instrumentalist reasons, and modern knowledge was valued as a means to an end (for government jobs) instead of being valued as an end in itself.[23]

On the one hand, instances of native excesses abounded where truth and falsity itself appeared to lose all meaning. Reason was unmoored without the force of the normative framework within which beliefs acquired their truth or falsity. On the other, various kinds of intellectual inconsistencies of the educated natives and their peculiar mental attitude were highlighted – that the Indian students lacked the faculty of historical reasoning, did not display any strength of belief which they could justify through principled reasoning, submitted to the teacher unquestioningly and opted for the path of least resistance, were untouched by contradiction and inconsistencies they harboured and failed to understand what giving one's assent to a proposition meant – and cited as examples of their immorality. That the natives gave consent to various propositions of equality and freedom in speeches and examination papers but in their everyday life often failed to meet up to the norms was also included within the ambit of immorality.[24] Both these effects were seen as results of an incomplete transition where the natives had rejected their traditions without embracing a true religion, thereby possessing no source of morality. The failure of the emergence of the morally autonomous subject who would develop the capacity to ascertain the truth of beliefs with certainty, rule out all contradictions and base one's actions on the true belief through principled reasoning became the axis along which the debate turned.

I would like to suggest that the British diagnosis at the *observational level* was not all wrong even if we disagree with their *evaluation* of it. At some level, the contours of our current narrative of crisis in the university can already be found here. However, for the British, these observations become *evidences* in a theory of education which orders civilizations vertically, culminating in European superiority, the hallmark of which is autonomy and 'inner-judgement'. We can remove the evaluative force of the British gaze and instead formulate the attitude that Indian students display as a knowledge disposition,[25] indicative of a *different* form of mental cultivation effected primarily through structures of family and community. In his *Subject Lessons*, Sanjay Seth suggests something along these lines. He argues that given the defining feature of modern knowledge is that it creates a knowing subject who is set apart from the objects to be known, he points out that the modern subject and the world as an object to be known ('the world as picture' or 'system') failed to emerge in India. This is partly so because 'another subjectivity', corresponding to indigenous modes of relating to knowledge, was diverting and frustrating the impact of modern education. Seth is aware that because he is posing the question within already available categories, the conclusion can only be presented as a 'different sort of subject' who can only be represented as an inadequate or unrealized version of the first. The challenge, he points out, is to 'search for forms of thought which allow us to recognize that there have been and are ways of thinking the world other than modern, occidental ones; but also ways of thinking difference without invoking the Subject' (Seth 2007: 45).

I would like to argue that the structures of formation and learning implicit in modern education appears to be interrupted not by the presence of 'another subjectivity', as Sanjay Seth puts it, but *another conception of education*. This is made evident in the nationalist problematization of education by Tagore and Gandhi who, unlike contemporary scholars who resort to 'external' factors to explain the crisis, sought an answer to the crisis *in the cultural difference*[26] *between Europe and India*. It is in their problematization of modern education that we find a diagnosis of the crisis as a crisis in *education and structures of moral/ethical learning*.

The nationalist problematization of education

The Indian national movement responds to the late 19th century debate on crisis in education and reopens the question on education and formation. Education emerges as the single most important problematic in early 20th century India. Many nationalist thinkers drew attention to the presence of distinct 'mental traditions' and forms of learning. Tagore, for example, is strongly wedded to the idea of the 'Indian mind' and an Indian ideal of education. Gandhi does not hypostasize anything called the 'Indian mind', but it is he who through his active ways of involving people in the act of spinning and satyagraha teaches people to understand the relation between the action, person, practices and ends. While we find them articulating their thoughts through the inherited vocabulary of 'nation' and 'religion', there is yet a sense in which their articulations on the subject constantly exceeds the conceptual limits set by the colonial, liberal framework. I would like to suggest that their response to the problem of national education is best understood not as a 'nationalist' answer, but as a way to *counter* the effects of nationalism and as an attempt to grasp something significant about the distinct patterns of learning and forms of mental cultivation specific to the traditions of the land, even if they do not have an adequate formulation of it.

The two thinkers forwarded a similar diagnosis of the educational problem: the crisis in education is not about institutional failure, a problem with the social fabric or one of bureaucratic apathy, but a crisis in *education and learning*. It is an interruption in the transmission of learning structures and concepts that help clarify and reflect on experience, factors essential to understanding and the full-fledged flourishing of ourselves. As a result, education had become an unreflective activity. Instead of enabling inquiry and understanding, it actively prevented them, thereby arresting the growth and development of the student. Therefore, it was not surprising that education had become merely a way to earn more money and get into government careers as clerks and interpreters.

What then was an obstacle to learning and 'knowing ourselves'? In his essay 'The Centre for Indian Culture or Visva-Bharati' (Tagore [1919] 2007b), Tagore locates the cause in our unassimilated acceptance of Western ideas and concepts which come to us like 'rigid truths'. For Tagore, institutions are more than just mere physical and administrative structures. It is precisely because we fail to acknowledge that the university is the outcome of a specific pattern of learning traditions distinct to Western culture, we also fail to understand the relation of Western thought and its institutions to its culture. As a result, Western thought which is flexible and living in the context of its origins, comes to us with certain immobility (Ibid. 523), merely as tools to deploy and reify or for reasons of external advantages rather than as a framework of ideas we can actively engage with. Tagore's charge is that our failure to understand the depth of the debates in the West from *our own* vantage point results in us not understanding the West or India and ourselves. Hence, one of the first steps towards a new university was that 'the mind of India has to be concentrated and made conscious of itself' (Ibid. 515). This acknowledgement of the distinctness of the Indian mind is crucial for Tagore, for the consciousness of the living traditions of India which shape our experiences and the way we go about the world was for Tagore not an ideological, nationalist position, but a recognizable, social fact for all to see and acknowledge. In short, it was given to us experientially. We had to acknowledge this distinctness, not merely to know our past, but because these intellectual traditions of the land continued to exercise their influence in the present, though running underground (Ibid. 541). To bring them to the surface was to make possible a certain fullness of life for all.

Thus, Tagore envisaged the Centre for Indian Culture, as an Indian and international centre of learning with a comparative thrust. The goals of the institution included the 'patient study' and scientific research of different cultures, specially the West and the East on the basis on their respective underlying unity.[27] It was a unity that Tagore recognized and researched into, in his own way, though he is unable to theoretically formulate the nature of this difference. His vision was one of a genuine complementarity of the East and the West where we would understand both in the most robust ways possible, making possible genuine understanding and cooperation, without succumbing to parochialism.

In his 'An Eastern University', Tagore ([1922] 2007b) poses the question of what should be the ideal that should govern the Indian Centre. Here, he gives us a startlingly different answer from that of the European thinkers on Bildung who emphasize education as the actualization of the self and the realization of the individual: 'The one abiding ideal in the religious life of India has been *Mukti, the deliverance of man's soul from the grip of self*' (Ibid. 656). Here, the influence of Indian traditions, especially the *Upanishads* on Tagore is unmistakable, and he makes no attempt to hide this influence. In some of his writings, Tagore would talk about India as a personality, the unique character of which has to be brought out, similar to the cultural idea of nation expressed by the thinkers on Bildung like Herder, Humboldt and other German Romantics. Yet, in his other writings, for instance in 'The Problem of Self', another conceptual layer leaps out where he draws attention to the fact that true knowing consists in understanding that the self which we think is real, is not a real, positive entity or an object at all:

> In the typical thought of India it is held that the true deliverance of man is the deliverance from avidya, from ignorance. It is not in destroying anything that is positive and real, for that cannot be possible, but that which is negative, which obstructs our vision of truth. When this obstruction, which is ignorance, is removed, then only is the eye lid drawn up which is no loss to the eye.
>
> (Tagore 2011: 159)

Such a mode of knowing, as he points out, *is negative in its operation*, removing the cognitive obstacles that come in the way of us learning and being attuned to the world around us. It is precisely the access to these resources that made it possible for Tagore to counter the effects of nationalism and other ideologies.

Tagore notionally recognizes the importance of the *Upanishadic* insight that the self is not a positive, real object. However, it is Gandhi who embodies and 'enacts this insight' performatively in the political arena, outside formal institutions. Gandhi locates the problem in the very nature of moral learning and structures of formation brought in by the West.

Gandhi on education

Gandhi is known for his sharp and uncompromising criticism of liberal education that we have inherited from the British. His diagnosis of the problem was stated in no uncertain terms: liberal education, he claimed, not only did not enable ethical learning, but was destructive of it. His solution took the form of education through craft as expressed in his idea of Nayee Talim (New Education). *Prima facie*, this is a puzzling response. In what way was learning through craft/arts tied to ethical learning?

Contemporary scholars have focused on the centrality of actions in Gandhi and shown how Gandhian action ruptures the traditional understanding of the relation between action and principles as embodied in the Western tradition, particularly as represented by Kant. In one of his pioneering articles, Akeel Bilgrami argues that in Gandhi, one can find a repudiation of the Kantian system of normative ethics with its focus primarily on ends, which involves a choice of an action based on a principle which applies as an *'ought'* or as an imperative to others in similar circumstances (Bilgrami 2003: 4159–4165). Since the principle generated or applied exemplifies a moral truth, any deviation from it would necessarily be wrong and invite moral criticism, something Gandhi repudiated. Instead, Bilgrami understands Gandhian non-violence as a practice of exemplarity where the concept of the *exemplar* replaces the concept of *principles*. Since no principle is generated with which we can criticize others for falling short of or violating any principle, violence or coercion is eschewed. At most, as Bilgrami points out, one can be disappointed that one's example has not set. Thus, he asserts that truth for Gandhi was not a cognitive notion where truth is the property of propositions that describe the world rendering the world as an object of detached study. Such a notion of truth, he notes, 'intellectualizes our relation to the world' by seeking principles that explain the diverse phenomena and removes the world we inhabit from the sphere of our moral experience. Instead, for Gandhi, truth is an exclusively experiential and moral notion that undergirds our practical and moral relationships.

Uday Mehta, similarly, recasts Gandhian exemplary action as an action severed from any teleology thereby divesting it of any 'deferred larger purpose' that modern institutions necessarily rely on, requiring the instantiation of larger notions of justice or equality (U.S. Mehta 2010). Thus, Gandhi, Uday Mehta points out, often accepts social life as it is, without taking recourse to an idealism (or a fundamental commitment to normative principles) that evaluates, finds experience incomplete or deficient and is transformative of given social particularities.

It is precisely Gandhi's emphasis on actions per se that contemporary thinkers focus on, recognizing it as departing from the Kantian frame. Consequently, their attempt is to rescue actions from a conception which sees them as executions of principled reasoning. If we push this insight further, we arrive outside the Kantian frame to formulate another way of thinking about reflection on action: *reflection on action can take the form of another action and is transmitted practically*. This is what Gandhi's emphasis on actions is about, which we shall henceforth refer to as 'practical knowledge'.[28]

Thus, when violence breaks out after chauri-chaura, Gandhi inserts the masses into *the activity of spinning*. He makes spinning central to the reconstruction programme and repeatedly asserts that it was the route to Swaraj. When Tagore objects to the 'cult of spinning' that he was creating, Gandhi maintains that 'I am an explorer and having discovered a thing I must cling to it. The Poet presents the world with new and attractive things from day to day. I can merely show the hidden possibilities of old and well-worn things' (Gandhi [1925] 1997b: 126). What had Gandhi discovered? I would like to suggest that what Gandhi had discovered was a new action *within the coherence of a form of life* which could serve to induce reflection on action at a nationwide level through the act of spinning, which suited the needs and demands of the time. This could be done not by asking or providing reasons for spinning (any or many would do, but that was beside the point), but by insisting on the very act of spinning. The action acquires its meaning from the current of moral activity within which it is enacted rather than from a fidelity to an external tradition of moral reasoning.

Gandhian exemplary action therefore is not as much about content, but about teaching *the ability to think without thinking about*.[29] Such an ability which aimed at curbing intentional, object-directed activity, could not be taught by giving propositions or instructions, but learnt only by doing and inserting oneself into a milieu of actions that enabled the cultivation of such ability. The insertion into the activity would help *sever external goals* imposed on oneself by the normative principles of morality underlying modern politics and education where one was prone to a third-person point of view of oneself[30] and others generated by various kinds of ideologies, thereby engendering violence. By inserting oneself within a tradition of learning, one is taught to orient oneself *to the long-standing goals internal to the practice*, thereby restoring a form of engagement with the world which is essentially practical. Gandhi here is drawing from traditions of India which transmitted such a practical form of knowledge, a form of reflection which could only be acquired through immersion in the practice and transmitted as know-how.

The dominant Western tradition envisages the acquisition of moral knowledge as acquiring prior normative principles and imperatives. In comparison with such a notion, underlying Gandhi's conception of education is ethical learning through actions and practice. Primary to this vision was the link that Gandhi made between the insertion of the body as a site of inquiry (Dhareshwar 2013b: 42) and the cultivation of virtue.[31] Gandhi had been developing the link from his days in South Africa which saw further intensification in his experiments in Sabarmati Ashram where Gandhi practiced spinning, fasting and silence. He recreated several practical domains – the domain of health and dietetics, erotic and economy, which served primarily as a milieu for the elaboration of practices of the self.[32] It is through inserting oneself into these practical domains that Gandhi problematized the nature of ethical action.

That action per se was central to Gandhi's notion of education is evident in his proposal for basic education or Nayee Talim, where Gandhi draws up the educational vision for India, completely oriented around practical forms of knowledge, with the spinning wheel once again at the centre of it. Gandhi's criticism of modern education was that the learners were removed from their milieu of action and practices. As a result, they were now lost to their parents. They had acquired a smattering of something, but whatever that was, it was definitely not education. Education through craft would not only reinsert them into existing domains of practices but would also enable the practitioner of the craft to learn the necessary ethical comportment for it, which could then be extended to other similar situations as well, possessing a wider range of reference than the practice of the craft.

Underlying Gandhi's emphasis on craft is immersion in an existing tradition of learning, of acquiring the expertise and skill in the practice of it, as well as training the learner's mind and developing the 'cunning of the fingers'. The student would learn how to make finer and finer distinctions, learn to distinguish good yarn from not so strong ones, the particular textures of cloth, the various processes involved in the picking of cotton and improve upon the practice. Learning to perform the necessary action in the process often involved cultivation of the right disposition, judgement, care, attention, awareness and mindfulness. Exactly like in learning music, the standard of correctness is internal to the practice and the idea of doctrines or beliefs remains irrelevant in these domains of actions. The practice of craft would be woven so much into one's everyday life that the article made would be part of our lives. History, arithmetic, geography and mechanics would all be integrally correlated to the learning of a craft, where practice precedes theory. In this way, a practitioner, with the necessary intellectual and ethical virtues is formed by inserting the student in the domain of activity and the ethical web and transactions the practice demands (*dharma*). Actions here are not subject-expressive (where person is seen as prior to actions), *but constitutive of the person* (the tradition of activity or the domain of action is seen as prior to the person).

If virtue is knowledge and cannot be codified in propositional terms, then how is it learnt and transmitted? Gandhi's stress on spinning, the significance of exemplary action and satyagraha as a mode through which one can become aware of the nature of action has some answers for the question. While in the West, a tradition of morality which proceeds on 'knowing that' in the form of prescriptions has been dominant, of late there has been greater attention to ethical practice as a 'know-how'.[33] This, perhaps, comes close to the Aristotelian conception of ethical learning where Aristotle sees ethical learning as closer to a know-how rather than dependent on theoretical exercise based on reasoning. In *Nicomachean Ethics*, Aristotle distinguishes between three forms of knowledge: *Episteme* or scientific knowledge which is that which cannot be otherwise, and involves knowledge of first principles and is demonstrable, *techne* and *phronesis* which are essentially *know-hows* (knowing how to make a product and knowing how to perform the right action where the outcome is not a product, but a specific form of social organization or human interaction). Aristotle emphasizes that *techne* and *phronesis* have much in common: both are knowledge of that which can be otherwise, knowledge of 'how to' rather than 'knowing that', and both are picked up similarly through practice and exercise (Aristotle 2004: 103–118). In other words, exactly as in the case of the arts or *techne* where we become good at an activity by doing it, we acquire virtues or *phronesis*, by previous exercise of those activities or by *doing them*. Just as we become good builders by building, become better lyre players by playing the lyre, good swimmers by swimming (and not by learning *about swimming*), similarly, it is by doing just acts, we become just, it is by doing generous acts that we become generous and by doing courageous deeds that we become courageous (Ibid. 24). No amount of instructions that tells one how to become courageous will help a person become courageous. Only the practice of the act will produce the desired disposition and the knowledge of what courage or fear is. Here, it is practice or actions, or more particularly, being inserted in traditions of activity, *which results in knowledge*. A failure to be courageous or to control one's desire is not a 'weakness of will' or a mental conflict as much as a failure to submit oneself to training, discipline, reflection and practices of the self in the past. Proper training results in mastery or what Varela calls 'spontaneous coping' (Varela 1999: 6).

Varela distinguishes between what he calls 'spontaneous coping' that springs from ethical know-how (a more pervasive mode of being ethical in everyday life) and ethical action based on rational judgement 'in which one experiences a central I performing deliberate willed action' (Ibid. 5), where we can own up to the action as 'our own'. Varela's contention is that those who study the mind, philosophers and scientists included, and those studying ethical behaviour have focused more on actions that are a result of 'deliberate and intentional analysis' with a focus on reasoning consisting mainly in application of principles, while neglecting a more pervasive mode of being ethical that comes closer to a skilled behaviour which is 'immediate, central and pervasive' (Ibid. 23). Varela's claim is also that this negligence is not universal, for according to him, the teaching traditions of the East have focused precisely on what has been neglected by the Western tradition. Thus, when Gandhi stresses on the cultivation of ethical learning which modern education neglects and organizes his vision around the learning of arts and craft, one could say that a similar assumption underlies his conception of education.

Such an education would also create the internal disposition to reflect on experience, to be a *satyagrahi*, one who dwells in truth by being able to sever action from subjective ends (Dhareshwar 2012: 269) and attain freedom in action. Hence, when violence breaks out and Gandhi is forced to withdraw the civil disobedience movement, spinning is the action through which he creates sites for people to reflect on the nature of human action. No amount of instructions that the protest has to be non-violent would work. This has to be individually realized only through insertion within a larger milieu of learning which is embedded in a network of social relations. One would then be able to extend the affinities and similarities to the freedom movement as well. By inserting people into the practice of spinning, Gandhi creates a milieu of learning where people, through action, learn to detach their actions from individual ends and from mistaken ends.

Here, Gandhi seems to be drawing from Indian traditions of learning which are practice based, where truth about the nature of self is arrived at through action and practice rather than given in advance doctrinally. Nayee Talim is perhaps still the best model to capture the way performative art forms such as music (or other performative-reflective practices such as *gamaka, yakshagaana, Taalamaddale* among others) continue to be learnt in India, with an emphasis on long years of arduous training or *riyaz* under a mode of discipleship to the guru and integrally bound to ethical know-how. Rather than see Nayee Talim as an outdated, historical model, I suggest that we see it as a model that even today best explains how learning pursuits that aim at creating practitioners and exemplars in various performative traditions continue to thrive outside the university. Such a conception of ethical learning, as scholars point out, permeates the Indian social fabric; and the traditions are repertoire of such action heuristics for various kinds of inquiry. Gandhi's vision, like Tagore's, is an invitation for us to understand our own learning traditions better.

Conclusion

Much of our contemporary effort at understanding the crisis in the university has focused on factors *external* to education and learning. By showing that the institutional crisis is linked to conception of education and forms of knowledge, the chapter compels us to understand and address the crisis differently. Just as the Bildung model of education gives rise to the idea of the university in Europe, we can see Nayee Talim as presenting us with an Indian model of learning where immersion in the practice is prior to theory, intellectual and ethical virtues come 'spontaneously' together in the exemplar, and it is learning and problem-solving in the domain that permeates the environment. Unlike in the Bildung model of self-development, the ends are internal to the practice, and one submits to these internal ends which have been elaborated over centuries. In other words, the self is not given prior to these domains, but one is constituted within these domains of actions.

The advantage of the Nayee Talim model is that it can recognize the various forms of performative-reflective endeavours outside the university as legitimate knowledge pursuits in their own right. At the same time, it can also be extended to accommodate the form of learning that the university embodies. The university brings to us a valuable practice which as practitioners of the art we need to preserve, refine and perfect. Different traditions of activity generate specific forms of knowing and develop corresponding means of transmission. The university, whose goal is formation through the pursuit of Science or *Wissenschaft*, then is *one* such tradition of learning (*however, not the only one and by no means the privileged one*) that initiates you into a study of objects through the cultivation of a theoretical and conceptual orientation. Here, we are introduced to disciplinary forms of knowledge which require us to learn the norms specific to each domain, work at inherited problems, learn the valid procedures, as well as acquire the intellectual distinctions necessary in order to learn, refine and improve upon the practice. However, if certain inherited theoretical and conceptual structures prevent learning and reflection because they are not universally valid, then *as practitioners within the university*, our concern should be to identify and make explicit the category habits that give rise to the dominant models of thinking. Such an endeavour allows us to mark our points of departure and difference, reformulate existing theories as well as make alternative models and lines of thinking from other cultures available for reflection and further development. It is here that we can place the Tagorean vision of Santiniketan, with its thrust on the comparative study of cultures.

Notes

1 This essay is a condensed version of the argument presented in my unpublished doctoral thesis titled 'Locations of Knowledge: The University, Liberal Education and the Case of India', pursued at The Centre for the Study of Culture and Society, affiliated to Manipal University, Bengaluru. I would like to thank Tejaswini Niranjana, Vivek Dhareshwar, Akeel Bilgrami, Narahari Rao and S. N. Balagangadhara for their valuable comments and encouragement. A revised version of the thesis, titled *Liberal Education and its Discontents*, is forthcoming.
2 An extensive body of literature on the idea of the university and liberal education has developed into a flourishing genre of philosophical writing in the West. One can immediately recall Nussbaum's *Cultivating Humanity* (1997), Derrida's *Eyes of the University* (2004), Pelikan's *The Idea of the University* (1992) and Bloom's *The Closing of the American Mind* (1987) among many others which are devoted to this subject. The absence of this genre of writing in India is particularly striking.
3 I use liberal education and liberal arts education interchangeably. For the confusion that surrounds the idea of liberal education in our context, see Srinivasan (2013: 2–5).
4 For different aspects of this issue, see Singh (2003), Shah (2005).
5 Refer to Agarwal (2009); Khurana and Singhal (2010) for a collection of articles that emphasize governance and quality management.
6 See particularly Chatterjee (1993: 1–13), Chakrabarty (2000: 3–23) and Kaviraj (2001: 287–323) and Nandy (2000: 115–123, 2002: 61–88) on the difficult question of the transfer of political concepts.
7 One could say that the report on the 'Social Science Research Capacity in South Asia' is an attempt in this direction. However, towards the end of the report, the authors admit that while the narrative of decline is neither simple nor general, it 'is not to say that it does not contain the proverbial grain of truth' (Chatterjee 2002b: 142). They go on to list the degeneration of several institutions, both within and outside the ambit of ICSSR. The

degeneration of so many institutions (across regions and time) remains puzzling and tends to undermine their thesis which attempts to locate the reasons for institutional decline in its historical and regional specificity.

8 See, for instance, Viswanathan (1989), Tharu (1998) and Kumar (2005) for various strands of the response.

9 Rao points out that 'to identify a category-habit is to identify a certain line of thinking by showing the structure of connections in that line of thinking. This is a constructive task, a task of constructing a model that can circumscribe a possible mode of thinking – or, in Ryle's terms, a category underlying a field of discourse' (Rao 1994: 5).

10 For the theological roots of Bildung, see Dumont (1994: 82–83), Koselleck (2002: 176–177) and Gadamer (2004: 8–17).

11 A revival movement within German Protestantism.

12 The Aristotelian idea of *form* or potential specific to man gets equated with the Image of God (*Imago Dei*) supposedly imprinted in him while being created.

13 Charles Taylor (1975: 15) observes:

> To talk about the realization of a self here is to say that the adequate human life would not just be a fulfilment of an idea or a plan which is fixed independently of the subject who realizes it, as is the Aristotelian form of a man. Rather this life must have the added dimension that the subject can recognize it as his own, as having unfolded from within him. This self-related dimension is entirely missing from the Aristotelian tradition.

14 In one of his early essays, 'Idea for a Universal History from a Cosmopolitan Perspective' written in 1784, Kant puts forward the idea of species-end and the march of universal history as one towards *morality* which involves willing the moral law (auto – self, nomos – law or to give the law to oneself). *Reason*, for Kant, is a capacity not identifiable with the reasonableness of individual human beings. *Reason is rather the ability to rise above natural instincts*, such as interests and desires. In other words, while we largely use our skills and knowledge to manipulate the material world in order to satisfy human needs and desires, one does not emerge as a moral agent till one goes beyond desire *to realize the rules of reasons* (Kant [1784] 2006).

15 Hence the importance of *Altertumswissenschaft*, the science of studying ancient Greek and Roman arts, literature and poetry, which would serve the purpose of 'harmonious development of all faculties in its pupils'.

16 See Balagangadhara (1994: 241–392) who argues that secularization was merely part of the universalizing drive of a religion. That secularization can no longer be understood as divested of religious elements and is part of a theological transformation within Christianity is emphasized by other scholars as well. See Martin (2007) and Gillespie (2008) for an analysis of this transformation.

17 The early 19th century documents are full of these observations. See Wilks (1805: 25–28), Jones (1807, VII: 28–29), Grant (1813: 251–52), *First Report from Select Committee of House of Lords* (1852: 500–530). References can be multiplied.

18 See Young and Jepanēcañ (1995: 51–52), Claerhout (2010: 325–380).

19 For scholarship that is sensitive to the shared framework between Orientalists, Anglicists and missionaries, see Viswanathan (1989), Niranjana (1992), Mani (1998), Tharu (1998). For more recent studies that elaborate on this shared framework, with a greater emphasis on the conception of religion as constitutive of the frame, see Gelders and Derde (2003) and Oddie (2006).
20 Harrison points out that for the deists, the record of history of not just religions but of society itself accordingly became not the narrative of how natural religion has been universal in all societies and in all times, *but the narrative of the corruption of a pure original religion by the priestly class which was deceitful and kept the laity buried in superstitions, drawn largely from their own cultural experience* (Harrison 1990: 68). This deistic influence and its thesis of corrupted 'original' doctrines looms large in all accounts of Hinduism and is a primary source for the diagnosis of immorality in India – beginning with the accounts of several Orientalists who were sympathetic to Hinduism.
21 Also see King (1999), Mandair (2009) and App (2010) for an account of the role played by religion in the birth of Orientalism.
22 By hermeneutic, I mean an orientation towards practices where they are regarded as texts to be interpreted. One unearths meaning or belief behind them to understand the actions of a community of people.
23 For an interesting analysis of this problem which I draw from, see Seth (2007: 17–46).
24 Observations with regard to scientists consulting astrologers, professors who hold forth on Kantian morality and then visit their ancestral shrine, social reformers marrying young girls despite leading struggles against child marriage and campaigning for widow-remarriage, educated natives assenting to principles of equality and liberty, but being different in their personal lives were commonplace and were the very stuff of the life of various social reformers. On this point, see McDonald (1966) and Seth (2007: 52–78).
25 Here, I draw from Rao who argues that attitudes or *stances* expressed in the way members of a culture lead their life can be considered as *a knowledge disposition, especially when the question is one of formulating the nature of cultural inheritances* (Rao 1996, 2002).
26 An argument of cultural difference should not be collapsed with an argument for cultural relativism. The idea of difference makes sense only against a common coordinate system on which you plot the difference. The existence of a common system denies the claim of incommensurability, which is central to cultural relativism.
27 The aim of Santiniketan, largely in the words of Tagore, is as follows:

> To study the mind of man in its realisation of different aspects of truth from diverse points of view. To bring into more intimate relation with one another, through patient study and research, the different cultures of the East on the basis of their underlying unity. To approach the West from the standpoint of such a unity of the life and thought of Asia. To seek to realise in a common fellowship of study the meeting of the East and the West, and thus ultimately to strengthen the fundamental conditions of world peace through the establishment of free communication of ideas

between the two hemispheres. And, with such ideals in view, to provide at Santiniketan, a centre of culture where research into and study of the religion, literature, history, science and art of Hindu, Buddhist, Jain, Islamic, Sikh, Christian and other civilizations may be pursued along with the culture of the West, with that simplicity in externals which is necessary for true spiritual realisation, in amity, good fellowship and co-operation between the thinkers and scholars of both Eastern and Western countries, free from all antagonisms of race, nationality, creed or caste and in the name of One Supreme Being who is *Shantam, Shivam, Advaitam*.

('Objectives of Visva-Bharati' 2015: n. pag.)

28 Here, I draw from Balagangadhara's hypothesis that practical or performative learning processes, which focus not on *knowledge about* but on practical knowledge regarding 'how to live' or know-how dominates configurations of learning in Asia (1994: 410–420). The hypothesis illuminates and renders the responses by Gandhi and other nationalists intelligible to us. For Gandhi and reflection on action in a practical form of life, see Dhareshwar (2010, 2012) from which I have drawn.

29 I borrow this term from Balagangadhara who singles out 'the ability to think without thinking about' (Balagangadhara 2005a: 1006), a form of reflection which is transmitted practically as one of the main features of Indian/Asian traditions.

30 In his 'What Is a Muslim', Bilgrami points out: 'Understanding a phenomenon is something that occurs in the third person. And, of course, we do often take such a third person stance toward ourselves. But, to allow such a stance to develop into defensive and reactive commitments is to rest with a third person conception of ourselves. It is to deny the first person or agent's point of view' (Bilgrami 1992: 1075). Gandhi's criticism of the extremists seems to indicate that even when one sees oneself as an 'agent', one is already inscribed into a third-person point of view. There seems to be some resonances between Bilgrami's 'third person' and Dhareshwar's 'Adhyasa', where he characterizes adhyasa as one's relation to oneself: 'Wherever experience gets covered over and misidentified there we have adhyasa' (Dhareshwar 2008). In other words, the nature of 'I' is covered over and misidentified with what it is not. In his insightful article 'On Experience Occluding Structures' (2005b), Balagangadhara describes avidya or ignorance, the learning strategy, as '*inducing* the *identification* of the structure of the experience with the structure of the explanation itself*' (Ibid. n. pag.). It very well describes what happens when 'self' and 'agency' is produced by various ideologies and the explanatory structures of social and political science.

31 See Akeel Bilgrami's brief but illuminating foreword to Devi Prasad's *Gandhi and Revolution* where he emphasizes the very different conception of moral education that underlies Gandhi's thoughts:

Gandhi conceived of education as something that should be founded on making, not on learning, that it should involve the body and its habits as a path to the cultivation of virtue as well as to the development of skills and understanding. This is a very different idea of moral education than the acquisition of principles and normative imperatives.... Much is made by commentators on Gandhi of the affinities between him and Socrates. But I think there is nothing in the celebrated dialectical or dialogical method, quite like this link between the dispositions of the body and virtue, on which Gandhi rested his ideal of education. Nayee Talim ... is a quite radical departure from even the heterodoxies of a Socratic conception of education.

(Bilgrami 2012: viii)

32 These domains of experience are very similar to Foucault's reconstruction of the practices of the self in ancient Greece. For an elaborate account of these practices, see Foucault's *Hermeneutics of the Subject* (2005). For why Foucault's account is important to understand the process of normativization of practical life in India and how Gandhi preserves the 'actional frame', refer to Dhareshwar (2012).

33 For versions of ethical know-how, see Balagangadhara (1987, 1988), Varela (1999) and Dhareshwar (2005, 2013b). Also see Rao who, in his *A Semiotic Reconstruction*, makes a persuasive case for taking 'knowing how' to be logically prior to 'knowing that', in opposition to the theories of knowledge dominant since the 17th century, which take 'knowing that' to be prior to 'knowing how' (Rao 1994). His thesis could be extended for ethical learning as well.

References

Agarwal, Pawan. 2009. *Indian Higher Education: Envisioning the Future*. New Delhi : Sage.

App, Urs. 2010. *The Birth of Orientalism*. Philadelphia: University of Pennsylvania Press.

Aristotle. 2004. *Nicomachean Ethics*. Trans. Roger Crisp. Cambridge: Cambridge University Press.

Balagangadhara, S. N. 1987. 'Comparative Anthropology and Action Sciences: An Essay on Knowing to Act and Acting to Know', *Philosophica*, 40 (2): 77–107.

———. 1988. 'Comparative Anthropology and Moral Domains: An Essay on Selfless Morality and the Moral Self', *Cultural Dynamics*, 1 (1): 98–128.

———. 1994. *'The Heathen in His Blindness. . .': Asia, the West, and the Dynamic of Religion*. Leiden, New York, and Cologne : E.J. Brill.

———. 2005a. 'How to Speak for the Indian Traditions: An Agenda for the Future', *Journal of the American Academy of Religion*, 73 (4): 987–1013.

———. 2005b. 'On Experience Occluding Structures', Working Paper, Comparative Science of Cultures, Ghent University, Belgium.

Beiser, Frederick. 2003. *The Romantic Imperative: The Concept of Early German Romanticism*. Cambridge, MA: Harvard University Press.

Bilgrami, Akeel. 1992. 'What Is a Muslim? Fundamental Commitment and Cultural Identity', *Critical Inquiry*, 18 (4): 821–842.

———. 2003. 'Gandhi, the Philosopher', *Economic and Political Weekly*, 38 (39): 4159–4165.

———. 2012. 'Foreword', in Devi Prasad (ed.), *Gandhi and Revolution*, pp. vii–xiii, New Delhi: Routledge India.

Bloom, Allan. 1987. *The Closing of the American Mind: How Higher Education Has Failed Democracy and Impoverished the Souls of Today's Students*. New York: Simon and Schuster.

Chakrabarty, Dipesh. 2000. *Provincializing Europe: Postcolonial Thought and Historical Difference*. Princeton: Princeton University Press.

Chatterjee, Partha. 1993. *The Nation and Its Fragment: Colonial and Post-Colonial Histories*. Princeton: Princeton University Press.

———. 2002a. 'Institutional Context of Social Science Research in South Asia', *Economic and Political Weekly*, 37 (35): 3604–3612.

———. 2002b. *Social Science Research Capacity in South Asia: A Report*, Vol 6. New York: Social Science Research Council.

Claerhout, Sarah. 2010. '"Losing My Tradition": Conversion, Secularism and Religious Freedom in India', Unpublished PhD dissertation, Ghent University.

Derrida, Jacques. 2004. *Eyes of the University: Right to Philosophy 2*. Trans. Jan Plug et al. Stanford: Stanford University Press.

Deshpande, Satish. 2008. 'Declining Simplistic Narratives', *Economic and Political Weekly*, 43 (5): 25–28.

Dhareshwar, Vivek. 2005 'Reconceptualising the Human Sciences', in Satish Poduval (ed.), *Re-Figuring Culture: History, Theory, and the Aesthetic in Contemporary India*, pp. 194–206. New Delhi: Sahitya Akademi.

———. 2008. 'Adhyasa and the "I": On Some Aspects of Stereotypes', Draft paper for the DEVHAS/ASIA-LINK meet at the University of Ghent, Belgium, May 3–11.

———. 2010. 'Politics, Experience and Cognitive Enslavement: Gandhi's Hindswaraj', *Economic and Political Weekly*, 45 (12): 51–58.

———. 2012. 'Framing the Predicament of Indian Thought: Gandhi, the Gita, and Ethical Action', *Asian Philosophy: An International Journal of the Philosophical Traditions of the East*, 22 (3): 257–274.

———. 2013a. 'Truth or Fact? Reframing the Gandhi-Tagore Debate', a draft paper Presented at *Convergences and Divergences: The Gandhi-Tagore Correspondence*, an International Symposium organised by Bangalore Human Sciences Initiative in association with *Srishti School of Art, Design and Technology*, Bangalore and *Indian Council for Philosophical Research*, December 26–27.

———. 2013b. 'Understanding the "Semblance of Objectivity": Critique, Genealogy and Ethical Action', *International Journal of Social Sciences and Humanities*, 2 (1): 31–49.

Dumont, Louis. 1994. *German Ideology: From France to Germany and Back*. Chicago: University of Chicago Press.

Foucault, Michel. 1999. 'About the Beginning of the Hermeneutics of the Self', in Jeremy R. Carrette (ed.), *Religion and Culture*, pp. 158–181. Trans. Thomas Keenan and Mark Blasius. Manchester: Manchester University Press.

———. 2000. 'Technologies of the Self', in Paul Rabinow (ed.), *Ethics: Subjectivity and Truth (Essential Works of Michel Foucault, 1954–84*, Vol. 1), pp. 207–222. Trans. Robert Hurley et al. London: Penguin.

———. 2005. *The Hermeneutics of the Subject: Lectures at the Collège de France, 1981–1982*. Trans. Graham Burchell. Frédéric Gros (ed.). New York: Palgrave Macmillan.

Gadamer, Hans-Georg. 2004. *Truth and Method*. Trans. Joel Weinsheimer and Donald G. Marshall. New York: Continuum Impacts.

Gandhi, M. K. 1997a. *Gandhi: 'Hind Swaraj' and Other Writings*. Anthony Parel (ed.). Cambridge: Cambridge University Press.

———. 1997b. 'The Poet and the Charkha', in Bhattacharya, Sabyasachi (ed.), *The Mahatma and the Poet: Letters and Debates between Gandhi and Tagore, 1915–1941*, pp. 125–129. New Delhi: National Book Trust, India.

Gelders, Raf, and Willem Derde. 2003. 'Mantras of Anti-Brahmanism: Colonial Experience of Indian Intellectuals', *Economic and Political Weekly*, 38 (43): 4611–4617.

Gillespie, Michael Allen. 2008. *The Theological Origins of Modernity*. Chicago: University of Chicago Press.

Grant, Charles. 1813. *Observations on the State of Society Among the Asiatic Subjects of Great Britain: Particularly with Respect to Morals : And on the Means of Improving It*. London: House of Commons.

Great, Britain. 1852. *First Report from the Select Committee of the House of Lords, Appointed to Inquire Into the Operation of the Act 3 & 4 Will. 4, C. 85, for the Better Government of Her Majesty's Indian Territories. . . : Together With the Minutes of Evidence and Appendix*. London: House of Commons.

Hamann, Johann Georg. 1996. 'Metacritique on the Purism of Reason', in James Schmidt (ed.), *What Is Enlightenment: Eighteenth Century Answers and Twentieth-Century Questions*, pp. 154–167. Trans. Kenneth Haynes. Berkeley: University of California Press.

Harrison, Peter. 1990. *'Religion' and the Religions in the English Enlightenment*. Cambridge: Cambridge University Press.

Hegel, Georg Wilhelm Friedrich. 1998. *Phenomenology of Spirit*. Trans. Arnold V. Miller. New Delhi: Motilal Banarsidass.

Herder, Johann Gottfried. 2002. *Herder: Philosophical Writings*. Trans. Michael N. Forster. Cambridge: Cambridge University Press.

Humboldt, Wilhelm von. 1970. 'On the Spirit and the Organisational Framework of Intellectual Institutions in Berlin', Trans. Edward Shils. *Minerva*, 8: 242–250.

———. 2000. 'Theory of Bildung', in Ian Westbury, Stefan Hopmann, and Kurt Riquarts (eds.), *Teaching as a Reflective Practice: The German Didaktik Tradition*, pp. 57–62. Trans. Horton-kruger. Mahwah, NJ: L. Erlbaum Associates.

Jones, Sir William. 1807. *The Works of Sir William Jones: With the Life of the Author by Lord Teignmouth*. Vol. VII. London: J Stockdale.

Joseph, Sarah. 2006. 'Modernity and Its Critics: A Discussion of Some Social and Political Theorists', in V. R Mehta and Thomas Pantham (eds.), *Political Ideas in Modern India: Thematic Explorations*, Vol. x. 7, pp. 419–436. New Delhi: Sage.

Kant, Immanuel. 1996. 'An Answer to the Question: What Is Enlightenment?' in James Schmidt (ed.), *What Is Enlightenment? Eighteenth-Century Answers and Twentieth-Century Questions*, pp. 58–64. Trans. James Schmidt. Berkeley: University of California Press.

———. 2002. *Groundwork for the Metaphysics of Morals*. Trans. Allen W. Wood. New Haven: Yale University Press.

———. 2003. *On Education*. Trans. Annette Churton. New York: Courier Dover Publications.

———. 2006. 'Idea for a Universal History from a Cosmopolitan Perspective', in Pauline Kleingeld (ed.), *Toward Perpetual Peace and Other Writings on Politics, Peace and History*, pp. 3–16. Trans. David L. Colclasure. New Haven: Yale University Press.

Kaviraj, Sudipta. 2001. 'In Search of Civil Society', in Sudipta Kaviraj and Sunil Khilnani (eds.), *Civil Society: History and Possibilities*, pp. 287–323. Cambridge: Cambridge University Press.

Khurana, Paul, and P. K Singhal. 2010. *Higher Education: Quality and Management*. New Delhi: Gyan.

King, Richard. 1999. *Orientalism and Religion: Postcolonial Theory, India and 'the Mystic East'*. London and New York: Routledge.

Koselleck, Reinhart. 2002. *The Practice of Conceptual History: Timing History, Spacing Concepts*. Trans. Todd Samuel Presner et al. Stanford: Stanford University Press.

Kumar, Krishna. 2005. *Political Agenda of Education: A Study of Colonialist and Nationalist Ideas*. New Delhi: Sage.

———. 2010. 'Quality in Education: Competing Concepts', *Contemporary Education Dialogue*, 7 (1): 7–18.

Mandair, Arvind-Pal Singh. 2009. *Religion and the Specter of the West: Sikhism, India, Postcoloniality, and the Politics of Translation*. New York: Columbia University Press.

Mani, Lata. 1998. *Contentious Traditions the Debate on Sati in Colonial India*. Berkeley: University of California Press.

Martin, David. 2007. 'What I Really Said About Secularisation', *Dialog* 46 (2): 139–152.

McDonald, Ellen E. 1966. 'English Education and Social Reform in Late Nineteenth Century Bombay: A Case Study in the Transmission of a Cultural Ideal', *The Journal of Asian Studies*, 25 (3): 453–470.

Mehta, Pratap Bhanu. 2006. 'Democracy, Disagreement and Merit', *Economic and Political Weekly*, 41 (24): 2425–2427.

Mehta, Uday Singh. 2010. 'Gandhi on Democracy, Politics and the Ethics of Everyday Life', *Modern Intellectual History*, 7 (2): 355–371.

Nandy, Ashis. 2000. 'Recovery of Indigenous Knowledge and Dissenting Futures of the University', in Sohail Inayatullah and Gidley Jennifer (eds.),

The University in Transformation: Global Perspectives on the Futures of the University, pp. 115–123. Westport: Bergin & Garvey.

———. 2002. 'The Politics of Secularism and the Recovery of Religious Tolerance', in *Time Warps: Silent and Evasive Pasts in Indian Politics and Religion*, pp. 61–88, New Brunswick: Rutgers University.

Niranjana, Tejaswini. 1992. *Siting Translation History, Post-Structuralism, and the Colonial Context*. Berkeley: University of California Press.

Nussbaum, Martha. 1997. *Cultivating Humanity: A Classical Defense of Reform in Liberal Education*. Cambridge, MA: Harvard University Press.

Oddie, Geoffrey. 2006. *Imagined Hinduism: British Protestant Missionary Constructions of Hinduism, 1793–1900*. New Delhi: Sage.

Pelikan, Jaroslav. 1992. *The Idea of the University: A Reexamination*. New Haven: Yale University Press.

Rao, Narahari. 1994. *A Semiotic Reconstruction of Ryle's Critique of Cartesianism*. New York: de Gruyter.

———. 1996. 'A Meditation on the Christian Revelations', *Cultural Dynamics*, 8 (2): 189–209.

———. 2002. 'Culture as Learnables', *Manuscrito* 25 (2): 465–488.

Schiller, Johann Christoph Friedrich von. 2005. *Letters Upon the Aesthetic Education of Man*. Trans. Charles W. Eliot. Raleigh: Hayes Barton.

Seth, Sanjay. 2007. *Subject Lessons: The Western Education of Colonial India*. Durham: Duke University Press.

Shah, A. M. 2005. 'Higher Education and Research: Roots of Mediocrity', *Economic and Political Weekly*, 40 (22–23): 2234–2242.

Singh, Amrik. 2003. 'Academic Standards in Indian Universities: Ravages of Affiliation', *Economic and Political Weekly*, 38 (30): 3200–3208.

Srinivasan, Shashikala. 2013. 'In Search of a Concept of Education: Liberal Education and the Case of India', *International Journal of Social Sciences and Humanities*, 2 (1): 1–30.

Tagore, Rabindranath. 2007a. 'An Eastern University', in Mohit K. Ray (ed.), *The English Writings of Rabindranath Tagore: Essays*, Vol. IV, pp. 639–658. New Delhi: Atlantic.

———. 2007b. 'The Centre for Indian Culture or Visva-Bharati', in Mohit K. Ray (ed.), *The English Writings of Rabindranath Tagore: Essays*, Vol. IV, pp. 515–548. New Delhi: Atlantic.

———. 2011. 'The Problem of Self', in Fakrul Alam and Radha Chakravarty (eds.), *The Essential Tagore*, pp. 159–169. Cambridge, MA: Harvard University Press.

———. 2015. 'Objectives of Visva-Bharati', Prospectus of Visva-Bharati/Santiniketan. n. pag.

Taylor, Charles. 1975. *Hegel*. Cambridge: Cambridge University Press.

Tharu, Susie J. (ed.) 1998. *Subject to Change: Teaching Literature in the Nineties*. New Delhi: Orient Longman.

Tilak, Jandhyala B. G. 2007. 'Knowledge Commission and Higher Education', *Economic and Political Weekly*, 42 (8): 630–633.

Vaidyanathan, A. 2008. 'An Overview', *Economic and Political Weekly*, 43 (5): 21–24.
Varela, Francisco J. 1999. *Ethical Know-How: Action, Wisdom, and Cognition*. Stanford: Stanford University Press.
Viswanathan, Gauri. 1989. *Masks of Conquest: Literary Study and British Rule in India*. New York: Columbia University Press.
Wilks, Mark. 1805. *Report on the Interior Administration, Resources, and Expenditure of the Government of Mysoor: Under the System Prescribed by the Orders of the Governor General in Council, Dated 4th September 1799*. Madras: Printed by Order of the Governor General in Council, Fort William.
Young, Richard Fox, and Es Jepanēcan. 1995. *The Bible Trembled: The Hindu-Christian Controversies of Nineteenth-Century Ceylon*. Vienna: Indological Institute of the University of Vienna.

2

IN-DISCIPLINE(S)
Diversity, disciplinarity and the humanities

Kailash Baral

Preliminaries

Diversity is our challenge. The concern is not how academic disciplines negotiate with diversity, but equally significant is how disciplinary singularity also seeks a plural horizon. 'In-discipline' and 'indiscipline', in the context of the present discussion, are conceptual categories; they bear upon disciplinary structure of a university as well as reflect upon the academic eco-system across Indian universities. Indiscipline as an antinomy of discipline is employed here not as a binary opposition, but as a hyphenated third position as 'in-discipline' to imply that indiscipline is not external but internal to any discipline as such. 'Indiscipline' with a hyphen therefore would imply the logic of disciplining a discipline that ascertains its boundary, and without a hyphen, it would mean something that is external to the discipline that defies the disciplinary logic. A similar dynamic also operates in academic protocols of preparing syllabi, setting pedagogic objectives, doing research, teacher recruitment, admission of students and so on in our universities. In this context, it is therefore pertinent to examine the force of 'in(-)discipline' as a referent in the context of Indian universities, wherein 'indiscipline' in general is not exclusively external to disciplinary formation, but a corollary to say politics of representation.

Following some of Arjun Appadurai's concerns in his essay 'Diversity and Disciplinarity as Cultural Artefacts' (1996), it is pertinent to ask how does diversity operate and what modalities does it seek at the domain of disciplinarity, as well as at the sites of higher education say in a postcolonial university in the production and dissemination of knowledge. Further, in engaging with the problematic, it is important to follow the way Appadurai sets forth his discussion on diversity and disciplinarity; to him, diversity means 'plenitude, having an infinity possibility and limitless variation', and disciplinarity means 'scarcity, rationing and policing' (Appadurai 1996: 23). To reduce his concerns to an opposition between a limitless plurality versus disciplinary particularity is not, I guess, Appadurai's intention; for, he examines diversity in a broader socio-political context of diverse constituencies of the American society in terms of the policy of affirmative action as well as funding of higher education and the way policy interventions impact the university system in terms of teaching and research. What is significant in Appadurai's analysis is a substantive deficit in addressing 'epistemic inwardness' that becomes problematic in a shift from cultural diversity to culture of diversity. Even though Appadurai's anxieties apparently seem to concern American Research Universities, they have serious implications in the Indian context. In the face of external interventions, what is important to Appadurai is how 'epistemic inwardness' is affected as a consequence resulting in disciplinary decadence. 'Epistemic inwardness' in the structure and mandate of a discipline to me would mean an in-built system of self-critique as well as self-reflection that could create the possibility of an open dialogue between the formation of a discipline with the codes of disciplinarity. This is a huge academic responsibility without alibi in view of competing social aspirations. It is more challenging than diversity because if the episteme is fractured and lacks coherence in terms of its structure and manifestation, then in what voice it would speak to itself and to others. This problematic is a double bind and a paradox. A double bind in the sense that if the foundational principles of a discipline get subverted by its own actions, its object of study gets obfuscated leading to an inevitable blindness that constrains the very process of seeing, and perhaps even seeing reason; a paradox because what is meant or supposed to be its objective gets vitiated when disciplinary mandate is compromised.

The scenario

In our postcolonial times, we who represent different constituencies of higher education are also implicated in its processes, often losing our voices to those who control and manage the system. There is an exponential growth of universities in the country today (when I joined Northeastern Hill University in 1979, it was the 7th Central University; now there are more than 40 Central Universities, hundreds of state and many private universities, including special universities such as forensic, petroleum, shipping and so on). We in India hardly discuss or debate what type of university we need; on the contrary, establishing universities has been either a government prerogative or it is left to private players for commercialization of education. The story becomes bizarre when Ajit Jogi allowed many foreign private universities to open shops in Raipur with the plea of getting FDI in education sector. Even the Ministry of Human Resource Development is keen to invite foreign universities using the same plea and justifying its stand in the name of quality education. Is quality a prerogative of foreign universities alone? Can't we ensure quality in our own universities? What stops us in doing so? The Supreme Court of India derecognized the universities opened in Chattishgarh. Is there a lesson for us to learn from this judgement of the Supreme Court? The story does not end there, for many deemed-to-be-universities were derecognized under a government fiat, and some are yet to be re-recognized. These facts underline the mess in higher education in the country.

It is high time that we debated on the type of university we actually need. Has the colonial grafting of a university into a multilingual, multicultural and multiethnic society like India outlived its mandate? If so, it would be pertinent to ask how the university as an institution could provide critical-intellectual direction to competing aspirations, while addressing some of our socio-economic conflicts. If education is a creative engagement with life, it is further pertinent to ask how is it integrated with our cultural practices and social life. These questions take us to the other relevant question, such as the status of the humanities education in Indian universities today. As the scientific-technology paradigm underwrites the intellectual quest for production of knowledge and pedagogic practice, we need to relook at humanities education critically. Challenged by new social conflicts, on the one hand, and afflicted by disciplinary decadence on the other, humanities education seems to be in a crisis in an ever-expanding university system in India. It is time we look at the humanities critically both in terms of diversity and disciplinarity. Until a few decades ago, the humanities education constituted the core of education in giving direction to the aspirations of a new nation; but somewhere, it lost its anchorage and moorings. Before getting into a discussion on the reasons for its decadence, it is proper to throw more light on the university as an idea and its implications in the Indian context.

The university as an idea

The university is not a physical entity as such but has evolved as an idea in the West. Wilhelm von Humboldt established the first modern university in Berlin in 1810 and this university became a model for all modern universities in the West. The idea of a university largely was a product of the Western Enlightenment and was held forth by Kant under his three regulations of reason, culture and excellence. Humboldt, a great advocate of liberalism, visualized a sublimation of the normative force of reason in a culture of liberal thinking that could make the university a place, reclusive in character, but suitable to pursue and produce knowledge for wider dissemination. The Kantian discourse of rationality was expanded by Weber with his argument of 'logical consistency that would systematize beliefs as much as organise actions' (Talgeri 1999: 74). Hence it was not just concretizing an idea, but translating the idea into organized action was the objective. Establishment of the modern university in the West coincided with radical transformation in the social context of knowledge production with the separation of religion from education that ensured the stability of scientific knowledge and its enquiry, and also ensured its institutional autonomy from the state. The epistemic shift from religious to secular learning was further reinforced with the stated motto of Wilhelm von Humboldt that a university is a place for the 'unity of teaching and research', which 'engaged not only in the assimilation, transmission of existing knowledge but also become centres for the creation of new knowledge' (Bèteille 2010: 22). Considering the roots of American universities in German philosophy, Bill Readings in his work *The University in Ruins* (1996) further dwells on the Kantian context as a story of modernity:

> The characteristic of the modern University is to have an idea that functions as its referent, as the end and meaning of its activities. . . . In general the modern University has had three ideas. The story begins, as do so many stories about modernity, with Kant, who envisioned the University as guided by the concept of reason. Kant's vision is followed by Humboldt's idea of culture, and more recently the emphasis has been on the techno-bureaucratic notion of excellence. The distinguishing feature of the last one in this list is that it actually lacks a referent. That is to say, the idea that functions as the University's referent – excellence – itself has no referent. The University of Excellence is the simulacrum of the idea of a University.
> (Readings 1996: 54)

Readings' argument exemplifies how an idea seeks a referent, hence a university seeks an epistemological mooring wherein ideas internal and external to a university stated and unstated keep on evolving and become generative. If the generative character of an idea is reduced to a techno-bureaucratic concept such as 'excellence', a non-referent, it remains as a simulacrum of that idea. The modern university in Germany has a philosophical foundation besides Kant's, in Hegel's understanding of institutional structures reflecting upon the 'objective spirit'; in Dilthey's attempt to balance natural science with humanities in using the modalities of explanation and understanding that continued to be reflected upon in Habermas's insistence on 'moral culture' in that 'the entire intellectual life of a nation can be focused in the institutions of higher learning' (Talgeri 1999: 7). In England, Cardinal Newman in his work *The Idea of a University* (1907) further elaborated on the context of a modern university adding to its function the true and adequate end of intellectual training wherein thought or reason is exercised upon knowledge (Newman 1907: 140). The instrumentality of reason seems to be the very life force of a modern university. However, it was never separated by implication and practice from the ethical. Robert Young in his essay 'The Idea of a Chrestomathic University' (1996), although critical of the older universities of England – Oxford and Cambridge, which were historically outside the provenance of the new universities – concedes to the inseparability of the ethical and the rational. What exactly is the ethical/rational frame within which a university functions? For me, ethicality is a process of self-discipline that defines a person's social character and is counted for the integration of the self. Self-discipline therefore is necessary to cultivate a habit of mind that works at the command of the rational. Hence at the site of intellectual practice, there happens a sublimation of the ethical-rational. Fichte has visualized this as the guiding principle of a university, for he considered the university as the birthplace of a future emancipated society. Of course, he did not mean emancipation in the political sense, but predicated emancipation to liberation of the mind in teaching, thinking, doing research and producing positive knowledge for good life.

However, the so-called moral consciousness of a university, a product of the integration of the ethical/rational, under industrial societies resulted in the 'disintegration of the unified metaphysical interpretation of the world as an ordered totality' (Talgeri 1999: 10). However, the modern university, in its structure, continues to be a composite totality that functions with a commonality of purpose and cooperative consciousness. As an institution, its objective among other things is to play a pivotal role in fulfilling the educational needs of a society through integration of curricular goals with intellectual pursuit of knowledge.

University in India: tradition and modernity

The university in India is a colonial transplant. The establishment of Calcutta, Bombay and Madras Universities by the colonial government in 1857 did not have any 'genealogical and historical connection with India's ancient and medieval centres of learning' (Bèteille 2010: 23). These universities are primarily extensions of the European-modernist paradigm. Through these universities, teaching of modern Western education was reinforced in that colonialism became a pedagogic enterprise. As a transplant, the colonial modern university in India overlooked or ignored the real India as an object of study with its socio-cultural complexities and their imperatives. For Venkat Rao:

> It [the university] is a European implant with all its political, philosophical and cultural baggage. It is a graft imposed with utter disregard for the tissue texture of the host culture. For the graft itself was conceived as a part of a whole good bestowed upon a 'nation' to be civilized.
>
> (Rao 2010)

The colonial civilizing mission was also defined in linguistic terms; Macaulay emphasized, among other things, the English language's 'intrinsic superiority of reason' (Talgeri 1999: 9). Be it as it may, there are other concerns and contestations that have been written about and debated, such as university education vis-à-vis Indian nationalism, secularism, Western knowledge systems, postcolonial modernity and translating the colonial agenda into action with the objective of producing an educated workforce for the colonial government and so on. The colonial pedagogic enterprise had two clear objectives: first, 'to teach Indians a diffusion of the improved arts, sciences, philosophy and literature of Europe; in short, European knowledge' (Seth 2007: 2); secondly, 'to supplant indigenous knowledge (Oriental knowledge) that was condemned as ' "superstitious," "mythic," "primitive," and, more generally, untrue' (Ibid. 1). European modernity through the agency of colonial rule reached India not only through the universities, but through other institutions and agencies as well: 'A textbook of 1897 told its audience of Indian school boys that the Penal Code, public works, railways, irrigation and civil works, schools, the post office and telegraph and a free press were all forces working to educate India' (Ibid. 2). To educate India was not certainly to emancipate India, but to mould Indians differently as knowing subjects of the European knowledge thereby creating a context for the negation of Indian knowledge.

Modelled after the newly established London University, the colonial Indian University was not a template of the European University as such with its philosophical foundation. It was simply a transplant, and its curricular goals were meant primarily to serve colonial objectives. Even so, the education that was imparted had consequences outside the colonial agenda. Macaulay's children were, however, not mechanical products of the debate between the Anglicists and the Nationalists; some of them, the deviants with university education, were able to reinvent themselves in the Indian cultural-national context even while adhering to the educational objectives of a colonial university.

The civilizing mission with its operative logic of reason worked to produce good (loyal) subjects instead of good Indians. Gauri Viswanathan's account of colonial–political–anthropological position in the context of religious conversions in India in her work *Outside the Fold: Conversion, Modernity and Belief* (1998) provides a window to another development in the mother country which had a contrary effect in the colony. The Tory Government at home awarding the Catholics and Jews equal political status and liberty to practice their religion freely had the agenda of having good Englishmen in England instead of 'good Anglicans', but not so in the colonies (Good Indians to serve the British not India). The participation of the missionaries in Indian education in general reinforced the argument that the colonial Indian university although secular in character was implicated in the Christian theological reason to produce good subjects for the colonial government; they would, it was assumed, like the faithful following the Church, loyally follow the colonial government. 'Since the colonial good was assumed to be an *a priori* good, the host's potential or possible response to the intruding good remains foreclosed' (Rao 2010). The colonial project of education succeeded in two ways: it did not overwhelm the traditional social hierarchies in India (including caste) but produced a group of loyal subjects to work for the colonial government. Further the dispassionate pursuit of science and scholarship in a liberal climate did not happen in British–Indian university from the very beginning unlike its counterpart in the West.

The postcolonial university in India continued with the colonial organizational structure and objectives because the university in India did not evolve as an idea. Hence its priorities and objectives were/are misplaced and misconstrued. The universities in India are continued to be challenged from within as well as from without. The Commissions on education, most famously of Radhakrishnan and of Kothari with Edward Shils as a member of the latter to reform Indian education system with their comprehensive and productive contributions did not result in their acceptance in entirety. The Indian universities in Shils's view have become mass universities where students come for degrees for suitable employment and not for enlightened knowledge. Further, the university, with the policy of inclusive education, in the Indian context, has to bear the responsibility of educating the diverse and differentiated social groups, thereby changing in character and moving away from its foundational goal of dispassionate pursuit of knowledge within an ethical-normative frame.

It is in this context that Andrè Bèteille's work *Universities at the Crossroads* (2010) is significant. The work is a compilation of his articles and convocation addresses on the state of Indian universities; it is an extended reflection on the history, curricular, non-curricular mandate and other challenges including the social dimension of higher education in the country. With his vast personal experience, having taught and held many positions at different universities in India, Bèteille expresses his anxieties and articulates forcefully the malaise that afflicts Indian universities today. He maintains, 'The awareness of the continuing changes taking place in our Universities – and the Universities throughout the world – obliges us to take a historical view of the University as both a centre of learning and a social institution' (Bèteille 2010: 4). Besides its history, what is more important for discussion here is the changing character of the university as a social institution.

The demographic challenge

The university today is challenged in trying to adjust to the changing demography and governmental policies. It is therefore important that the disciplinary economies need to be factored in the debates on caste, gender, tribe and marginality under whatever designations they may appear (protected under the policy of protective discrimination in the form of quotas and quotas within quotas). The marginal, the stigmatized and the excluded within the Indian society have arrived not seeking only education, but also with diverse aspirations where the 'top is easy to find not the bottom'.[1] With changing social aspirations, universities have to adjust to a new sociology that challenges the old ethical-rational structure of the university and its curricular mandate. Such a challenge has forced the universities to stretch their capacity in terms of admissions, accommodation, classrooms and other infrastructure.

The university, in spite of being conceived as a secular-democratic institution with policy interventions of the state, has become a centre for conflicting interests and competing ideological struggle. Such conflicts have a spiralling effect on ideological wars, caste skirmishes and community interests. In the process, new icons have adorned the university walls, and new slogans have dominated campus politics. The so-called commonality of purpose and cooperative consciousness with the university's reclusive character for dispassionate pursuit of knowledge about the world and the human society in transcending narrow grooves of social boundaries have come under serious stress and interrogation. Mass has replaced merit, and the voice of the enlightened minority is silenced.

Nehru's optimism that the university in India should promote equality as enshrined in the Constitution of India was sensitively articulated by Radhakrishnan that 'education is a universal right, not a class privilege' (Bèteilie 2010: 14), and was endorsed by Kothari in affirming that if a change has to happen without a violent revolution, social equality could be achieved only through the instrument of education. But social equality has taken an aggressive turn in the name of social justice. The two premises of Nehru: (1) that 'a university stands for the adventure of ideas and for the search of the truth' (Bèteilie 2010: 156–157) and (2) that the spirit of the age shall triumph in bringing about equality in society have been negated. Consequently, autonomy of the university is severely compromised with interventions from outside and with corrosive politics from within. The search for truth if equated to self-cultivation of the mind following the rigour of rational enquiry the question that arises is: can we ever have the truth that is self-reflexive and other-sensitive in a climate where truth is manufactured for ideological purpose?

Today the violence that haunts the universities speaks in many tongues and takes many forms manifesting in ideological, caste, class and gender wars reflecting upon the social that is overtly politicized. In such a scenario, I think Gandhi may be relevant. Mahatma Gandhi's Nai Talim is an integral part of his own vision of a 'good society'. Gandhi in 'basic national education' of 1937 advocated that Indian learners should prepare themselves to participate in a national society based on truth and non-violence; Gandhi, in other words, visualized a new social order totally different from the existing one. For Gandhi, education 'not only brings liberation but becomes a catalyst in the transforming process of society' (Sykes 1998). We have never given any importance to Gandhi's views; instead, we have followed an ambivalent policy towards education in general and higher education in particular at our own peril.

Institutional politics: the indiscipline and the outside

The ideological-intellectual frame upon which education has been envisaged either from the Western or from Indian sources, seems to be out of sync with the contemporary reality. Universities are no longer places of recluse for dispassionate pursuit of knowledge for advancement of society. The outside has been the force of indiscipline on university campuses. The outside plays out organized action often overwhelming the authority of the university. The ethical-moral concerns of university's authority become politicized with interest groups playing out from within for their constituents outside. The university that is supposed to move with a cooperative consciousness to participate in the undertaking of production and dissemination of knowledge is fighting with itself; the cooperative consciousness is fractured as exclusivity of caste, gender and other social issues constantly challenging such a consciousness. Hence the moral authority of the university is subverted from within throwing away its foundational principle of the ethical-rational. Therefore, indiscipline at the site of the university as an institution is generated internally and externally by political-ideological groups, caste groups and others. Social conflicts are getting transferred to the campuses where the university by its organizational structure and function is unable to handle such issues. The claim of diversity often calls on individual rights and freedom for the self and the group that some view as undermining democratization of education, and some others claim it to be a revolution in the name of social justice. Many universities are exposed to problems with student groups and their agitations often spill over to streets and even politicized at the national level. The so-called campus unrests that have little to do with education and learning compel us to rethink the idea of a university and its mandate in the Indian context. The old ethical-rational frame of the university seems to have outlived its mandate that needs to be redefined to accommodate diversity that issues out from our social conflict.

In-discipline: disciplinary protocols and the humanities

The concerns of in-discipline that I raised at the beginning of this chapter bear on disciplinary protocols. Disciplinary protocols have suffered acute cultural and intellectual alienation. Further, humanities disciplines on the one hand are challenged by the techno-scientific model of education that the state vigorously promotes and on the other by the new sociology of disciplinarity that goes against the grain. Some of the new disciplines such as Exclusion Studies refuse to negotiate with the old disciplines considering some of these as oppressive and socially dominant (often dubbed as Brahminical). When a discipline within the university becomes exclusive (although created by the UGC), it lacks 'epistemic inwardness' as well as negates meaningful dialogue and conversation with other disciplines. When plural conversations that is the life force of disciplinary protocols take a backseat, how can learning be democratized? There are meaningless departments (without having any disciplinary mandate) across universities, for example, the department of Resource Generation at EFLU, that are instituted not following 'rigorous analysis or interrogation of the ontological necessity of the disciplinary frame' (Rao 1999: 11). As a consequence, research at the universities has become an endeavour for aggregation of numbers instead of authentic contribution to knowledge in terms of worth and value (when we compare PhDs produced at Indian universities with those from Chinese universities). The value-coding of a discipline needs to be responsive to the university framework from where it originates in terms of teaching and research and then to society and to its representational contexts in terms of its relevance. Part of the discussion of 'in-discipline' may be examined by focusing on the humanities and disciplinary crisis.

Although the university is primarily a humanistic concept, the space for meaningful study of humanities is shrinking today. The university, a place for producing archival and referential knowledge in a broader sense advancing our knowledge and understanding of what makes us 'human' and the end of man, has to address concerns of humanities and humanistic education. In a general sense, it is assumed that humanistic education brings together the imaginative-creative and the rational with an objective of awakening in a learner an integrated consciousness. It must look at education as a cultural process in traditions, captured in the arts, histories, philosophy and in human sciences. Among the three basic functions of a university, 'the freedom to teach and learn' constitutes the core of the humanistic perspective of education. Unfortunately, hitherto valued parameters of producing knowledge and 'knowing' within the humanities are held suspect today. The domain of humanities is an embattled field now; challenged and interrogated by diverse forces and discourses. In the process, what has become central to the context is what and how to teach in ensuring the freedom to the learner from his or her discursive struggle bringing him or her to meaningful conversation. A scenario is created in which a learner instead of moving towards clarity on learning objectives is mired in pulls and counter pulls across identity politics and other sociological factors. There is a failure of dialogue in the university today that affects agency.

The problem of agency in today's universities concerns three major issues: structure, system and process. The structure of the university as a secular-democratic institution, with its mandate of dispassionate pursuit of knowledge and its dissemination with the objective of liberating minds towards a better society has been subjected to debilitating interventions. It is in this context that the question of agency of 'indiscipline' not of 'in-discipline' needs to be understood. In arguing against institutional and other regimes of power, Foucault advocates resistance to such power and also against subjugated knowledge. While speaking to power from a position of subordination/marginalization, Foucault acknowledges 'innumerable points of confrontation, focuses of instability, each of which has its own risks of conflict, of struggles, and of at least temporary inversion of the power relations' (Foucault 1995: 26–27). In a re-reading of Foucault in the Indian context, it may be argued that in the inversion of power relations, the authority of a university as an autonomous liberal humanist institution today is most vulnerable as it is challenged by the illegalities of 'the affirmation of inalienable rights' (Foucault 1995: 290). Such a situation leaves us with questions who then stands for the right of a university; how does a university structured within a legal-regulative frame address a particular type of 'liberty'; further how in such a scenario dissemination of knowledge/pedagogic transaction takes place? Reading Foucault elsewhere, the point I'm arguing becomes clear that power relations conceptualized as the power of action to induce other actions makes one realize that power relations are 'rooted deep in the social nexus, not reconstituted "above" society as a supplementary structure' (Foucault 1982: 222). As a result, no claim is made not to criticize the workings of an institution (the university) – supposedly neutral and independent – and examine its processes whether or not it fulfils its social obligations without compromising its mandate (meaning dispassionate pursuit of knowledge and truth), but it is hard to accept that its very foundational principles are rendered redundant. In our context, if 'a new politics of truth' (Foucault 1982: 133) has to manifest, there is a need to seriously engage with the 'indiscipline' of agency.

The new politics of truth can only arrive when we bring in the learning subject to conversation. This conversation is possible within the pedagogic frame. However, in our context, pedagogic transaction is pathologized to an extent that the caste of a teacher has become problematic not how he teaches or what he teaches; even ideological and genealogical motifs are attributed to texts (in case of Ramanujan's *Three Hundred Ramayanas*). The minority that stands for reasoned voice in a university is silenced even by legal intervention. It is no longer possible to ask whether a teacher enlightens or not; whether a text is deep and enriching or not. It has become 'normal' to accept many 'illegalities' that are constructed and forced upon by ideological imperatives. How do we then negotiate between the core values of the humanities and the dissemination of humanistic knowledge to enrich the self-knowledge of the knowing subject?

If teaching of the humanities has to be a sustained effort to strengthen the continuity of life and culture, as Steiner (1969) maintains, and to differentiate between the universal and the contingent, nature and culture, local and global, tradition and technology, we need to rethink many issues. Gadamer argues that the disciplines in humanities for their sustenance need to be placed in a philosophical hermeneutics that allows a diffusion of horizons (Baral [1977] 2002: 13). Unfortunately, Gadamer may not be relevant in our context today, for the humanities education no longer seeks a philosophical hermeneutics with a historical awareness and literary-aesthetic understanding; instead, its study is directed to challenge the idea of 'knowledge as culture' asking questions such as: whose knowledge? whose culture? In the process, it leaves little or no room to draw together diverse methods and pursuits for diffusion of horizons. Thus, to make a shift from social diversity to intellectual diversity is only possible if we follow Appadurai's reasoned argument for a move from cultural diversity to culture of diversity within disciplinary protocols.

Teaching of the humanities following its primary goal to know the world with an awakened self-knowledge is constrained by other considerations. The new humanities have paved the way to recast teaching in the changing times. Foucault's concern to 'ascertain the possibility of constituting a new politics of truth' bears upon our fresh endeavours to recast humanities with a deeper understanding of Gandhi's advocacy for a 'new social order' using education as a transformative process. This endeavour is possible if we take a call from critical humanities. Critical humanities with a theoretical orientation takes interdisciplinary study to a different level; for me, such an orientation would help in filling the deficit in 'epistemic inwardness' referred to earlier. It is possible to have new ways of thinking and directing research from critical humanities perspective as two of my colleagues have attempted to do so (even if in a limited way) with courses on 'Jati and Genre' (Venkat Rao) and 'Biopolitics and the Nation' (Dilip Das) with the intent to move away from the narrow boundaries of social division in producing positive knowledge in understanding our social malaise/strength in a deeper way. Often such courses face closure or erasure by the powers of those who perpetuate the politics of social division from within the university structure. Therefore, there is a need to create a space for production of alternative humanistic knowledge and its dissemination.

If teaching at the universities has to be on the side of truth and critical judgement allowing a learner to discover the depth, richness and beauty of the humanities, it is time we ponder over the crisis that afflicts the humanities education in our country. As it battles to survive in a techno-commercial-utilitarian academic structure and burdened with caste, class, gender and other social factors where truth is no longer self-evident, but manipulated and manufactured, there is a need for the humanities to redefine itself in the changing context of education.

Note

1 Arjun Appadurai while delivering the 4th Balvant Parekh Distinguished lecture on 'Disciplining India's Diversity' at Baroda has said that the politics of reservations in India is problematic, for the 'top is easy to find not the bottom'. His observation indeed is a statement of fact in today's reservation politics as many groups are fighting to come under reservation, often resulting in violent demonstrations (e.g., the Patel/Patidar community of Gujarat and the Kamma community of Andhra Pradesh). Besides these movements, the states are adding new groups to the existing lists of SC, ST and OBC for vote bank politics.

References

Appadurai, Arjun. 1996. 'Diversity and Disciplinarity as Cultural Artifacts', in Cary Nelson and Dilip Parameshwar Gaonkar (eds.), *Disciplinarity and Dissent in Cultural Studies*, pp. 23–36. New York: Routledge.

Baral, K. C. (ed.) 2002. *Humanities and Pedagogy: Teaching of Humanities Today*. New Delhi: Pencraft International.

Bèteille, Andrè. 2010. *Universities at the Crossroads*. New Delhi: Oxford University Press.

Foucault, Michel. [1975] 1995. *Discipline and Punish: The Birth of the Prison.* Trans. Alan Sheridan. New York: Vintage.

———. 1982. 'The Subject and Power', in Hubert Dreyfus and Paul Rainbow (eds.), *Michel Foucault: Beyond Structuralism and Hermeneutics*, pp. 208–226. Chicago: University of Chicago Press.

Newman, J. Henry. 1907. *The Idea of a University*. London: Longmans, Green and Co, 1907.
Rao, D. Venkat. 1999. *In Citations: Reading in Area Studies of Culture*. Hyderabad: Allied Publishers.
———. 2010. 'Anachronistic Reflections: of Critical Humanities', *Pratilipi*, March–June, Pratilipi.in (accessed on 26th December 2016).
Readings, Bill. 1996. *The University in Ruins*. Cambridge, MA: Harvard University Press.
Seth, Sanjay. 2007. *Subject Lessons: The Western Education of Colonial India*. Durham and London: Duke University Press.
Steiner, George. 1969. *Language and Silence*. Harmondsworth: Penguin Books.
Sykes, Marjorie. 1998. *The Story of Nai Talim*. Google books (accessed on 26th December 2016).
Talgeri, Promod. 1999. *Farewell to a Classical University: Essays on Education and Culture*. Hyderabad: CIEFL Publications.
Viswanathan, Gauri. 1998. *Outside the Fold: Conversion, Modernity and Belief*. Princeton: Princeton University Press.
Young, Robert. 1996. *Torn Halves: Political Conflict in Literary and Cultural Theory*, pp. 184–221. New York: St Martin's Press.

3
SITES OF LEARNING AND INTELLECTUAL PARASITISM
The case for new humanities

Vivek Dhareshwar

There have been inquiries in Indian traditions whose objective has been to enhance and expand the experiential world. Perhaps implicit in those inquiries was a meta-level inquiry about what kind of inquiries do that and how. We need to raise that question now because the gulf between cultural learnings and academic disciplines in the humanities and the social sciences (the human sciences for short) seem only to be increasing. If our 'education' at all levels has not made an attempt to connect with cultural learning, it is perhaps not too late to ask how the latter is being nourished and transmitted. It is certainly a research question for the human sciences, since, after all, they have to be concerned with experience, clarifying it, understanding it, expanding it. That the question has taken this form and the concern that the experiential world is increasingly losing its self-aware, that is, experiential, character as structures inimical or indifferent to it are distorting or undermining it, that such concerns are emerging in all sphere of life in India and elsewhere, go to show that we are already beginning the inquiry. It remains for us to explore how to deepen it and how to make the existing disciplines responsive to it. My suggestion is that we begin by reflecting on the way the academic life has been parasitic: we seem to be pursuing the disciplines for reasons other than intellectual discovery and the disciplines not only are not articulating any learning, but seem inimical to cultural learning. I am making a number of assumptions in beginning this inquiry. I hope to clarify and defend them in the course of this reflection, but none of them seems unjustifiable or unintuitive to start with. My strategy then is as follows: I will begin by motivating a certain kind of reflection about cultural learning arising out of what we ordinarily notice around us as a disturbing social phenomenon, whether it has to with the frenetic construction activity or commercialization of education. With some hold on the idea of cultural learning and parasitism, I distinguish between pragmatic and intellectual parasitism. Though they are interdependent, it's the latter that distorts our experience. The disciplines in the human sciences perpetuate parasitism either because they are unable or unwilling to examine how they end up severing all connection to cultural learning. To demonstrate my argument, I take up history and philosophy, both of which, in their different ways, render it impossible for Indians to access their past and its relationship to truth. The interrogation of history will try to answer why we have to give up our enslavement to it in order to access the past; similarly, questioning the process by which translation/interpretation of Indian thought transforms *aadhyatma* into philosophy will also force us to choose between *aadhyatma* and philosophy. It will turn out that our experiential discomfort with parasitism was already the beginning of *adhyatmic* inquiry in so far the latter is always seen by Indian traditions to be present in experience itself to reflect on and resist structures that occlude it (parasitism being a dimension of the *upadhis* Indian traditions were concerned to meditate upon).

Parasitism

When we look at the different domains of life in contemporary India, the metaphor of parasitism suggests itself. Can we use that metaphor to begin a serious inquiry into what might be a generalized phenomenon? Rather than using that metaphor as a moralizing judgement, would it be possible to theorize it as a social phenomenon? Let's work with a couple of examples to get clearer on what kind of social phenomenon we are talking about. Consider 'real estate': there is little doubt that it is an entirely parasitic activity. What is it parasitic upon? On the experience of home, the intimate relationship between land and dwelling, the web of relationships, of certain ethos and obligations.[1] The frenzied economics of real estate is entirely stifling the experience of *oikos*, even though without the latter, there is nothing for that frenzy to exploit. But the experience of home has, as it were no home to nourish it, to develop the intricate details of its webs, modulate its ethos. Instead the economics of real estate is constructing, through advertisement (parasitic activity par excellence), a phantasm of home, a living style, and simultaneously criminalizing the industry as the frenzy has to be driven, heightened and maintained. It is not only that in cities and towns people can no longer afford to have a home, but importantly their experience of home is being corrupted and criminalized in unheard of ways. The idea of home is in danger of being rendered homeless by the parasite 'real estate'. One needs to say a lot more both about how real estate is distorting, stifling and rendering homeless what it is dependent on and, even more importantly, about the kind of language and ethos 'home' needs to flourish. Even these brief remarks about 'real estate' as an example raises an important issue, namely whether such a social phenomenon, rather than being specific to postcolonial India, is a product of capitalism. Although very interesting, it is not an issue we need to address at the moment. For our purposes, it is enough that the example gives a sense of the social phenomenon parasitism designates and what it does to the experience (the organism, as it were) on which it is parasitic. To take another example which has a similar structure: consider health as an experiential domain and the healthcare industry. The economics of the latter, and its allied regimes, user experience studies, advertisement for big hospital chains and health tourism, create a phantasmatic world of fear and need that leave no room for another way of relating to health, namely health as part of ethical living (the fads such as veganism are perhaps a distorted attempt to give expression to the latter in the same way as *vaastu* perhaps plays a similar role in real estate sector).

With the help of these relatively straightforward examples of parasitism, where the parasitic structures distort and smother the experience that nonetheless sustain them, we can now move to cases or domains that seem to have a more complicated structure of dependency and creaming off. Both education and politics present examples of parasitism where the relationship between the experience and the parasitic structures is mediated (if that is the word we need) by disciplines and/or institutions that are inherited from colonialism. One could, of course, point out that here too we can get hold of the experience – learning and governance or self-governance – on which the parasitic structure are erected. Nonetheless, it is not difficult to see that the disciplines and institutions are perpetuated by Indians – academics and politicians – who seem to be parasitic on those disciplines and institutions; and unlike in the case of the flourishing real estate sector, there is no unambiguous answer why those institutions and disciplines are perpetuated. Are there cognitive or practical gain? There is of course a colonial story about why India must have political and educational institutions of the Western kind, but with the exception of Gandhi and Tagore, there has been no attempt really to fundamentally question that story, leave alone developing an alternative story about

SITES OF LEARNING AND INTELLECTUAL PARASITISM

how we want to conceive of education or politics. The enslavement to certain ways of looking at ourselves – which are embodied in the disciplines and the institutions – poses problems about how we understand the structure of parasitism here. If education "obstructs" the Indians' interaction with their conceptual world and at the same time produces enslavement to a frame that prevents any genuine cognition or action, what sustains such insulation and allows its reproduction?

The experience of learning present in the culture may not even impinge, or does so only tangentially, on the disciplines and institutions which perpetuate themselves through the process of cognitive enslavement. Herein lies the complication: unlike in the case of real estate where the domain of experience that was exploited could not be done away with even though it underwent distortion and deformation, in the case of education (we will stay with education in order keep the discussion manageable), the experience of learning has been actively disowned, disavowed and denigrated. It is as though the disciplines and the institutions are parasitic on the process of denying the experience of learning, the denial taking the form of denigration or disavowal of practices which embodied the learning in India! By saying this, I am not advancing any paradoxical claim, but merely noting our predicament. We rightly think of education as a process that abstracts from and elaborates on the learning implicit in a culture. In India, however, education has become a process that denies cultural learning. The parasitic perpetuation of the disciplines and the institutions has meant that new discipline (but not learning) has been instituted. The cultural learning cannot simply be denied in this fashion; so rendered mute, distorted and uncared for, it makes its presence felt by taking hold of the same institutional structures for pragmatic ends. The latter case might make us think of institutions such as the state universities, where everything – faculty selection, vice-chancellorship – is, to put it euphemistically, negotiated. But we would be overlooking the most corrosive aspect of pragmatic parasitism as opposed to the intellectual parasitism, with which we will largely be concerned, if we confine ourselves to the more obvious aspect of what I would like to term the 'creaming off' phenomenon, namely instrumentally exploiting a discipline, a practice or an institution, without being concerned for its integrity or its place in the larger context.[2]

Although there is clearly a distinction between intellectual and pragmatic parasitism, we should be aware of the more complex interdependency or even interchangeability between the two. The practice of natural sciences in India too is a victim of pragmatic parasitism, as indeed is the domain of the arts. The superficial success of Indian science manifested in the global integration of some scientific institutions (and scientists) should not mask the fact that the learning that produced the natural sciences has not been assimilated or made our own. The analysis of that situation has to be postponed to another occasion to focus on the phenomenon that I want to get hold of, namely cognitive enslavement and the intellectual parasitism that it perpetuates. The humanities and the social sciences are hollow because they do not transmit any learning, because they actively deny and denigrate the cultural learning whose incorporation alone could have led to their revitalization and reconceptualization. Ironically, though, if we were to do that, the disciplines which survive only because we are enslaved to them would disintegrate. How do we today, situated as we are in the parasitic structure of the education system, try to incorporate the cultural learning into our disciplinary practices? The task is both daunting and necessary because the cultural learning is not simply there to be appropriated. In fact, as I have suggested or hinted, it is muted and distorted. That is why the task is daunting – the case to be made is that education has to involve articulating that cultural learning, nourishing that experience, formulating new kind of theories for its extension and development. The task is at the same time necessary and urgent because without undertaking it, our intellectual and pragmatic parasitism will continue, making it impossible eventually to even glimpse what is being occluded.

I want to begin this process of interrogating our intellectual parasitism with history and philosophy. To the extent that the questioning I undertake here extends the framework and argument that I have been outlining in my other work, what follows will be simultaneously clarificatory and methodological, substantive and programmatic. My discussion of history will in large part be a commentary on Balagangadhara's provocative talk (Balagangadhara 2014b), which forces Indians to choose between history and the past. Reflecting on the grounds for setting up the choice that way clears the way for posing another, equally dramatic choice which is actually implicit in the first choice, namely: *aadhyatma* or philosophy?

History or the past? Historical consciousness as colonial consciousness

Irawati Karve's *Yuganta* used to be recommended to young people as an exemplary 'progressive' or 'historical' reading of Indian past through its 'mythology' (Karve [1968] 2006). Although I have forgotten most of the book, I still remember its attempt to calculate the age of Bhishma at the time of the Kurukshetra battle. Apparently Bhishma would have been in his late 90s. The image has stayed with me of a frail old man barely able to lift his bow. I must admit to being both angry and amused at that time; but even now when I think about that image, some feeling stirs in me. It is hard to name, perhaps akin to a sense of violation accompanied by a vague feeling of aimless reproach that this should not have happened. Rather than explain away this peculiar affect and its persistence, I want to look at it as the violation of an intuition that is transmitted through a form of what I have called cultural learning. I put it in this cautious and tentative way because no work has been done to understand the ways in which the *Kavyas* and *Puranas* are transmitted. They have of course been subjected to all sorts of analysis and categorization: studied as Hindu religious texts, analyzed as part of Indo-European mythologies, collected as theogony, considered as part of theology, scrutinized as history. When I say we have not studied the ways in which *Kavyas* and *Puranas* have been transmitted, I do not mean those analyses and classifications. They are the problems we inherit as part of our historical consciousness. As long as we regard historical past as exhausting the conception of the past, and historiography as the only approach to it, we will not be able to inquire into the cultural learning that transmits a certain way of relating to the stories and characters of the *Kavyas*.

As a discipline, it would be difficult to find a more eclectic and unself-conscious discipline than history. Not only are its presuppositions unclarified, but its functioning and method tend to be largely ad hoc. As Hayden White (White 2014: 265n5) has repeatedly pointed out, the various aspects of historiography are left unclarified because the vagueness surrounding them is essential to the belief that there is indeed a real referent for 'history'. It is a real miracle why history has such a hold on us! However, although history in its secular garb cannot answer the question about its referent, theology regards history as designating something real and true, namely history as expression of God's plan or intention. Indeed, for theology history tracks the God's Kingdom on earth – history is the history of the Christian *ecclesia*, the community of believers, past, present and future. The notion of truth and falsity too plays a central role in this theological conception, where it is all important to sort out lies about the human past to decipher God's plan for humans. Believing in false or imaginary things would endanger salvation itself. So, history ought to study the true past, which is biblical; by the same token, Christianity turns all the diverse pasts of humanity into so many false pasts that eventually 'ought' to lead to the one true biblical history. From Augustine to

Hegel, this vision was worked into a philosophy of history that was self-consciously theological, and precisely for that reason, there was clarity about what 'history' referred to, and what is truth and falsity in history. The historiographical space is thus a theological space, opened up to validate the story of Jesus' Christ nature as a 'true' story. Subsequently the space acquires many 'theological' properties such as God's plan, pattern, directionality, teleology etc.[3] However, in its secular garb, it can no longer provide these as answers, and as a discipline, it has not been able to come up with a convincing alternative conception of what 'history' refers to and what is historical truth. As the debates about the nature of historical explanation and role of narrative in history have made amply clear, there is not only no clarity about historical truth and historical causality, but history has not quite figured out why the only sense it makes is because of the implicit or explicit narrative structure, thereby making, ironically, the fictive elements or devices central to its intelligibility.

If we focus on the lack of rigour and cohesion of the discipline and its eclectic methods, it becomes hard to understand why anyone has bought into history and the historical attitude, especially in India. The only hypothesis is that somehow (some? considerable number of?) Indians have come to look at their past historically. That is to say, they have taken over the colonial view of Indian past. The 19th century demand to write our own history was the beginning of this process. Having history or wanting history meant taking over the historical attitude already written into the historiography produced. No matter what happens to the evaluations in nationalist or later leftist historiography, the enslavement to history remains. As Nandy has pointed out vividly and forcefully, both the left and the right are the 'illegitimate' children of the West who have now engaged in an epic battle, after escaping from the 'orphanage of history' (Nandy 1995: 65). The historical consciousness has indeed become a major part of the colonial consciousness: to the latter's parasitic use of the colonial descriptions of Indian social and intellectual world (the immoral caste system that is part of the evil Hindu religion), it adds the historical past as the only past. The search for historical truth or the transformation of the past into history creates the kind of problems that we have witnessed – Rama's birthplace, Basaveshwara's rebellion or his caste, or at a much larger and diffuse sense, Aryan invasion. Do the problems arise because of the establishment of 'truths', or something else? How do the factoids – 'Basava tore his sacred-thread' – by themselves create problems? What in the historical narratives has the potential to create problems? We need to understand in greater detail and depth the mechanism by which history destroys the past. Something that Hayden White, a contemporary sceptic about historical knowledge, says might be worth thinking about in this context. His general thesis is that all historical works at bottom rely on or presuppose a philosophy of history (in the theological sense).[4] He also argues that when historical narratives emplot factoids (say annals or chronicles), they necessarily moralize (White 1987). Is the historiographical space already a moralized space and that is the reason why collection of truths has the potential to create conflict and violence? But neither factoids nor narrative as a device have anything to do with moralization. Where does moralization enter? It is always already there in the parasitic acceptance of either the frames or the descriptions or both. When a community is given a 'true' past, which consists in a series of 'factoids' cobbled together as narrative, any 'truth' (that is, any factoid) can acquire great 'moral significance' and any perceived attempt to contest the 'truth' will give rise to conflict because those who are invested in the moral significance of the 'truth', those, in other words, whose history it has become, feel threatened. One cannot any more say that Rama is not an historical figure or that his Ayodhya is not our Ayodhya without incurring the wrath of those invested in the 'factoid'. It is out of the question even to point out that 'Basava tore his sacred-thread' is not an archivally verifiable fact because it has become central to the moralized narrative about Basava and the *vacanakaras*' fight against Brahmanism. The 'objective past' that history thus brings about is not open to intellectual inquiry; it can only be emplotted differently (as White would say). From the utterly derisory colonial to the chic postmodern subaltern historiography (via the earnest nationalist and the righteous leftist), the 'objective past' of India constructed by historiography has remained fixed, but the past has become inaccessible.[5]

Thus, the intellectual parasitism here consists in not only accepting the particular descriptions – say the caste system – but the evaluation that underlies it; similarly looking at the past historically implies not only certain classification and categorization of Indian textual material, but embodying a historical and historicizing view into those material. The attempt, therefore, to calculate Bhishma's age, however ridiculous it appears, is merely implementing the historical view. As do the Sangh Parivar view of Puranic figures, events and names (some of these views are so naive it is hard to believe they are not meant as silly provocation or baiting). When such a historical view comes to embody and endorse a nationalism then there is imminent danger that nothing of the saliences of the cultural learning remains anymore even as a discomfort caused by the intuition of loss. To accept the particular description with the classifications and categorization is to commit oneself to the frame it embodies; to subscribe to the frame implies being led to those descriptions. Doubtless starting one way rather than the other may allow for a limited variety of evaluative and terminological differences ('our historical past was so great we had flying machines and plastic surgery' or 'we will need to get an accurate view of the grisly, oppressive structures of Indian history'), but it is a loop which effectively keeps out any whiff of the cultural learning that might disturb the frame or the description. What is at stake is the loss of a conceptual capacity that the cultural learning had assiduously nurtured.

So the choice: history or the past. But if we choose history, whether the frame or the actual descriptions the frame has produced, we are in effect saying that there is no cultural learning that is likely to bring forth new saliences and knowledge. For some of us, there is no choice at all. When we turn to *itihasa*, our attitude, therefore, cannot be one of either reading it as history or of reading it historically (historicizing it, as they say). What might be thought of as a radical shift is really a natural one. Surely, we cannot be taking the Western frame to understand *itihasa* when *itihasa* has made the past a site of learning for us and has enacted the relationship between truth and the past! Rejecting history as disguised theology is a first step toward reaccessing our past. The next step is to ask what understanding *itihasa* itself embodies or how it makes the past a site of learning. The *iti* in *itihasa* presents truth anaphorically: it refers back to something, but that something is *adhyatmic* truth. However, truth ('*sat*') here is a radically different notion than the truth theology/history was after. The latter has to do with conventional truths, that is, with what exists. *Sat* is real but does not *exist*; it is real because it is not an existent, that is, what perishes and passes. What exists is what we can know cognitively or epistemically; what is real is what we can access experientially. That is why any experience is what it is because it can potentially access the real. Because we can access the real, we can also attain happiness of the kind that is not transitory. *Ananda* is what you experience then when you access or stand in *Sat*, which is not an existent. If accessing the past is accessing *adhyatmic* truth, it cannot be the case that the past is a temporal entity. So, when we say that *itihasa* presents truth anaphorically, the referring back relationship is akin to a logical relationship. The major source of difficulty, the real stumbling block in understanding this notion, has to do with the fact that historical consciousness is an important and particularly invidious component of colonial consciousness. I am wondering if it is due to historical consciousness that we now find it difficult to get away from the idea that the past is in essence a temporal entity. So, while it is undoubtedly true that the anaphoric kind of relationship between *itihasa* and *aadhyatma* or past and truth needs more elaboration than Balagangadhara has given (or I can give), it is important to appreciate the absolutely crucial insight it provides into how we can have a science of experience even though we cannot have a science of happiness. Since the next section will go some way toward clarifying this claim, I will confine myself to correcting what I think is a misleading formulation: after correctly arguing that Mahabharata initiates or sets the context for a learning process through stories about *aadhyatma*, Balagangadhara says that *Talamaddale* teaches by transforming *aadhyatma* into *anu-bhava*. *Aadhyatma* is not a thing, an existent, to be transformed. Since it is reflection about what is accessible in or through experience, I imagine we need to see the *anu* in *anu-bhava* as the transforming or extending or the completing of experience made possible by that access.

Balagangadhara's concern was to show how history effects a separation between *aadhyatma* and *itihasa*. Equally responsible for that separation is the discipline philosophy. We not only have to choose between the past and history, but we have to also confront another choice: philosophy or *aadhyatma*.

Aadhyatma *or philosophy?*

It would appear that all the branches of philosophy (except perhaps logic)[6] deal with problems inherited from theology. If some of them appear transformed, it's only because the new idiom derives either from a pervasive scientism or the use of formidable-seeming logical apparatus. So even though philosophy may shudder to think of itself as handmaid of theology, its problems still bear the imprint of theology. Some essential qualifications need to be noted before we examine how the presence and practice of philosophy could be a problem for Indians. Unlike historical consciousness, which appears to have sunk roots in the Indian sensibility, philosophical structuring of Indian thought seems to be largely confined to the academic field, such as it is. The filtering of Indian intellectual traditions through the classificatory categories and problem field of Western philosophy deforms our access to Indian thought (if we were taking the academic route). This filtering has close links with history to the extent it's the Western historiography of philosophy that influences the classification, thus feeding into and reinforcing the orientalist/indological enterprise of comparing Western theology/philosophy and Indian thought (e.g., the study of Indian 'soteriology' or 'eschatology'). There is yet another strand of Western philosophy that attempts explicitly to shape the historical consciousness, namely Hegelian Marxism. Whether through the scheme of dialectical/historical materialism or through transition and mode of production debates and discussion of class character of the state, the treatment of history and historical consciousness takes explicit philosophical form. Philosophy, then, plays an indirect role in re-elaborating the orientalist picture of Hinduism and its eschatology, its soteriology and spirituality. The separation of *aadhyatma* as philosophy/theology from *itihasa* as either history or mythology is due in large part to philosophy. This separation is then reinforced by the constitution of Indian philosophical texts as objects of philological and translational exercise. Despite this burgeoning scholarship on Indian 'philosophy', our discomfiture with the translation of terms such as *maya* or *sat* or *upadhi* into English (or any other Western language) has not gone away. It cannot be that after more than a century of translating and interpreting Indian thought into 'philosophy', we are still in search of better, more accurate equivalents for these terms. How do we then account for the persisting discomfiture with the English terms for what is regarded as the central concepts of Indian thought? Every time *dharma* is translated as 'religion', we wince; when we see *maya* translated as 'illusion', we protest; *atman* as Self or Soul mystifies us; *upadhi* as 'limitation' or 'obstruction' and *adhyasa* as 'superimposition', while seemingly accurate, just don't afford us any handle on them for the kind of critical thinking they are supposed to enable us to perform. Well, a sophisticated philosophical response would be to say that this discomfiture has to do with the nature of translation itself: given the problematic nature of 'meaning', we have to regard translation as, at best, difficult or, at worst, impossible. If you were a deconstructionist, you might see your task as translator to enhance the discomfiture; if you were a Quinean or a Davidsonian, you would reassure us, on behaviourist or pragmatist ground, that translation does indeed take place, no matter what one does with 'meaning'. Shifting the locus of the problem to translation, however, has the consequence of evading the real source of the discomfiture, which, I want to argue, stems from the transformation of *aadhyatma* into philosophy. Translation contributes to this transformation. The discomfiture will not go away until we realize that we may have to choose between *aadhyatma* and philosophy.

The term *aadhyatma* captures a distinctive kind of reflection on experience that is not specific to any one Indian tradition. When Gandhi, for example, refused to distinguish Buddhism from the traditions normally classified as Hinduism, I imagine this to be his reasoning. Each tradition practices that reflection in its own way. Therefore, while for convenience I might use categories such as Buddhism or Jainism or this or that Bhakti tradition, I want to depart radically from what those classifications mean in the 'philosophical' and 'Indological' literature on Indian traditions. Given our concern with 'translation', it would be appropriate to begin our elaboration of the seemingly simple characterization of Indian traditions as preoccupied with reflection on experience by noting that 'translation' as a problematic never figured in that reflection. None of the debates about poetics or *kavya* even remotely or obliquely talk about translation.[7] Doubtless, we appreciate the significance of this absence comparatively, that is, in relation to the obsessive preoccupation with translation in the Western intellectual traditions. However, once we register the significance of its absence, it is not hard to realize that it has to do with the nature of what we have been calling 'reflection on experience'. Let's begin from the other end and ask why translation/interpretation is such an obsessive problematic for the West. It clearly has to do with the importance of revelation for Christianity as a religion. In fact, rich and prolix body of discourse we call theology exists solely to explain the 'existence' of this extraordinary event and to interpret the 'text' of revelation to transmit the 'experience' of faith. This text has to be maximally consistent, and its intent and meaning has to be deciphered correctly, a challenging and perhaps impossible task given the finitude and failings of the readers. And a disturbing issue that emerges inevitably is: how other tongues especially the pagan ones can 'correctly' translate the message of this text without diluting or distorting or otherwise profaning the sacred word? The ones left out of the privileged community have to be saved by conveying the Truth to them, but what if their language obscures or worse falsifies the Truth? So, we have here the generation of interpretation/translation as a problem of theological hermeneutics; the power of the problem and the strategies of tackling it are later carried over to 'secular' disciplines dealing with texts – literary or philosophical – and their meaning. The relationship between philosophy and theology is a complex one, since philosophy – the Greek experience as Heidegger would say – precedes theology, but the latter fundamentally shapes the former from the early Middle Ages, as again Heidegger often notes and bemoans (Heidegger 1959: 13). No matter how 'secular' modern or even contemporary philosophy and its divisions (morality, epistemology and ontology) sound, at bottom, its problems are derived from theological concerns. So, translation/interpretation/commentary carries over the theologically determined model to the organization of philosophy and its auxiliary branches too. There are activities that are parasitic, second-rate, and yet unavoidable and even indispensable. In fact, one could argue that the problem of interpretation/translation is caught in the theological working out of the Christological dilemma, since the latter arises because the Christ nature can only be revealed to a community, and yet the truth of that has to be universalized even if that requires the shedding of the particularity of the Christ figure and the message he embodies.[8] Translation, the ultimate parasitic activity, is, therefore, always regarded in the West as a betrayal, but a necessary one.[9]

In contrast, what we find in India are different forms of preserving reflections on experience. When Gandhi takes to the *Gita*, he does so because it is, as he puts it, someone's experience and hence repeatable. That is to say, he is able to see it as someone's reflection that helps in clarifying experience. Of course, by the time Gandhi reads the *Gita*, the theological frame of European scholars and colonial institutions have turned it into a 'religious' text closest by some reckoning to the Bible (after all a god-figure is offering his discourse to a human-figure), one of the three important 'texts' of Hindu religion/theology/philosophy. The powerful classificatory enterprise of Western hermeneutics had slotted the epics as Indian mythology, the Vedas as in part theology and metaphysics and in part philosophy. This was 'classical' Hinduism to which the 'popular' Hinduism of the *Bhakti* traditions was counter-posed. What about the tradition of commentary (*Bhashya* and *Karica*) on the central texts? Aren't they very much like the biblical hermeneutics? They can indeed be made to appear that way if we look through the theological frame.[10] If we, as a thought experiment, try to set aside that frame and try to grasp the variety of traditions – ranging from the *advaitavedanta* with its triumvirate of 'texts' to *vacanakaras* of 12th century, from *Kashmiri Saivism* to *Bauls* of Bengal, reflection on experience is recognizably the organizing focus of them, but we would be hard put to show any central or foundational 'texts' for them. With the help of the theological frame, we could perhaps try to constitute a 'text' for them or even constitute them as texts, as the Indological enterprise has even now been busy doing. However, making sense of the texts seems an activity that can hardly be found except in some traditions, precisely the ones that the Western scholarship has held up as 'classical' Hinduism. As I pointed out earlier, it is not difficult to understand why the West constructed these entities to make sense of a culture that otherwise seemed bewilderingly different: understanding the 'text' is a matter of reinforcing the *faith* in an event, which is like no other

SITES OF LEARNING AND INTELLECTUAL PARASITISM

event. In contrast, for some Indian traditions texts, if this entity could be said to exist, are an aid to understand experience. Let's remember that it is the Vedantic tradition, supposedly text-centric, that regards *Vedas* themselves as potential *vaasana*. So there has been translation/interpretation of the 'texts' of Indian traditions within the theological frame, but no understanding of the traditions from which these texts have been extracted.[11] Contrary, then, to the well-known Davidsonian claim, translation/interpretation need not yield understanding of the other, especially when that activity construes the other as a variation of itself. This may appear a familiar story making a familiar point. The story may well be familiar, but the point is not. The bland constructivism that seems to have attained the status of a scholarly dogma has actually obscured the point and its consequences. The West-constructed, invented 'Hinduism' means just that, namely the latter is an experiential entity for the West. Evidence shows that it experienced Indian culture in that way. That does not mean that 'Hinduism' has now come to exist (ontologically real, as it were). It still is an imaginary entity in the ontological (or any other) sense of non-existing.[12] That is as clear as I can make it. What has created havoc in the meantime is the dogma I previously mentioned, according to which all things are invented, constructed, imagined – and so is 'Hinduism'.[13] One has heard that the Christian God is powerful, but one hadn't quite realized that his power endowed the religious culture he brought forth the further power of creating religions at will! So, if you accept (or more likely presuppose without realizing it since it is the common sense) this dogma, you have no way of appreciating the point I have been making about how things look if one accepts the theological frame. Whether it is the larger point about 'Hinduism' a religion or the regimentation of Indian thought along the familiar lines of Western philosophical disciplines, there is no reason to think that the frame is inescapable or compulsory. As long as that frame is firmly in place, and I believe it still governs the disciplines we are concerned with here, our discomfiture with the translation/interpretation will persist.

A framework distilled out of the self-understanding of Christian Europe was used to make sense of the intellectual and cultural world of India. This is a perfectly sensible and entirely defensible strategy, of course, since there is perhaps no other way to begin understanding another culture. The classificatory structures they used and the entities they postulated no doubt made experiential sense to Europeans. The only question that has not been addressed at all satisfactorily is why this frame has persisted even now when its disciplinary structures (I will not call it learnings) simply fail to capture the cultural learnings and salience of Indians that underlie the stories, the reflections, the practices that got so drastically regimented in that frame? But persist it has; whether or not the revelation has reached everyone, the theological/philosophical frame has imposed its structures and terminologies everywhere. Although we can always come up with exceptions such as Gandhi whose access to the reflection on experience is not distorted by that frame or the terminology it brings, in the academic world, it is indeed rare to find someone resisting the talk of Indian soteriology, Indian religious texts, Indian myths, leave alone the academically respectable field classification such as Buddhist epistemology, *Advaita* metaphysics, Jain morality and so on. The terminological issues may be secondary, though they are far from insignificant, but the formulation of the problematics is not. If the latter fails to capture the cultural saliences, or, worse, presents what is unrecognizable to the reader as a problem, one's intuition remains unengaged or is drastically misled. After all, what one calls intuition in this context is what results from the transmission of cultural learning; and once that transmission is disrupted, over time the cultural learning itself goes mute, leaving the disciplinary practitioners of philosophy without any intuitions.[14] Cultural learning and disciplinary practice have never come together in the case of philosophy in India. So, we have here a complicated structure of parasitism: the practitioners have perhaps unwittingly become parasitic on a discipline presumably for some cognitive gain which they are yet to realize, but the discipline itself, like a true parasite, is harming the nourishing soil, the cultural learning whose concepts and problematic as an intellectual discipline it should have been articulating.

Taking my cue from Gandhi's use of the *Gita* and, more generally, his engagement with Indian thought, I want to show that we can only fully understand the source of our discomfiture with the translation of the concepts of Indian thought when we realize that reflection on experience has its sole focus on the removal of structures of parasitism that inhibit and distort experience. A corollary of this large argument that has implication for translation is that instead of worrying about how to render *upadhi* and *maya* in English, we need to think of forms of parasitism and its self-concealment. That way, we will begin to understand how Indian traditions directed us to reflect on experience. Translation of Indian thought, even if possible in some obvious sense, may not be the route to reappropriate Indian thought. Although Gandhi, as I remarked earlier, borrows the terminology that came with the new frame, his intuition was seeking to use the resources of the

SITES OF LEARNING AND INTELLECTUAL PARASITISM

traditions in consonance with the cultural learning underlying those traditions. When he sought, therefore, to understand the effect of colonialism on Indians, he wanted to analyze the obstacles to self-knowledge. He realized that the structures of parasitism that colonialism was busy creating had contributed further to those obstacles by actively interfering in the transmission of what I have been calling the cultural learning. Gandhi was, of course, thinking of the separation between practice and learning rather than the much narrower problem of discipline and learning that concerns us here; the diagnosis, however, remains relevant. We must freshly wonder again at the striking novelty or, depending on your perspective, the complete oddity of Gandhi's route of inquiry into colonialism. When he formulated *swaraj* or self-knowledge as the only way of understanding and resisting colonialism, he was in effect practicing *aadhyatma* or reflection on experience. As he readily confessed, he had very little 'knowledge' of Indian 'philosophy'. He wasn't concerned about how to translate *Atman* or *Maya* or *Sat*, nor about their metaphysical or ontological character. Although he did not set out his reasoning in any detail, he realized that Indian thought concerns itself with ethical action (a pleonastic expression if we follow Gandhi's *Gita*) without metaphysics or ontology. If we want to term it philosophy, it's philosophy as activity.

What kind of activity is it? In one formulation, we could say that it is an activity that aims to fully realize experience. When talking about reflection on experience, it is important to realize that we invariably use experience to refer to what occurs or happens (*bhava*), as well as to the result of the activity of assimilating or understanding what happens, what we undergo (*anu-bhava*).[15] How to turn the happenings – sad or happy, ordinary or extraordinary, natural or social – into experience constitutes the *adhyatmic* inquiry. Clearly there are any number of ways of saliencing what is important and how to transform that into experience. Elsewhere I have coined the term 'practitional matrix' to conceptualize experiential inquiry that characterize the Indian intellectual traditions. The thought behind it is something like this: action is always action in a matrix, like a gesture in a dance, sound in a *raga*, or offering in a ritual. You learn to appease the ancestors and that involves engaging the past in a practitional matrix; you express your gratitude to the implements that have helped in your interaction with the world, so *ayudha puja* is a practitional matrix that engages the implements. Since there are no events or occurrences that are by themselves trivial or significant, and there may be multiple ways of engaging each event or aspect or dimension of what occurs, diversity of practitions is a given. Hence the diversity of Indian traditions. The central inquiry though is about awareness or self-consciousness – realizing the *atman* is the way one tradition speaks of it (*Vedantins*), another might speak of 'standing in awareness' (*arivinalli niluvu*, a phrase used by *Vacanakaras* writing in Kannada), but none speak of it as a 'religious' or 'mystical' event only manifest to some, and none can actually attain it, as is the case with monasticization in Christianity. The theological or normative frame has, unfortunately, turned the talk of *atman* into some sort of revelation, and the Bhakti traditions (so-called popular Hinduism) have been accorded the mystic status.

Every element that is potentially a way of completing experience is also a way in which experience could get distorted or occluded altogether. An architect concerned with understanding how space can enhance living or relationship of those who inhabit it begins to be parasitic on the real estate sector's exploitation of land for selling phantasmatic ideas of living. A singer begins to make her musical pursuit secondary to the fame concerts bring in. A politician begins to love his own exploits for the rewards and fame they bring in. A scientist becomes enamoured of the junketing that international collaborations bring in. These are not unusual examples by any means since any of us could be or are in that position. What it highlights is the peculiar structure of parasitism. Doing things for fame or making the latter motivate your pursuit has ways of occluding and perhaps terminating the really important things, namely the pursuit itself, because the phantasy supporting the desire conceals the parasitic structure. This is the case even if you are a human being not pursuing anything like science or music. The texture of the relationships could come under strain as you get caught in a phantasmatic conception of yourself as say attractive or tough and so on. What the parasitism ultimately occludes is experience that enables you to have self-knowledge. When Gandhi began to see that colonialism had begun to create parasitism through, for example, medicine, law and the state, and that these institutions were distorting or occluding experience, he was not distinguishing, as Marxists and Liberals were to do later, colonialism as some material process with no effect on experience (taken in a narrow sense as subjective). The violence of colonialism, he realized, consisted in very deeply fragmenting the saliences that had organized the practitional matrix, thereby in the long run undermining the very integrity of experience. His attempt to reorganize the saliences drew from the same resources that had indeed enabled him to see how the violence of colonialism had a disintegrating effect on experience itself.[16] Stripped of the practitional structure, actions tended to be automatism, occurrences and incidents traumatic. The result was perhaps the last great concept to come out of Indian traditions, namely, *satyagraha*, yet another concept that can indeed be translated (as it has been), but the translation 'truth force' simply makes no sense as it equates an epistemic concept – 'truth' – with an ontological one – '*sat*'. Could the structure and activities that have become parasitic be transformed through *satyagraha* into sites of learning? How can new sites of learning be brought into being so that the automatism of actions and trauma of occurrences be transformed into experience, and the phantasy that conceals the parasitic nature and perpetuates desire be therapeutically engaged if not removed? The crucial concept here is that of sites of learning. There is no limit to the kind of practical learnings there can be which enables one to transform structures, occurrences, emotions into experiences. The body, time, relationships, place . . . all these can turn into *upadhis*, or they could be transformed into sites of learning. And what is a site of learning for one tradition may not be a site of learning for another, or not in the same way. Erotics is way of learning for one tradition (think of Tantric traditions), for another it is austerity of a certain kind.[17]

The concept 'practitional matrix' enables us to understand the way experiential knowledge works and why it is necessarily an ever-expanding field. It helps us model how rich tradition of *kavyas* and *shastras* emerge in the process of tackling multiple aspects of living, whether it is engaging the past, arranging the living space, appreciating beauty, incorporating consideration of taste and health, elaborating erotics, and so on. The cultural learning that this process creates does not consist in any doctrine it yields (the *shastras* are not doctrines) but structures ways of doing things – practical knowledge, in short. What the process also produces is what we might term action-theoretic concepts, that is, concepts that one understands only by understanding their function in the matrix.[18] Concepts such as *manana*, *shravana*, *nidhidysana*, or *upadhi*, *avidya*, *maya* too are action-theoretic concepts; they are not (metaphysical or ontological) descriptions of the world. Looking for translation of them as though they are descriptions (even if metaphysical) of the world has the effect of turning them into obscure, mystic, religious entities. Entities in the world do not come with *upadhi* written over them, for instance. Whether my body or my past becomes an *upadhi* depends on my relationship to it. Nor is any entity, action or discipline parasitic in itself. When for example I become parasitic on fame, how am I supposed to understand 'fame'? What kind of *upadhi* is it? What makes it one? If, however, we want to understand how *upadhi* functioned in *advaita*, we do better by trying to understand parasitism in our contemporary experience. Are we thereby translating *upadhi*? Or are we drawing on Indian thought to understand ourselves critically? Does recognizing the self-concealment of parasitic structures and activities help us understand why *maya* was such a powerful insight?

Finally, to return briefly to the choice *aadhyatma* or philosophy: my claim has been that there is disjuncture between the practice of the discipline of philosophy and the cultural learning that underlies Indian thought and its diverse paths of organizing reflection on experience. This raises a large and difficult question about whether this claim implies that Western philosophy is inimical to experience or, less strongly, at least to certain ways of reflecting on it. Although the context of Indian thought regimented by philosophy has forced this way of formulating the question, it does nevertheless throw light on why there has been a significant strand of thinking within Western philosophy – from Marx and Nietzsche to Heidegger and Wittgenstein – which has sought the end of philosophy. It may well be that the destruction of the past goes hand in hand with the destruction of experience, if indeed it is not the same process. The unease generated by this process must have registered at some level and in some form in Western thinking.[19] Indeed, both philosophy and history come to be regarded with profound distrust by many thinkers after Marx, the most prominent being Nietzsche, Heidegger and Foucault (Wittgenstein too, but he questioned only philosophy). Maybe our attempt – following Gandhi – to bring to bear the cultural learning on the practice of philosophy provides a different, experiential route to that task. Worrying about interpretation/translation of concepts of Indian thought, however, will keep us within the fold of Western philosophy, making us parasitic without us realizing it.

Home

From real estate to philosophy, being parasitic means to be homeless. There was a time not so long ago when being at home meant being literally open to the world. In villages and even towns, once the door was opened in the morning, it would remain open till nightfall. We can take an historical view and argue that that arrangement depended on the way work was distributed and on patriarchy and so on. Even so one would be hard put to deny a conception of home that was still at work, that was if you like part of the cultural learning. In that conception home meant openness to the world, a place where the structure of learning through experience – what I have called the practitional matrix – was put in place. By making the past external to us, history denies such learning. It is historicized away as nostalgia. We glibly say that past cannot be retrieved, without realizing that we are disowning learning in our confused attempt to be historical. We regard figures such as Ramaksrishna Paramahamsa or Ramana Maharshi as mystics, and even if we feel certain awe toward them, we conceal that with expression of condescension. Gandhi gets treated as a benign father of the nation, his thought and action finding no resonance in our thinking. Both history and philosophy, the new tools we proudly use, render them alien to us. We discuss concepts such as *atman* and *upadhi* in the same way as we write commentaries on Hegel's essence and appearance. Without knowing how to understand the two traditions, we treat both traditions as charlatans. If history renders the past external and phantasmatic, philosophy insulates experience from reflection.

We are at home in thinking when our cultural learning is made available for articulation either as practitions or as theories. When, however, the disciplines of the human sciences actually make us disavow our cultural learning, and do so, moreover, without offering any new learning, we have no choice but to begin the slow work of re-understanding education as setting up of sites of learning, to recover, create, nurture and articulate our cultural learnings.

Notes

1 In Bangalore today, we are offered every possible 'dwelling' – Mediterranean, Californian, New York style etc., everything except the homely Bangalorean way, which either does not exist or the advertising industry has no use for it.
2 One can think of any number of examples, from the IT and bio-technology industries, which have exploited the market without in any way contributing to the growth of research, to the flourishing art market, which again contributes very little to creating institutions. This is not the place to undertake what would otherwise be a necessary analysis of this creaming-off phenomenon in postcolonial India.
3 Without scrutinizing its epistemic credentials, people tend to assume that it would be committing genetic fallacy to point out history's obvious connection with theology. When Nandy in his powerful and pioneering essay (Nandy 1995) wonders why history is not reflexive enough to critique itself so that it can realize the dangers of historical consciousness, the answer has to do with the fact that history in its secular guise has not been able to replace its theological assumptions or premises. That has to be the response also to those attracted by historical inquiry and narrative ask why we cannot have both *itihasa* and history. Within the comparative science of cultures' ambit (Balagangadhara 2012: Ch 3), the only way to argue for historiography is to show that historiography does not inherit any property from theology and that it is indeed an intellectual discipline or resource that contributes to the project of comparative science

of cultures. The latter is not interested in writing a history of (any aspect of) the West or of India. It has set itself the task of building a story of how a people come to be that people. But that's a story of how a configuration of learning emerges, what are the loops set up between it and social structures and social organizations.

4 Hayden White (2014) too agrees that we have to choose between the past and history, because (as he put it in his personal communication dated 18 February 2015), history brings with it too many prepackaged presuppositions and premises to be remade for liberation purposes. I think that Oakeshott doesn't quite realize, like Nietzsche and Foucault obliquely did, and as Balagangadhara and Nandy explicitly do, that one cannot have both a historical past and a practical past, that the former will destroy the latter. Indeed, one could argue that when history begins to destroy the past, the practical past will be forced to use the historical past to enact the kind of 'farce' Marx famously talked about.

5 If you want to destroy the past of a culture, Balagangadhara argues, give it history. Ashish Nandy makes the same point when he argues for alternative *to* history rather than alternative histories (always in the plural, of course) favoured by the cultural left (Nandy 1995). What implication does Balagangadhara's claim have for our understanding of the only truly historical culture we know, namely the West?

6 I say 'perhaps' mainly because it is unclear if the modal intuitions underlying the work on modal logic are universally shared.

7 See Rao (2014: Ch 8) for an illuminating discussion of this claim.

8 On the importance of the Christological dilemma for understanding the dynamic of Christianity as a religion, the indispensable work is Balagangadhara (1994).

9 As Salman Rushdie playfully suggests in his *Midnight's Children*, the dark-blue playful pagan god Krishna could be used in evangelization to illustrate the Christ figure, but the danger obviously is that the latter might end up becoming just another avatar, even if somehow the immorality and deceitfulness associated with Krishna could be overlooked!

10 I have elsewhere (Dhareshwar 2012) called it the quasi-cognitive/normative frame and contrasted it with the actional frame of Indian traditions.

11 When Derrida undertook to deconstruct the transcendental signifieds of Western philosophy, it's remarkable that he had to claim the world as a text! To claim that 'There is nothing outside the text' is therefore a deeply theological move, no matter how playful or ironic it is supposed to be. It would not be out of place, therefore, to propose, playfully and ironically, of course, a claim such as: There is no 'text' in Indian traditions.

12 Even Ian Hacking, otherwise so acute, misses the point when he discusses constructivism (1999). To add further confusion to an already muddled doctrine, he introduces a category called interacting kind. Thus, if we apply his scheme to the case at hand, not only the invented religion 'Hinduism' conveniently comes to exist (be ontologically real), by interaction with it, people become that category. It's all rather mysterious what property the invented kind has and how it lends that property to those interacting with it. Perhaps constructivism does indeed possess more powers than what even the most ardent theologians could not hope to find in religion.

13 Nicholas Dirks' *Castes of Mind* (Dirks 2001) is a near perfect enactment of the confusion created by the dogmatic application of constructivism.
14 For an illustration, see my discussion of Matilal (Dhareshwar 2012).
15 The term 'experience' will now have connotations that cannot be restricted to 'past experience, accumulated knowledge' and 'current experience, sensory or sensory like', which according to the linguist Wierzbicka constitutes the cultural legacy of English (Wierzbicka 2010).
16 I have set out a framework (Dhareshwar 2015), drawn largely from Tagore and Gandhi, which allows us to see how both these thinkers insist on seeking explanations of the Indian predicament, its indistinction, its having disintegrated into facts, from within the actional frame, so that the very activity goes toward making the frame distinct, even as the explanation offered illuminates what has rendered India indistinct and helps in seeking ways to strengthen the dharmic activity. The actional frame is what Tagore calls the rhythm of dharmic activity that helps 'assimilate truth'.
17 I have developed the concept of sites of learning to explain both Gandhi's response to colonialism and his understanding of ethical action in Dhareshwar (2011).
18 There is nothing mysterious in this: think of 'cover drive' or 'square-cut' which cannot be understood except by having some understanding of the practitional matrix, namely cricket, within which that concept/action has sense. Bernard Williams once contrasted thin concept such as 'right' with thick concepts that are action guiding and world guided. His claim was that under the sway of morality, thick concepts are disappearing (Williams, 1985). The action-theoretic concepts of the practitional world fit the bill better because they are truly action guiding and world guided. For a discussion of the practitional matrix in a comparative perspective, see Dhareshwar (2014).
19 Historians such as Pierre Nora have expressed their grave concern that the historical activity of constructing memorials and monuments – *the lieux de mémoire* – seems to be adversely affecting the *milieu de mémoire* (Nora 1989).

References

Balagangadhara, S. N. 1994. *'The Heathen in His Blindness. . .': Asia, the West and the Dynamic of Religion.* Leiden, New York, and Cologne: E.J. Brill.

———. 2014a. 'Comparative Science of Cultures: A Methodological Reflection', in *Reconceptualizing India Studies.* New Delhi: Oxford University Press.

———. 2014b. 'What Do Indians Need, A History or the Past? A Challenge or Two to Indian Historians', Maulana Azad Lecture 2014. ICHR website (accessed on 6th June 2015).

Dhareshwar, Vivek. 2011. 'Politics, Experience, and Cognitive Enslavement: Gandhi's Hind Swaraj', in A. Bilgrami (ed.), *Democratic Culture: Historical and Philosophical Essays*, pp. 64–86. New Delhi: Routledge.

———. 2012. 'Framing the Predicament of Indian Thought: Gandhi, the Gita, and Ethical Action', *Asian Philosophy*, 22 (3): 257–274.

———. 2014. 'Critique, Genealogy and Ethical Action', in A. Bilgrami (ed.), *Marx, Gandhi and Modernity: Essays Presented to Javeed Alam*, pp. 98–126. New Delhi: Tulika.

———. 2015. 'Truth or Fact? Reframing the Gandhi-Tagore Debate' (Unpublished).

Dirks, Nicholas. 2001. *Castes of Mind*. Princeton: Princeton University Press.

Hacking, Ian. 1999. *The Social Construction of What?* Cambridge, MA: Harvard University Press.

Heidegger, Martin. 1959. *An Introduction to Metaphysics*. Trans. R. Manheim. New Haven: Yale University Press.

Karve, Iravati. 2006. *Yuganta: The End of an Epoch*. 2nd edition. Hyderabad: Orient Blackswan.

Nandy, Ashis. 1995. 'History's Forgotten Doubles', *History and Theory*, 34 (2): 44–66.

Nora, Pierre. 1989. 'Between Memory and History: Les Lieux de Mémoire', *Representations*, 26 (Spring 1989): 7–24.

Rao, Venkat. 2014. *Cultures of Memory in South Asia: Orality, Literacy and the Problem of Inheritance*. New Delhi: Springer.

White, Hayden. 1987. 'On the Value of Narrativity in the Representation of Reality', in *The Content of the Form*, pp. 1–25. Baltimore: Johns Hopkins University Press.

———. 2014. *The Practical Past*. Evanston: Northwestern University Press.

Wierzbicka, Anna. 2010. *Experience, Evidence and Sense: The Hidden Cultural Legacy of English*. Oxford: Oxford University Press.

Williams, Bernard. 1985. *Ethics and the Limits of Philosophy*. Cambridge, MA: Harvard University Press.

4

WHY COMMUNALISM IS AN *INDIAN* PROBLEM

The relationship between communalism and Hinduism in colonial discourse

Sufiya Pathan

The rising domain of the 'critical humanities' raises several questions about the way the West has colonized the humanities and social sciences and seeks to find alternatives to this dominant discourse. One of its most pertinent concerns is the effect this dominant discourse has had on the way communities were conceptualized in the South by the forces of colonization and the impact of this conceptualization. For instance, one of the questions raised in the call for papers on critical humanities was the following: 'What is the place of the objectifying (constative) discourses among cultural formations which lived on for millennia by means of reflexive-praxial modes?' Before one answers this question, however, we must ask a prior question, as to whether we *understand* these constative discourses and can reconstruct them coherently. We have assumed that we do understand and can reconstruct these discourses with ease. In addition, we believe that we have also discovered the flaws within these discourses and have thus been able to move beyond them.

It is only with the work of S.N. Balagangadhara that these commonly held beliefs have found a strong challenge. He proposes that colonial discourse expresses the experience of the colonizer (Balagangadhara 1994, 2010, 2012). A crucial part of this experience is shaped by the Western engagement with Christianity. Without an understanding of this engagement, that took place over centuries, it is facile to claim that we have the tools to understand colonial discourse. The depth of this seemingly simple claim is staggering. Following from this insight, even a preliminary investigation shows that we have neither understood the premises of colonial discourse, nor have we been able to dismantle it and move beyond. This chapter attempts one such preliminary investigation into the colonial discourse on 'communalism'.

Let us begin with a simple question that should be easily answered if we are indeed in a position to reconstruct the colonial understanding of the problem of communalism. Why did so many British colonial officials and scholars see communalism as a problem unique to India? That is, if communalism is religious intolerance or antagonism (whatever else it may be in addition to this), then what made it a uniquely *Indian* problem, so much so that a new term had to be coined to talk about this phenomenon in India? The British were no strangers to religious antagonism in Britain and in Europe at large. There is no question that Europe faced a great deal of internal upheaval as well as interstate wars in the aftermath of the Reformation because of the irreconcilable differences between Catholics and the variety of Protestant Churches that sprang up across Europe at the time. Whether it is the massacres of St. Bartholomew's day in 1527 or the large-scale immigration of Puritans from England to the new promised land of America under the persecution of the Church of England in the 17th century, Europe had witnessed tremendous problems of religious difference and intolerance.[1] Much before the conflicts between different Churches, the popular anti-Jewish sentiment had often erupted into violence. Large-scale massacres of Jews took place during the First Crusade. These continued intermittently, and Jews were expelled from England in 1290 and from France in 1306.[2] Yet, the British did not see their struggles with religious differences as a parallel to the Indian situation. Why?

This chapter is an attempt to better understand and point towards an answer to this question. The chapter doesn't claim to provide a full answer to the question, but offers an important first step since contemporary scholarship has never seriously considered this question. Scholars may accuse British administrators and scholars of high-handedness for seeing communalism as a peculiarly Indian problem,[3] but do not consider whether the British actually did see this as a unique problem and how they could have held this to be the case.

The reason for contemporary scholarship to brush aside this question lies in one of its key assumptions about colonial scholarship. This is the assumption that colonial scholarship on India, in general, was a product of prejudice and colonial superiority. Thus, the colonial blindness to parallels with their own situation is easily dismissed as yet another product of prejudice. This assumption may be true or false.

However, it is important to gauge its impact on our ability to understand colonialism. The idea of colonial prejudice has come to act as a completely unverifiable *explanation* in contemporary scholarship. This rationalization does not give us any systematic answers to what we may reject as a product of prejudice and what we must deal with as a factual description of India within colonial scholarship. Thus, scholars are left free to reject, in an arbitrary manner, whatever does not fit into their own accounts and accept as an unprejudiced true description that which does fit. This leads to two problems: one, we remain unable to unearth the premises of colonial discourse and two, we are doomed to simply distort and reproduce them.

In such a scenario, for any systematic understanding of colonial discourse to emerge, we must give up our reliance on this rationalization and instead attempt to build a coherent account in relation to the colonial experience of India. The first section of this chapter makes a case for such a strategy by taking up an examination of two colonial writers, one representing the classical colonial administrative stand on India and the other, an India sympathizer. If the idea of colonial prejudice was to serve any purpose in our understanding of colonial discourse, we should find that the sympathizer would not express the same attitudes that the hard-core colonial administrator does. Yet, we find, this is not the case. The section shows that there are no significant points of difference in their understanding of communalism. Both of them corroborate that while colonial officials saw communalism as a problem of religious antagonism, they still saw it as a special problem unique to India.

The following section will bolster this point by investigating the colonial attitude to the notion of toleration. If communalism was the problem of religious intolerance, would Europe's solution to this problem serve the Indian case as well? Strikingly, the answer was negative. While many colonial observers conceded that toleration existed in much greater measure in India than it had in Europe, they were still convinced that India was also communal. Thus, unlike in Europe where toleration was posed as the cure for religious antagonism, in India, communalism and toleration coexisted side by side. The last section therefore considers the proposition that there are key assumptions that generate the idea of communalism in colonial accounts that we have not yet been able to identify or understand.

'Communalism': Indian or universal?

To begin with, one must note here that the term communalism became popular only around 1925. If one examines the Home files and Home

Political files of the Indian National Archives, we see that the use of the term 'communal tension' appears first in 1924 and refers to a question and answer session in Parliament related to the instrumentality of the vernacular press in inciting Hindu–Muslim clashes.[4] Before 1924, the term communal seems to appear only to speak of 'communal representation', which forms a large category of entries every year in the Home files and Home Political files since 1906. There are, of course, entries on 'riots' and 'disturbances' up to 1924 that are not called 'communal', but include incidents that did come to be called 'communal' once the term gained currency. In 1923, for instance, under 'riots', there are a large number of entries under 'Hindu–Muslim clashes' along with entries on the 'salt riots'. In 1925, there is a sudden spurt in the use of the term, with the Home Political files for that year containing three categories: 'communal disturbances', 'communal riot(s)' and 'communal tension'.

Thus, in the mid-1920s, colonial officials recognized some kind of violence as 'communal violence' that required separate attention. From this point on, 'communalism' became a common term of use amongst both colonial and Indian writers.[5] In this section, I take up only two major colonial writers post-1925 who took up communalism for analysis. These writings are fairly representative of the general opinion and are perhaps the most mature and well-considered colonial work on the issue until the work of the well-known W. C. Smith (1946). There is, of course, a great deal of attention paid to 'Hindu–Muslim antagonism' by colonial writers much before this. Part of this literature will come up for analysis in the following section on toleration.

One of the first essays specifically devoted to the new term, 'communalism', by a colonial authority was Hugh McPherson's 'The Origin and Growth of Communal Antagonism, Especially between Hindus and Muhammadans, and the Communal Award', published in 1932. McPherson's stand on communalism is one that would be echoed by almost all colonial thinkers after him and had no doubt been expressed by others, without the benefit of the term communalism, much before him.

Typical to the colonial position were the following assertions:

1 Communalism was not a British invention, but was a problem native to India and dated back at least as far back as the Muslim invasion of India.
2 It was essentially a *religious* problem. As McPherson puts it:

The differences which separate Hindu and Muslim are essentially religious. They may be reinforced by historical tradition, by political rivalries, or by economic contrasts, but for the great masses of the population it is the religious issue alone that counts.

(McPherson 1932: 109)

3   While the problem went long back in history, it had been aggravated by late 19th century and early 20th century developments in the nationalist movement and was partly the result of 'the general uneasiness induced in all minds by the fear of impending changes in the constitutional structure' (Ibid. 118).
4   The average Hindu and Muslim lived in harmony (more so in rural than in urban India), until some political or unexpected social clash stirred the underlying religious antagonism to come to the fore.

The great masses of the rural population, whether Hindu or Muhammadan, are simple cultivators, who at all normal times live in peace and amity.... The urban masses are more prone to communal strife, because life is more complicated in the towns. Here political friction often stimulates religious antagonism; temples and mosques are closer together; there is more danger of collision in the narrow streets, and a large admixture of the rowdy turbulent elements that love disorder for its own sake and for its opportunities. The educated classes of both communities, when their vision is not temporarily clouded by some communal issue, work harmoniously together in all walks of life.

(Ibid. 118–119)

5   And, while the problem of safeguarding minority rights was not unique to India, communalism was a unique problem in many ways.

Indian public men often refer with quite unnecessary shame to the necessity for communal safeguards under the new constitution. Mr. Gandhi has referred to it as a 'humiliation'. But the problem of minority safeguards is not peculiar to India.... The adequate protection of minorities against unfair treatment by the majority is now recognised to be a matter of international concern. General rules for securing the rights of minorities are becoming part of the international law of Europe and are embodied in the constitutions of at least ten States.

In many respects, however, the Indian communal problem stands alone and has no parallel elsewhere. The various communities have lived together for many generations. Their fundamental rights have been declared in Royal Proclamations on several historic occasions during the last century, and are taken for granted. But now that the British Government have declared their intention of conferring upon India a large measure of responsible self-government, the struggle of the various communities is for political power; for adequate representation in the public services, in the legislatures, in local bodies and in the provincial and central executives.

(Ibid. 122–123, emphasis added)

McPherson seems to claim that communalism is a universal problem of minority communities that is most acute in urban areas because of the presence of antisocial elements in these areas, while at the same time claiming that it is a problem specific to India and one that plagues every part of India. Where he claims a special status to the problem in India, he merely lists certain specific historical conditions. But, this is not an explanation for what makes the problem specific to India since every context of religious intolerance had its own specific historical context. That the two communities had lived together for generations did not make a special case in India. Whether it was the gypsies or the Jews, the early struggle with minorities in Europe was not with new immigrant communities, but with communities that had lived with the dominant group over centuries. Thus, McPherson's account, taken in isolation, does not provide a coherent picture. Perhaps other, more extended accounts would help us complete the picture?

The first book-length study on communalism was Clifford Manshardt's *The Hindu–Muslim Problem in India*, published in 1936. Unlike McPherson, who may be seen as a colonial administrator out to justify the need for British rule in India, Manshardt was sympathetic to India's anti-colonial nationalist movement. As an American living in India, a resident of Nagpada, Bombay, and the first director of the Tata Institute of Social Sciences, he claimed he had 'devoted the last nine years to a practical attempt to bring about communal unity' (Manshardt 1936: Preface). His account, however, reproduces all of the above points. Thus, even from the perspective of a sympathizer, communalism was native to India and also specific to India. This should render suspect the assumption of colonial superiority as an explanation for this attitude. While there is no way to ascertain that a sympathizer does not also have some deep-seated notions of superiority, such an explanation can only be a matter of speculation given the lack of clarity about how to identify such attitudes of superiority and what claims to take as evidence of the same.

The only point of difference between the two writers was that Manshardt did not entirely blame the nationalist movement for the recent rise of communal tension as McPherson did. In contrast to Indian nationalists, however, he was also reluctant to place the blame for communalism solely on the British constitutional reforms, which had made the provision of separate electorates for Muslims in India.

> We are fully alive to the arguments against communal representation, but we cannot think that it is the effective cause of this deplorable friction. At the same time we are no less clearly convinced that separate communal electorates serve to perpetuate political divisions on purely communal lines, and we have every sympathy with those who look forward to the day when a growing sense of common citizenship and a general recognition of the rights of minorities will make such arrangements unnecessary.
> (Manshardt 1936: 85)

It is striking that Manshardt shared all of McPherson's convictions, including the conviction that British policy may have been the immediate trigger for conflict, but it had certainly not *created* communal antagonism.[6] And, as McPherson had noted before him, the strife went along with daily harmonious coexistence, a point we will take up for examination in the next section.

> [I]t would be entirely wrong to convey the impression that communal conflict is always upon the surface of Indian life. It is not. All over India, Hindus and Muslims are living together in a peaceful fashion. But it is a fact that potential communal conflict lies just beneath the surface and it takes very little scratching to bring it to light.
> (Ibid. 51)

Manshardt's analysis explored a large number of diverse causes from the religious to the social, economic, historical and psychological. Anything and everything in the centuries of Hindu–Muslim relations could potentially be listed as a cause for communal strife. However, like colonial scholars, Manshardt was also clear that it was religious differences that really drove the problem of communalism: 'Differing religious practices are perhaps the most immediate causes of communal disorders' (Ibid. 40).

Thus, both Manshardt and McPherson proposed that 'communalism' is essentially religious animosity. Yet, they did not draw parallels to incidents of religious animosity from their own historical context. Where parallels were drawn, they were not to the European or American history of religious intolerance. For instance, McPherson drew a parallel with Europe's problem with minorities (while at the same time assuring his readers that the situation was special in the Indian context) after the end of the First World War. Manshardt drew a parallel with the American experience of nation-building.

> In the early days of my own country, the United States of America, each state or colony was extremely jealous of its own interests. They thought in terms of Virginia, or Maryland, or Massachusetts – but not in terms of America. But before many decades had passed, it became abundantly clear that if the new land was to flourish, the interests of the individual colonies must be subordinated to the interests of a united nation, in which each group would work for the interests of all. And that same transition must take place in India.
> (Manshardt 1936: 120)

It is important to note here that even when such parallels were drawn, they were limited to some aspect of what the authors saw as the problem of communalism. For instance, even though the above quote suggests that Manshardt saw communalism as a routine problem encountered in the process of nation-building, which would not be considered a problem in any way unique to India, there are other points in his narrative where he indicates a counter-view. For instance, citing a claim by another author that even the Hindus and Muslims of one village inhabit two different nations, Manshardt declared that the problem was even more pronounced in India since a Frenchman may live with a German family during his studies in spite of the great animosity between the German and French people, but Muslims and Hindus could never live on such terms (Manshardt 1936: 103–104).

There is a peculiar nature to the way colonial accounts deal with communalism. Even where parallels are drawn, there is a qualification that the problem of communalism exceeds in some way the parallel drawn with Western history. There are many questions that arise when we examine the parallels that these writers did draw with

Western historical moments.[7] However, this chapter cannot take up such an investigation. For the purposes of this study it is adequate to draw attention to the following features of the colonial description of communalism. The claims that communalism was specific to the Indian situation and that it was in its most basic form a matter of religious intolerance were consistently and coherently held by both sympathizers and critics of India. And although the problem was one of religious intolerance, the situation was not seen as a parallel to Europe's experience of religious intolerance. Before one asks what allowed colonial writers to hold such a position coherently, let us examine an added dimension of the colonial analysis of the problem. Not only was this religious intolerance specific to India, but it was an intolerance that was not solved by the European solution of toleration.

Toleration with conflict and communalism without conflict

The problem of religious antagonism was solved, to a great extent, by the principle of toleration in Europe. John Locke's formulation was not the only European model for the coexistence of different churches within one state. But some form or other of this principle was adopted across Europe in order to quell the disturbances that had plagued Europe over several centuries. However, it is striking that colonial authorities did not propose the same solution in India. What is more striking is that many colonial authorities noted, often with surprise, how tolerant Indian society was. Yet, this toleration not only had not prevented communalism from emerging, but it seems to have had little bearing on the problem of communalism in India.

Let us examine the evidence for this claim. Several colonial writers noted that what they took to be the various religious denominations in India had coexisted in relative toleration. In fact, this idea of harmonious coexistence was also a major observation in the work of McPherson and Manshardt. So, it was not a matter of differences of judgement – some seeing greater toleration, some seeing greater conflict. Toleration simply coexisted with communalism according to colonial observers.

In 1921, for instance, just four short years before the term communalism would completely take over almost all discourse related to Hindu–Muslim interaction, William Foster, in his preface to a collection of early travellers' accounts of India, contextualized these accounts by assuring the reader of the great accomplishments of the

English in India and the condemnation of the Indian despotism of the past. But he also observed,

> On the other hand justice, if rough and liable to be influenced by bribery, was fairly good; traders of all nations were freely admitted; and in religious matters toleration was more consistently practised than in any European country at that period. On the whole, our travellers, who were of course comparing Indian conditions with those of their own country, were not unfavourably impressed.
>
> (Foster 1921: x)

Although his reference to toleration is situated in the past, other colonial writers continued to observe harmonious coexistence and toleration along with the 'forever communal condition' of the Indian people. The irony deepens when we realize that not only did the presence of harmony, so to speak, *not* contradict the idea of communalism, but the actual presence of violence was *not* the basis for the proposition of communalism or Hindu–Muslim antagonism. Indeed, the use of conflict or violent outbreaks between the Hindus and Muslims as evidence for Hindu–Muslim antagonism occurs almost half a century after the consolidation of notions of Hindu–Muslim antagonism in colonial sources.[8]

Hindu–Muslim antagonism seems to become a feature of colonial discourse from the late 18th century onwards. Early colonial literature, for instance, Captain Alexander Hamilton's accounts, see no great rift occurring between these two major communities in India. Hamilton's accounts of India and Burma span the years 1688–1723. Consider the following observations on Calcutta:

> In Calcutta all Religions are freely tolerated, but the Presbyterian, and that they brow-beat. The Pagans carry their Idols in Procession through the Town. The Roman Catholicks have their Church to lodge their Idols in, and the Mahometan is not discountenanced; but there are no Polemicks, except what are between our High-Church Men and our law, or between the Governor's Party and other Private Merchants on Points of Trade.
>
> (Hamilton vol. 2. 1995: 13)

Bernier's account of India records the conflicts arising between the Mughals and Shivaji as well as the Sikhs. However, he does not draw the conclusion of Hindu–Muslim antagonism anywhere in his narrative. He does, in fact, record the relative toleration with which the Mughals treat the beliefs of the Hindus.

> The *Great Mogol* though a Mahometan, permits these ancient and superstitious practices; not wishing or not daring, to disturb the *Gentiles* in the free exercises of their religion.
> (Bernier 1989: 303)

The first accounts of Hindu–Muslim antagonism seem to emerge in the late 18th century. For instance, Alexander Dow proposed that British laws must be imposed in Bengal because of Hindu–Muslim antagonism, which would not allow either community to live by the other's laws:

> The inhabitants of Bengal are divided into two religious sects, the Mahommedan and Hindoo, almost equal in point of numbers. Averse beyond measure to one another, both on account of religion and the memory of mutual injuries, the one party will not now submit to the laws of the other; and the dissension which subsists between individuals, would without a pressure from another power, spread in a flame over the whole kingdom. It is, therefore, absolutely necessary for the peace and prosperity of the country, that the laws of England, in so far as they do not oppose prejudices and usages which cannot be relinquished by the natives, should prevail.
> (Dow vol. 3 1792: ci–cii)

Dow does not invoke incidents of violence as evidence for his claim. In fact, he does not give any evidence whatsoever. The claim takes on the status of a self-evident description to which causes and consequences may be attached in any number. This became the model for practically all claims for Hindu–Muslim antagonism. Thus, actual incidents of intercommunity conflict were not the source of the claim for Hindu–Muslim antagonism. This becomes clearer only when we see (as in the case of Foster, McPherson and Manshardt above) that the opposite of Hindu–Muslim antagonism, that is, Hindu–Muslim toleration, did not serve to contradict the idea of communalism within colonial discourse.

Often colonial writers relied specifically on the Maratha–Mughal conflict as evidence for communal antagonism.[9] One reason for treating the later colonial notion of Hindu–Muslim antagonism based on

Mughal–Maratha history with greater scepticism is the fact that both of the narratives above that stress the relative toleration practiced in India (Hamilton 1995; Bernier 1989) are written during the period of the Mughal–Maratha wars. What is it that made the later colonial sources see this conflict as a major source of antagonism between communities when their own sources of the time did not see this?

The point that the presence of toleration or absence of conflict did not serve as evidence against communalism (since communalism did not refer to the presence of conflict in society) is not to be understood as a denial of any historical conflict that has taken place or any conflicts that continue to take place. The point is rather to show that we do not understand what premises lead the colonizer to pose this description of communalism in relation to the Indian context. Thus, postcolonial accounts which seek to contradict the charge of communalism as a precolonial phenomenon[10] on the basis of the relative peaceful co-existence of communities or on the basis of pluralistic practices in the Indian villages,[11] fail to contradict the charge of communalism or even Hindu–Muslim antagonism, since these practices and the relative harmony of native society were all recognized by the colonizer. It was not in ignorance of these facts, but *in spite of* these facts that the colonizer reached the conclusion of Hindu–Muslim antagonism from the late 18th century onwards, and communalism in the 20th century. In addition, the solution to communalism was not toleration, but the reform or the eradication of religion in India (Thompson 1930; Smith 1946).

> The communal principle . . . cannot go unless the different systems of religion in India will overhaul their whole thought and practice, as freely as has been done with Christianity in the more civilised lands of the West.
> (Thompson 1930: 234)

The West did not see religious reform or the eradication of religion as a solution to its own inter-religious strife. Christian religious reform was aimed at eliminating the 'impurities' that had crept into the Church, never at resolving conflicts amongst religious groups.[12] Of course, the underlying assumption was always that under a 'pure' Church, there would be no conflicts. However, with the rise of conflicts (that were the outcome precisely of the search for the purer Church) came solutions in the political (and not religious) sphere such as secularism and toleration. Then why was it that in India it was *religious reform* that was seen as the solution for religious conflict? It is also curious that for India, secularism was never a convincing answer for the colonizer. The British state in India was a secular state after all. But the British did not propose that state neutrality towards religious groups would extinguish religious conflicts in India. Why is it that secularism was enough in the West, but not enough for India? This points towards the idea that it was not through the nature of the State alone that one could overcome communalism. One aspect that would require change was the nature of religion itself. It is this insight into the colonial conception of communalism that will answer the question raised at the beginning of the chapter: why is communalism said to be a problem unique (and perhaps even autochthonous) to India?

Indian 'religiosity'

Here then is what we know from a brief survey of colonial material on communalism. It is a religious problem. But, the solutions that Europe evolved for religious intolerance, that is toleration and secularism, do not solve this problem. Instead, as per the colonial understanding of communalism, the problem would not go away unless India underwent religious reform or, as some proposed, was 'purged' of religion altogether (Smith 1946). How does one understand these propositions about communalism?

One work that helps put the pieces together to some extent is W. C. Smith's analysis of communalism that remained most influential almost up to the 1990s. His basic proposition was that communalism had plagued India 'throughout the centuries' and was not the creation of British colonialism, even though colonial policy had been instrumental in fuelling it and pushing it into the direction of nationalism. Smith felt compelled to account for two distinct communalisms – Muslim communalism and Hindu communalism. Although his book-length study titled *Modern Islam in India* (1946), focused a great deal more on the former, it is his comments on the latter that shed light on our question about why communalism was seen as an Indian problem without parallel in Europe, and why it could coexist with (or be impervious to) toleration in Indian society.

> Religiously, it [communalism] is a reversion to tribalism: group solidarity is one of the sources of religion and vice versa. Through the centuries, religion has developed to serve many other functions besides that elemental one of expressing the life of a closed fraternity; and the great world religions had thought to outgrow such restrictedness. But in today's

embattled world, men readily press their religion again into the service not of its highest ideals but of the immediate interests of their own group. . . .

Hinduism has never outgrown its tribalism; has never aspired or claimed to be anything higher than the religion of a group, or rather a series of sub-groups eternalised in the caste system. To the Hindu, every Indian who is a Muslim is an outcast out-caste, an Untouchable with whom dealings must not be so intimate as to transgress certain formal rules. This exclusion is religious; but with Hinduism, 'religious' means 'social' in a highly evolved traditional way.

These facts therefore have presented India with a communal situation throughout the centuries. It has been sometimes less, sometimes more, a problem; has raised issues sometimes of acute, sometimes of devastating, import; sometimes it has raised no issues at all. . . .

The religious situation is, therefore, not in itself a disaster; though it has explosive potentialities. (And one may argue forcefully that the real welfare of India will wait until the country has been religiously purged.)
(Smith 1946: 188, 189–190)

There are several claims here that need to be differentiated to understand what Smith is saying about 'Hindu communalism':

1 'Hinduism' is a religion reserved for a group. Why does Smith make such a claim? Are not all religions 'group religions'? Here one must understand the distinction Smith is making between the 'great world religions' and those that remained at the 'lower level' of merely maintaining 'group solidarity'. The 'great world religions' had generated a mechanism to move beyond the confines of any given group – proselytization. In the absence of a mechanism for proselytization, 'Hinduism' could not but remain the religion of a particular group. You could only be a Hindu when born into the given group.
2 Thus, the mechanism of proselytization was at least one of the ways that transformed religion from *just* a form of group solidarity to something 'greater'.
3 Although he does not elaborate on what other functions religion serves when it expands from being just a form of group solidarity, he does assert that when it is only a form of group solidarity, it ends up serving 'only the immediate interests' of the group of adherents and not 'its highest ideals'.

How do we make sense of Smith's conviction that a religion that does not proselytize must express the narrow interests of its current set of adherents? There are at least two dimensions to this question. The first dimension, which is seemingly a logical one, follows from the contrast Smith wishes to draw between 'Hinduism' and the 'world religions'. A 'great world religion' cannot logically limit itself to the immediate interests of its present set of adherents since it is hard-wired to seek more followers from a larger set. It *must*, therefore, express 'higher ideals' or interests that are not limited merely to benefits for its present set of adherents.

But, in the case of Hinduism, the opposite is bound to be the case since, without the mechanism of proselytization, it never seeks to expand, and therefore, as Smith would see it, never needs to pursue 'higher ideals'. This is the 'restrictedness' of Hinduism as he sees it. However, this seemingly logical point follows from a much deeper set of assumptions about the nature of religion and what allows it to function for the welfare of Man. This leads us to the second dimension or perhaps it is better to describe it as the root of Smith's description.

Let us break the above question into two. What is the connection between religion and the interests of its adherents? And why would it follow that in the absence of the mechanism of proselytization, religion expresses only the 'immediate' (read narrow and worldly) interests of its present adherents? While we cannot answer the first question at the present time, we present a partial examination of the second. The answer provided is necessarily a limited one since a fuller answer must wait till we can answer the first question.

Let us break down the question further. When a religion seeks to proselytize, why does it do so? In the context of Christianity, the only real goal of religion is to seek the salvation of *all* mankind.[13] This is why it must seek to convert all without distinctions of any kind. A religion that does not do so is necessarily a corrupt (if not false) religion from this perspective, since it does not acknowledge God's message to all mankind and His beneficence to all who are willing to believe. (For instance, one of the central accusations made against the Catholic Church during the reformation was that the sale of indulgences went against the principle that salvation was for all who believed and not just those who could pay the priestly classes in the form of indulgences.)[14] A religion that does not proselytize, therefore, does not recognize the possibility of the salvation[15] of mankind. If so, it cannot seek anything but worldly happiness for its adherents since it is only salvation that brings eternal happiness.[16] This is necessarily a theological distinction – worldly as against eternal happiness. From this perspective then, it is inevitable that Hinduism was seen as a religion that does not pursue 'higher ideals' and sets its adherents only the goal of 'immediate', read, worldly interests.

On the other hand, the 'great world religions' are pressed into the service of the immediate interests of the group of adherents in the present day only under certain circumstances – in an 'embattled world', as Smith says in the quote above. This relates to his description of 'Muslim communalism'. When religion, which is meant to express 'higher interests', is pressed in the service of the 'immediate interests' of its present groups of adherents, this is *communalism*. If a religion cannot but express anything but the 'immediate interests' of its present group of adherents, it is doomed forever to be *communal*. Thus, 'Hinduism' by its very nature was doomed to be communal. But the rise of 'Muslim communalism' in India was contingent on special social, economic or political conditions. Consider the following two excerpts from Smith:

> In emphasising the fact that religion is not the efficient cause of communal riots, we do not mean to deny that when it is an accompanying factor it is an exceedingly important one. Religious passions are highly inflammable, and emotionally are of great driving force once aroused. . . .
>
> Few things infuriate some Muslim communalists more than to be told that communalism is not a religious problem. They know, from their own experience, and with all the intensity of their Muslim ardour, that it is religious. What they should be told is that it does not have a religious solution. The solution must be political and economic. Many of the religious factors can be allowed to remain; must be allowed to remain, even, for the opposition to interfering with them is too tremendous. But it is the economic and political factors that must be manipulated, in order to save the country from the horrors of communalist hatred. If these are properly manipulated, even though the religious factors do continue, communalist hatred will disappear.
>
> (Smith 1946: 211, 218)

This is the process Smith described in his account about Muslim communalism. In the context of the 'world religions', religion is not a sufficient condition for 'communalism', but requires other mitigating circumstances. It is this reasoning that underlies the idea that communalism is nothing but the 'politicization of religion'. However, it is crucial to note that this statement, which has become an axiom of sorts, only served to describe 'Muslim communalism'. This old adage, which has been repeated endlessly since the days of the nationalist struggle, does not express some deep insight. It merely echoes colonial assertions about India without understanding the assumptions that give coherence to these assertions.

If one does not make clear the differences that underlay the colonial understanding of communalism within the two groups – Hindus and Muslims – one will end up ascribing several contradictory positions to these colonial scholars. For instance, Smith seems to hold that India needed to be 'religiously purged' to solve the problem of communalism, while simultaneously holding that religion was not 'the efficient cause' of communal riots. One cannot reconcile these two stands without understanding that the first is a solution to 'Hindu communalism', while the latter characterization relates to 'Muslim communalism'. So, the question we should ask is: *which* religion must be purged from India to solve the problem of communalism?

In so far as Islam, as per Smith's characterization, is one of the 'great world religions', which can and does express higher interests unless constrained by particular economic and political circumstances, 'Muslim communalism' does not require a religious solution, but an economic or political solution. However, in so far as communalism is an amalgamation of both Hindu and Muslim communalism, complete solutions will have to wait until India is purged of Hinduism, because Hindu communalism has to do with the 'restricted' nature of Hinduism.

There is an important aspect of the quotation from Smith that I have not yet tackled. Hinduism is not simply the religion of a group, but a series of subgroups 'eternalized in the caste system'. The implication is that Hinduism's 'restrictedness' is twofold. Hinduism cannot but express only the interests of its present set of adherents in the absence of any compulsion to appeal to a larger set of adherents. In addition, each caste group within Hinduism is rigid. One cannot move from one caste to another. Thus, each caste group expresses an even narrower set of interests applicable only to its own set. And these narrow sets of interests have remained unchanged and unchallenged since eternity.

There is a further connection he draws between this rigid system of caste and communalism. He claims, as I have quoted above, 'To the Hindu, every Indian who is a Muslim is an outcast out-caste, an Untouchable with whom dealings must not be so intimate as to transgress certain formal rules' (Smith 1946: 188). Further, he says:

> The Hindu caste system both preaches and practices perhaps the most rigid social discrimination in the world. There are

many centuries of tradition and pressure of society, religion and economics, all urging the Hindu business man to treat the Muslim businessman as outside the pale.

(Smith 1946: 221)

How do we understand the connection he builds between the caste system and Hindu–Muslim relations? His characterization clearly suggests that the Hindu's model for the place to be attributed to the Muslim in society is drawn from the model the caste system provides for the treatment of the out-caste – the Untouchable. Why would Smith believe this to be the case? While there is no clear reasoning provided by Smith himself, one probable reason could well be the theory about Indian Islam that was dominant at the time. As per this dominant understanding, Islam had been extremely successful in gaining followers in India because of the existence of the caste system.[17] For instance, Manshardt claimed:

For our purposes it is sufficient to note here the most apparent weakening influences of caste viz. that consigning of a large section of the population to a permanent status of inferiority, which served in numerous instances as the seed of discontent which later helped to swell the Muslim harvest; and that fragmentation of society into groups, often hostile to one another, which has always been the enemy of national solidarity.

(Manshardt 1936: 14–15)

What can we understand as the place of the out-caste from Smith's account of Hinduism and the caste system? While his statements on the subject are very limited, it seems tenable to draw one inference. If caste groups are a set of subgroups which are driven to do nothing but express and pursue the narrow interests of the subgroup, the 'out-caste' is the set that is assigned no place in this system. Thus, Hinduism does not recognize any interests of the 'out-caste', only of particular caste groups that are within the Hindu fold. But being an out-caste means (as W.C. Smith sees it), that one is bereft of interest altogether. It is this that makes the caste system so immoral. However, until we unravel the connection between religion and the interests of groups, we cannot completely understand the nature of this claim.

Conclusion

Smith holds significant hidden theological assumptions, which must be spelt out to make his analysis coherent. Is it far-fetched to make such a claim when Smith does not explicitly express these theological assumptions? It is not far-fetched simply because it is not possible to give a non-theological background to the descriptions he provides. Even if the actual explanation I draw above is flawed, the significance of proselytization can *only* make sense within a theological framework. So, even though nothing in Smith's work may indicate either his faith in Christianity or his proclivity to theology, the nature of his claims cannot be rendered coherent except by reconstructing their underlying theological assumptions.

Admittedly, the above explication of his assumptions is not complete. We have yet to understand what exactly it means to say that religion pursues or expresses the *interests* of its adherents. It is extremely important to understand this claim since the British explicitly saw the Muslims and Hindus as conflicting interest groups (Pathan 2014). If communalism is an ancient and irresolvable problem of India, it makes perfect sense why colonial scholars spoke of the problem of communalism irrespective of the presence or absence of incidents of conflict in Indian society and why it was a problem without parallel in Europe's own history of religious intolerance. To the extent that it was a logical conclusion derived from the premises they held about Hinduism, communalism was alien to the European experience with religious conflict.

There are many questions that remain unanswered. How do we understand problems of conflict, especially between Hindus and Muslims that have come up since the late 19th century? In so far as the colonial conception of communalism does not help us understand these conflicts, what other tools can we employ to understand and solve these problems? Answers to these questions remain at least partially contingent on further explorations of how the colonial conceptualization of communalism still entraps our understanding of ourselves today. Unless we understand and reject these characterizations, we cannot reconceptualize the problem that is creating conflict.

Notes

1 While there is no dearth of literature on this issue, see Housley (2002), Kaplan (2007) and Marx (2003).
2 See Cohen (1983), Gerlach (2000), Michael (2008) and Sandgren (2010).
3 Well-respected scholars of communalism, like Gyanendra Pandey, have taken this line of reasoning. Pandey famously said, ' "Communalism" . . . is a form of colonialist knowledge . . . [which] stands for the puerile and the primitive – all that colonialism, in its own reckoning, was not' (1992: 6).

4 Pandey (1992) cites a 1924 Minority Report as making one of the first uses of the term. So, it seems we can quite precisely date the emergence of the term to this year.
5 While this chapter does not take up any Indian writers for analysis, such an analysis is certainly important to take up in the future since such a comparison should show that the premises that gave coherence to colonial discourse would be absent in the work of Indian writers.
6 This was an important point of contention in the 1930s since nationalists often claimed that communalism was not native to India, but a problem of British creation. It was also perhaps the only point of contention between the colonial and nationalist position on the issue!
7 W.C. Smith was perhaps the first to draw a parallel of Hindu–Muslim relations with 'Aryan–Jewish' relations in Nazi Germany.
8 Indeed, in sources up until the late 19th century, actual occurrences of violence between Hindus and Muslims do not often feature in their accounts of 'Hindu–Muslim antagonism'. The 'narrative of the communal riot' as Gyanendra Pandey traces it, begins in 1809, but becomes inflated and acquires predictable directions that show the entrenchment of a narrative pattern in 1907 (Pandey 1992).
9 Almost all British histories of India from the late 18th century onwards focused on Mughal–Maratha conflict. See Orme (1782, 1799), Mill (1826), Elphinstone (1841), Duff (1826) etc.
10 For a well-known confrontation of this kind, see Gyanendra Pandey's (1992) discussion of Christopher Bayly (1985).
11 All nationalist literature on communalism falls in this category, but even the more sophisticated approach that Nandy (1985) brings to the study of communalism shares this shortcoming.
12 The test for the purity of the Church was the continuing occurrence of miracles on earth. See www.newadvent.org/cathen/12700b.htm (accessed on 11 December 2016).
13 See, for instance, the entry on salvation in the New Advent Catholic Encyclopedia at www.newadvent.org/cathen/13407a.htm (accessed on 12 December 2016).
14 The classic text that took up this question was, of course, Luther's *Ninety-Five Theses*.
15 It is crucial not to fall into the trap of glib assertions like moksha is an equivalent for salvation. Moksha was a state to be achieved in life, while salvation is necessarily only possible for the soul after death.
16 See for instance the New Advent catholic encyclopedia entry on State and Church at www.newadvent.org/cathen/14250c.htm (accessed on 13 December 2016), which explains how the Church looks after the goal of 'perfect happiness' or salvation, while the State looks after the goal of 'temporal happiness'.
17 For a sound refutation of this theory, see Eaton (2000).

References

Balagangadhara, S. N. 1994. *'The Heathen in His Blindness. . .': Asia, the West, and the Dynamic of Religion*. Leiden: E. J. Brill.

———. 2010. 'Orientalism, Postcolonialism and the "Construction" of Religion', in Esther Bloch, Marianne Keppens, and Rajaram Hedge (eds.), *Rethinking Religion in India: The Colonial Construction of Hinduism*, pp. 135–163. London: Routledge.

———. 2012. *Reconceptualizing India Studies*. New Delhi: Oxford University Press.

Bayly, C. A. 1985. 'The Pre-History of "Communalism"? Religious Conflict in India, 1700–1860', *Modern Asian Studies*, 19 (2): 177–203.

Bernier, Francois. [1891] 1989. *Travels in the Mogul Empire AD 1656–1668*. New Delhi: Atlantic Publishers.

Cohen, J. 1983. *The Friars and the Jews: The Evolution of Medieval Anti-Judaism*. Ithaca: Cornell University Press.

Dow, Alexander. 1792. *The History of Hindostan*, Vols. I–III. London: John Murray.

Duff, James Grant. 1826. *History of the Mahrattahs*. Vols. I–III. London: Longmans, Rees, Orme, Brown, and Green.

Eaton, Richard Maxwell. 2000. *The Rise of Islam and the Bengal Frontier*. New Delhi: Oxford University Press.

Elphinstone, Monstuart. 1841. *The History of India*. Vols. 1–2. London: John Murray.

Foster, William. (ed.) 1921. *Early Travels in India 1583–1619*. London: Oxford University Press.

Hamilton, Captain Alexander. [1744] 1995. *A New Account of the East Indies being the Observations and Remarks of Captain Alexander Hamilton from the year 1688–1723*. Vols. 1–2. New Delhi: Asian Educational Services.

Housley, Norman. 2002. *Religious Warfare in Europe, 1400–1536*. New York: Oxford University Press.

Gerlach, Wolfgang. 2000. *And the Witnesses Were Silent: The Confessing Church and the Persecution of the Jews*. Lincoln and London: University of Nebraska Press.

Kaplan, Benjamin J. 2007. *Divided by Faith: Religious Conflict and the Practice of Toleration in Early Modern Europe*. London: Belknap Press of Harvard University Press.

Manshardt, Clifford. 1936. *The Hindu–Muslim Problem in India*. London: George Allen and Unwin.

Marx, Anthony W. 2003. *Faith in Nation: Exclusionary Origins of Nationalism*. New York: Oxford University Press.

McPherson, Hugh. 1932. 'The Origin and Growth of Communal Antagonism, Especially Between Hindus and Muhammadans, and the Communal Award', in Sir John Cumming (ed.), *Political India 1832–1932: A Co-operative Survey of a Century*, pp. 109–126. London: Oxford University Press.

Michael, R. 2008. *A History of Catholic Antisemitism: The Dark Side of the Church*. New York: Palgrave Macmillan.

Mill, James. [1817] 1826. *The History of British India*. Vols. 1–6. London: Baldwin, Craddock and Joy.

Nandy, Ashis. 1985. 'An Anti-Secularist Manifesto', *Seminar* 314 (October): 14–24.
New Advent Catholic Encyclopedia. www.newadvent.org. (accessed on 27th December 2016).
Orme, Robert esq. 1782. *Historical Fragments of the Mogul Empire, of the Morattoes and of the English Concerns in Indostan*. London: Strand.
———. 1799. *History of the Military Transactions of the British Nation in Indostan, from the year MDCCXLV: To which is prefixed a Dissertation on the Establishments made by Mahomedan Conquerors of Indostan*. London: Strand.
Pandey, Gyanendra. 1992. *The Construction of Communalism in Colonial North India*. New Delhi: Oxford University Press.
Pathan, Sufiya. 2014. 'Re-Examining "Communalism"', *Pragmata: Journal of Human Sciences*, 2 (2): 77–84.
Sandgren, Leo Duprée. 2010. *Vines Intertwined: A History of Jews and Christians from the Babylonian Exile to the Advent of Islam*. Peabody, MA: Hendrickson Publishers.
Smith, W. C. [1946] 1985. *Modern Islam in India*. New Delhi: Usha Publications.
Thompson, Edward. 1930. *The Reconstruction of India*. London: Faber and Faber Ltd.

5
SACERDOTAL VIOLENCE AND THE CASTE SYSTEM
The long shadow of Christian-Orientalism

Prakash Shah

The caste system is one of the most prominent global images of Indian culture and society. Putting the matter in different terms, Nicholas Dirks (2001: 3) opens his book on caste by stating that 'When thinking about India it is hard not to think of caste.' Multiple accounts and ideas of the nature of the caste system exist (e.g. Banerjee-Dube 2010). Given this diversity, it seems there is no consistent theory of caste out there. And yet the picture of the caste system is regularly projected both within India and increasingly so in diasporic settings such as the United Kingdom and United States, where Indians have settled in significant numbers over the past few decades. The constant reiteration of the caste system reinforces the impression that there is some stability to the idea. In this chapter, I examine one such invocation of the caste system during the enactment of the Equality Act 2010 in the United Kingdom. This Act contains the first provision on caste discrimination in the legislation of any Western country. To my knowledge, in the history of anti-discrimination law in the United Kingdom, it is the first time that the British Parliament has proceeded to legislate on the assumption that there is a problem to be dealt with and that an adequate conceptualizing of that problem is not needed until *after* legislation is put into place. The involvement of academics in the consultative and research exercises that surround the Equality Act's provision on caste has meant their co-option in and support of what has seemed like a pre-set juggernaut-like agenda for legislation in that field. Indians can be accused, as one of the academic proponents of the new law, Annapurna Waughray (2012), does, of practicing apartheid without a murmur of protest from any section of academia. Similar accusations have been made before the House of Representatives (2005) in the United States, inter alia, by Indian academics and non-governmental organization (NGO) workers. The example of the caste legislation instantiates a much larger Christian-Orientalist episteme which exercises its disciplinary power (Said 1978: 67), and against which every academic work on caste must measure up. This Christian-Orientalist episteme has become generalized by its secularization to constitute core ideas about the caste system including, as I argue here, its key presupposition of sacerdotal – Brahmanical – violence lying at the base of the caste system. In this chapter, I examine the debates with respect to caste during the passage of the Equality Act 2010, as well as the hardly discussed agenda of Christian proselytism that is being promoted by Western churches through the caste law. I then go on to explore just how it is that, even though we appear to lack a coherent idea of the nature of the Indian caste system, we can continue to talk about its existence with confidence. I propose that behind the descriptions of the caste system lies the idea of sacerdotal or priestly violence as a constitutive force, and that this background idea, which finds its source in Christian theological reflections on Indian culture and society, continues to inform and lend stability to accounts of the caste system. As such, the caste system fails to provide a true description of Indian culture and society. Seen on a broader canvass, this chapter contributes to the discussion on how problems of Orientalism (Said 1978) and colonial consciousness (Balagangadhara 2012) continue to inflect debates and law-making in the contemporary world, and we will see how the discourse on caste instantiates something about both Orientalism and colonial consciousness.

Legislating on caste in the UK: the Equality Act 2010

The UK's Equality Act 2010 creates a potential new ground of legal action for discrimination on the ground of 'caste'. Among other things, this will allow legal claims for damages to be brought for caste discrimination. The original wording of section 9(5) of the Equality Act made it *discretionary* ('may') for a Minister to make an order making caste an aspect of race. The Act was amended in April 2013 to make it *mandatory* ('must') for the Minister to make an order adding 'caste' to colour, nationality, and ethnic or national origins. The Minister is therefore obliged to bring the provision into effect. That has not yet happened because of the controversy the caste clause provoked, including opposition from Hindu, Jain and Sikh organizations. The position remains ambiguous despite the shift to a majority Conservative party government since the General Election of May 2015. At the time of writing, the government had announced that it would hold a consultation on how (not whether) protection against caste discrimination can best be provided for.

The Equality Act 2010 consolidates and builds on earlier anti-discrimination statutes, and allows for tort-like civil legal actions to be brought by claiming an act of discrimination, whether it is 'direct' or 'indirect' discrimination, victimization or harassment. Besides 'race' (of which caste is made 'an aspect'), such actions can be brought on grounds of age, disability, gender reassignment, marriage and civil partnership, pregnancy and maternity, religion or belief, sex, and sexual orientation. The Equality Act covers various domains such as employment, partnerships, entry to a profession, provision of goods and services, housing, education, bodies conferring qualifications, trade unions, professional or trade organizations, local authority activities and the exercise of public functions. Civil actions for caste could arise alleging the occurrence of any act of discrimination in the United Kingdom, no matter what the nationality of origin or the location of the head office of a business. An action for caste discrimination could therefore also be directed to an Indian company doing business, hiring employees, or having a branch office in the United Kingdom. Such civil legal actions can include claims for compensation, including for injury to feelings, aggravated damages for malicious behaviour, and interest on any compensation. In an employment case, an Employment Tribunal can also recommend that the employer take action to correct the situation or limit the damage done to the claimant. An official body, the Equality and Human Rights Commission (EHRC), also has legal powers to conduct investigations of any organization and these could be extended to cover caste discrimination. Other methods include inquiries, assessments, issuing unlawful act notices, and compliance notices. Indian (or, more widely, South Asian) businesses or community organizations could face specific investigations or other intrusive actions on grounds that caste discrimination is suspected to occur within those businesses.

The model chosen for caste discrimination claims in the Equality Act makes the United Kingdom a unique example of using its civil law anti-discrimination legislation for targeting caste discrimination. The Indian case presents a quite different model because it is focused on preferential reservations (quotas) for groups that are specifically listed in legislation. Such a list currently figures in the Constitution

(Scheduled Castes) Order of 1950 and varying legislation at the level of different Indian states, although the idea goes back to the British colonial period. Indian law therefore makes no demands on judges to define caste, and the Indian legislation is not an invitation for an open-ended set of litigation claims as the UK legislation is, although it has its dysfunctional effects, as outlined in the study by Shourie (2012). There is no tested model of the kind the United Kingdom is due to implement, and the Indian case law will not help establish guidance for when an act constitutes 'caste discrimination'. UK lawyers and judges will effectively be going alone into an area which they scarcely understand, and where the social science literature and expertise is not only confused but, as argued later, founded on Christian theological ideas of Indian religion as false. Pakistan and Bangladesh, the second and third largest South Asian countries respectively, have no specific legislation on caste. India also has criminal laws on caste atrocities, while Nepal passed a law in 2011, the Caste-based Discrimination and Untouchability (Offence and Punishment) Act, 2068, which is extremely widely drafted to capture many practices associated with tradition and authorizes the application of criminal penalties for transgression. Mauritius has a constitutional provision (section 16) providing that no law may discriminate inter alia on grounds of caste, but with wide exceptions for personal laws. If applied in India, a provision on caste such as that included in the Mauritius constitution would make unlawful the Indian system of caste-based reservations.

If we go by debates in the British Parliament during the passage of the 2010 caste clause and its 2013 amendment and, more broadly, in the accounts of various Dalit NGOs (e.g. Anti-Caste Discrimination Alliance et al. 2009) or other bodies such as the National Secular Society (2013), we will not find a reference to the spreading of the Christian message through proselytism, which is a key component of the current agitation in Britain surrounding caste. Proselytism is a key tenet of Christianity, and branches of Christian churches from Western countries are active in many parts of India as elsewhere in Asia. The fact that the Holy See voted in favour of inclusion of discrimination on grounds of work and descent in the World Conference Against Racism (WCAR) declaration of 2001 also indicates its investment in proselytism among Dalits in India. Attempts to convert have been identified as the cause of many a conflict in post-independence India and have become the subject of laws in some states where alarm has been raised over conversion activity (Sen 2010: 114–117). Many advocates of the cause of the so-called low castes in India are the Christian churches which continue to highlight cases of discrimination and oppression through whatever 'atrocity stories' they can find, thus reinforcing a picture of the corrupt nature of Indian society and its Brahmanical religion. This helps justify conversion.

The caste issue has been simmering in the United Kingdom since at least the second half of the 2000s. As Waughray (2009: 182–183, 2014: 359–360) recounts, when the proposals for a Single Equality Act were being mooted, the government carried out a consultation and had decided by 2007 not to include caste in the new legislation. In a document prepared as a response to the consultation on caste, the Hindu Forum of Britain (HFB) (2008: 25) had noted:

> HFB has found that there are strong links between MPs who have interns paid by CARE [Christian Action, Research and Education] and the Dalit lobby in the House of Commons. Several of the MPs who have CARE interns are also the most passionate advocates of Dalit Rights in Parliament and elsewhere. Some of them are also active members of Christian organisations like the Christian Solidarity Worldwide which advocate a strong case for Dalit Rights.

Meanwhile, the Lords Spiritual who sit in the House of Lords, some of whom have spoken out in support of the caste provision in the Equality Act, have remained conspicuously silent about their interests in keeping the caste issue high on the agenda. Among them, Lord Harries, a former Anglican Bishop of Oxford, led the charge to include caste in the 2010 Act and to move the 2013 amendment.

The different 'protected characteristics' in the Equality Act all have a distinct history and legislative context. The earliest British legal provisions against race discrimination date back to the 1960s and were influenced by Lord Lester, who is now one of the main proponents of the caste provision, and who had then worked for Amnesty for which he travelled to the United States to study the segregation against African Americans. Many reports and studies were issued regarding racial discrimination in Britain before legislation was passed and subsequently strengthened. Legislation against discrimination on religious grounds was introduced after a persistent campaign by Muslims (Meer 2010).[1] There was the European legislation, Council Directive 2000/78/EC, which obliged Member States to adopt laws against religious discrimination in the field of employment.[2] That Directive was implemented in 2003, but Britain went further making legal action for religious discrimination possible also in service provision, professions, housing, and education via the Equality Act 2006. This regime continues in the current Equality Act 2010. Meanwhile, the push to include caste in the 2010 Act has come from lobby groups linked to churches that, as noted, have an agenda that relates more to the situation in India than Britain. Briefly put, the aim is that efforts made towards gaining recognition for Christians' reservations for jobs and education places in India could bear greater fruit if it could be shown that Dalits, the broad political term employed for 'low-caste' people,[3] enjoyed the support of the British legislature without distinction as to their religion. It is well known that proselytism in India is directed more intensely among Dalits with a reportedly large proportion of Christians said to be Dalits and tribals (Tharamangalam 1996: 296; Hindu Forum of Britain 2008: 20–21; Robinson and Kujur 2010: 5). The move in Britain would also boost an internationally orchestrated campaign within UN organs and the European Union (EU) to have caste discrimination recognized in some form. Efforts for lobbying in the EU are organized by the International Dalit Solidarity Network (IDSN). That organization, based in Copenhagen and whose funding comes mostly from different churches in European countries or from governments of different European countries including Denmark and the Netherlands, is also seeking consultative status at the United Nations. A member of the IDSN, the Dalit Solidarity Network–UK (DSN–UK) is at the core of efforts to coordinate the legislative campaign in the United Kingdom, but with an array of other organizations, some with a barely disguised evangelical agenda, also playing a role.

So, the campaign for legislation in Britain comes not from any significant section of the Indian communities, but from select lobby organizations, which have put up a case that caste discrimination exists in Britain. Among the components of that case is the invocation of the size of the problem by citing the numbers of Dalits affected by caste discrimination in Britain, with estimates ranging from anywhere between 50,000 and 200,000 (Lord Avebury) to 500,000 (Lord Harries).[4] In the 2013 debates, Lord Deben compared size of the Dalit population to that of Jews and Sikhs respectively saying, 'There are, after all, fewer Jews in this country than there are Dalits. They are wholly protected under the laws. There are fewer Sikhs in this country than there are Dalits, but they are wholly protected under the laws.' In the 2011 Census, over 263,000 respondents in England and Wales answered 'Jewish' to the voluntary question on religion, while over 423,000 people identified as 'Sikh'.[5] Lord Deben must therefore have been suggesting that the number of Dalits was something over 423,000. In a House of Commons debate that took place in July 2014 to raise the question why the caste provision had not yet been implemented, Jeremy Corbyn MP, who is trustee of the Dalit Solidarity Network and member of the All-Party Parliamentary Group for Dalits, was not to be outdone by members of the Upper House. He declared 'There are roughly 1 million Dalit people in Britain.'[6] Whether a result of natural increase or immigration, or merely imaginary, the extraordinary inflation in the Dalit population helps to justify the need for legislation.[7]

Proponents of the legislation also portray the legal situation in South Asia, especially India, incorrectly or they simply appear not to have much grasp of it. For instance, Lord Harries, the former Anglican Bishop and a chief proponent of the 2010 and 2013 amendments on caste, argued for the United Kingdom to have 'very firm legislation in place, *as there is in India*, prohibiting discrimination in the areas of employment, public education and public goods and services'. In 2013, Lord Deben referred to Nepal and Bangladesh, arguing: 'All we are saying is that we would do in this country what other countries have already done. It has not been seen as an insult to religion there, so that is not a reasonable argument.'[8] In the July 2014 House of Commons debate, Jeremy Corbyn MP weighed in, referring to the celebrated Indian anti-caste politician and thinker, B. R. Ambedkar (1891–1956), who is widely thought of as the architect of India's constitution, arguing:

> The Ambedkar constitution is an excellent document. Dr. Ambedkar was himself a Dalit. *It absolutely outlaws discrimination* and has some provision for protected employment for people of the scheduled castes. It is a very effective document, but raising these matters with the Indian Government or the Indian high commission is extremely difficult; they are quite resistant to having good discussions about it.[9]

None of these parliamentarians grasped the scope of Indian or wider South Asian legislation on caste. In India, the legislation varies from state to state, applies reservations for jobs and in universities (which in some states does include Christians and Muslims) and otherwise criminalizes prohibitions on access to facilities such as water wells. There is, however, no general anti-discrimination law with civil law remedies in India applying to the fields to which the British Equality Act does. It is central government legislation in India which is the chief, but unstated target of the proponents of the UK law, since central legislation does not recognize Christians as qualifying for Scheduled Caste and Scheduled Tribe status, thus preventing their accessing reservations to jobs and education places on less merit, except if they do not declare their converted status. Although Muslims and Parsis also do not qualify for reservations, it is the churches that support the British law because of the potential advantages to Christians in India and, therefore, the potential for reinforcing proselytism efforts. The Nepali legislation, meanwhile, is extremely wide and tries to capture and punish criminally a whole set of activities including marrying, saying that committing or causing the commissions of such acts 'on the ground of custom, tradition, religion, culture, rituals, caste, ethnicity, descent community or occupation' deems a person to 'have committed caste-based discrimination and untouchability' (Caste-based Discrimination and Untouchability [Offence and Punishment] Act, 2068, section 4[11]). The law effectively criminalizes, with potential imprisonment, fines and restitution, actions that would ordinarily take place by virtue of traditional practices. Proselytism in Nepal has been afoot in a significant way during the past few years (Chowdhury 2014), and the assistance provided to proselytizers in Nepal by such a broad anti-caste law could well be a reason why Lord Deben spoke of it favourably.

Well before the caste discrimination legislation came onto the scene, there was a pre-existing, tried and tested model of anti-discrimination law to which different grounds have been added successively over the years. Different kinds of exceptions have also been made, for sex, disability, religion or sexuality, to limit the scope of actionable discrimination. So, in the past, legislators carefully considered the extent to which the public interest required the scope of legal provisions against discrimination on a particular ground to be reduced or enlarged. Religion, for example, enjoys very large exceptions that allow certain services to continue to be provided according to criteria which distinguish according to religion.[10] This is understandable in a culture such as the United Kingdom or the West, which is constituted by religion (Balagangadhara 1994: 391–392). Not to provide broad exceptions for religious conscience would create havoc in society because, suddenly, all types of highly disruptive claims may be coming forth. Not only has little debate taken place about the propriety of introducing caste as a ground for discrimination, but still less has it been considered what the proper scope of any such legislation should be. The issue of legislative coverage, in so far as it is aimed at curbing any mischief is ambiguous. The official report by the National Institute for Economic and Social Research (NIESR) (Metcalf and Rolfe 2010), commissioned *after* the reference to caste was inserted into the Equality Act 2010 showed no clear case for applying caste discrimination legislation often drawing on case studies involving temples and marriage, areas that do not otherwise fall within that Act's scope. Sometimes, the impression is given that the aim is to eradicate caste in general, not merely caste discrimination. The then Opposition spokesperson for Equalities, Labour MP Kate Green, declared in Parliament that, 'Everyone agrees that caste has absolutely no place in our society.'[11] This type of sweeping assessment is not surprising, given the default intuition among Europeans that caste is an inherently discriminatory and immoral institution. Kate Green's statement reads like a secularized, and much broadened, version of the plea by 19th century Protestant missionaries in India that caste has no place in the Christian Church (Oddie1979: 45–56). In Kate Green's account, the nation has replaced the Church. Although legislation exists in the form of the Forced Marriage (Civil Protection) Act 2007 to allow court orders to be made and criminal sanctions imposed in case of forced marriages (Grillo 2015: 59–91), no case has yet been made to *compel* a person to marry out of caste. However, while it might be assumed that no serious case can be made for extending anti-discrimination law to areas such as decisions to marry, a recent statement by Waughray (2014: 378) should be a very worrying indication to South Asian communities of the kind of slippery slope that arguments about the annihilation of caste might entail:

> Ambedkar identified endogamy as the vehicle by which caste is maintained and replicated, and intermarriage as the solvent of caste. Legislation prohibiting discrimination on grounds of caste should contribute to identifying and reducing caste prejudice, including in social and intimate relations, and thereby possibly to the eventual dissolution of caste in this country, in line with the present government's aim.[12]

Waughray and her co-authors of the reports written for the EHRC (Dhanda et al. 2014a, 2014b) also emphasize endogamy as a factor of caste. The aims of those promoting the caste provision in the legislation are thus far wider and constitute an attack on the social structures of the South Asian communities in the United Kingdom. Such a scenario as Waughray advocates may yet appear a distant reality in the United Kingdom, but in Nepal, the law on caste discrimination already imposes criminal sanctions for preventing an inter-caste marriage (Caste-based Discrimination and Untouchability [Offence and Punishment] Act, 2068, section 4[11]).

Legislators supporting the law on caste have shown great, albeit unjustified, confidence in their ability to see the mischief and act upon it. Some said that a single case of caste discrimination is enough to act. In 2010, Lord Lester, the leading human rights lawyer and one of the architects of the earlier Race Relations Acts, had initially tabled an amendment to introduce descent into what was then the Equality Bill to cover caste discrimination. Responding to the government's plea for research to establish the case for legislation, he noted, 'I simply do not understand why research is needed. The Minister has agreed that, even if there were one case of the kind that I described, that should be unlawful because it is wrong in principle.'[13] Kate Green MP stated, 'if there is even one case of such discrimination, proper action must be taken and there must be proper access to redress.'[14] The hyperbolic reference to the single case can also be regarded as an admission that such writing as has been produced to justify the caste law hardly succeeds in making the case for it.

Those favouring the caste provision in the legislation have never explained why they think the existing model of equality law is important for caste, nor was the question raised during the parliamentary debates. As we have seen, legislators had no real idea of the nature of the Indian legislation and how it compares to the British legal context, although they used references to caste in Indian law as an argument in favour of legislating in the United Kingdom. Lord Avebury and Lord Harries spoke as if the NIESR report endorsed their stand in favour of the caste provision, while the EHRC also recommended the Equality Act be given the widest possible scope on caste on the strength of the same report.[15] It is possible that the seeds of ambiguity are contained in the NIESR report itself. While the NIESR study did state that there is evidence of caste discrimination, it also stated that it could not establish its extent and whether it was dying out, and recommended a full research programme to answer these questions (Metcalfe and Rolfe 2010: 63). Lord Dholakia, the only Asian peer in the House of Lords to have maintained an explicit stance against the legislation noted that 'in essence, there is a lack of evidence on caste matters' and that the NIESR report clearly acknowledged that 'there is no evidence to suggest the existence of large-scale discrimination in this country based on caste'.[16] Thus Lord Dholakia was able to cite the same report in argument *against* the need for legislation and to criticize the fact that such legislation had been pushed through. A Member of Parliament for a Leicester constituency since revealed, 'I have never seen any evidence of caste discrimination in Leicester.'[17] This statement becomes more significant if one considers that the density of the South Asian population (Indian, Pakistani and Bangladeshi) in Leicester is some six times that in England and Wales as a whole.

The Western framework that gives life to the idea of an immoral caste system means that evidence is not required for legislating against it; its immorality is already clear. Remarkably, Asian peers in the House of Lords played a significant role justifying the law, and it is worth noticing how the framework of Indian moral corruption has been internalized by some of those who spoke. This is Lord Singh of Wimbledon:

> Caste has a very precise meaning attached to practices associated with the Hindu faith. It has its origin in the desire of the Aryan conquerors of the subcontinent in pre-Vedic times to establish a hierarchy of importance, with priests at the top followed by warriors, those engaged in commerce and then those engaged in more menial tasks. The conquered indigenous people were considered lower than the lowest caste. Accident of birth alone determined a person's caste. Sadly, thousands of years latter [sic], and despite legislation by the Indian Government, which has been referred to, this hierarchy of importance still lingers on.[18]

Interrupting Lord Singh's erudition, Baroness Flather offers her insights:

> The caste system was established very early in Hinduism. The Sanskrit for caste is "varna", which is also the word for colour. The noble Lord mentioned the Aryan conquerors, who were supposed to be lighter skinned. They wanted a division not only on the basis of who would do what but on the basis of colour.[19]

The link between Aryan conquerors, the caste system and different Indian races seems quite solidly in place even among those who are assumed to, in some special way, 'represent' and 'speak for' the British-Indians. When these Asian peers speak in this colonized manner, they solidify the Western account of Indian immorality and corruption since they are often seen as spokespersons who may say things that white Europeans would not get away with.

An important dimension of the Western discourse on caste is its situation within a framework of normative ethics. A key normative postulate in Western culture is that everybody is equal, and it is derivable from that postulate that there ought not to be any discrimination on grounds of caste. Attracted by Western Enlightenment ideas,

Ambedkar had said that Brahmanism was the very 'negation of the spirit of Liberty, Equality and Fraternity' (cited by Roy 2014: 51). Such a normative framework is, however, further circumscribed in the British legal context in as much as the UK's Equality Act 2010 deals with discrimination in certain delimited spheres. As noted, the Act covers certain domains including employment, partnerships, entry to a profession, provision of goods and services, housing, education, bodies conferring qualifications, trade unions, professional or trade organizations, local authority activities and the exercise of public functions. Although there is a distinction to be made between strictly legally actionable prohibitions in those domains and other, ethical norms covering a wider range of areas, such as marriage or temples, they are often fused together in the broader normative ethical framework that is at play when official legal reforms are discussed (Waughray 2014: 378; Dhanda 2015: 38–39). Indeed, Westerners also do not see why Indians, or Hindus, should be insulted at the prospect of a law against caste discrimination. As one of the proponents of the legislation, Lord Deben, stated in the House of Lords, 'The idea that passing this law would in some way be insulting to Hindus seems to me to be absolutely out with sense, and we have to make that absolutely clear.'[20] Other British politicians have reportedly been taken rather by surprise at the reaction against the legislation within the Indian community in the United Kingdom. Given that hierarchies exist in human societies and cultures, including Western culture, we will try to inquire into what gives a peculiar normative tint to the idea of the caste system. As argued in this chapter, a combination of Orientalism and 'colonial consciousness' stands in the way of our discovering how Indians actually make sense of caste, if at all they do. We will see later in chapter how missionaries identified caste as a major obstacle to conversion, how a society based on religiously sanctioned caste stratification was counter-posed as inimical to core Protestant ideas about equality of status, and how the Aryan invasion theory was brought in to explain caste as a religiously ordained racial order. The idea of a violent sacerdotal or priestly Brahmanical order is a core aspect of Indian religion providing support to secular theorizing of the oppressive caste system and the corruption of Indian culture and society.

Colonial consciousness

One may say with Balagangadhara (2012: 82–85) and Venkat Rao (2014: 308–315, 327–328) that Indian culture lacks a framework of normative ethics and thus an idea like equality as an ethical norm makes no sense in such a cultural context. When Indians talk about equality as a legal or political ideal, distortions inevitably occur. Meanwhile, given the anti-traditional nature of the Western ethical order, Indians can legitimately feel under threat, although they may not be able to pin down what that threat consists of and why they feel threatened. Even when Indians try to challenge those portrayals of their traditions that they do not like, they end up partly accepting the premises on which they are built. So, for example, when challenging the caste discrimination legislation, members of the Indian diaspora might argue that the caste system is a problem, say, in India but not in Britain or the United States. Or they might contend that the caste system existed once upon a time, but it is not of relevance now. Or they might even say, as M.K. Gandhi (1869–1948) or the philosopher Radhakrishnan (1888–1975) did, that the original caste system (*varnavyavastha*) was a good one, but it has since degraded (Inden 1990: 72–73; Bayly 1999: 251–253; Dirks 2001: 234). They could even say that British parliamentarians have not paid attention to the far more important problem of class discrimination, while they hypocritically legislate on caste. However, this indicates a failure to acknowledge how caste acquires a very peculiar tone of immorality in Western accounts. At the same time, such responses seem to accept that something of the Western account of India, which includes the idea of the caste system, represents true knowledge about India.[21] We might say, following Balagangadhara (2012: 95–120) that, being a result of the intrusion of the colonial account of Indian culture and society, and compelled by the accompanying violence of colonialism, they instantiate 'colonial consciousness'. Colonial consciousness thus involves the compelled acceptance of the colonizer's account of the moral inferiority of the culture of the colonized on the part of the latter even though such a claim is not rationally justifiable.[22] In the process, the colonized is prevented from accessing his own experience, even as he lacks access to the experience of the colonizer.

We will see in the following sections how the idea of sacerdotal or priestly violence lies at the core of normative ideas about the Indian caste system. Anti-clericalism has a long-standing pedigree as a common theme in Christian polemics of Indian religion (Gelders and Balagangadhara 2011). Building on this theological framework, Protestants drew on their critiques of Catholicism and Judaism, and said that the false religion of Hinduism or Brahmanism also mandated discriminatory practices based on a hierarchy. This constituted the background, discussed in more detail later, around which Orientalist accounts of India and its caste system then crystalized. The Aryan invasion theory justified claims about the caste system by adding the idea that there are different races in India. In its simplest form, this meant the aboriginals and the Aryan immigrants, with the caste system said to be the outcome of their resulting interaction. These ways of constructing discourse about Indian society have their roots in Christian, theologically driven assessments of Indian culture and traditions. However, this background framework has been accepted as a fact in the theories of those conducting studies on India and Indian communities abroad. Mantras against Brahmanism and the caste system can be heard from every corner of the secular academic establishment in India and among academics abroad (Gelders and Derde 2003).

In repeating such mantras of which one recent instance is given by Dhanda (2015), who also headed the investigation on caste sponsored by the EHRC in Britain, Indian intellectuals show they cannot access their own experience. On the one hand, the world of the West cannot be theirs. On the other hand, their world is no longer accessible to them due to the Western mantras which prevent them from seeing and reflecting upon their own experience. Indian intellectuals have been suborned by the colonial visions of their society, described by Venkat Rao (2014: 6) as a state of 'postcolonial destitution'. Pointing to how 'European epistemic violence disrupted the prevailing cognitive sense of the colonized people' (Ibid. 19), Venkat Rao argues (Ibid. ix):

> It seems to me that one acid test for contemporary Indian intellectuals (and most of the generally educated persons) pertains to their position on caste/*jati*. Invariably the response is caught between the related poles of political correctness and 'feudal benevolence' (Spivak's politically correct formulation). These responses reel under the enormous burden of unexamined guilt and stigmatize *jati* in their responses. They reduce the *jati* person (especially the so-called 'scheduled caste') to an abject figure. Strangely, Gandhi and Ambedkar remain in complicity in this conception.

The sense of stigma is well reflected in the vision articulated some years ago by Chetan Bhatt, now the Director of the Centre for the Study of Human Rights at the London School of Economics. In his assessment of the Hindu diasporic presence in Britain, Bhatt (1997: 249–250) argued that

> Hindu organizations, including most temples, many of which may be opposed to the extremism of the RSS, are universally

structured through caste (*jati*) membership, as well as *gotra* (exogamous clan), *sampradaya* (a movement or loose community based around a spiritual leader), religious sect and regional origin. Every Hindu council is composed mainly of caste defined organizations. These Hindu councils receive significant local state, Labour and Conservative Party patronage, as well as some local authority funds. The persistence of caste prejudice in Hindu communities has barely received attention or opposition from black socialism. It also represents a considerable underdevelopment in secular thinking within multiculturalist and antiracist efforts in Britain.

Thus, some years before the agitation for legislation on caste took hold in Britain, Bhatt had begun to castigate the Hindu community in Britain for 'caste prejudice' and had considered that 'black socialism' would be an antidote to such prejudice. On secularist grounds, he also opposes the funding of any Hindu caste-based organization. Bhatt's stance reflects the kind of dilemma that faces an Indian scholar working in the contemporary academic context. He articulates the shame of caste and the necessity for a deracinated future of his own culture, which some kind of secular black socialism should replace. Western scholars are unable to accept this as a problem because, one assumes, they have little at stake in the questions posed, and the Western culture does not really prepare them to ask questions in ways that are relevant for Indian culture. On the contrary, taking the stance that normatively degrades Indian traditions, which Bhatt does, may well be a passport to being serenaded by Western scholars and courted by Western universities.

Dhanda (2015), who argues against my claim that the caste system trope is Orientalist, says that she and other Indian scholars who challenge the caste system cannot be Orientalist. I agree with that, but on grounds that she does not consider. Indians taking her sort of position, arguing that Indian society is rife with caste discrimination originated by Brahmins and encoded in texts such as *Manusmriti* and the *Gita* that constitute historical evidence for such discrimination, are actually in a worse position than the Orientalists or their contemporary Western descendants. Orientalism, as Balagangadhara (2012: 34–59) shows, can be seen as a cultural project; Western culture gave rise to it, and Orientalists display a Western 'culturality' about them. In that sense, Orientalism does not tell us anything about Indian culture, but studying it tells us something about the Western culture, how Westerners make sense of, and how they are thus able to go about, in India.

Indian writers like Dhanda cannot have access to the Western culture or the Western experience of the Orient that gave rise to Orientalism. Instead, in their work, 'Orientalism is reproduced in the name of a critique of Orientalism' (Balagangadhara 2012: 47). This reproduction involves mimicking or merely decorating the Christian-Orientalist picture of Brahmanism. To make matters worse, such writers may feign an understanding of it and impute it to others: Dhanda argues that 'pre-existing ideas of equality, coupled with their incongruent socio-economic realization, made the victims of castism [sic] receptive to the colonizers' offer of legal equality in the latter period of colonization' (Dhanda 2015: 39). This makes them and those they describe inauthentic people, as indeed the West has described Indians (Balagangadhara 2012: 117–120).

Despotism and priestcraft

Reading contemporary accounts of the caste system, it may be easy to see why there is no escaping the conclusion that Hindus have a caste system which they are (im)morally compelled by their religion to defend. In the opening sections of the chapter on 'Hindus' in his widely circulated book, *Ethnicity, Law, and Human Rights: The English Experience*, Sebastian Poulter (1998: 239) wrote, 'One of the most striking elements of Hindu belief and practice – and certainly the most widely criticized – is the classification of individuals and families by caste.'[23] This observation underscores the fact that there is a fertile soil onto which ideas about India cultivated over the past centuries can be worked over if only because they have become common sense Western notions about Indian culture. As seen in the summary of the British Parliamentary debates above, such ideas go into the making of legislation against caste discrimination too.

Centuries apart, we can see common themes in how pictures of the caste system were painted. James Mill (1817, Vol. 2: 186–187) shared his polemic against India's caste system in his influential text, *The History of British India*:

> We have already seen, in reviewing the Hindu form of government, that despotism, in one of the simplest and least artificial shapes, was established in Hindustan, and confirmed by laws of Divine authority. We have seen likewise, that by the division of the people into caste, and the prejudices which the detestable views of the Brahmens raised to separate them, a

degrading and pernicious system of subordination was established among the Hindus, and that the vices of such a system were there carried to a more destructive height than among any other people. And we have seen that by a system of priestcraft, built upon the most enormous and tormenting superstition that ever harassed and degraded any portion of mankind, their minds were enchained more intolerably than their bodies; in short that, despotism and priestcraft taken together, the Hindus, in mind and body, were the most enslaved portion of the human race.

An image of priestly or sacerdotal violence upholding an oppressive caste system drowning those in its sway in superstitious ignorance comes through from James Mill's account here. This image of sacerdotal violence underpins and precedes the building of theories of the caste system. Even though at some variance from one another, these 'theories' have endured.

Having renamed latter-day Orientalism to Area Studies (Said 1978: 2, 19, 106–107, 275–276; Inden 1990: 36–38), Americans now vigorously cultivate European ideas about the oppressive Indian caste system. In his *Spirit of Hindu Law*, Donald R. Davis (2010: 106) writes thus of his field of study:

> This brings us to an ugly side of Hindu law, specifically its view of property. One must acknowledge that the system of castes and life-stages (*varnāśramadharma*), the notion of *dharma* that underlies all Hindu law, is an inherently hierarchical and exploitative system of social stratification by birth. Since the system also undergirds and materially manifests in a differential ownership of property, it is worth pausing to point out the, from a modern perspective, plainly unjust and unequal notion of inherent status that theoretically and practically produces particular relationships to property. Modern Hindus rightly often deny that this view of caste difference must continue as part of their religion today, but it would be both disingenuous and incorrect to suggest that the system of castes and life-stages never typified Hindu theologies or was never defended by them. Theological defenses of human inequality are by no means exclusive to Hinduism, but we must forthrightly state the form which this theology takes in the Hindu tradition in order to understand a crucial part of the spirit of Hindu law.

In his reading, the writers of the *dharmashastra* texts, which Davis refers to as 'Hindu theologies', typically defended an inherently exploitative and unjust social order. Contained as they are in their theologies, Hindus must be compelled to defend the inherently immoral system of caste. If they do not, then they must at least accept that their forbears did so and reject their inheritance. The question might follow that if one rejects the theology of one's religion, whether one can possibly adhere to that religion. Perhaps the groundwork for conversion is laid out here. Certainly, there is little space here between the barely disguised Protestant polemic against the false religion of Hinduism implicit in James Mill's account and that proffered by Davis, even though Davis thinks he is writing from a 'modern' context. Davis (2010: 173) nails his point arguing by reference to Hannah Arendt's study of totalitarianism:

> Arendt's studies of the plight of stateless persons in relation to the law points to the most significant shortcoming of classical Hindu law. By emphasizing the ethical goods of the Veda and of *varnāśramadharma*, classical Hindu jurisprudence measures the worth of individuals against those standards, in the hierarchical manner so familiarly associated with India. In so doing, what we today consider to be fundamental rights of human existence could be, as in totalitarian regimes, suppressed with little ideological dissonance. More specifically, lower castes were denied status within the scheme either of the Vedic world or of the *dharmas* of caste and life-stage. Lower castes had no rights (*adhikāra*) in those domains. Without legal status, these groups could have no voice and no standing from which to effect changes and improvements to their condition, at least within the system.

These images endure despite the fact that simple scrutiny undermines the claims therein. The quotes from Davis are also remarkable in that he reads the *dharmashastras* as if they are legal code-like 'authoritative texts' (Lubin et al. 2010: 3) that provide a 'scriptural foundation' (Ibid. 6) for a totalitarian regime. Quite how the Brahmin writers of the *dharmashastras* would have enforced the oppressive structure across the Hindu world that Davis pictures is unclear.[24] Davis (2010: 119) himself contradictorily acknowledges, after all, 'the primacy given to non-legislative sources of legal authority in Hindu jurisprudence', while Lubin observes (2010: 151) that 'There seems to be hardly any example of a king publishing a generally applicable law on his own authority, let alone promulgating an entire code.'[25] Despite the obvious contradictions, an image of sacerdotal violence effuses from the passages by Davis, as does the deprivation of agency of the lower castes, which appeared so unashamedly in Mill's account nearly two centuries before Davis's, and which we will continue to see, again and again.[26]

Christian moral themes

We have seen how a violent and despotic priestly core was present in Western accounts of the caste system. In this section, we can draw connections between older and contemporary Orientalism and how it has been shaped around the Christian polemic about Indian culture and religion. We can therefore see a thread running through older and contemporary accounts of India and its caste system. The references to 'Christian-Orientalism' highlight the fact that Orientalism builds on a theological structure of knowledge that is already present in the Western episteme. When Europeans encountered India and related stories about it, they were influenced by their background theological assumptions, which already told them that Indians have a religion and that that religion is a false one. Gelders and Balagangadhara (2011) have shown that prior to the British colonial takeover of India, there was already a 'generic' Christian theological framework that concerned itself with defining non-Christian traditions as the proto-Christian or the post-Christian evidences for the existence of religion. It centred on the idea of a 'sacerdotal nucleus' behind the plethora of Indian traditions. This analytical format overarched Protestant and Catholic models of the history of religion and, within this context, the contemporary forms of Hinduism were recognized as 'post-Christian' expressions of religion in the East. Europe therefore always had to accept that religion existed in India and that it was centred upon a priestly nucleus, which facilitated the move from truth to falsehood. It was thus already in the early modern period, and prior to the colonial Orientalist efforts, that 'Brahmanism' was identified as the core around which multiple Indian traditions coalesced, and which were self-evidently false given the hold of the priesthood. The idea of a sacerdotal nucleus seems to be at the core of subsequent attempts to provide theories about India's caste system. Its pervasive presence in the background may account for the endurance of the story of the caste system and how various seemingly contradictory accounts of that system have coexisted without the idea being abandoned.[27] Intellectuals supporting legislative actions such as the caste provision of the UK's

Equality Act 2010 appear to show little awareness of this background. Yet they want to have it both ways; they repeat the mantras of anti-Brahmanism but claim, as Dhanda (2015) does, that they do not rely on Orientalism.

The theme of the corrupting hold of the priesthood in India became more elaborated as Protestantism gained ascendancy, enabling Europeans to experience Indian culture in terms of a caste system that was integral to Indian religion, Brahmanism or Hinduism. One dimension of this was how caste was believed to be single greatest obstacle to conversion, while their efforts at proselytism tended to bear fruit among the so-called lower castes (Oddie 1979: 61–64; Dirks 2001: 26–27). Oddie (1979: 48–49) refers to discussions among missionaries in India during the 19th century regarding the retention of caste status among converts to Christianity, giving rise to the question whether caste among Christians was a civil or a religious institution:

> By 1850 the great majority of British and American missionaries believed they had found the answer – that caste among converts was *primarily a religious institution based on the concepts derived from Hinduism*. . . . Thus, in retaining caste, converts retained an important part of their former religion, caste being 'one of the evils of heathenism which has unwarily and most unfortunately been allowed to accompany the native convert in his passage to Christianity' (italics added).

The theologically driven linkages made by Protestant missionaries between the caste system and Hinduism (or Brahmanism) entered secularized discourse on the Indian caste system and also explain why it has acquired a very peculiar moral connotation. Bayly (1999: 110) refers to the influential four-volume polemical work (published 1817–1820) by the Rev. William Ward, an Evangelical Protestant missionary, which characterized the Hindu faith as a 'fabric of superstitions' concocted by Brahmins as 'the most complete system of absolute oppression that perhaps ever existed'. Bayly (1999: 110) goes on to note that:

> Christian polemics like Ward's were clearly a major if unacknowledged source for later academic theorists, including those modern anthropologists who came to regard the Brahman as arbiter and moral centre of Hindu social order. . . . This vision of immoral Brahman despotism clearly drew on popular English Protestant mythology of a priest-ridden,

tyrannised papist Europe awaiting liberation by the triumph of the Reformation spirit.

One consequence of the transfer of Christian moral themes into secular academic discourse is that contemporary writers have, as we saw earlier, few qualms talking of caste as based on Hindu 'normative values' and 'theological doctrines' (Lubin et al. 2010: 3n).[28] As the 19th century progressed, two strands of work began to offer explanations for the caste system, and both of these have remained influential in informing contemporary understandings of the Indian caste system. As Bayly (1999: 126–143) shows, one strand was focused on caste as an occupational division of labour, while another developed theories about caste and the racial classification of Indian society, referring back to earlier Orientalist ideas about the links between various 'Aryan' languages (Inden 1990: 59–60; Bayly 1999: 113–115).

The occupational theorists appear to have developed merely secularized versions of the Protestant account of Indian religion, which referred back to post-Reformation debates in Europe. De Roover and Claerhout (2015) have demonstrated how this connection between social structure and religion came to be established. They show that while Catholic writers saw caste as part of the secular world of the Indians, Protestant accounts instead firmly linked caste to the false religion of Hinduism. Protestants saw in the Indian culture a variation of the kind of stratified social system, with priests, noblemen and labourers, which theologians in the West had already used to describe their own societies. Protestant thinkers despised the priestly hierarchy and emphasized equality of all before God. They also got riled about the idea that vocation could be prescribed in such a way that an ecclesiastical calling was restricted to the priests of the Catholic Church and, by extension, the Brahmins in India. As Marx (2008 [1844]: 51) had said, Luther had 'turned priests into laymen because he turned laymen into priests'. They held that vocations performed by persons of any station are important in the sight of God, and a hierarchy such as caste prevented people the freedom of taking up any occupation to fulfill their calling.[29] Moreover, as Davis (2010: 106) wants us to believe, the Hindu law sanctioned 'an inherently hierarchical and exploitative system of social stratification *by birth*' (italics added). In more recent research, De Roover (2017) builds a hypothesis proposing that at least ideas about Hinduism or Brahmanism as a false religion also drew upon Christian polemic against the Jews and their priestly tribe of Levites, who were both keepers and interpreters of the divine law and decided on matters such as purity and excommunication. This tribe, who falsely passed off human laws as being of divine origin, could thus function as an analogue to the Brahmins in the Indian religion.

The Brahmins thus constituted one of three castes of the Indian system, the second of which were the *kshatriyas*, who were the warriors, and the third were the *vaishyas*, the agricultural, pastoral or trading groups, together making up Indian caste society. Anybody else who could not be fitted into this framework of the *varna* system belonged to a fourth group, the *shudras*. Westerners later identified other groups, the 'untouchables', as being outside this fourfold structure altogether. The scheme was explained and underpinned by the Aryan intervention onto the Indian scene sometime in the past, which subjugated the *shudras* and other non-caste groups. Speakers of Dravidian languages, like Tamil, were also thought to have been a separate race subjugated by the Aryans. So the story went, variations of which we find having a strong currency and repeated time and again, not least, as we have seen, in the British House of Lords. What gave endurance to this story was a mystery about which we have some more clues now thanks to research by Marianne Keppens (2015). The notion of an Aryan race had wide currency in Western intellectual circles until its discrediting after the genocide during the Second World War. However, it continues to rear its head when India's population and caste system are brought into discussion. Many scholars of India working in different disciplines assert that there was indeed an Aryan intrusion; whether it was an invasion or a series of migrations is a secondary matter of some debate. The basic idea is that the Aryans were followers of a particular religion, Brahmanism, they had civil and religious institutions, and spoke a sacred language called Sanskrit. They subjugated the indigenous Indian peoples who did not enjoy access to the laws and institutions of the 'Hindus'. Versions of this story have persisted since Orientalist writings predating the British colonialism in India. In these accounts, the Brahmins and those who followed them because of the religion they espoused, the language they spoke, and the institutions and laws they established, made them one people, race or nation, the Aryans. Others came to be regarded as people of different races upon whom the Brahmanical religion and laws was imposed but who, being a different people, were at the same time excluded from the laws and institutions of the Hindu Aryans. As we have seen, Davis (2010: 173) not inconsistently observes that the lower castes had no 'status', 'rights', 'voice' or 'standing' in this caste structure.

According to some European accounts from the 19th century, the Brahmins had brought a version of the true religion to India, which had since become corrupted. Even earlier reports of European missionaries told of how the Brahmins prevented their followers from converting to Christianity (Balagangadhara 1994: 86–89). As such, they were the priests of a false religion who kept their people languishing in idolatrous ignorance.[30] It fell upon the European Aryans with their superior religion, Christianity, to bring civilizing light to the idolatrous Indians. Behind such thinking lay the idea that the Europeans were evidently an Aryan race given that linguistic connections had earlier been found between Sanskrit and European languages. Despite its Semitic origins, for some, Christianity even became an Aryan religion. In these narratives, espousing a common religion and speaking a common language and having common laws and institutions provided the basis for making a nation, a people or a race. Describing the documents produced by the anthropologist and Census Commissioner Herbert H. Risley and their outgrowths as the location of the 'hegemonic discourse on caste of the Anglo-French imperial formation', Inden (1990: 59) notes Risley's argument that 'caste was the result of interactions between two racial types, a white and a black.' The anthropological categorization of Indian people from the late 19th century can be seen as founded upon and in turn influencing subsequent thinking about them. Anthropometric measurements were enlisted to section out which parts of the Indian population belonged to which race. That Indians were constituted of peoples of different races also informed the formulation of ethnographic reports of the Indian population, which then went into the framing of the colonial Indian census from 1891 to 1931 (Inden 1990: 56–66; Bayly 1999: 119–126; Dirks 2001: 48–52, 173–227).

The colonial construction of caste

An examination by recent scholarship of the Orientalist and colonial impact has led to some claims that, upon closer analysis, do not withstand scrutiny. One of the key American thinkers on caste, Nicholas Dirks (2001), may be justified in attributing to colonialism and its methods of fashioning knowledge of the idea of caste as typifying a way of *talking about* Indian society. His research (Ibid. 63–80) shows that pre-European societal classifications were immeasurably complex with a variety of different indexes being relevant depending on the context (for a similar claim, see Bayly 1999), which the colonial regime reconstructed in discursive terms. However, one cannot agree he is correct in assuming, as he does, that the way the British classified Indian society has taken on a reality of its own (also Bayly 1999:

7). For instance, he refers to the 'power of the colonial leviathan to produce caste as the measure of all social things' (Dirks 2001: 8), to the 'powerful history' through which caste 'has been constituted as the very condition of the Indian social' (Ibid. 8), and to how the transformation wrought upon caste by colonialism 'had immense implications for everyday social life' (Ibid. 12). To argue that is to accept that 'colonial governmentality' (Ibid. 6) somehow brought *into existence* that which the Europeans *falsely described*; that Indians were passive recipients of such 'colonial power/knowledge' (Ibid. 8); and that those descriptions actually made sense to them. Dirks fails to show how that could be.

There is another problem with Dirks's treatment of the impact of Orientalism and colonialism. He refers (Ibid. 10) to the manner in which some of those subject to colonial rule took on a narrative of caste thus:

> [T]he colonized, sometimes in direct reaction to the colonial lie of universality, would appropriate tradition as resistance and as refuge, but under conditions of colonial modernity tradition was simultaneously devalued and transformed. As a result, tradition too suffered from loss, even as it was tainted by its evident historicity. In the case of caste, many Indian social reformers and critics mistook this history as linear decline, the degradation of a noble system into a corrupt structure of power and dominant interests . . . attempts at historical recuperation typically took the form of finding an Orientalist golden age, a time when caste was an ideal system of mutual responsibility, reasoned interdependence and genuine spiritual authority. Only a few non-Brahman and Dalit voices rejected this kind of Orientalist nostalgia, all the while feeling increasingly trapped by the demands of anticolonial nationalism to downplay, and defer, all critiques of Indian culture and civilization.

One may well agree with Dirks (see also Inden 1990: 72–73) that the application of colonial historiography to tradition that he describes would inevitably result in an unrecognizable distortion, because of the onset of the 'colonial consciousness' that Balagangadhara (2012) identifies. However, when Dirks refers to 'non-Brahmin and Dalit voices', the colonial power/knowledge framework somehow recedes into the background and, instead, Dirks makes anti-colonial nationalism responsible for strangulating their voices (see Dhanda 2015, similarly, relying on Gandhi and Radhakrishnan).

Like many other writers, both Indian and Western, Dirks is prone to see authenticity in the kind of account of Hinduism and its caste system that figures like E. V. Ramaswamy Naicker ('Periyar', 1879–1973) and B. R. Ambedkar produced, whereas a figure like M. K. Gandhi would most likely be classed as someone who revels in 'Orientalist nostalgia'. Yet, as Gelders and Derde (2003) show, the criticism of Hinduism and caste that Ambedkar mounted was as much, if not more firmly, framed within the Protestant-Orientalist accounts of Indian culture and its caste system. Although Dirks (2001: 255–274) does not read the evidence in that way, his own account of the thoughts and actions of both his representative Indian anti-caste figures, Periyar and Ambedkar, supports the contention that, indeed, they had thoroughly imbibed the Protestant accounts of the caste system, so much so that they both routinely attacked Hinduism, Brahmanism and Brahmins; both also burned copies of the *dharmashastra* text, *Manusmriti*.[31] In Periyar's case, it also amounted to physical attacks as his followers 'beat priests and idols with shoes' (Dirks 2001: 261), while 'on more than one occasion, he implied that Brahmans should be murdered' (Ibid. 262). Such attacks have carried on in post-independence India by adherents of Periyar's ideology (Seshadri 2014). Ambedkar was meanwhile adamant that destroying caste required destroying the religion, Hinduism (Dirks 2001: 267). As noted, Ambedkar celebrated the European Enlightenment values of liberty, equality and fraternity (Roy 2014: 48, 51), while neither he nor Periyar wanted the British to leave India (Shourie 1997; Ambedkar 2014: 237n).

Part of the problem Dirks faces is to do with the fact that a critique is normally directed against the background of a dominant account or theory (Balagangadhara 2012). If he is right about the power of the colonial state, then how could 'Indian culture and civilization' be the object of critique by non-Brahmins and Dalits, except by their being parasitic on already existing Western accounts of India? The point is of more general importance because of the widespread tendency among Indian and Western intellectuals to want to critique 'Brahmanism', as recently attempted by Dhanda (2015). One can only assume that such critiques of 'Brahmanism' are extensions of Christian theological accounts of Indian culture or secularized variations thereof. Dirks (2001: 257) describes Periyar and Ambedkar as 'revealing in their particular ways the *extraordinary tyranny* of nationalist ideology' (italics added). If Dirks's thesis is true that it is colonial governmentality that shapes the caste system as postcolonial India inherited, then one may have expected him to ask why Periyar and Ambedkar did not rail against the colonial state for its attempts to construct and thereby bring into existence a caste system where none had previously existed. He doesn't pose the question though. Instead, he regards their lives as having 'made manifest' that 'oppression has been enclosed within the Brahmanic fold of Hindu civilization' (Ibid. 274). While seemingly adopting a critical stance on the Orientalist archive, Dirks presupposes and brings back to reapply from that archive the narrative of the 'sacerdotal nucleus', consistent with the 'most complete system of absolute oppression' that Ward saw (Bayly 1999: 110), the cocktail of 'despotism and priestcraft' that Mill spoke of (Dirks 2001: 33) and the tyranny of the *dharmashastras* that Davis diagnosed. So invidious is the tendency to locate the oppressive structures of Indian culture that such contortions have been read even into archeological evidence. Stanley Wolpert's 2000 edition of *A New History of India*, where the historian speaks of brick dwellings found in an archeological dig at Harappa as 'similar to those occupied by most Dalit labourers', is cited by Keane (2007: 13) one of the legal writers supporting the British caste legislation, in order to buttress his case for a caste system in India. Wolpert continues: 'Although hidden from view for thousands of years, the ruins of Harappa reveal the extensive history of oppression in India.'

Conclusion

I have argued here for the persistence of Christian-Orientalism in the way caste in India and the Indian diaspora is talked about. The language is the secularized one of the social sciences, but the framework and the background pre-theoretical assumptions that give it life can be found in the Christian polemic against Indian religion. Its violent sacerdotal core simultaneously underlined the falsity of that religion and provided the normative orientation to the caste system trope. The embedded presuppositions about the violent sacerdotal basis of the caste system generate further anomalies. Jalki and Pathan (2017) report finding it impossible to locate instances of Brahmins engaged in violence against so-called low-caste people in past volumes of the *Economic and Political Weekly*, which seems counter-intuitive if one assumes the truth of the priestly violence hypothesis. Broadly speaking, however, the climate is currently unfavourable for going out on one's own and raising the problem of the caste system as a vestige of Western Christian-Orientalist episteme in Western, or indeed Indian, universities. The evidence presented here demonstrates that Western academic institutions, political organs, and statal and non-statal bodies remain in the grip of this framework, viewing Indian traditions as inherently immoral and as legitimate targets for destruction.[32] The Western Churches and their missionaries had done the groundwork in centuries past, and their agenda for proselytism keeps the framework alive and reinforces its hold. They are able to garner the support of postcolonial Indian intellectuals who are parasitically dependent on the West for sustenance, and parrot out the need to annihilate caste, while simultaneously denying their dependence on Christian-Orientalism. Tragically, many decades after independence, Indian scholars do not appear to have broken away from the influence of this framework. Energy for removing the malign influence of the Christian-Orientalist episteme will, however, have to be harnessed in the Indian context. In talking about the internally differentiated biocultural formations known as *jatis*, Venkat Rao makes progress towards a non-normative, mnemocultural framework in which to understand Indian performative and reflective traditions. He explains why the West will be unable to produce an understanding of such biocultural forms and charts a method how to begin to understand them. Defunct theories of the caste system should then naturally collapse because that they are not only cognitively unsustainable, but there now exist genuine alternatives for understanding caste.

Notes

1 In Northern Ireland, where different concerns prevail, legislation against religious discrimination was introduced earlier.
2 The Directive 2000/78/EC also extends to disability, age or sexual orientation discrimination.
3 The term 'untouchables', also a political term, is used in place of Dalits by proponents of the legislation. See e.g. Lord Harries, House of Lords Debates, 11 Jan 2010, col. 334 and 22 Dec 2010, col. 1099.
4 See Lord Avebury, House of Lords Debates, 11 Jan 2010, col. 332, also citing the lack of detailed research, and Lord Harries, House of Lords Debates, 11 Jan 2010, col. 335.
5 See 'Religion in England and Wales', Office for National Statistics, www.ons.gov.uk/peoplepopulationandcommunity/culturalidentity/religion/articles/religioninenglandandwales2011/2012-12-11#toc, last accessed on 27 December 2016.
6 House of Commons Debates, 9 July 2014, col. 138WH.
7 How the number of Dalits and other information was presented in Parliament is encapsulated in the video, 'The Lying Lords of London' issued by the National Council for Hindu Temples (NCHTUK), www.youtube.com/watch?v=z5-XQdinqHo#t=75, last accessed 27 December 2016.
8 Lord Harries, House of Lords Debates, 22 Dec 2010, col. 1099, italics added and Lord Deben, House of Lords Debates, 22 April 2013, col.

1309. On the contrasts between India and Britain, see the essay by Menski (1992).
9 House of Commons Debates, 9 July 2014, col. 138WH.
10 See, e.g. Equality Act 2010, section 29(8), section 33(6), Sch. 23, para. 2, and Sch. 9, para. 273.
11 House of Commons Debates, 23 April 2013, col. 791.
12 Indeed, Ambedkar (2014: 285–286) had identified inter-marriage across caste lines as one of the tools for the annihilation of caste.
13 House of Lords Debates, 11 Jan 2010, col. 344.
14 House of Commons Debates, 23 April 2013, col. 791. To similar effect, see Lord Deben, House of Lords Debates, 22 April 2013, col. 1310.
15 See remarks of Lord Avebury, House of Lords Debates, 22 Dec 2010, col. 1098, where his interpretation comes through in the following question: 'My Lords, does the Minister agree that the research shows that discrimination based on caste does occur within the areas covered by the Act, and that it would be reduced if Section 9(5) of the Act was activated?' Also, Lord Harries, House of Lords Debates, 22 Dec 2010, col. 1099.
16 House of Lords Debates, 22 April 2013, col. 1312. Similarly, on the NIESR report concerning the extent of caste discrimination and any change regarding it, see Jo Swinson, Equalities Minister, House of Commons Debates, 16 April 2013, col. 220; also Alok Sharma MP, House of Commons Debates, 16 April 2013, col. 233–234.
17 E-mail communication from Jon Ashworth MP, 5 June 2013. Similarly, see Alok Sharma MP, House of Commons Debates, 16 April 2013, col. 234.
18 House of Lords Debates, 4 March 2013, col. 1304.
19 House of Lords Debates, 4 March 2013, col. 1305.
20 House of Lords Debates, 22 April 2013, col. 1309.
21 Inden (1990: 69–74) places such ideas in the context of the Romantic accounts of India.
22 Jakob de Roover (2015) elaborates on how Western normative ethics propels the idea of the immorality of non-Western cultures like India.
23 Later on in the same passage, Poulter describes caste as 'largely invisible'. Waughray (2014: 359) writes, 'Caste was largely invisible in Britain as a social phenomenon and as a ground of discrimination until 2005, when the then Labour Government announced a major overhaul of Britain's equality framework.' The invisibility theme chimes with the claim by Anti-Caste Discrimination Alliance et al. (2009) of 'hidden apartheid'.
24 The citation to Lubin et al. here is convenient and reflects what I believe to be Davis's influence in that co-authored text.
25 For a sustained critique of legal and non-legal writing asserting the code-like, positivistic status of the *dharmashastra* texts, see Menski (2003: ch. 3).
26 Postmodern scholars play with agency relentlessly of course. They can read agency deprivation in any text or presentation but, contradictorily, many Dalit rights supporters argue that Dalits enjoyed agency and autonomy in cultural production of all kinds. The recently diagnosed rise of low-caste political assertion is seen as one such affirmation of low-caste agency.
27 For an analogue for this claim, we can point to the argument by Balagangadhara (1994) that the presence of religion in Asia is founded on a pre-theoretical theological idea which informs all subsequent theorizing

on religion in Asia/India. For elaboration on the contradictory accounts of caste and the anomalies they produce, see Farek et al. (2017).

28 The claim that there is some Brahmanical or Hindu theology (see also Lubin et al. 2010: 6, and, more persistently, Davis 2010) is merely a projection of India as yet another culture having religion. On this problem, see in detail Balagangadhara (1994) and Balagangadhara and Jhingran (2014), and specifically on the 'textualization' of Indian religion antedating colonial Orientalism, see Gelders and Balagangadhara (2011: 123–127).

29 The contrasting perspectives between the Protestant missionaries and the Catholics can also be seen in the account by Jesuit missionary Abbe Dubois, whose famous text circulated widely in the early 19th century in which he had also claimed that caste was a kind of civil institution that protected Hindus from falling into barbarism, while he was repulsed by the religion of Hinduism (Dirks 2001: 21–26). Meanwhile, Bayly (1999: 111) cites the missionary Rev. William Ward describing the *varna* system as an attempt to 'cramp the human intellect, and forcibly restrain men within bounds which nature scorns to keep'. His fellow evangelicals appear to have followed him in this assessment.

30 It is interesting to note in this light that the monumental work by Pollock (2006: 39–44) on Sanskrit also departs from the problem (and assumption) that although Sanskrit knowledge was denied to lower orders of society, it spread so widely in Asia. Its analogue lies in the Protestant critique of the Catholic Church hierarchy that they held back knowledge of revelation written in the Latin language from the generality of believers. Invariably, contemporary annihilators of caste repeat this idea. On the role of Christian polemic against Jews, see Dr Roover (2017).

31 The focus of both Ambedkar and Periyar on a written text, *Manusmriti*, as a foundational legal document indicates the degree to which colonial consciousness had set in. Venkat Rao (2014: 10) instructively argues that, 'Despite various efforts to show the intrusion of writing into "Sanskrit knowledge systems" neither the scribal mode gained significance, nor, more importantly, did it in any palpable way affect the mnemocultural reflective ethos'. Dhanda (2015), taking an Ambedkarite line, remains oblivious to these questions.

32 A further instance of this tendency is provided by the attempted rejection of a review of my book, Shah (2015) by the journal *South Asia Research* whose editorial team consists of members of the South Asia Institute at the School of Oriental and African Studies. In the event, the review by Werner Menski was published on condition that another, more hostile review by Annapurna Waughray be published in the same issue. The reviews can be found in Vol 36(3), November 2016, of *South Asia Research*.

References

Ambedkar, B. R. 2014. 'Annihilation of Caste', in S. Anand (ed.), *The Annihilation of Caste: The Annotated Critical Edition*, pp. 181–317. New Delhi: Navayana.

Anti-Caste Discrimination Alliance, Roger Green and Stephen Whittle. 2009. *Hidden Apartheid – Voice of the Community: Caste and Caste*

Discrimination in the UK, A Scoping Study. Anti-Caste Discrimination Alliance.

Balagangadhara, S. N. 1994. *'The Heathen in His Blindness. . .': Asia, the West and the Dynamic of Religion.* Leiden: Brill.

———. 2012. *Reconceptualizing India Studies.* New Delhi: Oxford University Press.

Balagangadhara, S. N., and Divya Jhingran. 2014. *Do All Roads Lead to Jerusalem? The Making of Indian Religions.* New Delhi: Manohar.

Banerjee-Dube, Ishita. (ed.) 2010. *Caste in History.* New Delhi: Oxford University Press.

Bayly, Susan. 1999. *Caste, Society and Politics in India from the 18th Century to the Modern Age.* Cambridge: Cambridge University Press.

Bhatt, Chetan. 1997. *Liberation and Purity: Race, New Religious Movements and the Ethics of Postmodernity.* London: Routledge.

Chowdhury, Jayant. 2014. 'Nepal Struggles with Christian Conversions', 28 December. Swarajyamarg.com (accessed on 27th December 2016).

Davis, Donald R. Jr. 2010. *The Spirit of Hindu Law.* Cambridge: Cambridge University Press.

De Roover, Jakob. 2015. *Europe, India and the Limits of Secularism.* New Delhi: Oxford University Press.

———. 2017. 'A Nation of Tribes and Priests: The Jews and the Immorality of the Caste System', in Martin Farek, Dunkin Jalki, and Sufiya Pathan and Prakash Shah (eds.), *Western Foundations of the Caste System.* Basingstoke: Palgrave Macmillan and Springer.

De Roover, Jakob, and Sarah Claerhout. 2015. 'The Caste Connection: On the Sacred Foundations of Social Hierarchy', *Theatrum Historiae*, 17: 9–36.

Dhanda, Meena. 2015. 'Anti-Castism and Misplaced Nativism: Mapping Caste as an Aspect of Race', *Radical Philosophy*, 192: 33–43.

Dhanda, M., D. Mosse, A. Waughray, D. Keane, R. Green, S. Iafrati, and J.K. Mundy. 2014a. *Caste in Britain: Experts' Seminar and Stakeholders' Workshop.* Equality and Human Rights Commission Research Report no. 92. Manchester: Equality and Human Rights Commission.

Dhanda, M., A. Waughray, D. Keane, D. Mosse, R. Green, and S. Whittle. 2014b. *Caste in Britain: Socio-legal Review.* Equality and Human Rights Commission Research Report no. 91. Manchester: Equality and Human Rights Commission.

Dirks, Nicholas B. 2001. *Castes of Mind: Colonialism and the Making of Modern India.* Princeton: Princeton University Press.

Farek, Martin, Dunkin Jalki, and Sufiya Pathan and Prakash Shah. (eds.) 2017. *Western Foundations of the Caste System.* Basingstoke: Palgrave Macmillan and Springer.

Gelders, Raf, and S.N. Balagangadhara. 2011. 'Rethinking Orientalism: Colonialism and the Study of Indian Traditions', *History of Religions*, 51 (2): 101–128.

Gelders, Raf, and Willem Derde. 2003. 'Mantras of Anti-Brahmanism: Colonial Experience of Indian Intellectuals', *Economic and Political Weekly*, 38 (43): 4611–4617.

Grillo, Ralph. 2015. *Muslim Families, Politics and the Law*. Farnham: Ashgate.

Hindu Forum of Britain. 2008. *Caste in the UK: A Summary of the Consultation with the Hindu Community in Britain*. London: Hindu Forum of Britain.

House of Representatives, Subcommittee on Africa, Global Human Rights and International Operations of the Committee on International Relations. 2005. *India's Unfinished Agenda: Equality and Justice for 200 Million Victims of the Caste System*. One Hundred Ninth Congress, First Session, October 6, Serial No. 109–102.

Inden, Ronald B. 1990. *Imagining India*. Oxford: Basil Blackwell.

Jalki, Dunkin, and Sufiya Pathan. 2017. 'Are There Caste Atrocities in India? What the Data Can and Cannot Tell Us', in Martin Farek, Dunkin Jalki, Sufiya Pathan, and Prakash Shah (eds.), *Western Foundations of the Caste System*. Basingstoke: Palgrave Macmillan and Springer.

Keane, David. 2007. *Caste-Based Discrimination in International Human Rights Law*. Aldershot: Ashgate.

Keppens, Marianne. 2015. 'The Mysterious Ways of the Aryans: Caste and the Aryan Invasion Theory', *Theatrum Historiae*, 17: 63–89.

Lubin, Timothy. 2010. 'Indic Conceptions of Authority', in Timothy Lubin, Donald R. Davis Jr, and Jayanth K. Krishnan (eds.), *Hinduism and Law: An Introduction*, pp. 137–153. Cambridge: Cambridge University Press.

Lubin, Timothy, Donald R. Davis Jr, and Jayanth K. Krishnan. (eds.) 2010. *Hinduism and Law: An Introduction*. Cambridge: Cambridge University Press.

Marx, Karl. 2008. 'Contribution to the Critique of Hegel's Philosophy of Right', in Karl Marx and Friedrich Engels (eds.), *On Religion*. Mineola, New York: Dover.

Meer, Naser. 2010. *Citizenship, Identity and the Politics of Multiculturalism: The Rise of Muslim Consciousness*. Basingstoke: Palgrave Macmillan.

Menski, Werner F. 1992. 'The Indian Experience and Its Lessons for Britain', in Bob Hepple and Erika M. Szyszczak (eds.), *Discrimination: The Limits of Law*, pp. 300–343. London: Mansell.

———. 2003. *Hindu Law: Beyond Tradition and Modernity*. New Delhi and Oxford: Oxford University Press.

Metcalf, Hilary, and Heather Rolfe. 2010. *Caste Discrimination and Harassment in Great Britain*. gov.uk (accessed on 27th December 2016).

Mill, James. 1817. *The History of British India*. London: Baldwin, Cradock and Joy, 6 Vols.

National Secular Society. 2013. Briefing on 'Caste Discrimination'. Secularism.org (accessed on 27th December 2016).

Oddie, G. A. 1979. *Social Protest in India: British Protestant Missionaries and Social Reforms 1850–1900*. New Delhi: Manohar.

Pollock, Sheldon. 2006. *The Language of the Gods in the World of Men: Sanskrit, Culture, and Power in Premodern India*. Berkeley: University of California Press.

Poulter, Sebastian. 1998. *Ethnicity, Law and Human Rights: The English Experience*. Oxford: Clarendon.

Robinson, Rowena, and Joseph Marianus Kujur. (eds.) 2010. *Margins of Faith: Dalit and Tribal Christianity in India*. Los Angeles: Sage.

Roy, Arundhati. 2014. 'The Doctor and the Saint', in S. Anand (ed.), *The Annihilation of Caste: The Annotated Critical Edition*, pp. 15–169. New Delhi: Navayana.

Said, Edward. 1978. *Orientalism*. London: Penguin.

Sen, Ronojoy. 2010. *Articles of Faith: Religion, Secularism, and the Indian Supreme Court*. New Delhi: Oxford University Press.

Seshadri, Badri. 2014. 'Periyar's Followers have a Perverse Sense of Justice', in *Swarajyamag*, 21 April. Swarajyamarg.com (accessed on 27th December 2016).

Shah, Prakash. 2015. *Against Caste in British Law: A Critical Perspective on the Caste Discrimination Provision in the Equality Act 2010*. Basingstoke: Palgrave Macmillan.

Shourie, Arun. 1997. *Worshipping False Gods*. New Delhi: ASA Publications.

———. 2012. *Falling Over Backwards: An Essay Against Reservations and Against Judicial Populism*. Noida, Uttar Pradesh: Harper Collins.

Tharamangalam, J. 1996. 'Caste Among Christians in India', in M. N. Srinivas (ed.), *Caste: Its Twentieth Century Avatar*, pp. 263–291. New Delhi: Penguin.

Venkat Rao, D. 2014. *Cultures of Memory in South Asia: Orality, Literacy and the Problem of Inheritance*. New Delhi: Springer.

Waughray, Annapurna. 2009. 'Caste Discrimination: A Twenty First Century Challenge for UK Discrimination Law?' *Modern Law Review*, 72 (2): 182–219.

———. 2012. 'The New Apartheid?' *New Law Journal*, 6 January newlawjournal.co.uk (accessed on 27th December 2016).

———. 2014. 'Capturing Caste in Law: Caste Discrimination and the Equality Act 2010', *Human Rights Law Review*, 14: 359–379.

6
CASTE AS AN IMPEDIMENT IN THE JOURNEY OF A BHAKTA
Lingayat Vachanas, jati and aadhyatma[1]

Dunkin Jalki

An ever-increasing dissatisfaction with the studies of culture and life in Asia is a norm today. The boom in postcolonial studies, in the aftermath of Edward Said's *Orientalism* (1978), is not only testimony to this dissatisfaction, but has also, one may say, institutionalized it. There are two dominant strands in these studies of the past three and a half decades. There is, on the one hand, a criticism of colonialism. This is an attempt to understand how colonialism affected Indian traditions, their self-understanding and their preferred ways of existence. There is also, on the other hand, a criticism of problems and structures that are said to be inherent to Indian culture. The caste system, for instance, is generally considered to be one such structure inherent to Indian culture. Today, there is a new realization, as this collection reminds us, to go beyond these criticisms and expression of dissatisfaction. Criticism of something, if it ought to be worth human resources and time, should lead us towards solutions to problems, progress in human knowledge and, more importantly, a better world to live. Unhesitatingly we can assert that postcolonial studies have begun this process decades ago and have contributed, what they could, to this endeavour. Today, we have to build on the work done by postcolonial scholars. This is a task of, as the call for papers puts it, 'new inquiries into humanities'. Referring to the work of S. N. Balagangadhara, the call also warns us that no inquiry into human sciences 'is likely to happen unless we undertake the task of thinking from our "backgrounds"'.

The task that this chapter sets itself is of the nature of *thinking from our 'backgrounds'*. The focus is not on contributing to the existing criticism of writings on Indian traditions. It will rather provide an outline of a new model for understanding bhakti traditions, by focusing on the way the Lingayat tradition and the Lingayat *Vachana* literature talk about *jati* or caste. This, however, needs some stage setting. We should first confirm whether or not the existing model of understanding the Vachanas and their stance with regard to caste is problematic. This will be done in the first two sections, and in the third and larger section, we will develop a new way of understanding the Vachanas' take on the 'caste question'. This is not a hermeneutic exercise that humanistic disciplines are familiar with. It is part of S. N. Balagangadhara's efforts to build a comparative science of cultures, which would include a theory about Indian traditions.

Modern interpretation of Bhakti

A glance through the colonial and the modern literature on Indian traditions reveals a consensus on dividing Indian traditions into two broad categories: those that opposed the caste system and Brahminical ideology and those that did not oppose them, or what is worse, even promoted them. Over the last 150 years or so, the former traditions have been dubbed 'anti-Brahmanical traditions' (Stephenson 1839; Stevenson 1846), 'Little Traditions', following Redfield and Singer (Ramanujan 1973), 'non-caste Hindu traditions' (Lorenzen 1987) and, more popularly, 'bhakti traditions'. For ease of use, we will refer to them in this chapter by their most popular name: bhakti traditions. The dominant way of speaking about the bhakti traditions and the literature attributed to them is to see them as a social movement against the deeply negative impact of Brahminical Hinduism on Indian society and the ensuant caste system. The view in the following excerpt is typical of this currently dominant understanding.

> Bhakti had a wide appeal from the very beginning, not only because it recognized the emotional approach to God as fully valid, but also because it broke down all the barriers of privilege. . . . Bhakti became the way of salvation for everyone: women and children, low castes and outcastes, could become fully recognized members of the bhakti movement. Some of the great *bhaktas* are saints for Hindus, Muslims, and Sikhs alike. Even Christians in India are beginning to accept them as theirs, finding the religiosity of these *bhaktas* to be deep and genuine and utilizing their hymns in their services. Some of the universally revered *bhaktas* were outcastes, like Nanda

and Cokamela, some were women like Mirabai and Antal; others were great sinners for whom orthodoxy could not find means of salvation. Kabir, one of the finest Hindi poets of medieval India, reputedly was a Muslim weaver; his songs are a favorite with countless Hindus in northern India even today.
(Klostermaier 1989: 184)[2]

As scholars have pointed out over the years, there is something deeply unsatisfactory about these readings of the Indian bhakti traditions. These readings thrive 'on the crudest kind of anachronism: Buddha the reformer, Ashoka the secularist, Akkamahadevi [a Vachana composer] the feminist, and so forth' (Dhareshwar 2010). They render the entire tradition extremely inconsistent and ambiguous. Kabir and his followers, for instance, seem ambiguous to David Lorenzen (1987: 267). Scholars have resolved this ambiguity simply by breaking the tradition into two: the true and false traditions, or the founder's original and noble ideals and the followers who seem to bring soon their sect into the fold of Hinduism and the caste system (Thapar 1989). As we see in the case of the Lingayat tradition, scholars simply hold that it diverted from its founding anti-caste ideals and soon became a caste itself (Lorenzen 1987: 267, 275; Schouten 1995). Scholars have also dubbed some of our prominent saint-poets themselves inconsistent.[3]

Such arguments render these saint-poets and the entire tradition built around them immoral and hypocritical. They seem often to indulge in practices that they are said to preach against. Eleanor Zelliot finds such 'ambiguity' and puzzles in the writings of the 14th century saint-poet Chokhamela. While Chokhamela is 'the first authentic voice of the Untouchable in Western India', he also seems to accept karma, because of which he 'and his family are rejected as models for the current-day [anti-caste] movement' (in Lorenzen 1995: 212, 217). Talking about the 15th century Lingayat saint-poets, J. P. Schouten notes that they 'were ultimately more interested in washermen mystics than in the social position of contemporary washermen' (1995: 67).

Commenting on Schouten's work, Robert Zydenbos notes that Schouten has been misled by 'certain modern authors in Karnataka [who] cultivate an image of Basava [the Lingayat saint-poet] as a successor to the Buddha and a predecessor of Dr. Ambedkar, as a champion of the socially oppressed.' And they thus present the Lingayat tradition as 'a hybridized form of religion which ... has imbibed Western secular and Christian ideas' (Zydenbos 1997: 527, 535). This, as we will see ahead, is an apt comment about modern scholarship on the Lingayat tradition.

Modern interpretations of the Vachanas

The Lingayat tradition is a bhakti tradition largely from the Kannada-speaking (and to some extent the Telugu- and Marathi-speaking) region of South India. As it is popularly considered today, it came into prominence in the early part of the second millennium with an 'anti-caste movement', called the Lingayat or *Virashaiva* movement. The Lingayat saint-poets who were part of this movement composed the Vachanas over the next 800 years, giving expression to the very views that shaped the movement. Hence, the movement is also popularly called the Vachana movement. The Vachanas are a body of work in Kannada associated with this 12th century 'movement'. Over the years, this body of work has come to be treated as the most prominent body of 'Literature' produced in Kannada, mainly because the Vachanas are ostensibly one of the earliest indigenous forms of expressing a 'subaltern' revolt against 'the caste system'. This image of the Lingayat tradition, community and the Vachanas has been quite dominant in modern Lingayat studies.

The following comments of a few leading contemporary scholars are typical of this scholarship. First, the views of a well-known Kannada epigraphist, M. M. Kalburgi: 'India is a land of a "culture of discriminations" [*bhedasamskruti*] – class discrimination, varna discrimination, gender discrimination. In a society constituted by a culture of discriminations, only experiments of spiritual welfare can have some impact, and not social welfare.' The Lingayat reformers of the 12th century, like Basava and Allama, he asserts, did both.[4] Elsewhere, he writes,

> The 12th century was the period of temples. . . . Temples had become the centre of exploitation and extremely powerful. They had everything, from priests to prostitutes and indulged in all kinds of activities from receiving gifts to money laundering. As a centre of exploitation and a forum of ignorance, they had come to control everything. It was a period when the rich were building temples. Building temples was a way of spending the money earned in sinful ways. . . . Poor people were unable to build temples. Therefore, Basavanna stood for them, and said "I'm a poor man, what can I do."
> (Kalburgi 1998: 282–283)

In the words of another Kannada scholar, 'the Vachanas are full of the wise sayings of Virasaiva saints, which condemn the caste system. Several Vachanas of Basava unequivocally condemn caste and stress conduct, and not birth, as the criterion for deciding who is good and who is bad' (Sadasivaiah 1967: 43).

According to Hiremallur K. Ishwaran (1997: 118), a reputed Kannada sociologist,

> The intentions of the Vachanas were three-fold: (1) social change, (2) establishment of [egalitarian social] practices and philosophy, and (3) spiritual development. Of these three, social change was important for the Sharanas.[5] Their aim was to turn the hierarchy-ridden society towards equality.

D. R. Nagaraj, a prominent Kannada literary critic, claims that 'anti-caste philosophy was the fundamental stance of the Vachana movement' (1999: 183). According to Chidananda Murthy, one of the most important epigraphists to do substantial historical work concerning the Vachanas and the 'virashaiva movement', 'Kannadigas should be proud of the fact that historically eight centuries ago . . . a movement against the caste system was carried out by the Vachana-composers in Karnataka' (2004, 4: 726–727). This view has the support of the most popular Western scholars from Karl Marx[6] and Max Weber[7] to the recent ones, such as Sheldon Pollock (2006: 433). In his lengthy book on the Lingayats, J. P. Schouten, claiming ample support from inscriptions, accounts of foreign travellers and epigraphic records, says,

> When Basava and his fellow preachers appeared in the twelfth century, the society was completely under the spell of the caste structure. . . . [A] rigid caste system prevailed then in South India. . . . The bottom of the status pyramid was formed by the large masses of untouchables who were not at all entitled to participate in religious and social life. . . . The working conditions of the lowest castes were harsh and slavery was [a] rather common phenomenon. . . . The untouchable class had long come into existence. Free intercourse among castes and classes was restricted and the rules regarding interdining and intermarrying were rigid. It was in this caste-ridden society that the Virasaiva movement came into existence. The preaching of the leaders of the movement, under the charismatic leadership of Basava, is preserved in their little poems, the *Vachanas*. It will become clear from these texts, how the Virasaiva leaders protested against the social values and their days and what the inspiration for such radical criticism was. Caste is [a] frequent subject in the vacana literature of the

twelfth century. In various ways, the conviction is expressed that the traditional division of people into hereditary caste groups is untenable. The arrogant attitude of the higher castes is severely criticized and in particular the pretensions of the Brahmana caste are attacked. . . . *The Vachanas give ample testimony to this egalitarian way of thinking. Especially Basava wrote many poems on this topic, in which they clearly express his radical ideas on the equality of all people.*
(Schouten 1995: 24–25; emphasis mine)

In fact, the view that the Vachanas take an anti-caste stance and criticize Brahmanism (if not Brahmans) seems to be so dominant and hegemonic in our times that scholars have rarely laboured to justify it either with textual or with historical evidence. Yet, increasingly scholars are also finding such interpretations of the Vachanas unsatisfactory (Niranjana 1992; Punekar 2004; Zydenbos 1997).

Over the last decade, the research group working with S. N. Balagangadhara has raised the strongest criticism of such readings of the Vachanas and the Lingayat tradition (Hegde and Shanmukha 2015; Jalki 2009; Jalki and Balagangadhara 2012). Here is a brief and partial summary of the argument. Let us begin with the popular assumption that the Vachanas represent a movement against casteism. If this argument were to hold, we may reasonably expect that most of the Vachanas, if not all, should speak about 'caste'. It can hardly be the case that the Vachanas are part of a movement against the caste system without caste forming the central focus of their attention. Hence, if we can demonstrate that the focus of the Vachanas is not caste, then the argument that they are caste-critiques is proved untenable. The argument here is simple: modern Vachana scholarship will fail in this empirical test since its arguments are based on a highly selective and an extremely small number of Vachanas. Here is a sample of the data that this argument presents:

- The total number of Vachanas published by the state government of Karnataka so far: 21,788.[8]
- The total number of Vachanas that apparently *talk about*[9] Brahmans: 195.
- The total number of Vachanas that apparently talk about jati, *kula* and related topics: 458.

By any standard, 195 and 458 out of 21,788 Vachanas (which is 0.89 and 2.1 per cent of the total Vachanas, respectively) are insufficient to justify the argument that the Vachanas deal with Brahmans and the caste system, let alone allowing us to argue that the entire corpus criticizes either of the two. Let us focus on the Vachanas that contain some reference to the Brahmans. What complicates our task of inferring an anti-Brahman argument from these 195 Vachanas is the fact that a considerable number of these Vachanas make positive remarks about Brahmans, while many Vachanas do not make much sense to us today, both linguistically and (more importantly) conceptually. That leaves approximately a third of the 195 Vachanas (or 0.30 per cent of the total) that say something against Brahmans. Even here, sometimes the Brahmans they criticize are mythical characters and not contemporary people, and often the remarks made against Brahmans are incidental rather than stereotypical. This leaves an extremely insignificant number of the Vachanas for us to make the argument that is so popular in modern Lingayat scholarship: 'the social and political project of the [Vachana] movement was self-consciously anti-Brahman and anti-caste' (Pollock 2006: 433).

As far as this problem in modern Vachana scholarship is accepted and reflected upon, scholars have tried to point out two sources of this problem. One, it is suggested that such popular understanding of the Lingayat tradition and the Vachanas has to do with the tendency 'to see many Christian or other recent Western values in' the writings of the Lingayat poet-saints (Zydenbos 1997: 525). In Tejaswini Niranjana's words,

> attempting to assimilate *Saivite* poetry [the Vachanas] to the discourses of Christianity or post-Romantic New Criticism, these [modern] translators [of the Vachanas] . . . try to show how the Vachanas are always already Christian, or 'modernist,' and therefore worthy of the West's attention. Their enterprise is supported by the asymmetry between English and Kannada created and reinforced by colonial and neo-colonial discourse. This is an asymmetry that allows translators to simplify the text in a predictable direction, toward English and the Judeo-Christian tradition and away from the multiplicity of indigenous languages and religions, which have to be homogenized before they can be translated. . . . Both European and Indian commentators persist in discussing *Virasaivism* in terms of Puritanism and Protestantism, suggesting that the poems of the *Virasaiva* saints are part of a Pilgrim's Progress.
>
> (Niranjana 1992: 180–181)

Two, scholars have tried to show that we will not be able to extract a sound anti-caste stance from the Vachanas because: (a) the tradition as a whole is inconsistent with regard to its anti-caste stance. The argument here is that in a matter of a few centuries, the tradition lost its founding ideals. In fact, it went on to strengthen Brahmanism. (See, for some discussion of this issue, Niranjana 1992: 176.) (b) More importantly, even a single saint-poet is not consistent in his own stance about caste. According to Rahmat Tarikere,

> Basava did not propound his ideas scientifically and logically as a philosopher, like Karl Marx or any experienced scientist.... Consequently, there is no consistent thesis in his Vachanas, as one can find in a philosophical text. What we can see here is different and contradictory voices and struggles of a poet and an activist.
>
> (2008: 65)

As Zydenbos asks, if Basava was such a revolutionary, as he is generally taken to be, 'why [do] some vacanas by Basava clearly show that he stressed inequality and criticized those who did not believe in his form of religion and whose ways of life differed from his?' And in a footnote, he adds: 'we must note that Basava's stance was apparently not very consistent.... Or there may be a deeper consistency which is not immediately apparent' (1997: 529).

The first point, which links the current understanding of the Lingayat tradition to a Christian framework, hints at (but leaves unanswered) one crucial question: What does it mean to see an Indian tradition from a non-Western, non-Christian, non-Orientalist framework? The second point, unless exhaustively substantiated, which no scholar has done so far, remains a mere accusation. The *principle of charity* demands that we do not dismiss offhand a tradition that is in existence for well over 800 years. We must attempt to show under what conditions Vachanas and the arguments they put forth would look maximally consistent to us today. Additionally, we must also be able to show what makes them inconsistent. After all, if Lingayats held a saint-poet, like Basava, as important to their tradition over the centuries, then it is unlikely that they saw him as an inconsistent thinker, unless of course all Lingayats of the last 800 years were intellectually challenged. This line of argument leads to the following claim: a non-Christian alternative way of understanding the Vachanas, if it has to challenge contemporary scholarship, should be able to unearth 'the deeper consistency which is not immediately apparent'.

CASTE AS AN IMPEDIMENT IN THE JOURNEY OF A BHAKTA

This chapter is an attempt to do this. It will show that these contradictions and ambiguities that scholars find in Bhakti literature like the Vachanas are a result of reading them through the framework of Christianity and Orientalism. It will do so not by analyzing the existing readings of bhakti literature, but by developing a 'new' way of analyzing the Vachanas. This 'new' method of analysis, it will show, will substantially decrease the seeming contradictions and inconsistencies within the Vachanas. This is not, as noted earlier, a hermeneutic exercise. That is, it does not offer a fresh 'literary interpretation' of the Vachanas that will redress all the contradictions. Situated within the research of S. N. Balagangadhara, this is part of an effort to develop a theory about the Indian traditions.

A new hypothesis

If the Vachanas do not talk about the *caste system*, what do they talk about when they talk about jati and related issues? This question has been one of the standard responses to the arguments put forth by S. N. Balagangadhara and his team that the Vachanas do not talk about the caste system. It is an indisputable fact that the Vachanas say something about jatis and about a 'problem' or two about the way people relate to them in their life. As it has been shown, this cannot be rendered into an anti-caste stance in any straightforward way (Jalki and Balagangadhara 2012). What, then, one may reasonably ask, are Vachanas saying when they talk about jati, *jati-difference* ('*jati-bheda*') and so on? Let us spend some time on this question here.

What follows in the rest of the chapter can also be seen simply as an attempt to provide a coherent view of the way the Lingayat tradition talks about caste. Such a view is available within the tradition. This chapter, in its attempt to formulate this traditional view in the current conceptual language, also tries to gain insight into the meaning the Vachanas had for the precolonial Lingayat scholars or saint-poets.

Let me propose here, in the form of a hypothesis, what the Vachanas are saying about jati. The core of this hypothesis is proposed and elaborated upon by S. N. Balagangadhara and other members of his research team in some of their recent published writings (Balagangadhara 2013; Hegde 2013; Hegde and Shanmukha 2015), as well as the unpublished and ongoing work. This hypothesis, as I formulate it here, consists of three interconnected claims: (a) compared to other Indian traditions, the Vachanas say nothing new or different about jati; (b) when Vachana composers speak about jati, they deal with a relatively minor problem within the limited context of their immediate surroundings; (c) the context within which they speak about jati is the *aadhyatmic* progress of those who belong to the Lingayat tradition. Let us discuss each point in turn and reflect on some of their implications.

(a) *Vachanas say nothing new or different about jati*

As noted in the first part, much of the importance bestowed upon the Vachanas in the past 100 years or so is based on an assumption that they resumed the war against caste system that the Buddha and the Mahavira had started more than two millennia ago. 'The Buddha and Mahavira were born into Hindu families . . . rejected the caste system, the authority of the Brahmins, the ritualism of the Vedas and abstract thinking.' Similarly, the 'Lingayats, or Virasaivas [and] . . . [t]heir founder, the radical poet Basava (b. AD 1106), wrote passionately against the caste system, mocked the Brahmins and preached complete surrender (bhakti) to Shiva' (Lal 2010: 42, 71). This popular belief suggests that the Vachanas say something about caste system, in line with the early Buddhists and the Jains, which was radically new and different from what all other Indian traditions have to say about the issue.[10]

It is necessary to note the following before we proceed further. How do we know that the Vachana composers took an anti-caste stance? There is only one source today to talk about the so-called anti-caste movement of the Lingayat saint-poets: Vachanas and perhaps a handful of other literary texts (Desai 1968). By implication then, the claim that the Vachanas say something new about jati should be and can only be proved through textual analysis of the Vachanas. There is nothing wrong with this situation. If we want to show that Adolf Hitler was a virulently anti-Semitic, we can, among other things, analyze his speeches and writings and show how he consistently spoke against Jews. Similarly, by analyzing the writings of Martin Luther King Jr., we can learn that he was against apartheid in South Africa. What happens if we find no difference between the way Martin Luther King Jr. speaks about the blacks and those who explicitly supported apartheid in South Africa?

The situation regarding the Vachana composers and their anti-caste stance confronts us with one such peculiar situation. The Vachanas are full of 'insulting language' and 'negative stereotypes' about the so-called lower castes. For example, they frequently and unapologetically use the names of the lower castes, like *Holeya* and *Madiga*, as abusive curse words.[11] At this rhetorical level, then, Vachanas do not differ from other Indian traditional literature, including those texts that are supposed to uphold the caste system, like the *Manusmriti*. The popular belief that the Vachanas 'fiercely questioned' and 'ridiculed' the caste system and its various aspects, like, 'classical belief systems, social customs and superstitions, . . . image worship, . . . the caste system, . . . [and] the Vedic ritual[s]' (Ramanujan 1973: 30), is then simply and patently wrong.

This leaves us with one other option. The anti-caste stance of the Vachanas is to be located not at the rhetorical level (i.e. in the way the Vachanas speak about different castes), but in the ideas that they put forth about, say, social life, ethics and so on. This way of arguing is also popular among scholars writing in Kannada. However, at this abstract or philosophical level too, there is nothing much to distinguish the Vachanas from other traditional Indian texts. The way the *Mahabharata* speaks about jati (Hegde 2014), or the way Buddha or Buddhism speaks about it (Balagangadhara 1994: chap. 7) or the way Chaitanya Vaishnava writers wrote about Brahmins vis-à-vis caste (Farek 2015), is indistinguishable from the way the Vachanas deal with it. The following conclusion, therefore, is inescapable: in comparison with other Indian traditions, the Vachanas say nothing new or different about jati.

The feeling that the Vachanas take an anti-caste stance is mainly the result of European misinterpretations of the anti-Brahmin polemics of the Vachanas. As noted already, the Vachanas are full of abuse against those who do not belong to the Lingayat traditions. In our study, we have found that there are more Vachanas (327 Vachanas, that is) that engage in 'abusing' non-Lingayats than the Vachanas that talk about jati. Basava's Vachana #752 is a good example. Here Basava says that unless one slits the mouth and the cheeks of the person who says there is a *daiva* ('god') other than Shiva, his anger will not subside. And he concludes the Vachana by urging lord Shiva to kindly consider his wish.[12]

Let us spend time on a more general aspect of this intercommunity polemics in India. That the communities, traditions and castes are polemical about each other is intuitively known to all of us. But, as it often happens, proving the known is next to impossible. The traditional Indian writings of various traditions as well as European writers on India are full of indications of how communities are (often innocuously) antagonistic about each other's practices, rituals and ways of living. What we lack is an understanding of the cultural and social context of such polemics. There are many reasons for our lack of understanding of this polemics today. First, our access to Indian traditions has deteriorated so much that it is almost impossible to see what those traditions were fighting about. For example, it is unclear to us today when is someone called a *pashandi* or for what reasons. Second, the writings in languages other than Indian vernaculars, like the colonial literature, either do not report the actual words and contexts of polemic or use a morally and theologically charged translation of the verbal expression of polemics between communities. Furthermore, English translations of the polemical texts form India (and Asia) make them inaccessible for our purpose.

Consider the following excerpt from the well-known poet Milarepa. It is an English rendering of his 11th century Tibetan text.

> Meanwhile Milarepa . . . opened the books that Rechungpa had brought back from India, and said with great compassion: '. . . I sincerely pray to all Guards of Dharma to destroy all *heretical books of vicious Mantras that will certainly bring great harm to the Doctrine and to sentient beings*!'
> (Chang 1962: 442 italics added)

Unless one knows the Tibetan language, the cultural context and the relationship between various Indian traditions in the 11th century, it is not possible to reconstruct what are 'heretical books' that contain 'vicious Mantras' and bring harm to both the 'Doctrine' and to 'sentient beings'. Third, there are two modern developments that have further aggravated this problem. In the contemporary atmosphere of 'political correctness', a public expression of criticism of another community and recording such a criticism attracts great censure. Not just public censure, with the enforcement of laws against casteism in post-independence India, but even the use of caste names in public, with the 'intent to humiliate', has become a punishable crime.

Notwithstanding these problems, available records of intercommunity polemics in India are sufficient to make one important claim: ridiculing and criticizing Brahmans or other castes is neither idiosyncratic to the Vachanas and the Lingayat tradition nor is it a sign of Lingayats' alleged anti-casteism. Here are three random examples from the literature. The first one is from Francis Buchanan, who makes a perceptive observation about the native pundits he had come across.

> However well these men may be instructed in certain dogmas, and the art of disputation, they are not qualified to give any satisfactory information concerning the origin of their order,

or the means by which it came to prevail over others; for, of the sectaries which differ from themselves, such as those of Budha, Jaina, or Siva, *they profess an almost total ignorance, and sovereign contempt.*

(Buchanan 1807: 142 italics added)

In Jain texts the Brahmans are held in contempt and are represented as opponents of Jain religion. Frequently the term *dhijjai (dhikjati)* or 'condemned caste' is used for them contemptuously. In Jain *Suttas* . . . generally the primary position in society is assigned to the *Khattiyas* instead of to the *Bambhanas*. We have seen that no *Tirthankara* was born in a family other than the Ksatriyas. It is laid down that no great men are ever born in low, miserly beggarly or in Brahmanical families.

(Jain 1984: 187)

And in a footnote appended to this paragraph, the author adds the following. A 'similar view is expressed in the *Nidankatha* [a Buddhists text] . . . that the Buddhas are born in one or of other two highest classes, the Khattiya or the Brahmana castes and never in the low caste' (Ibid. 187, 187 n.1).

Among the three communities from whom my informants were drawn, there was no lack of mutual criticism and recrimination; but the idea that one might prefer to have been born in another caste was never expressed. One's own caste role was taken for granted, and so were those of one's own social superiors, and those of the menial groups.

(Carstairs 1957: 57)[13]

According to T.R.V. Murti, a well-known expert in Buddhist and Vedanta studies,

polemic (*parapakshanirakarana*) is an integral part of each (Indian) system. It is an evidence of the maturity not only of one system, but of several contemporary ones from which it is differentiated. In spite of the heroic language used, polemics does not mean that rival systems are refuted out of existence; they are only differentiated from each other. Confusion of standpoints is warded off, and clarity results.

(Cited in Klostermaier 1979: 60)

That is, an intercommunity polemics seems to be how the communities and traditions relate to each other in India. Admittedly, one needs elaborate studies to see the apparently mutually abusive language used by the communities as a polemic between two different schools of thought. Nevertheless, in the case of the Vachanas, at least, this looks more plausible than not. This plausibility is not taken as a proof for the claim made here, but an indication of the fact that the claim is not far off the mark. In line with the claim about the polemics made here so far, we can further observe the following about the Vachanas: even the so-called lower-caste Vachana composers use similar idiomatic expressions, which make use of lower-caste names as abusive swear words. For example, the Vachanas of Ambigara Choudaiah (see his Vachanas, #77, 111, 116, 176 in Kalburgi 2001) and Urilingapeddi (#1277, 1390 in Kalburgi 2001), the two most representative 'low-caste' Vachana composers, use names of lower castes, such as *holeya* and *madiga*, as invective.

It is true that anti-Brahmin polemics seems to be more pronounced in the Lingayat literature. However, as scholars have pointed out, anti-Brahmin polemics have 'surface[d] periodically in the South Indian literature. . . . [For example, anti-Brahmin] rhetoric played an important role in the writings of some of the Siddhars, a group of Tamil ascetics, the majority of whom lived between the fifth and tenth centuries' (Richman 1991: 189). It seems that European scholars have interpreted this anti-Brahmin rhetoric as a mark of an anti-caste stance and therefore a sign of progressive nature of the Lingayat tradition.[14]

(b) *Jati for the Vachana composers is a minor and a local problem*

Jati and all the related topics are a relatively minor issue and a local problem. That it is a minor issue can be empirically ascertained by showing that the Vachana composers spend much less time talking about jati. They, for instance, spend more time denouncing relationships with a *'para-stri'* and offering puja to or following an *'anya-daiva'*. In contemporary idiom, scholars generally consider the former as an issue of adultery and the latter an issue of 'monotheism' or 'monism', in the sense of worshipping no deva other than Shiva.

It is a local problem in the sense that discussion of jati in the Vachanas is specific to a context and a domain: the followers of the Lingayat tradition and their adhyatmic progress are situated within the cultural context of the region where the Vachana tradition emerged and lived. The Vachanas do not speak about 'all human beings' or people belonging to 'all castes or traditions'. They do not even address 'all Kannadigas' or 'all *bhakta*s'. More needs to be said about these claims, which we will do in the following section.

(c) *Jati is an aadhyatmic issue for Vachana composers*

This brings us to the last and the more important part of our hypothesis. The talk about jati is a reflection on obstacles that a seeker faces in one's *aadhyatmic* journey. What I intend to do here is to give a sense of what the previous sentence means, by making use of S. N. Balagangadhara's (2005, 2013) writings.

Indian traditions teach us that everyone can be happy, if one wants and tries to be happy. A programme of teaching one to be happy is *aadhyatma*. The most misunderstood and difficult term here is 'happiness'. Indian traditions would use terms like *ananda* or *anubhaava* to refer to it. It is not a feeling, but living in a 'contented state of being happy', which is beyond the transient feelings of happiness and sadness.[15] The Lingayat tradition uses various words like *Shiva-sayujya*, *shunya* and *bayalu* to talk about this way of being. One should aspire for and strive to attain this end. Indian traditions are a way of helping one to attain this end. For the economy of language, we will use 'happiness' in this essay to refer to this way of being. It is important to clarify at the very outset that this chapter will not ask or answer questions about the possibility or properties and the modes of attaining such happiness. It assumes that, at the very least, the Lingayat tradition believes that one can live such a life and sets out to help the seekers to attain it. The Vachanas reflect this stance, as they are part of the way the tradition teaches this to its followers. This section, and in fact the entire chapter, is an attempt to show that when one understands the Vachanas outside of this context, one grossly misunderstands and distorts them.

Adhyatma, then, is about how one lives on this earth as a human being and all those things that are useful or required to attain this happiness. An Indian tradition, like Lingayat or Advaita, is that which has developed a specialized set of instructions and plans, for those who come to it, to live a rich life full of happiness (Balagangadhara 2005). That means, when the Lingayat tradition speaks about attaining happiness, it is also speaking about this physical world and how one lives in the world. It not only has a deeply philosophical idea of what life is, what it means to live the life at its best and so on, but also a set of practices, Do's and Don'ts, and anything (albeit under several constraints) that helps one attain happiness. Consequently, the following two aspects will shape a tradition to a considerable extent:

its philosophical stance about the question of happiness and the local cultural and social context from where its followers come. Much of a tradition, thus, belongs to the seekers who approach it. It addresses them and their specific requirements, which depend on their social background, among other things. The tips and tricks that a tradition will suggest to its followers may therefore involve criticizing other traditions and their practices.

One must understand the pragmatic purposes of such criticisms. The end of the pragmatic purpose is to convince the seekers that they can be happy in the very world they are living. The problems that a seeker faces are human problems, conditioned both by the physical world we live in, the biological animal that we are and the cultural and social environment that one belongs to. Hence, when a tradition addresses the problems of its seekers and develops solutions for those problems, it is addressing both human problems in general and the problems specific to the cultural and social environment of its seekers.

The Vachanas and what they say about any issue, including jati and kula, seen from this perspective, are therefore composed of some of these things: (a) empirical claims about the world we live in, (b) empirical and psychological claims about the human animal that we are, (c) claims about happiness and (d) the relation between these things. As though this is not sufficient, they may reflect elaborately on these issues or merely refer to them through various idioms and signs, whose meanings are embedded within a specific tradition. Note that the meaning of such idioms and signs may have substantially changed over the centuries, and thus, are completely lost to us today. The Vachanas may indulge in a highly philosophical discussion or merely make a sneering joke about other traditions and castes. They may tell a story or, like a Zen koan, use a provocative image, metaphor or a statement. Consequently, anyone who intends to use the Vachanas as textual evidence for any argument must recognize and distinguish between these elements in the Vachanas. In other words, this is a demand to develop a theory of the Vachanas and of Indian traditions, thereof.[16]

This is true about all Indian *aadhyatmic* traditions. That is, the way they address the problems of the seeker has two dimensions: cultural, psychological and social on the one hand and the biological and physical on the other hand. In other words, these problems may be specific to the seekers' cultural and social context or they are universal and applicable to all human beings. By adding a premise to this, that India is one culture (Balagangadhara 1994), we can derive the following conclusion: all Indian *aadhyatmic* traditions that address a seeker's problems deal with the problems that the Vachanas address when they speak about kula and *jati-mada*. And, if jati and kula are how Indians relate to each other, to the world and to oneself, one should also be able to see deep similarities in the way different Indian traditions speak about jati. The difference between different traditions will be in the language usage, context and the actual examples and the situations that those traditions refer to, the form of literature and so on.

A tradition in Kashmir, for example, will not have the same social context as the Lingayat tradition of Karnataka. A 3,000-year-old *itihasa-purana* will speak about jati in a different way than a *pada* written by a Kannada *haridasa* of the 16th century. A Sanskrit *shloka* in the *neti neti* format will be different in its approach to jati than a Kannada *bhajan* or Vachana. Thus, while an *itihasa-purana*, like the *Mahabharatha*, uses stories to talk about jati, Adi Shankara's 'Nirvana Shatka', composed in the *neti neti* style, would write, 'na me jatibhedaha' ('I have no caste distinctions'). A famous pada of Kanaka Dasa, a 16th century Kannada saint-poet, says, 'Do not fight in the name of kula, do you even know the root of kula?'

A Lingayat Vachana, as we can see, speaks in an idiom that looks more like a set of instructions or social commentaries. After all, unlike what Ramanujan (1973) made them look like, the Vachanas are not free-verse poems. The argument here is that despite a shift in time, space and the mode of writing, what Indian traditions say about jati revolves around one basic claim: jati is a hurdle that a *bhakta* (or a seeker) encounters in one's adhyatmic journey.

Aadhyatma and jati

A few words now about what aadhyatma means within the context of the Lingayat tradition, borrowed from a short piece by S.N. Balagangadhara (2013; see also his contribution to this volume). Seen from the perspective of a seeker (of happiness), human life is a journey from a stage where one is caught in the affairs of this world (which is a state of bondage), towards happiness. In the *aadhyatmic* idiom of the Vachanas and the Lingayat tradition, it is a journey from being a bhavi (worldly person) through the life of a bhakta or a sharana (a devotee) to the 'attainment' of the bayalu.[17] The journey, therefore, is the journey of a Lingayat bhakta. A bhakta is one who undertakes this journey; a seeker on the path of aadhyatma.

A standard way of understanding this journey, which the Lingayat tradition has developed over the ages, is to divide it into various stages. The most popular is a six-stage division called the *shat-sthala* division. '[E]ach Sthala is a preparation for a further rise. In the *Vacana-Sastra* it is frequently found in this sense' (Nandimath 1942: 164). The six *sthalas* are *bhakta, mahesa, prasadhi, pranalingi, sharana* and *aikya*. The journey that begins in the *bhaktasthala* culminates in the *aikyasthala*.

When a bhavi adopts the lifestyle that the Lingayat tradition suggests, and sets out on her or his journey of becoming enlightened, she or he becomes a bhakta or a sharana/e. As a first step in the journey, a bhakta must be made aware of the obstacles one would face, because of the nature of the being that she or he is and the nature of the world that she or he lives in. This can take several different methods and modes. The discussions on caste in the Vachanas should be seen in this context. A bhakta can neither afford to indulge oneself in hopping from one tradition to another, from one technique to another, nor keep shuttling between the life (of a bhavi) one has left behind and the life one has adopted (Lingayat bhakta). The concentration required here is attained in the form of focusing one's attention on one *deva*, Shiva in this case. The journey continues, and a bhakta is taught to 'think' (or experience/realize) that one is himself or herself a linga. In the final stage, even this difference goes, and one attains enlightenment.[18] Hence, we are not arguing that the Vachanas do not 'deny kula and jati'. However, the Vachanas are not making anti-caste statements the way we understand anti-casteism today. They deny everything that comes in the way of becoming enlightened. Therefore, if we forget who the Vachanas are written for or are addressing, our understanding of what they are saying loses direction. The Vachanas are surely not public speeches.[19]

What does a discussion about jati look like from within this context? As noted earlier, *aadhyatma* is about attaining happiness in this world. If so, the obstacles that *aadhyatma* deals with belong to this world. Jati is one such obstacle that hampers our attempts to live happily in this world. In this sense, jati can be called a 'social problem'. Given the context, we can hypothesize the following. If the Vachanas treat the hurdle called jati as a relatively minor problem of a seeker in the *aadhyatmic* journey, and the journey is divided into six progressive steps, then jati and related affairs of the world should be dealt with at an early stage in one's journey, rather than at a later stage.

Before we go to the Vachanas, let us find out whether we are on the right track in our argument. Here is an example from another *aadhyatmic* tradition from a different time and context. This is not to provide evidence for the argument, but to show that the argument that this chapter presents is not attributing anything new to these traditions. The example is from the 19th century Bengali saint, Ramakrishna Paramahamsa. A visitor asks Ramakrishna the following:

CASTE AS AN IMPEDIMENT IN THE JOURNEY OF A BHAKTA

'The Brahmo Samaj preaches the freedom of women and the abolition of the caste system. What do you think about these matters?' In answer, Ramakrishna says,

> Men feel that way when they are just beginning to develop spiritual yearning. A storm raises clouds of dust, and one cannot distinguish between the different trees – the mango, the hog plum, and the tamarind. But after the storm blows over, one sees clearly. After the first storm of divine passion is quelled, one gradually understands that God alone is the Highest Good, the Eternal Substance, and that all else is transitory.[20]

Let us now see how the Vachanas treat the issue of caste. As an issue, it is neither more important nor more serious or severe than any other problems that they write about. As noted earlier, the Vachanas spend more time talking about issues such as a relationship with a *'para-stri'* and following an *'anya-daiva'*. Let me elaborate some of the arguments proposed here by focusing on the Vachanas of a prominent Lingayat saint-poet, Basava or Basaveshwara (1134–1196).[21] There are 60 Vachanas in Basava's available 1,414 Vachanas that are relevant to the discussion of jati. Of these 60 Vachanas, only 45 Vachanas belong to the shat-sthala Vachanas.[22] Of these 45 Vachanas, 42 appear in the first two sthalas: nine in the first sthala and 33 in the second sthala.[23] One out of the remaining three Vachanas appears in the third (prasadhi) and two in the penultimate (sharana) sthala, and none in the final sthala. Here are some of the major themes in the first 42 Vachanas of Basava that talk about jati and kula.

1 A non-Lingayat person is a 'low-caste' person (Vachana #142, 596, 605, 606).
2 Lingayats have no caste (#286, 345, 418, 568, 718, 732, 770).
3 Abusing Brahmans for flaws in their rituals and lack of bhakti (and not for caste-related issues) (#575, 577, 578, 581, 582, 583, 585, 587, 588, 592, 595, 596, 601).
4 Lingayats are *kulaja* (best or noble caste), or they are the best people (#583, 589, 590, 591, 600, 602, 657, 715, 718); they go to *kailasa*, the abode of Siva (#570).

Consider the way the Lingayat tradition talks about the first two sthalas: the *bhaktasthala* and *maheshvarasthala*. A person starts his or her *aadhyatmic* journey by becoming a bhakta, a devotee. Hence the 'devotional stage' is the first stage. Here the 'devotee meditates on *"ista-linga"* [a linga of one's choice] offered by the Guru as a symbol of the supreme Shiva and observes ethical code.' Observing the 'ethical code', here, suggests that a devotee 'must have control over all his senses'. A devotee should abstain from all those things that will disturb his or her journey: 'Thus the *Bhaktasthala* emphasises internal purity of a devotee and his unshaken faith' in linga. One moves on from this stage to a stage where the intensity of one's devotion and observance of the ethical code increases. In *maheshasthala*, the second sthala, therefore, 'the devotee should have unwavering loyalty to Shiva. He should not have any temptation for wife, wealth, and gods of others and should be loyal to *"Ista-linga"*.... It is a stage of endurance and ordeals' (Patil 2002: 27). Thus, while 'the chief characteristic of *Bhakta Sthala* is devotion,' the second sthala is 'the phase of ordeals and temptations'.[24]

It is not difficult now to see the issues that the Vachanas deal with when they speak about jati. They begin by segregating the Lingayats from the rest of the society, which includes those who have not taken up the journey of *aadhyatma* (bhavi) and those who belong to different traditions (like, Brahmans). (See Basava's Vachana #711; also 613.) This is followed by a constant reiteration that Lingayats are the best people, since they have no jati affiliation. One should be careful in understanding the word Lingayat here. It refers to a bhakta, a seeker, and not a bhavi, a layperson.[25] Similarly, the Brahmans that the Vachanas refer to are also bhaktas and not any random Brahmin bhavi. As we move into the second sthala, the question of the loyalty of a Lingayat devotee takes centre stage. It is here that all the Vachanas targeting the Brahmans appear. Note carefully that when Basava criticizes Brahmans, he is criticizing only those Brahmans who are walking the path of the *aadhyatmic* journey. Hence, they are criticized for not being followers of the Lingayat tradition and/or for not being true bhaktas. The criticism of Brahmans, thus, is a criticism of the *aadhyatmic* tradition of Brahmans and not the sociological category of the caste called Brahmin caste. There is no Vachana where Basava criticizes a Brahmin bhavi, except when he is criticizing all bhavis in general.

Not only is the criticism of other castes and daivas ('gods') almost restricted to the first two stages, but there is another important difference to take note of. As noted earlier, there is one Vachana of Basava in the third (the *prasadhi*) sthala and one in the fifth (the *sharana*) sthala. The former, in some sense, reiterates the claim that 'Lingayats have no caste.' However, the way this claim is made here is noticeably different from the way it is made in the second sthala. The harsh criticism and polemics have made way for a more reflective and 'philosophical' tone. And all that this Vachana says about caste is a one-line remark, in the form of a rhetorical question: is there pollution where there is linga; is there kula where there is jangama (#770)? A jangama, put roughly, is a Lingayat seeker in an advanced stage of his journey.[26] Expectedly, therefore, there is no question of jati troubling him. The later Vachana (#869), the *sharana-sthala* Vachana, says, again in the form of a rhetorical question, 'Why become a sharana if the pride of kula (*kula-mada*) is not shed?' Put in a more accessible language, since all rhetorical questions involve a claim, this question is claiming the following: one would not reach the sharana stage, if one has not shed *kula-mada* (which must be shed early in one's journey). (See further for comments on the Vachana #879.)

The Vachanas, thus, talk about jati, but only as one other (and not even the most important) impediment on one's path to happiness. And in the process, they sometime chide and poke fun at people and often resort to a 'politically incorrect' way of talking about castes and communities. However, the jati issue that they try to tackle is not what is called the caste system and casteism in contemporary parlance. It must be understood within the context of the 'spiritual' development discussed so far. If not, the Vachanas will become 'a mass of contradiction'.[27]

Conclusion

One point needs to be highlighted from the foregoing discussion. The discussion about progressive stages in the *aadhyatmic* advancement of a seeker must be common across Indic traditions, and not specific to just the Lingayat tradition.[28] That further means, the discussion about jati that we enumerated in the chapter is not idiosyncratic to the Lingayats. Indian traditions as a whole should have a similar attitude towards jatis.

An important outcome of the hypothesis that this chapter puts forth is that we can now begin to see the kind of mistakes one can make when one sees the Vachanas, and bhakti literature, outside of the traditional notion of *aadhyatmic* progress. The Vachanas seem contradictory, inconsistent and ambiguous because, modern critics mix the Vachanas from different stages of *aadhyatmic* development. Here is one example. Shouten notes that while 'the traditional classification of people into castes is rejected' by Basava and the Lingayat tradition, 'another division takes its place: devotees versus worldlings. And it seems that this new division is no less strict than the old one.' Thus, the Vachana composers, it is often said, merely replaced one immoral hierarchical system (the caste system) with another one (devotees versus worldlings). 'However', Shouten soon asserts, 'there are also a few Vachanas in which Basava transcends all divisions and propagates the ideal of the equality of all people' (Schouten 1995: 27). This is a classical mistake of not understanding the progressive stages of the sthala and its importance in understanding the Vachanas. First, as noted earlier, the division of bhavi and bhakta ('devotees versus worldlings') is not a moralistic division of society into good and bad people. It is a division that separates seekers from non-seekers. In the absence of such a distinction, a tradition like the Lingayat cannot even come into existence. Second, Basava's Vachana that Shouten quotes (Vachana #879)[29] as proof for the claim that 'there are also a few Vachanas in which Basava transcends all divisions' – thus suggesting a contradiction in Basava's stance vis-à-vis caste – appears in the Sharana, the penultimate, sthala. By the time one has reached this sthala, there is no place for the preliminary divisions drawn between a devotee and a layperson. Hence, this does not show a problem in Basava's thinking but in the modern Vachana scholarship. Such errors in our understanding of the Vachanas and the demand for consistency from saint-poets like Basava based on these errors, turns some of the best scholars India has seen, like Basava, into hypocrites. Or, to put it in Balagangadhara's words, we turn some of the best examples of enlightened people, like Basava, into those who are still writhing in the earliest stages of the spiritual journey.

Notes

1 This chapter is a slightly modified version of 'Lingayat Tradition, Aadhyatma and Caste: How Bhakti Traditions Understand Caste', *Journal of Contemporary Thought*, 41: 165–190, 2015.
2 For more examples, see Champakalakshmi (2000); Hawley (2005); Mahalakshmi (2000); Milner (1993); Prentiss (2000); Ramanujan (1989); Spivak (2001).
3 For some examples from scholarship in Kannada, see Jalki (2009, chap. 1).
4 The reference is to his editorial preface, 'Prastavane', to Basava's complete Vachanas brought out by the state government of Karnataka, India (Kalburgi 2001: 21). It may be noted: (a) All translations from Kannada into English, in this chapter, unless otherwise specified, are mine. The translations provided here are rather *free translations* than literal word-to-word translations. (b) Diacritical marks are also omitted from the text cited here for the ease of reading and consistency. However, Indian words have been italicized across the chapter, including the texts cited from

various sources. (c) All the web pages cited here were last accessed in June 2015.
5 A *sharana* is a Lingayat *bhakta*, a seeker. The saint-poet Basava, for example, is a sharana.
6 In his 25 June 1853 contribution to the *New York Daily Tribune*, Marx wrote, 'Hindostan is an Italy of Asiatic dimensions. . . . Yet, in a social point of view, Hindostan is not the Italy, but the Ireland of the East. And this strange combination of Italy and of Ireland, of a world of voluptuousness and of a world of woes, is anticipated in the ancient traditions of the religion of Hindostan. That religion is at once a religion of sensualist exuberance, and a religion of self-torturing asceticism; a religion of the Lingam and of the juggernaut; the religion of the Monk, and of the *Bayadere*.'

In a footnote added to the word 'religion of the Lingam', the editors of *Marx Engels Collected Works* Vol. 12 write the following. '*Religion of the Lingam* – the cult of the God Shiva, particularly widespread among the southern Indian sect of the Lingayat (from the word '*linga*' – the emblem of Shiva), a Hindu sect which does not recognize distinctions of caste and rejects fasts, sacrifices and pilgrimages.' See, www.marxists.org/archive/marx/works/1853/06/25.htm (accessed on 1 May 2016).
7 Weber describes the Lingayats as 'a type of particularly sharp and principled Protestant reaction to the Brahmans and the caste order' (cited in Aho 2002: 92).
8 The 14 volumes of the Vachanas, and a Vachana dictionary, were first published in 1993 (second ed. 2001), by the Kannada Book Authority, Bangalore. The website maintained by the Directorate of Kannada and Culture, www.vachanasahitya.gov.in/, hosts all the Vachanas published in these volumes (accessed on 4 December 2015).
9 When I say they 'talk about' Brahmans or caste, I mean they contain one or more words which is generally considered to refer to some aspect of the caste system, in the *postcolonial Indian context*.
10 Only the early Buddhists and Jains were an exception, since they themselves became a caste soon, like the Lingayats themselves were going to become one soon (Ramanujan 1973).
11 Besides the examples given earlier in the chapter (i.e. the context 4 Vachanas), here are two random examples. Kada-Siddeshvara (circa 1725) derides those who go to another teacher for instructions and boast around of having received *Linga* and the guru's compassion as *mulaholeya* (dumb *holeya*). He then asserts that his anger will not subside even if their mouths are slit and whacked by the shoes of the Lingayat bhaktas (#113, vol. 10, Samagra Vachana Samputa). Shanmukha-swami (circa 1639) calls *Chandalas* and *Holeyas* and Brahmins *adhamamadiga* (an inferior *Madiga*) in a Vachana (#323, vol. 14). As noted in a previous section, of the 465 Vachanas (out of 21,788) that speak of jati and the related issues, 145 Vachanas (i.e. one-third of the 465 Vachanas) are merely using caste-related words as curse words.
12 For a discussion of the Vachana, see http://sampada.net/article/801 (accessed on 13 May 2016).
13 For more examples of such polemics, see: Vaisnavas versus Sufis (Stewart 2013); Bhakti versus Tantra (Burchett 2013); Jains against Lingayats

(Veerabhadraswami 2010); intra-community polemics among Jains (Jaini 2008); 'Hindus' versus Buddhists (Klostermaier 1979); Alvars versus Buddhists (Jamanadas 1991). A great source of such intercommunity polemics in India are the traditional *gadhe*, as they are called in Kannada. In English, a gadhe is translated as a '(wise) saying' or 'proverb'. Here are two examples of such gadhes: 'There are three blood-suckers (butchers) in this world – the bug, the flea, and the Brahman.' 'The wealth of the Chetty will be known after death.' For more such gadhes, see (Kittel 1999; Percival 1843; Risley 1915).

14 Surely, this issue needs to be shown. This essay, however, is not an occasion for this. For a brief discussion of this issue, see Dunkin Jalki (2009). The larger project, of which, this chapter is a small part, focuses closely on this issue.
15 There is an immense urge to use scare quotes on almost all these English words, while explaining concepts that belong to Indian traditions. If I restrain from doing so, it is to maintain the readability of the text.
16 In the first part of this chapter, the Vachanas are not used to make any argument about them, but only to show how the current dominant understandings of the Vachanas are wrong. To this extent, this chapter does not need a theory of the Vachanas. The second part of the chapter, however, is to be seen as a step, however small the step is, towards building such a theory of the Vachanas.
17 Also known as, in different contexts and in the writings of different thinkers, *anubhaava*, enlightenment, *jnanodaya*, *shunya* etc.
18 I neither intend to explain what this stage is like nor do I claim to have understood it. For this chapter, it is sufficient to know that this is what the Lingayat tradition claims, and to understand the Vachanas, one has to take this into account. For an attempt to explain the Indian notion of Enlightenment in the 21st century language, see S.N. Balagangadhara's 'On the Indian Notion of Enlightenment: Reflections Based on Experience'. (www.academia.edu/7866603/On_the_Indian_Notion_of_Enlightenment_reflections_based_on_experience), (accessed on 13 December 2016).
19 This is a free translation of a passage from S.N. Balagangadhara (2013).
20 From a conversation dated Sunday, 19 November 1882 (M 2007: chap. 6). The book is available at www.belurmath.org/gospel/ (accessed on 13 October 2016).
21 This is a research in progress and as it progresses, it will analyze the Vachanas of all the Vachana composers.
22 According to the Lingayat tradition, during the reign of Deva Raya II (r.1424–1446 CE) of the Vijayanagar empire, certain 101 *Viraktas* (ascetics) began the task of 'reviving' the Vachanas. Their task

> ramified into three directions: 1) compilation of the Vachanas, 2) their systematic classification and 3) writing extensive commentary on them so as to make them intelligible to the ordinary folks.... They culled and collected the sayings of the *Sharanas* into an anthology of Vachanas called "Sarva-puaratanara Vachangalu". They arranged them according to the stages essential to the further progress of the pilgrim. The Vachanas thus organized became known as "Sthalada Vachangalu".
>
> (Sri Kumarswamiji 1993)

Today, the Vachanas of important composers, like Basava, Allama and a few others, are available in two major chunks: those that are traditionally divided into *shat-sthala* and the miscellaneous Vachanas. The 14 volumes of the Vachanas that the state government of Karnataka has published, which this chapter refers to, follow this pattern of Vachana division.
23 Serial numbers of those 9 and 33 Vachanas are # 81, 142, 263, 286, 306, 344, 345, 348, 418; and #568, 570, 575, 576, 577, 578, 581, 582, 583, 585, 587, 588, 589, 590, 591, 592, 595, 596, 600, 601, 602, 605, 606, 613, 622, 652, 657, 710, 711, 714, 715, 718, 732.
24 Excerpted from 'Philosophy of Basava Dharma' (www.sridanammadevi.com/basava-phil.htm). See also, 'Shatasthala'. (http://lingayatreligion.com/LingayatBasics/Shatasthala.htm), (both accessed on 12 October 2016).
25 This is true about any caste name in India. 'Brahmin' picks out both a person who is born in the Brahmin caste and a wise person. Similarly, 'Holeya' or 'Madiga' too is used both as a caste name and as an invective.
26 Here is how a Lingayat website defines the term: Jangama 'is one who is endowed with the true knowledge, sacrificed his life for the society, and avoided all the worldly happiness and attained the divine happiness' (see, http://lingayatreligion.com/LingayatBasics/Jangama.htm). In 'the technical' sense of the term, 'sharana' 'refers only to the aspirant of the fifth stage [*sharana-sthala*] of spiritual journey' (see, http://lingayatreligion.com/LingayatTerms/Sharana.htm). (Both accessed on 3 November 2011.)
27 Nandimath (1942: 208) warns us that 'If we neglect this feature [i.e. the sthala division] of Sivayogi Sivacarya, his book, the *Siddhanta-Sikhamani*, becomes a mass of contradiction.'
28 For a similar notion in different Buddhist traditions and Agama, see Apple (2003). (Scholars trace the origins of the *Shat-sthala* to the Agamas.) The similarity extends beyond a mere division of stages. Even the description of these stages, description of those who are not part of these stages of the journey, the activities associated with each successive stage, the end of the journey and so on.
29 This Vachana states, in its first line, 'there is one earth under a Shiva's temple and a *holageri* (the place where *holeyas*, live).' One has to assume too many things to derive an anti-caste stance from this sentence.

References

Aho, James. 2002. *The Orifice as Sacrificial Site: Culture, Organization, and the Body*. New York: Walter de Gruyter.

Apple, James. 2003. 'Twenty Varieties of the Samgha: A Typology of Noble Beings (Ārya) in Indo-Tibetan Scholasticism (Part I)', *Journal of Indian Philosophy*, 31 (5–6): 503–592.

Balagangadhara, S. N. 1994. *'The Heathen in His Blindness. . .': Asia, the West, and the Dynamic of Religion*. Leiden: E. J. Brill.

———. 2005. 'How to Speak for the Indian Traditions: An Agenda for the Future', *Journal of the American Academy of Religion*, 73 (4): 987–1013.

———. 2013. 'Vachanagalannu Adhyatmika Sandharbadallittu Nodidaga. . .', *Prajavani*, April 18.

Buchanan, Francis. 1807. *A Journey from Madras through the Countries of Mysore, Canara and Malabar: For the Express Purpose of Investigating the State of Agriculture, Arts and Commerce, the Religion, Manners, and Customs, the History Natural and Civil, and Antiquities*. Vol. 1. 3 vols. London: Printed for T. Cadell and W. Davies.

Burchett, Patton. 2013. 'Bitten by the Snake: Early Modern Devotional Critiques of Tantra-Mantra', *The Journal of Hindu Studies*, 6 (1): 1–20.

Carstairs, G. Morris. 1957. *The Twice-Born: A Study of a Community of High-Caste Hindus*. London: The Hogarth Press.

Champakalakshmi, R. 2000. 'From Devotion and Dissent to Dominance: The Bhakti of the Tamil Alvars and Nayanars', in R. Champakalakshmi and S. Gopal (eds.), *Tradition, Dissent and Ideology: Essays in Honour of Romila Thapar*, pp. 135–163. New Delhi: Oxford University Press.

Chang, Garma C. C. Trans. 1962. *The Hundred Thousand Songs of Milarepa*. Boulder and London: Shambhala.

Chidananda Murthy, M. 2004. *Sthavara: Jangama*. Vol. 4. Chidananda Samagra Samputa. Bangalore: Sapna Book House.

Desai, P. B. 1968. *Basavesvara and His Times*. Dharwar: Karnataka University.

Dhareshwar, Vivek. 2010. 'Render unto Wood', review of *I Keep Vigil of Rudra*, by H.S. Shivaprakash, *Tehelka*, 48 (7), Tehelka.com (accessed on 8th December 2016).

Farek, Martin. 2015. 'Caste or Qualification? Chaitanya Vaishnava Discussions About Brahmanas in Colonial India', *Theatrum Historiae*, 17: 91–118.

Hawley, John Stratton. 2005. *Three Bhakti Voices: Mirabai, Surdas, and Kabir in Their Time and Ours*. New Delhi: Oxford University Press.

Hegde, Rajaram. 2013. 'Vachana Chaluvaligala Saiddhantika Hinneleya Kuritu...', *Prajavani*, April 1.

———. 2014. 'Brahmananendare Yaru? Mahabharatadalli Baruva Charchegalu Haagu Adhunika Jati Mimamse', *Chintana Bayalu*, 2 (3): 11–22.

Hegde, Rajaram, and A. Shanmukha. (eds.) 2015. *Kotta Kudureyaneralariyade: Vachanagala Adhyayanadalli Adhunikara Purvagrahagalu mattu Avugalaachege*. Bangalore: Nilume.

Ishwaran, Hiremallur K. 1997. *Lingayata Dharma: Ondu Adhyayana*. Bangalore: Priyadarshini Prakashana.

Jain, Jagdishchandra. 1984. *Life in Ancient India as Depicted in the Jain Canons, with Commentaries*. 2nd rev. and enl. ed. New Delhi: Munshiram Manoharlal.

Jaini, Padmanabh S. 2008. 'Jain Sectarian Debates: Eighty-Four Points of Contention (Cauryāmsi Bol) Between Svetāmbaras and Digambaras (Text and Translation)', *Journal of Indian Philosophy*, 36 (1): 1–246.

Jalki, Dunkin. 2009. 'Vachanas as Caste Critiques: Orientalist Expression of Native Experience', Unpublished PhD dissertation, Centre for the Study of Culture and Society (Manipal University).

Jalki, Dunkin, and S. N. Balagangadhara. 2012. 'Vachana Sahityavu Jativyvastheya Viruddha Maatanaaduttadeye? Vachanagala Adhunika Adhyayanagalu Ondu Maruparisheelane', *Chintana Bayalu*, 1 (3): 25–44.

Jamanadas, K. 1991. 'Hostilities of Alvars Towards Buddhism', in *Tirupati Balaji Was a Buddhist Shrine*, pp. 58–59, Dalit E-Forum. www.ambedkar.org (accessed on 13th June 2016).

Kalburgi, M. M. 1998. *Marga 3: Samshodana Prabhandagala Sankhalana*. Bangalore: Karnataka Book Agency.

———. (ed.) 2001. *Sankirna Vachana Samputa: Ondu*. 2nd edition. Samagra Vachana Samputa 6. Bangalore: Kannada Book Authority.

Kittel, Ferdinand. 1999. *A Kannada-English Dictionary*. New Delhi: Asian Educational Services.

Klostermaier, Klaus. 1979. 'Hindu Views of Buddhism', in Roy C. Amore (ed.), *Developments in Buddhist Thought: Canadian Contributions to Buddhist Studies*, pp. 60–82. Waterloo, Ontario: Wilfrid Laurier University Press.

———. 1989. *A Survey of Hinduism*. 3rd edition. Albany: State University of New York Press.

Lal, Vinay. 2010. *Introducing Hinduism: A Graphic Guide*. London: Icon Books.

Lorenzen, David N. 1987. 'Traditions of Non-Caste Hinduism: The Kabir Panth', *Contributions to Indian Sociology* (n.s.), 21 (2): 263–283.

———. (ed.) 1995. *Bhakti Religion in North India: Community Identity and Political Action*. Albany: State University of New York Press.

M [Mahendra]. 2007. *The Gospel of Sri Ramakrishna*. Trans. Swami Nikhilananda. Chennai: Sri Ramakrishna Math, Belurmath.org (accessed on 14th October 2016).

Mahalakshmi, R. 2000. 'Outside the Norm, Within the Tradition: Kâraikkâl Ammaiyâr and the Ideology of Tamil Bhakti', *Studies in History*, 16 (1): 17–40.

Milner, Murray. 1993. 'Hindu Eschatology and the Indian Caste System: An Example of Structural Reversal', *The Journal of Asian Studies*, 52 (2): 298–319.

Nagaraj, D. R. 1999. *Allama Prabhu mattu Shaivapratibhe*. Heggodu: Akshara.

Nandimath, S. C. 1942. *A Handbook of Virasaivism*. Dharwar: The Literary Committee.

Niranjana, Tejaswini. 1992. *Siting Translation: History, Post-Structuralism, and the Colonial Context*. Berkeley: University of California Press.

Patil, S. H. 2002. *Community Dominance and Political Modernism: The Lingayats*. New Delhi: Mittal Publications.

Percival, P. 1843. *Tamil Proverbs with Their English Translation*. 2nd edition. Madras: Dinavartamani Press.

Pollock, Sheldon. 2006. *The Language of the Gods in the World of Men: Sanskrit, Culture, and Power in Premodern India*. Berkeley: University of California Press.

Prentiss, Karen Pechilis. 2000. *The Embodiment of Bhakti*. New York: Oxford University Press.

Punekar, Sankara Mokashi. 2004. 'Basavannanavara Vacanagala Shilpavidhana', *Basava Sahitya (no vol. no.)*, 198–242. Bangalore: Karnataka Sahitya Academy.

Ramanujan, A. K. 1973. *Speaking of Siva*. Harmondsworth: Penguin.
———. 1989. 'Where Mirrors Are Windows: Toward an Anthology of Reflections', *History of Religions*, 28 (3): 187–216.
Richman, Paula. (ed.) 1991. *Many Ramayanas: The Diversity of a Narrative Tradition in South Asia*. Berkeley: University of California Press.
Risley, Herbert. 1915. 'Caste in Proverbs and Popular Sayings', in W. Crooke (ed.), *The People of India*, 2nd edition, pp. 128–153. Calcutta: Thacker, Spink & Co.
Sadasivaiah, H. M. 1967. *A Comparative Study of Two Vīrasaiva Monasteries: A Study in Sociology of Religion*. Mysore: Prasaranga, Manasa Gangotri.
Schouten, J. P. 1995. *Revolution of the Mystics: On the Social Aspects of Virasaivism*. New Delhi: Motilal Banarsidass.
Spivak, Gayatri Chakravorty. 2001. 'Moving Devi', *Cultural Critique*, 47 (Winter): 120–163.
Sri Kumarswamiji. 1993. 'The Genesis of Shunya Sampadane – I', in S. Munavalli (ed.), *Veerashaivism: Comparative Study of Allama Prabhu and Basava, Shunyasampadhane and Vachanshastra*. Virashaiva.com (accessed on 13th October 2016).
Stephenson, D. D. John. 1839. 'On the Ante-Brahmanical Worship of the Hindus in the Dekhan [part 1]', *Journal of the Royal Asiatic Society of Great Britain and Ireland*, 5: 189–197.
Stevenson, Rev. Dr. 1846. 'The Ante-Brahmanical Religion of the Hindus', *The Journal of Royal Asiatic Society of Great Britain and Ireland*, 8: 330–339.
Stewart, Tony K. 2013. 'Religion in the Subjunctive: Vaiṣṇava Narrative, Sufi Counter-Narrative in Early Modern Bengal', *The Journal of Hindu Studies*, 6 (1): 52–72.
Tarikere, Rahamath. 2008. *Dharma Parikshe: Rajakarana-Dharma-Samskruti Chintanegalu*. Bangalore: Navakarnataka Publications.
Thapar, Romila. 1989. 'Imagined Religious Communities? Ancient History and the Modern Search for a Hindu Identity', *Modern Asian Studies*, 23 (2): 209–231.
Veerabhadraswami, N. 2010. 'Jaina Kavigalu Kanda Basavanna Charitre', *Aruhu Kuruhu*, 2 (5): 17–25.
Zydenbos, Robert J. 1997. 'Virasaivism, Caste, Revolution, etc.', *Journal of the American Oriental Society*, 117 (3): 525–535.

7

RIVER LITERACY AND THE CHALLENGE OF A RAIN TERRAIN

Dilip da Cunha

Rivers hold a prominent place among natural entities on the earth surface. Referred to as lifelines, spines of civilizations and ecological wonders, they are celebrated features in history, ecology, settlement design and development plans. However, they raise some troubling questions. Why, for example, are they seen to violate their banks and the land adjoining them when they cross a line asserted by human beings who then assume them to be 'natural entities' prone to 'flood'? The fact is that ecologies, histories, policies, design and the increasingly popular fields of disaster management and risk assessment depend on the existence of flood as much as they depend on the existence of rivers. Again, why are rivers seen to have a point of origin even when rain falls all over and when hundreds of square miles of snowfields are melting? Numerous scientific treatises and school textbooks say, for example, the Ganga River originates in the Gangotri glacier, and the Mississippi River begins in Lake Itasca; and as much as hydrologists want to introduce a 'basin' logic to the reading of rivers, they are bound to lines that begin in discrete points. Why are rivers drawn with lines at all? The fact is that some rivers run dry, seasonally, or exceptionally. Yet they continue to hold their definition of 'flowing water in a channel with defined banks'. Evidently, the lines that call out rivers 'flow' even when water between them does not. They are the basis of administrative decisions and planning agendas that have tended to exclude populations – human and non-human – that live less by fixed land uses and exclusive spaces and more by temporal appropriations and trajectories of movement.

Are rivers products of a visual literacy – the literacy of the drawn line separating land from water – before they are natural entities that they are believed to be? Does this literacy privilege a moment in time when water is *not* precipitating, seeping, soaking air, soil and vegetation, collecting, evaporating and transpiring in ways that defy delineation? The fact is that in the time of this chosen moment of apparent 'clarity', the earth surface is drawn in maps, maps upon which battles have been fought, properties demarcated, infrastructure designed, the past described and plans drawn up. More seriously, in the time of this moment, 'things' have been called out on the earth surface, things that are given the status of natural entities with a significant role to play as agents of change in everyday life. The river is among the most notable of these things. It is inconceivable without lines that separate water from land, confine that water to a course and calibrate its flow from source to destination.

But then are rivers products of a material literacy as well, one that constitutes water as a substance separate from land so that when we speak of water, when we feel, think and imagine water, we acknowledge the land from which it is separated? This land is not only a subject of controversy and conflict in concepts such as territory, property, settlement and city; it also puts water to work for it. Rivers then, as 'flows of water', are made to drain land, to provide it with transportation corridors, energy, water supply, waste disposal routes and popularly today, a 'riverfront' for development and real estate consumption. As such, if rivers are polluted, exploited and endangered today, it is not just because they are violated; it is because they are set up by a material literacy to be dominated by land.

As products of a visual and material literacy, rivers are extraordinary works of human creation. They are credited with generating great wealth, remarkable feats of engineering and significant thresholds in 'development', including cities and civilizations. But they do not work everywhere, especially in places of rains like those which come with the monsoon. These places are not surprisingly found chaotic and messy, chronically poor, underdeveloped and largely 'informal'. They also happen to be places that perhaps not coincidentally were until recently colonized by European nations otherwise known as the 'west'; and today, after decades of independence, they still strive to catch up with those nations. These places include India. Here, rivers flood devastatingly, run dry, are terribly polluted and increasingly contested. After decades of efforts to solve these problems, efforts that hold out an elusive hope of wealth and development, we need to ask: have rivers been imposed upon 'rain terrains' that refuse to conform to the line of rivers?

This chapter looks at one of many trajectories by which rivers have constructed a particular imagination, unfolding it by way of three ideas – Oceanus of mythology, lines of geography and the water cycle of hydrology. It makes the case that rivers are a moment of choice rather than necessity and paves the way for rain as the possible basis of a new imagination.

Oceanus to geographic flows

Rivers have deep roots in the word Ocean, which before it came to refer to the vast expanses of sea that cover 70 per cent of the earth surface, referred to a river that flowed back upon itself. Homer in the 8th century BCE declares this river 'the source of all rivers and all the seas on earth and all the springs and all the deep wells'. 'All', he says 'flow from the Ocean' (Homer 1990, 21: 194). He images it on Achilles' shield made by Hephaestus, the god of fire and patron of craftsmen, for the Greek hero's battle against Hector in the Trojan War, describing it from centre to periphery as Hector may have seen it in battle. At its centre, he says, are the earth, sky, sea, sun, moon and stars. Around them in consecutive rings are cities, fields and vineyards, and pastureland, and, finally, around all, he says, Hephaestus forges 'the Ocean River's mighty power girdling round the outmost rim of the welded indestructible shield' (Homer 1990; Book 18, 560–700; Figure 7.1).

Scholars see this as a portrayal of the earth surface seen from above, a proto world map depicting a disc-like landmass bound by a circumfluent river (Figure 7.2).[1]

What Homer did textually, it is said, Anaximander did geometrically with a diagram that is widely accepted as the 'first' world map. This natural philosopher of the Milesian School positioned his eye high above the earth from where, looking down, he could see the extremities of a landmass. With this view, observes Charles Kahn, he could diagram the earth in a way that poets like Homer did not and perhaps could not or maybe resisted because diagramming, he says, 'requires not drama but a precise geometric arrangement, and nothing could be more alien to the poet's state of mind' (Kahn 1960: 81).

There is no record of Anaximander's map, but it reportedly showed the earth surface seen from above, that is, in plan, making the correspondence between ground and diagram with points and lines (Figure 7.3).

The points did not interfere with the transfer as they had neither length nor breadth and, as such, transcended scale. And the lines connecting them were of measurable length but no breadth and so outlined 'things' in the map that remained true to their form on the ground. With points and lines, Anaximander could plot the edges

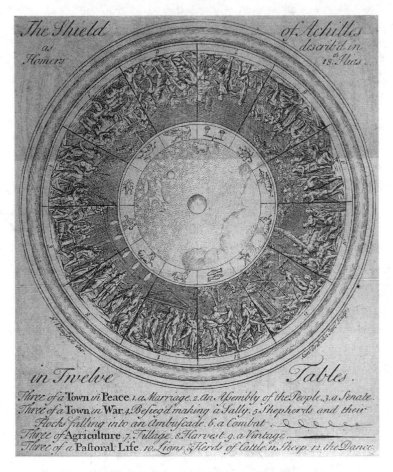

Figure 7.1 Achilles' shield in Alexander Pope's *The Iliad of Homer*, Vol. 5. London, 1736.

of continents as he could settlements, islands, mountains, lakes, rivers etc. He may not have been the first to use points and lines in this manner, that is, to construct a geographic map, but it is widely believed that he is the first in a tradition that captured, or sought to capture, the entirety of the earth in a 'world map'. He apparently saw this earth as a nearly circular island-like landmass carved out of *apeirōn* or infinity, a concept that he is credited with conceiving to refer to what, according to classicist James Romm, early Greeks saw as a vastitude of formless diffusion or void. The line

RIVER LITERACY AND THE CHALLENGE OF A RAIN TERRAIN

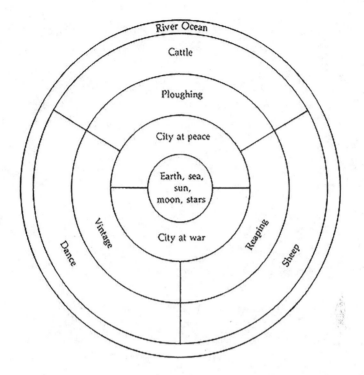

Figure 7.2 Achilles' shield in Malcolm M. Willcock's *A Companion to the Iliad*. Chicago: The University of Chicago Press, 1976, 210.

Note: 'The river Oceanus,' writes Willcock, 'forms the rim of the Shield, as the Ocean itself was thought to run round the perimeter of the world.'

then with which he marked the edge of the landmass in his map was of particular significance. It kept out, writes Romm, 'the terrifying *apeirōn* of primal chaos . . . where flowed the stream of Ocean, so as to permit a more formal ordering of its central spaces' (Romm 1992: 32).

But why, asks historian E. H. Bunbury, did the ancients see

> *not a sea*, surrounding the earth, as it became in later works on geography, but a mighty *river*, *flowing* all round the earth. This is repeated again and again. . . . It is termed also 'gently flowing' 'deep flowing', and 'back flowing', i.e., flowing back upon itself, in allusion to its circular course.
>
> (Bunbury 1883: 760)

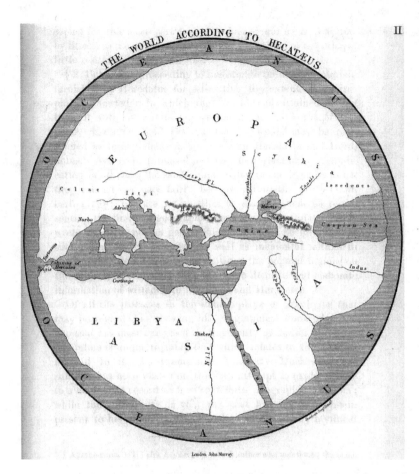

Figure 7.3 There is no record of Anaximander's map. But it likely resembled a map by Hecataeus which scholars have been able to reconstruct from fragments of writings. Edward Herbert Bunbury, *A History of Ancient Geography among the Greeks and Romans from the Earliest Ages till the Fall of the Roman Empire*, Vol. 1. London: John Murray, 1883.

Note: This is a historical map and is included here for representative purposes. The international boundaries, coastlines, denominations and other information shown do not necessarily imply any judgement concerning the legal status of any territory or the endorsement or acceptance of such information.

Bunbury does not have an answer, but Aristotle did. He thought it possible that by Oceanus the ancients referred to the transformative nature of the 'watery element', in particular, the ability of this element to become air-like and earth-like besides being water-like, doing so in a process that seemed to 'return' it to a 'previous' state.

> The earth is at rest, and the moisture about it is evaporated by the sun's rays and the other heat from above and rises upwards: but when the heat which caused it to rise leaves it . . . the vapour cools and condenses again as a result of the loss of heat and the height and turns from air into water: and having become water falls again onto the earth. . . . This cycle of changes reflects the sun's annual movement. . . . One should think of it as a river with a circular course, which rises and falls and is composed of a mixture of water and air. . . . And in this order the cycle continues indefinitely. And if there is any hidden meaning in the 'river of Ocean' of the ancients, they may well have meant this river which flows in a circle round the earth.
> (Aristotle 1952, II: 133; I: 69, 71)

If Aristotle is correct, the extraordinariness of Oceanus lies in it being a river that flows not on the surface of the earth, but on, in and through earth, air and sea. It is a flow that eludes the map, its edge being far too complex, fluid and ephemeral to mark with points and connect with lines in the view from above, particularly when it is in the form of mist, fog, clouds and currents, and when it is evaporating, precipitating, melting, sublimating, seeping, soaking and blowing, not to mention moving within the earth and through living organisms.

Thales, Anaximander's teacher at Miletus, who Aristotle considered the first natural philosopher is famous for declaring this watery element the first principle of matter and for asserting that earth rested upon it. It is said that he arrived at this belief on his travels to Egypt and Sumer (Brutsaert 2005: 560). Thales, however, was perhaps drawing on another account of Achilles' shield given by Homer. In this account, Homer does not describe the face of the shield; he rather describes its crafting in layers from a base up. Oceanus is this base, the first layer which Hephaestus thickens with four additional layers each smaller in diameter so that the shield is thickest toward the centre. 'And first Hephaestus makes a great and massive shield,' writes Homer,

> blazoning well-wrought emblems all across its surface, raising a rim around it, glittering, triple-ply with a silver shield-strap

run from edge to edge and five layers of metal to build the shield itself, and across its vast expanse with all his craft and cunning the god creates a world of gorgeous immortal work.

(Homer 1990, 18: 558–564)

Oceanus in this articulation of the shield is foundational rather than peripheral, a layer on the datum of the sea not just as a level, but also a beginning. From here, the watery element extends into the earth and air as wind, precipitation, streams, the moisture that is 'the nourishment of all things' (Figure 7.4).

Following Thales, Anaximander may well have conceived his map in two layers with Oceanus commanding its own layer or sphere as the ancients saw it, a sphere. Distinguished from the sphere of earth that lent itself to the points and lines of geometry, Oceanus is a sphere of water that performed by the cycles and transformations of hydrology. It meant that wherever a line marked the 'edge of earth', whether it was on the farthest sea or on the Nile or on a puddle or drop, it was not shared by Oceanus. Oceanus was its own tier (Figure 7.5).

But Anaximander's map is not seen as a two-tiered artefact; it is rather seen as maps are today, as single-layered geometric diagrams. It is a reading that reaches back to at least Herodotus who found Anaximander's map and others of his time, of which he says there were many, ridiculous and not based on experience.

> Legend says that Ocean is a great river running from the east all round the world, but there is nothing to prove this. . . . I cannot help laughing at the absurdity of all the map-makers – there are plenty of them – who show Ocean running like a river round a perfectly circular earth.
>
> (Herodotus 1954, IV: 8, 37, 44–45)

Elsewhere he writes, 'I know myself of no river called Ocean, and can only suppose that Homer or some earlier poet invented the name and introduced it into poetry' (Herodotus 1954, II: 23). In place of a river 'flowing' endlessly around in a sphere of its own, he sees an outer sea lapping against a shore and in place of the progeny of ocean, he sees rivers flowing on the surface of earth, emptying into the sea.

The shift is significant. The watery element is now subject to the terms of earth, paving the way for the coastline and riverbank, two lines tasked to separate land from water, each in its own way, land being the earth surface free of water. The coastline is familiar for its advances and retreats that marine biologist Rachel Carson famously

RIVER LITERACY AND THE CHALLENGE OF A RAIN TERRAIN

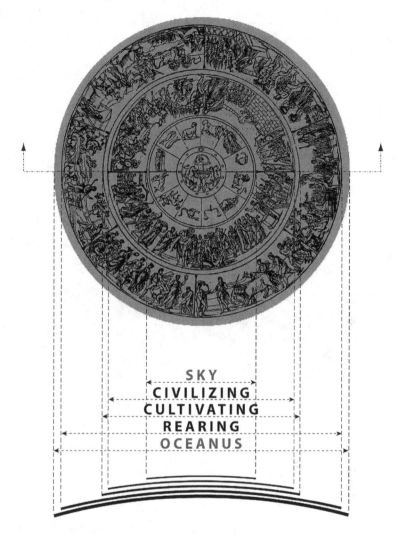

Figure 7.4 A section cut through Achilles' shield shows an artefact crafted with layers. Oceanus in this crafting is not circumfluent; it is foundational, a first presence. The shield is by Quatremere de Quincy from *The Penny Magazine of the Society for the Diffusion of Useful Knowledge*, September 22, 1832.

and tellingly called 'the edge of the sea' (Carson 1955). It has been studied for its ecology, energy and art; and it has been described as 'wrapped up in a sense of unceasing mobility' and 'infinite and folded' (Ryan 2012: 9; Carter 1999: 130–131). Riverbanks on the other

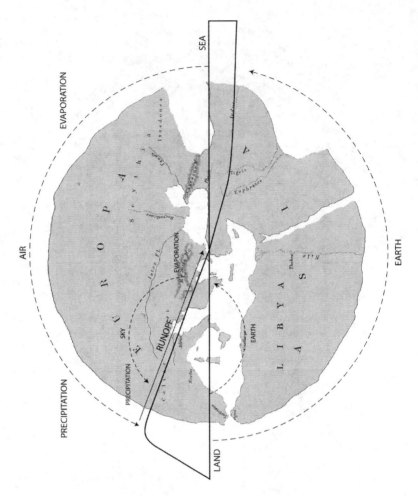

Figure 7.5 Anaximander's and Hecataeus's maps may well have been two-tiered artefacts: a tier of Oceanus performing by the cycles and transformations of hydrology, terms that are familiar today in the hydrological cycle; and a tier of earth performing by the points and lines of geography. Water here has no edge.

Source: Figure 7.5 is a reworking of Figure 7.3 by the author.

hand are lines that do not advance and retreat as much as flow along. Flow, writes T. S. McMillin in *The Meaning of Rivers*, 'is one of the most (if not the most) characteristic features of rivers. Rivers are rivers, one might say, because they flow; flow is what rivers do' (McMillin 2011: 153).

Geographic flows to riverbanks

Rivers are indeed inseparable from the idea of flow, but also from the two banks that call them out. Both feature prominently in the definition of a river as 'flowing water in a channel with defined banks'.[2] The definition can be more complex, such as 'a natural stream of water of fairly large size flowing in a definite course or channel or series of diverging or converging channels' or 'a large natural stream of water flowing in a channel to the sea, a lake, or another, usually larger, stream of the same kind'.[3] Accordingly, the image is more elaborate with multiple points on high ground, each generating a pair of lines that connect to those on either side of a 'main' flow before this flow divides in a delta where the lines multiply to link at many places with a coastline on a sea or a lake or upon occasion fade into the ground. Indeed, without lines, rivers are inconceivable, which is to say that to hear or speak the word 'river' is to think flow *and* see lines, lines like the one that the Greek academic Heraclitus in the 5th century BCE famously calls his readers to cross in order to know that 'you cannot step twice into the same river; for other waters are ever flowing on to you.' Not all will learn the lesson which Heraclitus believed this experience would impart, viz., that change is in the nature of things. Some will even disagree that this was the lesson he intended. But all will 'see' the line that he is asking them to step across, a line dividing stationary land from moving water (Figure 7.6).

The lines of riverbanks are unique, quite different than, for example, lines that convey meaning in alphabets, signs and symbols or lines that communicate measures like hachures and contours. Their difference lies in three tasks which they perform: they separate water from land, confine water to a course and calibrate time along their length from an 'origin' to a 'destination' or at least from an earlier to a later. All three tasks are necessary, but the first is fundamental. It brings a river into being, calling out something that can be named, touched, and recognized in its whole and its parts, but also something that can be extracted and drawn to scale on paper. On paper, it can be modified to look and perform differently before the changes are transferred back to the earth surface. What facilitates this back and forth are the lines of riverbanks. Indeed, mythology and history are replete with instances of gods and kings working these lines to command 'water'. Heracles, who has been called 'the greatest of river engineers', literally picked up the Alpheus by its banks and diverted it to clean the stables of King Augeias of Elis of the dung that had piled over 30 years. It is one of his famous Twelve Labors performed for Eurystheus, king of

Figure 7.6 G.W. Colton, 'Mountains & Rivers', in *Colton's Atlas of the World, Illustrating Physical and Political Geography*. New York: J.H. Colton and Company, 1856.

Note: This is a historical map and is included here for representative purposes. The international boundaries, coastlines, denominations, and other information shown do not necessarily imply any judgement concerning the legal status of any territory or the endorsement or acceptance of such information.

Tiryns (Herendeen 1986). Cyrus, King of Persia in the 6th century BCE, is known to have punished the Gyndes, a tributary of the Tigris, for sweeping away one of his sacred white horses by splitting it into 360 separate channels so as to make 'it so weak that even a woman could get over in future without difficulty and without wetting her knees' (Herodotus 2003, I: 189). Engineers today perform even more muscular tasks with the lines of riverbanks. They embank them with dikes or levees, pinch them with jetties and extend them with canals, gutters, aqueducts, ditches and pipes.

Some believe it is easy to call out a river. All it takes, writes the naturalist John Muir, speaking of the Merced River in California, is a high point. From here, he says, the river 'as a whole, is remarkably like an elm-tree, and it requires but little effort on the part of the imagination to picture it' (Muir 1907: 102). But it takes more than a prospect. It requires the clouds to pass, the rain to stop, a level of water to be set, and a host of other things that have taken centuries since Herodotus to cultivate. The cultivation has involved ideas, beliefs, stories, facts, but perhaps most significantly the art of the drawn line: its beginning in a point, its extension with a stroke and its ready modification by erasure. These acts, not coincidentally correspond to three essentials of a river – source, course and flood. It is a close correspondence that has made the river one of the most recognizable things on earth despite never being seen in its entirety. Even an aerial position – contrary to Muir's assertions – does not guarantee seeing an entire river. It is something made evident by the drawn line.

Indeed, more often than not, riverbanks speak louder than the flow of water for rivers do not cease to exist when they are without water. It is accepted that they 'run dry', some seasonally, others exceptionally, and yet others in geological time. What remains is a space between lines which continues to be seen as a 'river' or 'river bed', suggesting that it is the line more than water that is essential to rivers. This line 'flows' even when water does not.

The riverbank also features prominently in the identity of a river's source, the point where its two banks meet – its two 'longest' banks.[4] This definition has driven numerous expeditions across the world. Only recently, a group of explorers in 2006 declared that they had found the source of the Nile in a 'muddy hole' in the Nyungwe Forest of Rwanda at the head of a tributary of the Kagerain River flowing into Lake Victoria. 'All the greatest names failed – until now,' they write, referring to men including John Hanning Speke who 'discovered' Lake Victoria, Napoleon, Alexander III of Macedon and Herodotus. 'We know we are correct because we have studied the maps in detail and have now physically traced the longest source on the ground.' 'We've measured the river electronically using GPS tracks and now have the electronic data to prove the Nile is 6,719 kilometres in length' (Lovgren 2006).

It is in flood though that the riverbank features most prominently, paradoxically in its erasure, which hydrologists believe can occur 'naturally'. Flood, they say, is a 'naturally occurring, temporary inundation of normally dry land' (Schultz and Leitch 2008). Thus, when floods have tragic consequences, as they often do, there is much reflection on the nature of the line, its strength, position, height, fixity, temporality and management, but little if any on its necessity. Floods, in fact, have reinforced the line on the ground and in the imagination even as it has reinforced the belief that without their order there will be chaos, a belief best articulated by Niccolò Machiavelli in the 16th century. History he writes is

> one of those ruinous rivers that, when they become enraged, flood the plains, tear down trees and buildings, taking up earth from one spot and placing it upon another; . . . But although they are of such a nature, it does not follow that when the weather is calm we cannot take precautions with embankments and dikes, so that when they rise up again either the waters will be channelled off or their impetus will not be either so unchecked or so damaging.
> (Machiavelli 1985: 98)

The fact is that the lines which create a river also create flood.

Today, the lines of riverbanks are everywhere without question in pictures and in words, in textbooks, folklore, practices, rituals, policies, structures and conversations. Certainly, when historians and archaeologists speak of early civilizations on rivers, they invoke these lines. When geographers describe a landmass drained by rivers, they draw these lines. When engineers devise embankments, dams, barrages, drains, diversions and bridges, they work with these lines on the drawing board where such interventions are more easily conceived and tested. When surveyors draw a river, they draw these lines. When urban designers envision cities on rivers, they conceive these lines as 'riverfronts'. When ecologists speak of a river basin, they see these lines gathering from multiple points like branches of a tree and dispersing like roots into the sea and when they speak of a riparian zone, they thicken these lines to interface between land and river. When scholars translate ancient texts or the spoken word, we dare say, they are already disposed to seeing a terrain marked by the lines of riverbanks.

When activists, in their drive against displacement by dam projects or pollution, speak of 'lifelines' to which so many disempowered people are bound, they are referring to the lines of riverbanks. And, of course, when people see flood, which is an increasingly common event across the world, they see water transgressing these lines.

Riverbanks to infinite river

The lines of riverbanks have for centuries anchored much more than a flow from source to sea; they have also anchored a flow from the sea to source. This flow had its beginnings in the observation that the sea despite so many rivers entering it, does not fill. To Aristotle, this was because water evaporates more rapidly when its surface area increases as when

> one spills a cup of water over a large table, it will vanish as quick as thought. This is what happens with rivers: they go on flowing in a constricted space until they reach a place of vast area when they spread out and evaporate rapidly and imperceptibly.
> (Aristotle 1952, II: 355b)

He positions his view against Plato and others who believed that the sea does not fill because its water descended into 'a chasm which is the vastest of them all, and pierces right through the whole earth; this is that chasm which Homer . . . called Tartarus' (Plato 1937: 496).

But neither does the sea dry up. To Plato, this was because Tartarus was not just an end; it was also a beginning. Waters rise from it 'through subterranean channels and find their way to their several places, forming seas, and lakes, and rivers, and springs' (Plato 1937: 496). To Aristotle, it was because what the sun drew up, the rain brought down, from which 'It follows that the sea will never dry up: for before it can do so the water that has left it will fall again into it, and to admit that this happens once is to admit it continues to happen' Aristotle 1952, II: 356b).

While Aristotle and Plato read the observation that the sea does not fill or empty as an opportunity to clarify its equilibrium, others saw in it as an opportunity to explain a river's return to source. 'All streams flow into the sea,' it says in the *Book of Ecclesiastes*, 'yet the sea is never full. To the place the streams come from, there they return again.'[5] Attention here is returned to rivers. However, while flows to sea were straightforward – a matter of following a riverbank – the return to source was not.

For centuries, the dominant belief was that this return was through the earth. The water of the sea entered the earth and by some means – pressure, capillary action and vaporization – rose to springs. 'Openly it comes to the sea; secretly does it return,' wrote Seneca (Seneca 1971, III: 11.6, 5.1). This view apparently reaches back to Thales and carries forward to Leonardo da Vinci in the 15th century and then on to Athanasius Kircher in the 17th century. Springs, da Vinci says, are 'burst veins in the summits of mountains'. The water that emerges through them

> which with the utmost admiration of those who contemplate it raises itself from the lowest depth of the sea to the highest summits of the mountains, and pouring through the broken veins returns to the shallow parts of the sea, and again rises with swiftness and returns in like descent, and thus in course of time its whole element circulates.
> (MacCurdy 1958: 739)

Kircher thought the same, focusing his attention on the mechanisms by which water could be made to run upward and salt removed and diagramming a host of 'machines' that performed these tasks with pressure, vacuum, fire and other means (Figure 7.7). 'He then points out,' writes Frank Dawson Adams, 'that there is reason to believe there are in nature, conditions which parallel those which exist in the case of these machines' (Adams1938).

Some individuals though dared to ponder the return route through the air, although this was found difficult to imagine. 'Rainfall', wrote Seneca, 'can make a torrent but is not able to form a river gliding along with even flow between its banks. Rains do not make a river; they only make it flow faster.' It required a 'scientific proof' to establish the adequacy of rain – or more broadly, precipitation – to rivers. It was provided by a Frenchman, Pierre Perrault. He measured the volume of rain that fell in the 'upstream catchment' of the Seine (from its source to Aignay-le-Duc) and found that it was six times the amount that flowed in the river at Aignay-le-duc. He published his findings in 1674 under the title *On the Origin of Springs*. These findings were corroborated by Edme Mariotte a decade later with research that established the catchment as seven times the flow in the river. The remainder Mariotte said fed aquifers, wells, life or returned to the air (Brutsaert 2005: 572). Their 'true explanation' was so long coming, writes geologist Frank Dawson Adams of Perrault's and Mariotte's work, because scholars,

> seeing the great volume of water which rivers bore to the sea, could not believe that the rainfall of the country was

RIVER LITERACY AND THE CHALLENGE OF A RAIN TERRAIN

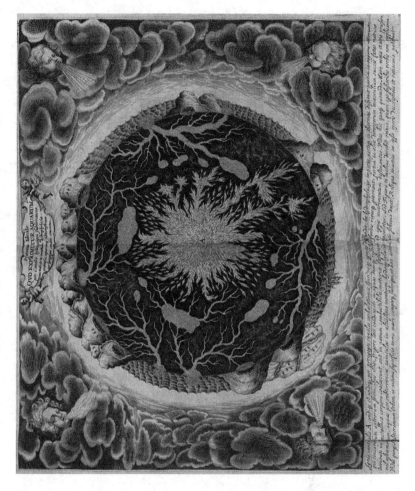

Figure 7.7 A section through the centre of the earth showing rivers descending from the sea to reservoirs near the fiery centre of the earth presumably before rising to *hydrophylacia* in mountains where they began their flow on the surface.

Source: Athanasius Kircher, 'Systema Ideale Quo Exprimitur Aquarum', *Mundus Subterraneus*. Amstelodami: Apud Joannem Janssoniuma Waesberge & filios, 1678 [University of Pennsylvania].

sufficient to supply so great a quantity of water. They did not know what vast expanses of the earth's surface were covered by the waters of the ocean, nor did they recognise how great a volume of water was raised from its surface by evaporation. . . . It was not until it had been demonstrated by actual measurements that the rainfall was more than sufficient to supply rivers with their water and that the water derived from the ocean was freed from its saline contents by the process of evaporation, that the true origin of springs and rivers was finally established.

(Adams 1938: 460)

With precipitation, more than adequate to rivers, the extended route of water was settled. Biologist William Amos calls it the 'infinite river'. It flows, he says, from sea to sky to earth and back to sea, where it is 'born again as it had been and would be, every moment of earthly time' (Amos 1971). Children learn it today as the hydrologic cycle, a flow that is diagrammed not with an eye positioned above the earth as maps are, but with a mind that travels with water through its many states (liquid, solid and vapour), processes of transformation and places, some of which can be obscure and elusive (Figure 7.8).

In other words, this water does not lend itself to being engaged visually in terms of the points and lines of *geometry*. Instead, it lends itself to being engaged materially in terms of a unit of hydrology that was not known until the late 17th century. This unit, which endures through liquid, solid and vapour, is the *molecule*. It was discovered by the French chemist Antoine Lavoisier, surprising him with the fact that water was not an element, but a chemical compound combining hydrogen and oxygen, later clarified as H_2O, that is, two atoms of hydrogen and one atom of oxygen (Linton 2010).

The infinite river does not have a singular source. It can begin anywhere anytime, writes hydrologist Robert Horton, in an

> isolated tree, even a single leaf or twig of a growing plant, the roof of a building, the drainage-basin of a river system or any of its tributaries, an undrained glacial depression, a swamp, a glacier, a polar ice-cap, a group of sand dunes, a desert playa, a lake, an ocean, or the Earth as a whole.
>
> (Horton 1931: 192)

It can also flow many ways. 'We speak of *the* water cycle as if there were only one,' notes Robert Kandel, 'but in fact there are many: some circuits are completed in a few days; but in others it can take months, years, millennia, even millions of years to go the course' (Kandel 2003: 6–7).

RIVER LITERACY AND THE CHALLENGE OF A RAIN TERRAIN

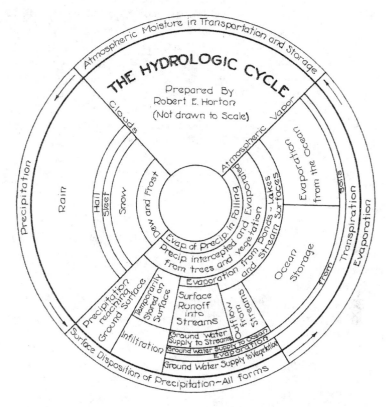

Figure 7.8 Robert E. Horton's 'The Hydrologic Cycle' in Robert E. Horton, 'The Field, Scope, and Status of the Science of Hydrology', *Transactions of the Geophysical Union*, Vol. 12, 1931.

Infinite river to rain terrain

The infinite river may seem to suggest the return of Oceanus. Yet it cannot be more different. Firstly, what circulates endlessly is not the watery element, but a chemical compound, H_2O, a colourless, odourless and tasteless substance. Secondly, the place of this substance is not the limitless *apeirōn* beyond the edges of a finite earth that it was to Anaximander, but the 'hydrosphere', popularly understood as a 'discontinuous layer of water at or near Earth's surface. It includes all liquid and frozen surface waters, groundwater held in soil and rock, and atmospheric water vapour.'[6] And thirdly, and most importantly, the infinite river is anchored in the moment of terrestrial rivers and orchestrated by the language of flows despite these flows occupying less than half a per cent of the hydrosphere. This language of flows has long provided the terms of infrastructure that has brought water to faucets and fields even in places considered 'un-serviced' by rivers. Today, this infrastructure is extending to capture the more elusive and ephemeral moments in the water cycle when water does not flow, but falls, dissolves, blows and soaks with the purpose of bringing these waters into rivers and their extension in canals, pipes, ditches and drains. To this end, rainwater is being harvested, seawater desalinated, groundwater pumped out of aquifers and clouds seeded. Here, the hydrologic cycle provides what a pioneer of national water policy – the National Water Committee in the United States of the 1930s – describes as a framework for 'understanding of the relationships among precipitation, run-off, evaporation, groundwater movement, soil condition, vegetation cover, transpiration (the breathing of moisture from vegetation) and many other associated phenomena' (Natural Resources Committee 1936). It also provides a framework for an integrated model of water supply and flood control, 'a means', writes Jamie Linton, 'of pulling together all water, at all scales, within a single integrated model' (Linton, Jamie 2010: 149).[7] That these frameworks are on the terms of flows is hardly noticed perhaps not surprisingly given that it is on the terms of the river that the cycle was conceived to flow infinitely.

Rivers then hold their course in the shift from the earth surface where they flow from source to sea to the hydrosphere where they flow endlessly. Here, defined as they are by their banks on the terms of geometry, they are not just another moment in the hydrologic cycle; they are a mediating moment. Being entities that flow both on the earth surface and in the hydrosphere, they mediate between water's more elusive moments (*aqua fluxus*) and land (*terra firma*). Indeed, rivers seem to have long played this mediating role of *terra fluxus* between water and land, reaching back to Heraclitus and his famous observation quoted earlier about not being able to step twice into the same river. He sees these waters moving against the backdrop of land on which he draws the line that he invites his readers to cross. It is easy to miss the human agency in this line today amidst the many design interventions that channel, extend, divert, dam and link rivers, interventions that tend to consume the conversation, particularly when they cause conflict or, worse, fail. But here perhaps lies the most significant revelation of the hydrologic cycle, seeding perhaps its own undoing: the exposure of flowing water as a moment of choice, a moment in which maps are drawn, properties are marked, histories are written and plans are made, a moment when water is *not* evaporating, blowing, precipitating, soaking, transpiring and doing all the things that blur lines. Indeed, waters in these 'other' moments are made transitional, on their way to becoming flowing water.

One can imagine choosing another moment in the cycle, the moment of, for example, precipitating water instead of flowing water. It will anchor a time that demands a representation as yet unfamiliar, a representation that will inspire an infrastructure and a construction of past and future as yet unimagined. It will of course, in its turn, make flowing water transitional.

Herein lies the possibility of a *rain terrain*, a ground that diverges in many ways from the *river landscape* that dominates the 'inhabited earth' through the agency of the (single-layered) map. Certainly, Alexander III of Macedon, a student of Aristotle, used this map to reach India even as he contributed to its extension with 'discoveries' such as the River Ganges, which he is first on record to call by that name, even if history says he did not reach it.[8] It is one of the many 'things' that he sought to capture for empire and empirical science but was kept from doing so by the refusal of his men to go on, defeated as they were by a ground where water was everywhere before it was somewhere. This was the case particularly in the monsoon when rain soaked and softened the earth, caused treacherous overflows, thickened the air, darkened the sky, and cultured a flora and fauna alien to these men who had come across the mountains from the rain shadow of West and Central Asia. Diodorus Siculus writes that this rain 'had been going on for seventy days, to the accompaniment of continuous thunder and lightning' before these men decided that they had had enough (Diodorus 1933: 17). Even Alexander, we are told, had his doubts. Quintus Curtius writes that 'He scorned the enemy and his beasts, but dreaded the nature of the terrain and [what he saw as] the violence of the rivers' (Curtius 1946, IX. Ii: 8–9). Alexander returned west to die shortly thereafter in Babylon in 323 BCE; but he had already seeded a river landscape in a rain terrain, the making and maintaining of which continues today against all odds.

Perrault and Mariotte had provided a glimpse of a 'rain terrain' when they 'proved' the adequacy of precipitation to rivers. Through their investigation, they were also saying that water falls before it flows; and that it challenged the separation of water from land on an earth surface. Precipitation after all falls indiscriminately and unpredictably in a moment when surveyors choose not to practice their art of mapping because precipitation fuzzes, even erases, the 'things' that they need to see and plot on the ground, rivers being important among them. Yet little was done to erase the lines of rivers. On the contrary, they have been extended as if to reach every point in a river's basin. Perhaps too much is invested in riverbanks and the moment of flow; or perhaps an alternative moment is yet to be articulated.

Few in India need proof that rain is adequate to rivers. But more importantly, rain has always been a choice here, not just in rain-fed agriculture versus river-fed irrigation or rain holdings as against piped water supply, but also in myths and stories that reveal a hidden, perhaps suppressed, imagination. The 'descent of Ganga' is a case in point.

As told in several texts, such as the epics *Mahabharata* and *Ramayana* and the *Puranas*, Ganga's descent was initiated by King Bhagiratha. Only this goddess, he was told, could revive the 60,000 sons of his ancestor, King Sagara. They had been reduced to ashes by Sage Kapila whose meditation they interrupted when they found him in possession of their father's sacrificial horse. This horse was sent out by the king to roam the world, and its possession by anyone meant a call to war. Indra, the god of rain, apparently worried about the dominion that could be claimed by the king, planted the horse in Sage Kapila's vicinity, thus setting up the events that followed. The king's grandson, Ansuman, was sent by the king to perform the last rites of his uncles. He found their ashes in a netherworld, but was told that to perform their last rites terrestrial water would not do; he required the Celestial Ganga. After neither he nor his son Dilipa could persuade Ganga to come down from her abode in the sky, it was left to Dilipa's son Bhagiratha to find a way. He renounced the world to beseech the gods who impressed with his asceticism convinced Ganga to descend. But they worried that the earth would shatter under her fall. Shiva offered to mediate by taking her fall on his head. Ganga, it is said, then flowed down his hair and, led by Bhagiratha, reached the netherworld where she reconstituted Sagara's sons.

Millions of people read this story today as portraying a river descending by the 'locks' of Shiva's hair. They see this river beginning in Gangotri in the Himalayas, flowing 1,569 miles before meeting the sea at Gangasagar (Figure 7.9). Jawaharlal Nehru called it the 'river of India', and the Government of India declared it a 'National River' in 2008. It was called Ganges by Alexander of Macedon in 327 BCE and was drawn for the first time on a world map a couple of generations later by Eratosthenes of Alexandria.

The story however can be read with another eye and imagination. What if Shiva let the goddess down, not the locks of his hair, but each of his infinite hairs? Her descent then does not picture a river as much as it does rain. Here, Ganga does not flow as the Ganges does, in a

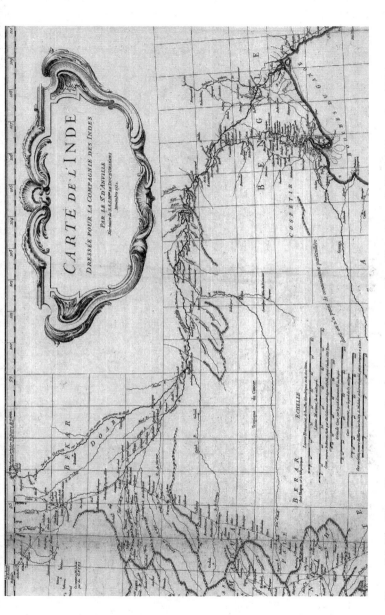

Figure 7.9 The River Ganges in Jean Baptiste Bourguignon d'Anville's *Carte de l'Inde*, November 1752.

Note: This is a historical map and is included here for representative purposes. The international boundaries, coastlines, denominations and other information shown do not necessarily imply any judgement concerning the legal status of any territory or the endorsement or acceptance of such information. For current boundaries, readers may refer to the Survey of India maps.

course to the sea; she is rather held in soils, aquifers, glaciers, living things, snowfields, agricultural fields, tanks, terraces, wells, cisterns, even the air, all for a multiplicity of durations that range from minutes and days to centuries and eons (Figure 7.10). Here she soaks, saturates, and fills before overflowing her way by a multiplicity of routes. Bhagiratha's task of leading her to a netherworld is much more challenging, much more mysterious, much more befitting of the infinite capacity of the gods. Unlike the Ganges, her source is not in a point or points, but in clouds. Also unlike the Ganges, her course cannot be drawn in

Figure 7.10 Rain does not flow; it rather holds before overflowing, extending like a stain across a blotting paper. With saturation and nearer the level of the sea, these overflows get deeper and move faster, appearing to the uninitiated to flow.

Source: Photographs by the author.

a map because her 'routes' are too complex, emergent and changing besides occurring across a vast depth rather than on a surface.

The only anchor she offers people is the time of her descent. It is celebrated each year at the coming of the monsoon with the festival *Ganga Dasahara*.

This Ganga, which holds and overflows, is not the River Ganges that flows and drains the land; nor is it the Ganges, which ever since it was named by Alexander, has served with a handful of other rivers as a river of paradise, a river of civilization, a paradigmatic sacred river, a case study river for hydrology and ecology, and today, an endangered river. It refutes the many texts that assume it to be the Sanskrit 'original' of the word Ganges. Indeed, this Ganga has refused time and time again to conform to the lines of a river. But rather than question the river literacy that does not belong in a place of rain, her non-conformance is read as a resistance and a call for more control, driven in large part by ideas such as progress and development that are themselves arguably inspired by the linearity, containment and calibration of a river imagination.

Given the massive edifice of belief, knowledge, practices and imagination built upon the banks of rivers, another order to the earth surface is difficult to imagine. But after nearly seven decades of 'independence' from a European nation that implemented the literacy of rivers as few rulers had since Alexander, it is perhaps time to ask if India is a land drained by rivers or a rain terrain. The question gains significance as the nation moves closer to implementing a 'mother of all projects' – interlinking India's rivers. This project aims to move surplus waters of rivers like the Ganges to areas of the country facing water shortage, thus solving two persistent problems simultaneously – flood and scarcity. It is an idea made seductively simple and efficient with simulations of complex flows by computers in an era of 'smart design'. Here, the nonlinear ground of a rain terrain is removed even further from consideration. Yet if one is aware of the existential difference between river and rain, Ganges and Ganga, it becomes clear just how much the flow of rivers are inappropriately and unfairly imposed upon the moment of rain to make the latter appear an illogical, impractical and often backward choice.

Today, given the reach of rivers into nearly every discipline, appreciating Ganga on its own terms requires a transdisciplinary effort. It calls for looking beyond not just the many lines that divide disciplines, but the one line that unites them – the line separating water from land. Here, a rain terrain puts forward another moment of the 'natural state', a moment in which we do not just see the world differently, but see a different world.

Notes

1. This is a popular reading of Homer that reaches back to Strabo who considered Homer 'the founder of the science of geography' and says that to him 'Oceanus touches all the extremities of the earth; and these extremities form a circle round the earth' (Strabo 1954, 1.1.7).
2. *The New Encyclopædia Britannica*, Vol. 26, 843. Encyclopædia Britannica Inc., 2007.
3. *Webster's Encyclopedic Unabridged Dictionary of the English language*. New York: Portland House, 1989; *Oxford English Dictionary*. Oxford University Press, 2012.
4. Cecil Rawling, an explorer in Tibet in the early 20th century, defines it as the point at the beginning of 'the longest visible branch of a river system and, if there are two branches of equal length, then that which carries most water at its greatest flood' (Rawling 1909: 424).
5. *Book of Ecclesiastes* in the Bible, Chapter I, verse 7. New International Version, 1984.
6. www.britannica.com/science/hydrosphere. Accessed June 23 2015. The hydrosphere is estimated to be 1.4 billion cubic kilometres and is popularly visualized as a 2.7-kilometer thick cover over the entire earth (De Villiers 1999: 35).
7. For this reason, Linton, following Ivan Illich, calls the substance of the hydrosphere 'modern water'. See Illich (1985).
8. Men who accompanied him say that he uttered the name in a speech to his soldiers on the banks of the Hyphasis. To reach it he says would take 'a journey of twelve days through desert waste'. It was 'the greatest river of all India', something that he wanted to cross and sail down to the 'eastern sea'. He believed it to be the last thing in the capture of Asia (Arrian 1983, V.26.1–3).

References

Adams, Frank Dawson. 1938. 'The Origin of Springs and Rivers', in *The Birth and Development of the Geological Sciences*. Baltimore: The Williams & Wilkins Company.

Amos, William H. 1971. *The Infinite River: A Biologist's Vision of the World of Water*. New York: Random House.

Aristotle. 1952. *Meteorologica*. Trans. H. D. P. Lee. Cambridge, MA: Harvard University Press.

Arrian. 1983. *Anabasis Alexandri*. Trans. P. A. Brunt. Cambridge, MA: Harvard University Press.

Brutsaert, Wilfried. 2005. *Hydrology: An Introduction*. Cambridge: Cambridge University Press.

Bunbury, Edward Herbert. 1883. *A History of Ancient Geography Among the Greeks and Romans from the Earliest Ages till the Fall of the Roman Empire*, Vol. 1. London: John Murray.

Carson, Rachel.1955. *The Edge of the Sea*. New York: The New American Library.
Carter, Paul. 1999. 'Dark with Excess of Bright: Mapping the Coastlines of Knowledge', in Denis Cosgrove (ed.), *Mappings*. London: Reaktion Books.
Curtius, Quintus. 1946. *History of Alexander*. Trans. John C. Rolfe. Cambridge, MA: Harvard University Press.
De Villiers, Marq. 1999. *Water: The Fate of Our Most Precious Resource*. Toronto: Stoddart Publishing Co. Ltd.
Diodorus, Sicilus. 1933. *Diodorus of Sicily*. Trans. C. H. Oldfather. Cambridge, MA: Harvard University Press.
Herendeen, Wyman H. 1986. *From Landscape to Literature: The River and the Myth of Geography*. Pittsburgh: Duquesne University Press.
Herodotus. 1954. *The Histories*. Trans. Aubrey de Sélincourt. New York: Penguin Books.
Herodotus. 2003. *The Histories* (Reissue Edition). Trans. Aubrey De Selincourt. London: Penguin Books.
Homer. 1990. *The Iliad*. Trans. Robert Fagles. New York: Penguin Books.
Horton, Robert E. 1931. 'The Field, Scope, and Status of the Science of Hydrology', *Transactions of the Geophysical Union*, 12: 192.
Illich, Ivan. 1985. H_2O *and the Waters of Forgetfulness*. Dallas: The Dallas Institute of Humanities and Culture.
Kahn, Charles H. 1960. *Anaximander and the Origins of Greek Cosmology*. New York: Columbia University Press.
Kandel, Robert. 2003. *Water from Heaven: The Story of Water from the Big Bang to the Rise of Civilization, and Beyond*. New York: Columbia University Press.
Linton, Jamie. 2010. *What Is Water? The History of a Modern Abstraction*. Vancouver: University of British Columbia Press.
Lovgren, Stefan. 2006. 'Nile Explorers Battled Adversity, Tragedy to Find River Source', *National Geographic News*, April 19.
MacCurdy, Edward. 1958. 'The Nature of Water', in *The Notebooks of Leonardo da Vinci: Arranged, Rendered into English and Introduced*. New York: George Braziller.
Machiavelli, Niccolò. 1985. *The Prince*. Trans. Harvey C. Mansfield Jr. Chicago: University of Chicago Press.
McMillin, T. S. 2011. *The Meaning of Rivers: Flow and Reflection in American Literature*. Iowa City: University of Iowa Press.
Muir, John. 1907. *The Mountains of California*. New York: The Century Co.
Natural Resources Committee. 1936. *Deficiencies in Basic Hydrological Data*. Washington, DC: United States Government Printing Office.
Plato. 1937. *Phaedo*. Trans. B. Jowett. New York: Random House.
Rawling, Cecil. 1909. 'Discoveries in Southern Tibet: Discussion', *Geographical Journal*, 33 (April): 4.

Romm, James S. 1992. *The Edges of the Earth in Ancient Thought: Geography, Exploration, and Fiction*. Princeton: Princeton University Press.

Ryan, Anna. 2012. *Where Land Meets Sea: Coastal Explorations of Landscape, Representation and Spatial Experience*. Farnham, Surrey: Ashgate Publishing Limited.

Schultz, Steven, and Leitch, Jay A. 2008. 'Floods and Flooding', in Stanley W. Trimble (ed.), *Encyclopedia of Water Science*, Vol.1. Boca Raton: CRC Press.

Seneca. 1971. *Naturales Quaestiones*. Trans. Thomas H. Corcoran. Cambridge, MA: Harvard University Press.

Strabo. 1954. *The Geography of Strabo*. Trans. Horace Leonard Jones. Cambridge, MA: Harvard University Press.

8
ACCENTS OF MEMORY
Critical humanities and the question of inheritance

D. Venkat Rao

The concept of responsibility has no sense at all outside of an experience of inheritance. Even before saying that one is responsible for a particular inheritance, it is necessary to know that responsibility in general ('answering for', 'answering to', 'answering in one's name') is first assigned to us, and that it is assigned to us through and through, as an inheritance. One is responsible before what comes before one but also before what is to come, and therefore before oneself (Derrida 2004a: 5–6).

Institutions of humanities

The field of humanities (even HASS – history, arts and the social sciences) is the legacy of Europe in cultures that faced colonialism. This legacy pervades the institutional and intellectual formations of the humanities in India even to this day. In the context of such a historical legacy any attempt to reorient teaching and research in the humanities in India is required to confront two related questions: (1) How does the field of humanities configure cultural forms and formations in India? (2) How do these forms and formations relate to communication technologies – oral to digital – in their millennial existence? Intellectual and institutional futures of the humanities in India depend on how one addresses these questions.

With 723 universities, 35,539 colleges, over 40 institutes of technologies (IITs, NITs, IIITs)[1] and scores of other higher education institutions, India has a substantial public and private academic infrastructure (this is, though, hardly adequate in a population of

1.2 billion). Over 20 million students enrolled (only) in higher education institutions in 2011.[2] The humanities and arts subjects dominate the enrolment lists in colleges and the universities. Over 37 per cent (i.e. over 6.5 million [about 9 million according to NEP 2016]) opted for the humanities subjects (in contrast to about 18 per cent in the sciences). Predictably, the humanities (and HASS) produce more graduate and doctoral students every year (over 450 doctorates in science and technology studies against thousands in the arts and humanities every year) (UGC Annual Report 2012: 4,61,66; MHRD Annual Report 2012: 100–101).

It must be noted here that the student composition enrolled is not a homogenous 'Indian' population as such. Over 50 per cent of this enrolment comes from what is called the 'reservation' ('affirmative action') category. This category itself is divided into three components, each of which gives only the illusion of a unifying totality, although even a cursory look at these components reveals that each one is composed of thousands of significantly varied communities called jatis (which the Portuguese turned into *casta*). On even a most conservative estimate, these jatis (as currently configured) run into about 5,000 communities. Four separate federal ministries[3] of the Indian state are entrusted with the task of safeguarding reservations and thus maintaining jati compositions. If one were to figure out the jati compositions of the other 50 per cent of student population, one can imagine the radically heterogeneous nature of the Indian classroom. The British abandoned such an enterprise to count the jatis in the 1930s (Samarendra 2011: 51–58). The institutions and the modern system of thought they (the British) established foreclosed any new reflection or inquiry into the heterogeneous jati formations and the alienating but (now) ineluctable structures of colonial modernity. Critical humanities must affirm their task of addressing the questions posed earlier in this double bind.

If the faculties of humanities are concerned with human creativity and reflection, and the question of what does it mean to be human, are these faculties in a position to grapple with the creative and reflective forces and forms of these diverse jati formations of India today? Do these forms and forces have any serious epistemic space at all in the teaching and research in the humanities in the Indian context? The negative answer that awaits these questions goes to prove that the structure, method, content and pedagogy in the humanities (let alone in the sciences) are dominated by the Euro-American paradigms. Caught in a juncture of such a glaring cognitive asymmetry, what is to be done?

The enigma of jati

Given the tenacity and resilience with which jatis sustained the heterogeneous cultural fabric of India, one is impelled to face the enigma of *jati* as a cultural formation. One learns to confront this much maligned phenomenon called jati once again from within the portals of modern institutions. Neither Buddhism, Islamic rule, European colonization, the (ultra) Left movements, nor globalization has succeeded in eliminating (let alone 'annihilating' as the rhetoric goes) the jati phenomena in the last 25 centuries. Neither originated nor controlled and regulated by any singular agency or person, jatis come forth, proliferate and sustain themselves. In their heterogeneous spread across millennia jatis seem radically unstructured or wild phenomena. Why and how they live on, what is their enduring essence (if any) and above all, what is there in them that tethers (and divides) groups of individuals to cherish jatis remain unanswerable questions.

As biocultural formations, jatis internally self-divide and disseminate themselves; as such jatis cannot be seamlessly grouped into homogeneous unities. They divide and disperse into newer formations. Jatis are infinite and no one can count them, says a medieval Sanskrit composition.[4] Therefore, the current reckoning of jatis mentioned earlier cannot be said to measure the quanta of jatis historically. Consequently, jatis bring forth biological and cultural formations ceaselessly. As jatis cannot be calculated so do their forms of learning and art, says the text cited above.[5] Indian classroom exposes the student, teacher and researcher to such heterogeneous singularities of biocultural formations. Indian classroom is barely prepared to respond to the immeasurable diversity of these cultural formations and their creative reflective inheritances. The inheritors who compose the classroom are epistemically (if not experientially) wrenched away from their inheritances. European colonialism inaugurated and sustained this epistemic violence by reducing jati to a closed system of hierarchy and oppression ('caste'). Consequently, 'colonial consciousness' stigmatizes caste and lives on with the colossal burden of unexamined guilt. Colonial modernity and its institutions thus foreclose the possibility of productively confronting the millennially inherited cultural forms and formations of jati singularities.

The 30 million students who enrolled in higher education institutions in 2015 represent a fractal segment of a much more gigantic and internally varied configuration of biocultural formations of India. While instituting the faculties in the form of civilizational education, the field of humanities sets out to measure this colossal conglomeration by one jati (the Brahmin) as an object of inquiry into the native culture. Consequently, accumulation and translation of 'Sanskrit knowledges' became the most cherished intellectual activity in the colonial period and later. This resulted in the creation of European humanistic field called Indology. Even to this day, Indology's driving impulse is to accumulate tangible objects in centralized repositories. Many universities in Europe (especially in Germany) and in the United States maintain such (largely scribal) archives. Apart from archivation, Indological work exposes Sanskrit knowledges to European interpretive gaze. Questions that were dominant in European intellectual history (questions concerning the origin, historicity, rationality, agency, literacy and progressivity, etc.) continue to govern contemporary Indological investigations. Two such noteworthy intellectual efforts can be noticed today in the US and US–Europe-based projects (supported by NSF and NEH) of 'Sanskrit Knowledge Systems on the Eve of Colonialism'[6] and the SARIT (Search and Retrieval of Indian Texts).[7]

Undoubtedly Sanskrit reflective and creative traditions are of immense human value. But they signify the singularity of one specific jati formation – though even this 'one' itself is significantly varied internally in its formations and in its creations. Secondly, colonial and Indological archives largely reduce Sanskrit to its scribal appearance; for, archives require tangible objects. The fact that no such archival impulse or repositories gained any prominence in Indian cultural formations received any significant attention in inquiries into India's pasts. One striking feature that enables us to relate the radically diverse jati formations of India pertains to their relation to communication technologies. All the biocultural formations for millennia augmented and proliferated their inheritances mnemoculturally.

Accents of memory

Mnemocultures signify cultural formations that articulate their memories essentially by the most primordial communicational technologies of speech and gesture. Cultural memories are/were composed, expressed, mediated, transformed and disseminated through the medium of the body. The body circulates as the quintessential medium and destination of articulated inheritances. Such embodied and enacted cultural forms have had no use for archives and museums – which emerged as the surrogate bodies of memories elsewhere. Mnemocultures remained indifferent for millennia toward external retentional systems of memory. Mnemotechnologies[8] such as writing, print, audiovisual analogue techniques and even digital technologies are destined toward surrogate retentional systems like scriptoria, archive, museum, database or data-lake. The historical ascendancy of mnemotechnologies marginalizes and enframes the embodied and enacted articulation of mnemocultures. Even after the invasion of mnemotechnologies (from scribal to digital) mnemocultures sustained their embodied articulation of memories in the Indian context. This cultivated indifference toward disembodied or surrogate retentional systems of memory distinguishes and differentiates mnemocultures in general and Indian jati cultural formations in particular from the cultures (of the West) that are haunted by the archival passions.

Cultures are said to differ from each other in different ways. The Indic cultural formations from Gandhara to Brahmaputra and Sangam took the lithic (inscriptional) and plastic (sculptural) turn rather belatedly within their predominantly mnemocultural soils and rhythms; but these turns to the lithic have had radically different consequences in these diverse cultural formations and their cultural forms than the impact they are claimed to have had in the Euro-Abrahamic contexts. Even over a millennium after writing was intruded into the Gandhara constellation, Sanskrit traditions preferred to sustain and proliferate themselves mnemoculturally – as they did for two millennia before the Common Era. Similarly, though in different ways, the Tibeto-Burman, Sino-Burman cultural flows bring forth literacy into the Brahmaputra constellation in the Common Era long after some of these cultural formations have made the valleys and ranges their habitat. The *Chaitharon Kumpapa*, the *Poireiton Khunthoke*, the Buranjis and the Rajmalas of the first and second millennia indicate the signs of archival output (the slow and belated emergence of surrogate bodies.)

Yet neither in Manipuri Meetei formations nor in Bodo, Assamese cultural forms, these scribal accretions anywhere appear to displace the heterogeneous manifestations of mnemocultural impulse. Madhav Kandali and Srimanta Sankaradev and numerous others remain eloquent currents in the lively archives even to this day; they barely become the hermeneutical objects of philological decipherment as scribal objects became elsewhere. Similarly, the Maibis of Meeteis and the Lai Haraoba performers, like the Paddana-Teyyam performers in Sangam constellation (to be explained in the next section) are not driven by any scribal commandment in their immersive enactments. In fact, the cherished Meetei *Cheitharon* has little to say about the lively traditions of Lai Haraoba or Sanamahi or even about Maibis (Parratt 2005).

In the same way the plastic creations, iconic or aniconic artefacts, material articles, tattoo designs, woven fabric and figures and morung ornamentations or decorations (as in diverse cultures of the northeast – Nagas, Adis, Miris, Noctes, Luceis, Meeteis, Kukis and Khasis, etc.), are all significant parts of ritual-performative cultures rather than distanced objects of a surrogate repository. It is von Heimendorf who first turns these into objects of photography and museum – artefacts for the externally retained memory spaces – in the middle of 20th century. Yet more sustained inquiries into the mnemocultural difference manifesting in their singular reception of and response to the lithic and iconic/pictorial turn must be advanced across these cultural clusters.

As is well known, the lithic turn in certain cultures (especially the Abrahamic ones) has aggravated the archival fevers – the passion for accumulation and preservation of inscriptional artefacts. Archives and museums are the external retentional systems of memory; they are the surrogate receptacles that claim to transcend the ephemerality and unreliability of the finite embodied memories. Whereas in contrast to the celebration of external retentional systems from the scribal to digital repositories, mnemocultures, even after the ascendancy of these communication systems, persist in acoustic-performative enactment of cultural forms. From ritual ceremonial recitations, temple song-cultural performances (say, of Nayanmars and Alwars, or at namghars), Khasi dances and *phawar*s to Naga feasts of merit, from funeral ritual chants to marriage ceremonial celebrations jatis and jan-jatis across the cultural clusters of the subcontinent and beyond, the body and its gestural-acoustic efficacy get foregrounded in mnemocultures.

Mnemocultures appear to grapple with the enigma of the body by putting it to persistent play as the medium and effect of existence. They do not seem to indulge in exclusive theoretical discourses about the body. The articulations of the body and the cultivated modes of tending the body thus become critical sources for configuring cultural difference among these constellations. If the archival cultures obsessively expand external retentional systems, the un-archival mnemocultures proliferate and disperse heterogeneous *lively archives* of embodied existence. If mnemocultures put the lively body to work, archontic cultures pursue the disembodied technical systems or surrogate bodies. But the latter are fundamentally articulated memories that are alienated from the lively bodies and immortalized or embalmed in virtual bodies. How to respond to these immemorial cultural forms and formations from within the archivally oriented disembodying institutional structures is the most urgent and demanding question in our contexts of humanities research.

A certain notion of knowledge is premised on the necessity of positing objects. Entities (organic or inorganic) must be turned into objects for probing and representation for the purpose of generating knowledge – knowledge 'about' objects. The accomplishments of modern sciences are essentially based on such translation of entities into objects – and into 'facts' of science. Objects are exhausted once they yield the partial knowledge for which they are posited. The field of HASS is not entirely free from this epistemophilic paradigm of positing objects and accumulating knowledges. In other words, entities are reduced to mediated objects of knowledge. The very constitutive principle (of reason) of the university institutes such an epistemological paradigm (Derrida 2002: 202–237, 2004b: 129–155).

Mnemocultures today are covered by such objectivizing and representational mechanisms in modern universities. Ill-thought categories such as 'folk' are imposed on jati cultural formations. 'Folk' emerged as an object of inquiry when industrializing societies were violently dividing cultural formations in the West. Whereas the vibrant biocultural formations (jatis) – resilient against all kinds of pressures – reaffirm themselves even to this day. In their enduring traversal across millennia, the jati formations do not demonstrate much archival or objectual impulse. There are rarely any life-narratives (until very recent times) that posit any jati into an *object* of inquiry. All genealogical compositions of jatis are lived on in performative embodiments and enacted spectacles. Jati cultural formations, therefore, cannot be reduced to the totalizing category called the folk. But covered by the cognitive violence of colonial modernity, the faculties of humanities have not risked any inquiry into the relationship between jati and culture. All the 12 folklore departments and about 18 Tribal Research Institutes[9] of India – marginal in their existence in the fields of HASS – are barely in a position to inquire into the co-constitutive relationship between mnemocultures and jati formations. They are forced by their disciplinary demands to retrieve (forage), accumulate and museumize – in a word: succumb to archive fevers and lobotomize jatis into folk. No new initiative to reflect on jatis and cultures can be seen from these organizations.

If jati and culture are co-constitutive entities over millennia, one notices a curious asymmetry in their existence in the modern period. Indology as a segment of European humanities devoted its time and energy relentlessly to frame Sanskrit (including Buddhism) in relation to the 'Brahmin (jati) ideology'.[10] European and the US federal funding sustains this intellectual venture. Consequently, Sanskrit as an object of inquiry moves across (ambivalently) various faculties of humanities (linguistics, religious studies, anthropology, art and philosophy, etc.). Whatever may be their position with regard to this ('Brahmin ideology') phenomenon, these inquiries cannot help confirming the relation between jati and culture in inquiries into India; but these inquiries have little to offer in examining the relation in any productively novel ways. Yet the relationship remains denegated.

If Sanskrit as an 'ideological formation' of Brahmins receives sustenance in Europe and the United States as a legacy of such framing, jati gets figured in two related ways in contemporary India: (1) As an object of 'reservation' (yet another denegated category) and (2) as an ideological formation (of the 'upper castes'). Consequently, the millennial relationship between jati and culture remains foreclosed for any further productive inquiry. Given the colonial stigmatization of jati, neither European (Indological) nor the US ('area studies') scholarship initiated any significant inquiry into the jati cultural formations beyond foregrounding some putative Brahmin ideology. No wonder, one barely finds any repositories of any of the divergent jati cultural formations and their mnemocultures in Europe or the United States. The post-war US philanthropic work in India (Ford Foundation) barely led to any fundamental inquiry into jati cultural formations. The latter mainly reinforced the archival impulses. As pointed out earlier, more than half of the composition of students (not only) in higher education today is directly enrolled in the name of jati. But the double barrels of stigma and ideologization of jati prevents any engagement with these extraordinary biocultural phenomena. More productive ways of *re*-turning to this Indian cultural singularity must be explored. The only way to reorient teaching and research in the humanities from the receiving ends in India appears to be to reinvigorate, reorient and rearticulate the enduring relationship between jati formations and mnemocultures of India.

Cultural constellations

Cultural passageways do not abide by territorial and cartographic borderlines. Cultures, like jatis that multiply, bring forth each other, miscegenate and proliferate transgressively and transgenerationally. Mnemocultures of India disseminate across and beyond the subcontinent even as they conserve singularities of jati. As a preliminary effort to measure the immeasurable, we can tentatively configure palpable rhizomic mnemocultural roots and routes. These nodes can be mapped under seven constellations as follows:

1 Gandhara[11]
2 Brahmaputra[12]
3 Indus[13]

4   Kham-Patha[14]
5   Madhyadesha[15]
6   Dakshinapatha[16]
7   Sangam[17]

The Indian cultural fabric is woven by the textures, flows and plasmas from these constellations. The traces and weaves of these formations spread across the Silk Route and Spice Route and disseminate elsewhere.

One possible invisible thread that might run through these constellations is that they all are mainly un-archival cultures for millennia (whether Indus/Harappans had a script or not is a hotly debated issue in recent times. [Farmer et al. 2004]).

Excepting the Indus/Harappa civilization, which archaeologically exists, all other constellations mentioned above have a lively and enduring mnemocultural presence in the Indian cultural formations. Curiously, even in the case of Harappans, although they were in exchange with ancient Mesopotamian and Egyptian inscriptional cultures, they did not appear to maintain any seal archive (like the cuneiform archive of Assurbanipal). But none of the constellations indicated above can be treated as a homogeneous unity. All the constellations are differing conglomerations of jatis and jan-jatis (or cultural formations). If there are about 5,000 jatis in the recent reckoning, there are over 800 jan-jatis (or 'tribes') spaced across the constellations of the subcontinent and beyond.[18] Each of the internally varied jatis and jan-jatis has deeply spread-out cultural genealogies (the washerman jati and the Savara jan-jati are rooted in the *Ramayana*). Extended cultural genealogical memories of these jatis and jan-jatis pulsate in the mnemocultural forms of song, story, *purana*, performance, music and the graphic.[19] These immeasurable *vidya*s (forms of verbal-acoustic learning) and *kala*s (patterns of visual, graphic and performative articulations) are enlivened in heterogeneous languages and idiomatic utterances, embodied rhythms and enacted gestures that would dwarf the achievements of the sciences of language and theatre. Here the force of creation defies the sciences of pattern finding. The template of constative-performative opposition is of little use here. Generative and improvisational impulses transgressively disseminate mnemocultural forms and formations.

Lively archives

Indian classroom is decisively composed of such resilient but protentive cultural genealogies. How to respond to such heterogeneous inheritances from inside (i.e. from the jatis and jan-jatis) *and* from *outside* (that is, the university)? What can be done with these embodied articulations of millennial memories? Here we are guided by the hypothesis that we are dealing with un-archival inheritances – intangible inheritances embalmed in no preservative warehouses excepting the body. In this context, we may propose to receive such embodied inheritances that are driven by generative and improvisational impulses as 'lively archives'. Lively archives refer to the singularity of embodied memories – memories or inheritances that get articulated in the living on of the bodies immemorially. Lively archives bring forth genetic, generative and generic memories that are inherited but exposed to improvisation in each of its traversals and in its rhizomic rhythms. In other words, the body as the medium and effect of the inherited memories rearticulates, remediates and responds to what it receives transgenerationally.

In contrast to the necrophilic haunting of the traditional archive which fabricates surrogate bodies (museum, database etc.), and longs for immortality of the embalmed, lively archives throb with an intuitive sense and impulse of *responsive reception* and live on with improvisational element. Lively archives may yield necrophilic archives – but mnemocultural force cannot be reduced to the embalming of the received. Consequently, lively archives can receive and transform interminably and infinitely (let's recall the improvisational basis of Indian musical traditions) what they receive or what has preceded them; lively archives can only be open-ended passageways of variants – variants without any definitive terminal. Thus the 'lively' in the lively archives implies the incalculability of what will be and what might be on the basis of what has been. That is to say that the 'promise', if there is any, of the received cannot be calculated on the basis of or reduced to the 'given'. The future anterior (*karma sanchita* – unpredictable coming forth of what might have been in action) cannot be calculated – the future of the past is contingent upon how the past is remediated in a given articulation of it.

The Indian classroom is nothing but innumerable unstructured clusters of inheritors of lively archives. Jatis and jan-jatis articulate India's genomic and cultural heterogeneity. The embodied memories of these biocultural formations are exposed to a whole range of communicational technologies from oral to digital today. As the mnemocultural media (speech and gesture) remain the most preferred forms of these jatis and jan-jatis, the lively quanta of articulated memories that are generated and disseminated remain immeasurable. Although archivation is not the driving impulse of these cultural formations, their articulated memories get captured by ascendant technologies across history. Thus, even the quintessentially mnemocultral formation that Sanskrit/

Brahmin cluster is, the estimated yield of scribal quantum of Sanskrit manuscripts is believed to cross 30 million texts (which exceeds all European manuscripts put together by 10^3 figure).[20] Added to this, the emerging digital corpuses of texts (in Europe and the United States) exponentially magnify the externally retained memories of this cultural formation. If one supplements these galaxies of articulated (and externally retained) cultural memories with the stand-alone retentions of memories (from oral to digital – manuscripts, audiovisual repositories, PC scans, downloads, DVDs, memoirs, archives), one can easily sense the inexhaustible quanta of (unstructured) cultural memories that circulate in the Indian context.

How to retain these colossal constellations of articulated memories beyond their prevalent abodes and enable them to live on unconditionally – 'without alibi' – is both the most urgent question and interminable but challenging task (not only) in the Indian reflective cultural institutional context.

These multiple repositories of cultural memories can be retained and enhanced only when the cultural inheritors of these heritages learn to affirm their inheritances. For this to happen, the primary steps of unlearning the two centuries' old internalized jati stigmatization and learning to reflect on the deeply sedimented but unexamined guilt must be undertaken. Today such urgent steps can be initiated only in the academic-research institutional context. For, nowhere in Indian history can one find such a powerful and singular, institutional structure that promises to 'contain' the jatis and jan-jatis in unifying categories (but disavowing and denegating) than the modern educational system (the university).

As pointed out earlier, all the 30 million (and increasing numbers of) students enrolled in courses recently are constituted by jatis (here one can include the minorities as variant jatis without, of course, reducing their internal complexity) and jan-jatis of deeply interwoven pasts. They populate and sustain about 60,000 higher education institutions in the country. Their force perennially demands more such institutional shelters. As pointed out earlier, at least four different ministries (apart from several other apex organizations – such as Niti Aayog, Parliamentary Committees and many others) regulate and execute matters pertaining to the jatis and jan-jatis through institutional mechanisms. The resources and provisions possessed by these ministries and institutions can be harnessed to reconfigure the colossal jati-janjati cultural memories mentioned earlier. If there were to be a future (or renewed future) of the humanities, it critically rests on the jan-jati cultural inheritances in India.

Critical humanities

If the field of humanities is fundamentally concerned with human creativity and reflection, and the question of what is proper to man, the future of critical humanities in India is deeply contingent upon what we do with these jan-jati cultural inheritances that we are composed by. The question of cultural memories concern not just humanities studies only, but is inescapably related to the entire orientation of education in the country as such. The questions pertaining to who are we educating and what are we educating them for cannot be dissociated for long from the question of cultural inheritances and their difference. Colonial education was aimed at permanently altering the relationship between jati and culture, what we think and how we live, cognitive and experiential realms. The definitive consequence of this epistemic violence can be seen in the severe disorientation in our humanities studies in particular and our educational telos in general.

A reconfiguration of the humanities teaching and research from the Indian context can be experimentally broached by attending to three immensely explored and related nodes: vidya, kala and tattva. The immeasurable mnemocultural proliferations across clusters and constellations of jati cultural formations are accomplished through these divergent cultural forms. Vidya is embodied sonic-musical verbal compositions accented through the face. Kala refers to gestural enactments which the body's articulations bring forth even from the verbally silent.[21] Then tattva can be configured as the parxial meditative reflection on the relationship between the symbolizing forms of vidya (speech) and kala (gesture) on the one hand, and para the 'weak' force that constitutively inhabits as a silent, unagentive, non-sovereign, 'power-less' witness in the individuated lively millions (*prani koti*), on the other. In other words, tattva is an interminable mnemopraxal inquiry into the relation (without relation) between the co-originary 'phenomenal' and the 'non-phenomenal' in the instance of existence. As vidyas and kalas are infinite, the tattvik activity remains at work as long as the lively millions live on. This nodal string with its other openings can help conceiving praxial-reflective teaching and research initiatives across institutions and cultures within and beyond the constellations indicated earlier.[22]

The critical humanities nodes indicated above will provide the possibility of facing the disciplinary structures currently in place and contribute to the possibility of reorienting the latter from the Indian context. The most significant disciplines of the humanities – literature, art (in the extended sense of visual and performative forms) and philosophy – have offered little in exploring and questioning the provenance, purpose and possibilities of humanities teaching and research in the Indian context.[23]

They have not helped us to grapple with in a theoretically informed way the intellectually destitute situation that we persist in our postcolonial era. The critical humanities nodes suggested earlier have not found any place in the disciplinary structures and reflections of the university – let alone the urgent task of unravelling these received structures from the vantage of the nodes outlined.

I must hasten to add that the point being made here does not pertain to use of Sanskrit terms or defining Indian terms as such. State-funded (and controlled) cultural organizations have been for decades doing precisely this kind of activity.[24] Yet such work has barely contributed to advance any theoretically viable reorientation of the humanities studies in India. On the contrary, these institutions and their work hardly show any awareness of the problem of the prevailing intellectual destitution in the humanities studies in the country. By default, each of these organizations (all the TRIs and even the IGNCA) invests in unthinking documentation of cultural practices; at the most such archivational work functions as showcasing 'cultural wealth' to the deracinated natives and academic or touristic foreigners.

The intellectual crisis we are pointing to has little to do with linguistic or definitional issues. The problem has to do with our continued failure to figure out cultural difference on the basis of patterned inheritance of salient cultural resources. It has to do with the failure to find reflective alternatives to institutionalized disciplines of thought of the colonial epoch and the absence of any theoretically informed configuration of the latter on the basis of their European religious-cultural/philosophical provenance.[25]

If onto-theology constitutes the cultural difference of the West, as many thinkers have argued, how do we configure the cultural difference of Indian cultural formations? Intellectual ventures in the social sciences, argued S. N. Balagangadhara, have never taken the risk of configuring this difference in any theoretically informed ways (Balagangadhara 2012). As a result, the disciplines of social sciences and the humanities, Balagangadhara goes on, simply derivatively repeat inquiries that emerged from European cultural framework. A situation where we do not know what kind of inquiries we should pursue and how one should respond to the inherited resources can only be an intellectually destitute situation. *This postcolonial destitution continues to grip our institutional and intellectual life today.*

Surely the task of advancing such inquiry is that of the universities, one can say. But the universities are barely prepared to address the issue. The humanities disciplines and their practitioners seem to know little about why they exist, what they can do and how they should move about in their work in the locations of their existence. From Kerala to Arunachal, Jammu to Kanyakumari, Mumbai to Odisha, the practitioners of the humanities have become, to cite a formulation Gayatri Spivak coined years ago, belated disc jockeys playing repeatedly old numbers created elsewhere. The distance between, for example, a philosophy or literature department and the blatantly marginal bhasha-based literature or 'folklore' department is so enormous in all the universities to expect the possibility of any communication among them. But even the former (the bhasha-based disciplines) apologetically genuflect before the supposedly vanguard disciplines of English and philosophy (and more prominently, philosophically impoverished social sciences) for their methods and materials. No wonder why the postcolonial destitution continues to persist in our higher education or intellectual life; no wonder why there are no autonomous intellectual inquiries in our contexts today.

It may appear preposterous to suggest that the intellectual destitution is deeply related to the invasion of the modern educational institutions, their discourses and methods. But the epistemic and epistemological disjuncture with our inheritances remains an undeniable fact in our everyday practices. Colonial education and its discourses deeply ruptured and displaced the millennial relationship between cultural formations and their cultural forms. In other words, colonial education manoeuvred to breach a permanent epistemic rupture between jatis/jan-jatis and their cultures. Subjugated and stigmatized, jatis and cultures were reduced into the object of colonial interpretative gaze. If this gaze appropriated the classical cultural forms (of Sanskrit, especially) into European humanities (such as Indology) as native ideological discourses, it enframed heterogeneous jatis and their cultural forms as heathen practices initially (in the colonial period) and as fodder for the social science machines later ('area studies' of the decolonization period). No wonder these disciplines of the university have an inherent suspicion toward any bhasha-reflective notions. The latter are by default subjected to the disciplinary protocols of the university. Consequently, the critical epistemological potential of these notions remains foreclosed for inquiry.

It is precisely in such a destitute situation that one must take the risky task of initiating inquiries into the three nodes of vidya, kala and tattva (as specified earlier) along with the other much maligned node – jati. For, the latter is deeply braided with the other three nodes. In this three plus one formation, none of the nodes is hermetically sealed barring any inward or outward relays. Each node is a complex of infinite fibres forever articulating the possibility of drawing from and responding to intimations from other fibres across other nodes. The three-plus-one frame operates as a peculiar fractal, which in turn composes and diversifies each cluster of cultural formations and its cultural forms on the one hand and all the constellational clusters of clusters on the other. Thus, the micro-fractalic unit of the three-plus-one formation with its radical internal dynamic of *vivarta* (internal mutation) transfigures itself into a series of gigantic constellations of cultural forms and formations. Despite apparent similarities of the compositional units, it is impossible to homogenize the three-plus-one frame either within a cluster or across clusters and constellations. Like the internally self-differentiating biocultural formation of jati, each of the fractalic folds too is perennially open to the force of *vivarta*. The mutations of the Mahabharata, the Ramayana, the *Puranas* and the Panchatantra across the constellations would have been inconceivable without heterogeneous jatis receiving and transfiguring them through their singular heritages of verbal sonic-melodic forms and gestural performative visual patterns – their vidyas and kalas – across millennia.

Actional nodes

Whoever is inclined to reflect on the critical possibilities of Indian bhasha-reflective cultural forms will, perhaps, be more open to the three-plus-one frame sketched here. Wherever mnemocultural lively archives are in circulation, even in an orphaned context (as in our ailing educational institutions), there such critical humanities initiatives can be advanced. Such lively archives, as is well known, continue to circulate predominantly in rural areas, on the margins of small towns and even in the interstices of metropolitan cities. As pointed out earlier, even the classrooms of any metropolitan universities are surely composed by the inheritors of mnemocultures. Yet, they often denegate their biocultural inheritances. How to rekindle the mnemocultural element and resuscitate it from the very institutional context that tore apart the biocultural formations is the most demanding task in the context of the university in India today. This impossible-seeming task can be initiated by outlining the mnemocultural compositional form and suggesting minimally the possible ways of inquiring into it.

Although it is impossible to decisively identify and delimit the heterogeneity of mnemocultural forms or mnemotexts, one can point to certain patterned aspects of a mnemotext as composed of five crucial strands of (1) allusion, (2) citation, (3) numeration, (4) melopoeia and (5) reasoning imagination. Mnemotexts allude to each other, quote without reference, number their components situationally with precision and performatively bring forth the composition in metrical-melodic tones as enactments of the body. These compositional elements are woven with a reasoning imagination through figural thinking in actional contexts which connects the immemorial and the contemporary (synchronizing the diachrony and diachronizing the synchrony) in varied ways. The impulse that is at work in the compositional weave can be designated as a responsive reception. Each composition receives the (selective) elements from earlier manifestations in other weaves – and responds to them in a different weave. That is, each weave, like each rendering of a raga, transmutes the received or existing acoustic or visual motif and improvises on it in bringing forth another composition. As an effect of this, what appears to be a musical process, varied and new compositions come forth and the dynamic of responsive reception moves on without any terminus.

Now, in the university context, one can thematize, describe and analyze these elements and variations they undergo in specific compositions. This exercise can move on a comparative basis. Universities can easily accommodate this kind of exercise into their curricular and research agenda. Whatever the value of this approach, one must notice that (1) such an approach demarcates the composition from the method that sets out to unravel it as an object; (2) (whereas) the impulse of responsive reception does not categorically differentiate mnemocultural compositions from the analytic method of unravelling. In fact, the division between creative and critical in mnmeocultural compositions has little value. Every worthy response breathes variedly into what it receives – and brings forth a different composition from the preceding one. Programmed by the intellectual tradition that categorically divides what is called critical-analytical from the creative-productive – the university must prepare itself to face the challenge of mnemocultural responsive reception: how to respond to such a compositional dynamic? As this challenge does not appear local/regional (although it manifests in the local/regional singular nodes) but traverses across clusters of clusters of jatis and across constellations, the university must bring forth newer ways of receiving this dynamic.

To move beyond the intellectually destitute situation sketched earlier, it should be possible to open up the tasks of critical humanities initiatives indicated above. Critical humanities, while emerging from within the modern institutional sites and responding to the intellectual and material resources (mnemotechnological systems from scribal to digital) of these sites (of European heritage), foreground the jati cultural inheritances articulated in diverse media and open up lively archives for deeper creative and reflective engagement. Critical humanities initiatives can unfold in practically distributed series of scalable courses, programmes, researches for the rejuvenation of humanities teaching and research in/from India (and possibly beyond). All these initiatives draw on, bring forth and create extensive and inexhaustible forms of cultural inheritances – such as song, narrative ritual, performative, graphical, gestural and any other material articulation of the culturally marked bodies.

At a primal level, critical humanities affirm the idiomatic survival of humanities (biocultural communities) on the verge (critical). If we can suggest a working account of culture as what we do with our inherited resources and what we or others say about what we do with them, critical humanities initiatives underwrite the necessity of engaging with the extensive sets of 'representations' of cultures and cultural formations of these critical communities. This cluster would include discourses of anthropology, folklore, the state, non-governmental organizations, the indigenous on the one hand and the (social) mediatized representations in the forms of film, photographs, documentaries, TV productions and YouTube renderings – in a word, all the mediatized clusters of representation, on the other. In this regard, the critical humanities initiatives will be entirely theoretical and practical. Specific theoretical explorations into mnemocultures and concrete practical project works on cultural memories and inheritances can be developed.

Given the extraordinary magnitude of critical humanities' initiatives, no single or stand-alone department or university can materialize such activities: the point is to unravel and displace the disciplinary institutional structure implanted in colonial modernity. In this context, the activities suggested are all eminently scalable sets which can be undertaken in related ways across all the existing departments and disciplines. A single individual, department or university can initiate them in one's own location. But this adventure can also be effectively undertaken across the networked constellations identified earlier. The cultural constellations specified earlier are composed of multiple internally divided clusters of jatis and jan-jatis; as cultural formations, they traverse across geopolitical territories of modern nation-states. Now each of these territories or regions contains numerous (though limited) academic institutions. But the (millennial and colossal) cultural formations and modern institutional set ups have no symbiotic (or only a denegated) relationship; in fact, the latter were implants which disrupted the relation between cultures and communities. The critical humanities initiatives aim at suturing this rupture. This can be envisaged by networking the clusters of institutions located within the cultural constellational zone of a nation-state territory with the other constellationally grouped clusters located within the geopolitical territory. This centripetal dynamic would connect, say, the Gandhara constellation with the Sangam one or the Madhyadesha with the Brahmaputra one within India; the permutations and combinations of such dynamic will be unforeseeable. That is, the divergent constellations (with their internally varied clusters of clusters) within the single territory of India (with its jati–cultural–academic formations) will create incalculable possibilities.

Now the demanding task of critical humanities confronted with the measureless weaves and proliferations of cultural forms and formations might appear to be a humanly forbidding task. Yet one of the ways of possiblizing this apparently impossible task is, as suggested above, by affiliating institutions and biocultural clusters in constellationally demarcated cultural territories. Thus, one can envisage the possibility of, for example, affiliating the universities of the northeast (the Brahmaputra constellation) with the approximately 518 internally divided cultural formations (of which 263 are 'tribal' clusters). On an experimental basis, these new initiatives can be explored with the cluster of the ten central universities located within the northeast. Similarly, a mnemocultural map can be envisaged in the context of the Gandhara constellation by affiliating the 1,063 plus cultural formations (SC, ST, OBC and OC)[26] and the 16 central universities of the zone. And so on and so forth with other constellational zones (with Sangam 464 cultural formations and three Central universities; Dakshinapatha with 549 cultural formations and five central universities; Madhyadesha with 1,335 formations and six central universities and the Indus constellation with 290 formations and two central universities) can be envisaged.

A more daring move of critical humanities initiative will be to supplement the centripetal dynamic with a centrifugal force – a force which can be said to have formed the constellations we have identified in the first place. Thus, the Gandhara constellation (say, from India) will enable us to connect the centripetally formed cultural institutional clusters located in the national territorial boundaries of Pakistan, Afghanistan and Iran. Similarly, the Brahmaputra constellation can centrifugally lace together via Kham-Patha the cultural/institutional clusters of Myanmar, China, Nepal, Bhutan, Vietnam, Tibet and Laos and beyond. The Sangam constellation would extend itself to Sri

Lanka, Malaysia, Myanmar, Thailand, Indonesia and China. On the western side (of India), the Indus constellation would spread relays beyond the African coastline to the Mediterranean.

The range and reach of critical humanities initiatives can be sensed when we suggest, for example, the possibility of linking the cultural flows of Gandhara constellation alone. The biocultural formations of these regions can be connected through the networking of the institutions developed in the Gandhara area spreading from Uttar Pradesh and Bihar (in India) to Kabul and Herat (in Afghanistan) via Lahore and Quetta (in Pakistan) and beyond these to Iran to the west. Here one can envisage the possibility of connecting approximately 140 universities and 2,400 colleges in the Indian wing of Gandhara to the universities of Pakistan (148), Afghanistan (55) and Iran (250).

Needless to emphasize, in suggesting the possibility of connectivity of these modern academic institutions, one is in fact foreseeing the deeper possibility of bringing together the jan-jatis (tribes and communities) and cultures – an exchange that has shaped cultural formations of Asia (and other continents) over millennia. Similarly, one can see the possibility of filiating the Brahmaputra and Kham-Patha constellations by connecting the 40 and odd universities and 430+ colleges located in the territories of the northeast (from Assam to Manipur and Tripura to Arunachal Pradesh) with the 40 universities and 25 colleges of the northern and western regions of Myanmar (Kachin state, Sagiang Division and Chin and Mandalay divisions) and the 25+ universities located in the five regions of the south–west China (mostly the former Kham domains – but today's Chingquing, Sichuan, Yunnan, Guizhou, Quanzhou and Tibet areas.)

These extensive constellations with their internally spread-out clusters can further be centrifugally and centripetally linked (needless to say without a centre!). This can be achieved, for instance, by tracing the ways in which the Gandhara constellation (with the prominent Sanskrit cultural formations in it) has permeated across other constellations within the Indian subcontinent on the one hand; and how these Indian constellations relate to other Asiatic and other continental cultural formations (Australian, European etc.), on the other. Such an initiative will open up unforeseen comparative studies of thought and culture of these cultural constellations, beyond but along with the universalized European episteme.

The critical humanities initiatives work with the givens in a given context and as a task move beyond them. That is, these initiatives of mapping mnemocultures, aimed at resuscitating and reorienting the lively archives, experimenting with the three-plus-one nodes of cultural formations and accentuating centripetal communications beyond the geopolitical territorial cartographies centrifugally can be undertaken from within the existing university structures and also from outside of them. But the initiatives, if pursued as envisioned and, in the process, improvised upon, will expose the university to upheavals of radical cultural tectonic grinding. For the university has all along been a centralizing and unifying national geopolitical unit, whereas the cultural formations we are immersed in have lived on outside and beyond such formations for millennia; and more importantly, these non-European and pagan-Asian cultural formations have not felt the need for any philosophical nationalism until their encounter with the European violence. The critical humanities initiatives are after all aimed at reorienting teaching and research in the humanities from within the interstices of these colonially entrenched institutions of higher learning. But these initiatives are impelled by the impetus to configure transinstitutional and transcultural critical humanities from the Indian context. But such an experiment can be undertaken from any galactic node of the planet (say from Africa with its earliest dispersals).

Dispersed networks

The critical humanities passageways sketched here do not sound all that outlandish when we recall the fact that extraordinary cultural and economic routes were chiselled open on the Silk Route and Spice Route from pre-Christian epoch. It is these routes that took Buddhism and the *Panchatantra* (apart from silk, condiments, medicines, astrology, music and other cultural forms) across the planet. Cultural flows transgress territorial boundaries. Today, all the cultural constellations and territorial domains we referred to so far (and beyond them too) are subterraneanly laced together and terrestrially woven together already by digital fibres. Every region mentioned above is wired and surveyed by digital forces (mobiles, iPhones, marine cables, satellite beams).

Critical humanities focus mainly on the nodes that run through the extended sets or clusters of territorially regulated institutions. For these are the very places that are peopled by biocultural formations of our planet. The Indian subcontinent today possesses hundreds of thousands of such nodes (spread across thousands of institutions). The Indian state pours in billions of rupees annually to sustain and enhance these digital routes and claims to provide access to these routes to millions (cf. e.g., the MHRD's venture National Mission on Education through ICTs alone was allocated 4,612 crores in 2009. [MHRD Annual Report 2012: 120–121]). Yet the faculties of humanities have barely any presence in all these efforts in the country. (The NMEITC is mainly devoted to content development in science and engineering fields.) The fact that – irrespective of the field of study – all the 30 million students populating the institutions today come from distinct biocultural formations and half of them are enrolled precisely on the basis of affirming their cultural-biological basis does not seem to attract the much-needed attention to jan-jati formations of India. And such much needed attention can be provided only by critical faculties of the humanities.

A serious and vibrant humanities inquiry alone can provide the basis for a meaningful and just education in the country. Yet, as pointed out throughout here, such education even into the cultural forms and formations requires profound attention to and extensive innovation in the domains of communicational technologies. The initiatives of critical humanities repeatedly affirm the fundamental need to reflect on the relation between communicational technologies and cultural articulations (from oral to digital). Today, all the cultural inheritances of the varied constellations discussed earlier can be woven together only through the digital fibres that permeate our planet. Critical humanities initiatives such as (1) forging critical curricular frames for epistemic comparative inquiry, (2) the centripetal and centrifugal dissemination of the lively archives within and beyond clusters and constellations of their provenance, (3) 'representations' of biocultural formations, (4) the ways and modes of networking of extended clusters of institutions and a whole range of related issues throw up challenges for thought, imagination, design and resources.

The challenges pertain to the task of generation of varied forms of liveable learning (performative reflections), their organization, dissemination and innovative transformation on an unprecedented scale. The magnitude and the radically unstructured nature of the tasks involved can be comprehended with a digital vision even as the embodied mnemocultural formations live on. One would require extended institutional and individual collaborative support of mnemotechnological resources for materializing such a project. For, no single institution can master and control such a gigantic project of projects. The impulse of the lively archives which permeates all the clusters and constellations makes the project interminable and inexhaustible.

Setting to work

The (transnational and trans-institutional) critical humanities initiatives outlined here from the context of India (but which far exceed

India), inexhaustible but manageable, can be productively launched through and extended collaborative work at two levels: (1) academic/research level and (2) policy level.

The Academic/Research team is required first to conduct a series of workshops on the thematics of critical humanities for drawing up a map for navigation of action. The action plan must be extensively discussed with other set of stakeholders – the policy makers from various ministries. Such an action plan moves with the basic navigational roots/routes of clusters and constellations. Within these sets of units, specific institutional sites can be identified for coordinating the set's work. But this can begin to happen only after a certain (ICT) infrastructure is put in place. The infrastructural issues are deeply related to the extraordinary quanta of diverse (Image, Music, Text and Performance) forms and levels to be interlaced. The infrastructural issues will be discussed by specific members of the two task forces. The action plan must aim at critical nodes in clusters and constellations becoming operational by the third year out of a five-year plan. The critical nodes must be chosen from rural based minority/tribal institutional clusters and local jan-jati formations.

The critical humanities initiatives aim at reconfiguring the humanities in crisis and reorienting teaching and research from the receiving ends of cultures that faced colonialism. If jati and jan-jati cultural complexes are the enduring source of creativity and reflection in the Indian subcontinent (and beyond) over millennia, the field of humanities must strive to learn to explore the singularity of this relationship and affirm a priori their (jan-jatis and their cultures) inheritances without alibi. Only then the humanities from the receiving ends will be able to continue and move beyond their European legacy. It is only through tracing such jati-jan-jati nodes across clusters and constellations of cultures that one can envisage the possibility of a transnational critical humanities teaching and research in the years to come. Hence the credo of critical humanities: *what do you do with what you have!?*

Notes

1 Indian Institute of Technology (IIT), National Institute of Technology (NIT), International Institute of Information Technology (IIIT) are the leading ICT institutions in the country.
2 In contrast, according to Chinese Ministry of Education, higher education recruitments were estimated to reach 30 million by 2010 (Kirby 2013). However, the draft report on New Education Policy submitted in April 2016 indicates that there are 711 universities, 40,760 colleges and 11,922 stand-alone institutions in higher-education sector in India

in 2015. NEP figure for student enrolment in 2015 is 30.3 million (NEP 2016: 30).
3 Ministry of Human Resource Development (MHRD), Ministry of Social Justice and Empowerment, Ministry of Tribal Affairs, Ministry of Minority Affairs. Cf., www.socialjustice.nic.in/sclist.php, http://ncbc.nic.in/Centrallistifobc.html for lists of jatis; and jan-jatis, cf., the Annual Report of the Ministry of Tribal Affairs at www.tribal.nic.in/WriteReadData/CMS/Documents/201305090204592676637Annualreport.pdf, pp. 55–68 (accessed on 22 July 2013.)
4 *Jatyaanantyam tu sampraptam tadvaktum naivashakyate* (jatis come forth endlessly (infinitely) and no one can recount or name them) (*Sukraneetisaramu* 2002: 4:3:11, 284).
5 *Vidyahyanantaschakalah sankhyatum naiva shakyate* (Recitational learning and gestural and handiworks are infinite and counting or reckoning them is impossible) (Ibid. 4:3:23, 236).
6 This project (spread from 2001–2004) was funded by NEH (National Endowment for the Humanities) and NSF (National Science Foundation) – US federal funding agencies for the advancement of knowledge in the fields of the humanities and the sciences http://www.columbia.edu/itc/mealac/pollock/sks.
7 This project integrates its archival initiative with the ongoing projects of the Heidelberg and Columbia (Sanskrit Knowledge Systems) https://www.neh.gov/search/content/SARIT.
8 On the relationship between memory and mnemotechniques in European cultural and intellectual history cf. Stiegler (2010: 64–87). Curiously memory's relationship to embodied communicational forms of speech and gesture barely receives any critical attention in Stiegler.
9 http://socialjustice.nic.in/pdf/anne9tri.pdf as accessed on 22 December 2013.
10 Among many other works for a more recent set of accounts, cf., Jan E. M. Houben (2012).
11 The Gandhara Constellation includes the states of Punjab, Haryana, Delhi, Himachal Pradesh, Jammu and Kashmir, Uttarakhand, Uttar Pradesh, Bihar and West Bengal. Its relays go beyond Indian territory and spread across Pakistan (Lahore, Punjab, Islamabad, Quetta, Peshawar), Afghanistan (Kandahar, Kabul, Heart) and Nepal.
12 The Brahmaputra Constellation includes the states of Arunachal, Assam, Meghalaya, Sikkim, Nagaland, Tripura, Manipur, Mizoram and extends across Myanmar, Bhutan, Bangladesh and Tibet.
13 The Indus Constellation includes the states of Rajasthan and Gujarat and extends to Pakistan, Oman, Yemen and beyond them to, Persia (Iran) and Mesopotamia (Iraq).
14 The Kham-Patha Constellation is actually composed of the region south of China, north of Myanmar and east of Tibet. This provided the crucial passageway for migrations into the Brahmaputra valley.
15 The Madhyadesha Constellation includes the states of Maharashtra, Jharkhand, Madhya Pradesh, Odisha, Chattisgarh, Goa, Daman, Dieu and relays into Sri Lanka.
16 The Dakshinapatha Constellation includes the states of Andhra, Telangana, Karnataka and its relays expanded up to Africa and Rome.

17 The Sangam Constellation includes the states of Tamil Nadu and Kerala and extends up to Sri Lanka, Thailand, Cambodia, Indonesia, Laos, Malaysia, West Asia, the Arabian Gulf and the Mediterranean.
18 Cf., Ministry of Tribal Affairs, www.tribal.nic.in/WriteReadData/ CMS/ Documents/201305090204592676637Annualreport, pp. 55–68, (as accessed on 22 July 2013).
19 It may, however, be noted that the use of Sanskrit-based terminology here may give the impression that one is silently erasing the heterogeneity of the Brahmaputra Constellation. The Tibeto-Burman/Sino-Burman cultural formations (Naga, Mizo, Meetei, Adi, Bhutia and many others) are *not* reducible to the Indo-European formations. Although well intentioned, such is the approach of Verrier Elwin in his work on NEFA: he routinely draws parallels between Sanskrit and NEFA myths. He also makes a curious and rather confused defence of the Baptist missionaries who banned the converted from participating in native cultural ceremonies. Elwin thinks that the Baptists were only rejecting the native cultural practices (which the Baptists thought were evil and wished to eradicate), but not their religion. Elwin does not inquire into whether these practices and customs can be said to constitute a 'religion' at all; although, he, by default as it were, approximates them to Christianity (he thought their stories contained 'Biblical dignity'). But he tries to extract 'NEFA religion' and chalk out 'religious aims' of NEFA from the very cultural ceremonies and customs which he wished to differentiate in his defence of the Baptists; he also recommends that the ritual dances of the tribals 'should not [be] introduce[d] . . . into educational curriculum'. Further, he goes on to compare the NEFA myths with the tribal myths of what we called the Madhyadesha Constellation (Elwin 1957: 78–88; the phrase 'Biblical dignity' appears in Elwin 1999: 7).

The arguments about mnemoculture that are being developed here are neither derivative of nor reducible to only Sanskrit cultural formation. Sanskrit cultural forms provide just one eloquent instance of the mnemocultural complex. The planet that we inhabit is replete with (discarded and marginalized) mnemocultures still living on across all the continents. (In the African context, for instance, one can at random mention the Gikandi performative exchanges, the Ozidi epics, the Gikuyu Rwimbo (song, dance and ritual ceremonies) and Kirira (oral and written compositions), the Maasai and the Gambian dances; and a whole range of mnemocultures affirm the intimate relations between the multiple 'tribes' (jan-jatis or cultural formations) and their cultural forms even to this day. Ngugi's whole theory of orature is drawn precisely on these lively resources (Ngugi 2012). One could, therefore, continue one's inquiry in the context of Meeteis, for example, drawing on the cultural categories of Salai (numbering seven) and Sagei (numbering over 400) to designate clusters of cultural formations. Similarly, in the Mizo context, we come across Hnams ('tribes' numbering 11) Hnam hming ('sub-tribes' numbering 60) and Chungkaw hming ('clans' numbering over 1,000) forming Mizo cultural formations. Among the Khasis, such clusters can be seen emerging from Shnongs (village level), Raids (group of villages) and Himas (conglomeration of Raids). These clusters form both cultural and administrative structures of the Khasis (and also Jaintiyas). One can enumerate similar clusters among the

Nagas (60 divergent 'communities'), Arunachali and other cultural formations. The hypothesis advanced here is that these clusters can be explored as mnemocultural formations. The Sanskrit words (jati, jan-jati, *vidya* etc.) are not deployed merely as linguistic units; they are drawn mainly to formulate and examine the mnemocultural hypothesis and inquire into the relationship between cultural forms and cultural formations by focusing on communication technologies (oral to digital). What is contended here is that the mnemocultural hypothesis can be explored across different cultural formations by drawing on the resources that the divergent clusters and their cultural forms provide. (I wish to thank Kishan Thingbaijam and Lalmin Sangi Pachauau for discussing the Meetei and Mizo cultural formations and forms with me. They are in the process of developing more comprehensive works on these mnemocultural formations.)

20 This number is suggested by the Indira Gandhi National Centre for the Arts; whereas the National Mission for Manuscripts suggests about 5 million manuscripts as the extant Indian scribal collection (Krishnan 2006: ix; Pollock 2007: 87). David Pingree is said to have observed that the worldwide spread of Sanskrit manuscripts runs into 30 million (Wujastyk 2009).

21 A Sanskrit composition cited earlier, *Sukraneetisaramu*, for instance, hazards the 'definition' and enumeration of genres under the categories of vidya and kala. In a rather unusual definitional move, the *Sukraneetisaramu* pronounces the mnemocultural significance of vidya and kala with simplicity and clarity. It must be noted that this definition and enumeration of Vidya(s) and Kala(s) take place here in a section that begins with the drift and proliferation of generations (jatis), where vidyas, kalas and jatis are said to be infinite (*Sukraneetisaramu* 2002: 236):

> *Yadyatsvadvaachikam samyakkarma vidyabhisanjnakam*
> *Shakto mookopi yatkartum kalasanjnam tatsmrutam*

> (Anything that is properly, efficiently organized/composed by Vak ['speech'] goes under the name of Vidya. That which even the speechless ['dumb'] can perform without the use of the mouth goes under the name of Kala.)

22 Two seminal and related compositions on the significance of vidya and kala can be instanced here to suggest the magnitude of creative reflective reckoning of the domains. There is nothing in the world, declares Bharata in his *Natyasastra* (c. 3 CE) while composing his response to what all he had received from the past, that the embodied and performative articulations of dance cannot show (Bharata 2014: 79):

> *Na tad jnanam na tad chilpam na sa vidya na sa kala /*
> *Nasau yogo na tat karma natye 'smin yan na drushyate //*

> (No knowledge, craft, wisdom, art, yoga, ritual-act exists which cannot be shown in the dance-drama/theatre. [Textual allusions and traces recede into intractable past.])

A few centuries after Bharata the poet-thinker Bhamaha transformatively receives Bharata and suggests the burden of the poetic composition (vidya) as follows (Bhamaha 2004: 106):

*Na sa sabdo na tadvachyam na sa nyayo na sa kala
jayate yanna kavyajna maha bharo mahan kaveh*

(There is no sound, no meaning, no law, and no art that has not been made into poetry. What a burden the poet has to carry!)

Similarly, drawing on the *sastra-vangmaya* (vidya), one of the inaugural compositions (of the 6 century CE) on the plastic visual forms, the *Citra Sutra*, begins with the most fundamental aporetic question: what is the relation between para, the universe (the domain composed and accessed by the complex of the *bhuta*s – the phenomenal-perceptual resources) and the (visual) 'arts' (kala)?

*Rupagandha rasairhina sabdah sparaa vivarjitaha
Purusastu tvaya proktas tasyarupam idam katham*

(How can one give form to *para [here named purusha]* which is said to be devoid of form, smell, taste, and who is said to lack sound and touch?)
                (*Chitrasutra* in *Sri Visnudharmottara
                          Purana* 1988: 153.)

23 K. C. Bhattacharya observed this several decades ago:

Our education has largely been imparted to us through English literature. The Indian mind is much further removed by tradition and history than the French or the German mind from the spirit of English literature, and yet no Indian, so far as I am aware, has passed judgments on English literature that reflects his Indian mentality . . . how many of us have had distinctively Indian estimates of western literature and thought?
                (Bhattacharya 1984: 386; the sentences in the
                quotation have been slightly rearranged)

24 National cultural institutions like IGNCA and Sahitya Akademi have been carrying on such tasks. The huge amounts expended from meagre budgets to organize conferences and workshops and research activities in such organizations remain largely stand-alone acts – more as precious exhibits in the profiles of the organizations (e.g.: the two conferences of Sahitya Akademi on the *Ramayana*, the *Mahabharata* and the two conferences of the IGNCA on the *Mahabharata*; the latter's extended work on orginary texts of kala and the multivolume lexicons on kala, and its Janapada Sampada and many such activities; similarly, as mentioned earlier, the various folklore studies departments and the 18 tribal research institutions of the country continue such work).

25 'The theologians and everything that has theologian blood in its veins: our whole philosophy,' says Nancy, quoting Nietzsche. Nancy's work here is a fundamental attempt to return to Christianity as the essential source of European thought: 'We know that our tradition is Christian, that our source is Christian. Yet . . . at bottom it is never confronted head on' (Nancy 2008: 139). But curiously his own confrontation (like that of Derrida) seems to take place firmly from within the onto-theological inheritance. Derrida's persistent practice has been, articulated especially in the context of his discussions on the university, is to acknowledge and move beyond the 'heritage of a barely secularized theology', of the West (Derrida 2002: 207). Derrida, however, works entirely from within these traditions to question and move beyond the spurious binary (believed to be an oppositional binary – between faith and knowledge), inaugurated during the Enlightenment. As is well known, the conceptual twin 'faith' and 'knowledge' is fundamentally theological and inherent to the Abrahamic traditions, and it is not a cultural universal (Derrida 1998, 2002). For a powerful unravelling of this intellectual heritage from outside the fold of Abrahamic traditions, see Balagangadhara (1994).
26 These are the categories through which the state classifies (and thus denegates) the extended *jati* formations in the Constitution of India. SC stands for Scheduled Castes, ST for Scheduled Tribes, the OBC for other Backward Castes and the OC for Other ('forward') Castes.

References

Balagangadhara, S. N. 1994. *'The Heathen in his Blindness. . .': Asia, the West and the Dynamic of Religion.* Leiden: E.J. Brill.

———. 2012. *Reconceptualizing India Studies.* New Delhi: Oxford University Press.

Bhamaha. *Kavyalankarah.* [1979]. 2004. Trans. Pullela Sriramachandrudu. Hyderabad: Sanskruta Bhasha Prachara Samiti.

Bharata. 2014. *Natyasastram.* Trans. Pullela Sriramachandrudu. Hyderabad: P. S. Sastry.

Bhattacharya, K.C. [1928]. 1984. 'Svaraj in Ideas', *Indian Philosophical Quarterly*, XI (4) (October–December): 383–393.

The Court Chronicle of the Kings of Manipur: The Cheitharon Kumpapa. 2005. Trans. Saroj Nalini Arambam Parratt. London: Routledge.

Derrida, Jacques. [1998]. 2002. 'Faith and Knowledge: The Two Sources of "Religion" at the Limits of Reason Alone', in Gil Anidjar (ed.), *Acts of Religion*, pp. 42–101. Trans. Samuel Weber. New York: Routledge.

———. 2002. 'The University Without Condition', in *Without Alibi*, Trans. Peggy Kamuf, (ed.). Stanford: Stanford University Press.

———. 2004a. 'Choosing One's Heritage', in Jacques Derrida and Elisabeth Roudinesco (eds.), *For What Tomorrow . . . : A Dialogue.* Trans. Jeff Fort. Stanford: Stanford University Press.

———. 2004b. *Eyes of the University: Right to Philosophy 2.* Trans. Jan Plug and others. Stanford: Stanford University Press.

Elwin, Verrier. [1958]. 1999. *Myths of the North-East Frontier of India*. New Delhi: Munshiram Manoharlal.
———. 2009. *A Philosophy for NEFA*. 1957. New Delhi: Isha Books.
Farmer, Steve, Richard Sproat, and Michael Witzel. 2004. 'The collapse of the Indus-script thesis: The myth of a literate Harappan civilization'. *EJVS*, 11 (2): 19–57.
Houben, Jan E. M. (ed.) [1996]. 2012. *Ideology and Status of Sanskrit: Contributions to the History of the Sanskrit Language*. New Delhi: Motilal Banarsidass.
Kirby, William C. 2008. 'On Chinese, European & American Universities', *Daedalus*, 137 (3): 139–146 (accessed from ProQuest website on 15th July 2013).
Krishnan, Sudha Gopala. 2006. 'Introduction', in Sudha Gopalakrishnan (ed.), *Tattvabodha*, Vol. 1. New Delhi: National Mission for Manuscripts and Munshiram Manoharlal Publishers.
Ministry of Human Resource Development. Annual Report. 2011–2012, MHRD website (accessed on 22nd July 2013).
Ministry of Social Justice. 2013. Ministry's website (accessed on 22nd July 2013).
Ministry of Tribal Affairs. 2013. Ministry's website (accessed on 22nd July 2013).
Nancy, Jean-Luc. 2008. *Dis-Enclosure: The Deconstruction of Christianity*. Trans. Bettina Bergo, Gabriel Malenfant, and Michael B. Smith. New York: Fordham University Press.
National Endowment for the Humanities. NEH website (accessed on 19th June 2013).
New Education Policy (Draft). 2016. NUEPA website (accessed on 25th June 2016).
Padmanabh, Samarendra. 2011. 'Census in Colonial India and the Birth of Caste'. *Economic and Political Weekly*, 46 (33): 51–58.
Pollock, Sheldon. 2007. 'Literary Culture and Manuscript Culture in Precolonial India', in Simon Eliot, Andrew Nash, and Ian Willson (eds.), *Literary Cultures and the Material Book*, pp. 77–94. London: The British Library. Columbia University website (accessed on 23rd May 2013).
Sri Vishnudharmottara Purana. 1988. Trans. K. V. S. Deekshitulu, D. S. Rao, and P. Seetaramanjaneyulu. (ed.) 3 Khandas (parts). Hyderabad: Sri Venkateshwara Arshabharati Trust.
Stiegler, Bernard. 2010. 'Memory', in W. J. T. Mitchell and Mark Hansen (eds.), *Critical Terms for Media Studies*. Chicago: University of Chicago Press.
Sukraneetisaramu, Trans. 2002. Kandlakunta Alaha Singaracharyulu. Nalgonda: Sahiti Sanmana Samithi.
The University Grants Commission. 2012. Annual Report. UGC website (accessed on July 2013).
Wa Thiongo, Ngugi. 2012. 'The Oral Native and the Writing Master: Orature, Orality, and Cyborality', in *Globalectics: Theory and the Politics of Knowing*. New York: Columbia University Press.
Wujastyk, Dominic. 2009. A mail to Indology listserv. INDOLOGY@liverpool.ac.uk on LISTSERV.LIV.AC.UK (accessed on 19th March 2009).

9

INDIAN CULTURE AND ITS SOCIAL SECURITY SYSTEM

S. N. Balagangadhara

One of the most striking things about the global economic meltdown in the 21st century is that it is a crisis generated primarily by managers and CEOs from the banking and financial sectors. Whatever might be the economic 'logic' behind the problems surrounding mortgages, sub-primes and derivatives, one of the psychological premises that functioned as a 'rationality assumption' of free-markets is no longer tenable. It was the following: no CEO would ride his firm to its death; doing so would kill the goose that lays golden eggs.

Today, we can see that this is not a 'rationality' assumption, but a claim about human psychology. After all, if the CEO can arrange his contract in such a way that he receives a huge bonus for every profitable quarter, then neither the enduring health nor the continued existence of the firm is of any concern to him. Indeed, he is indifferent to whether the goose that lays the golden eggs survives or not, if he can lay claim to a few of those eggs. He is driven by a focus on his share of the golden eggs; such a motive is called 'excessive greed' today. Many politicians, correspondingly, call for a cap on executive compensations. Even those who resist any such move do agree that 'greed' played a very important role in precipitating the crisis. The difference between these two camps is merely about restraining this greed. They agree that it played a significant role in the behaviour of the CEOs.

We need to reflect about this extraordinary consensus between the two competing parties. Both the free market proponents and those who call for massive state interventions in the economy share the same set of anthropological assumptions. By nature, human beings are greedy. The current discussion is merely about how to restrain the excess. Of course, the CEOs were greedy and acted greedily: this is indeed the 'phenomenon', or how the situation appears to our eyes.

But appearance is not always the truth: the sun appears to move around the Earth, but this is not the truth about our solar system. Therefore, the question is: in acting greedily, did the CEOs express a typical human behaviour? The answer to this question depends on how we understand human beings.

It is my suggestion that the anthropology which undergirds our economic and management theories, for example, is Christian in origin. Our deeply held intuitions that guide thinking about economics and management are not the results of scientific reflections about the nature of human beings. Instead, they have emerged due to *the kind of marriage* that has taken place between the religion that Christianity is and most of our theories in the domains of economics and management.

In this chapter, I want to explore two anthropologies. For the sake of convenience, call one 'a Western, Christian approach', and the other 'an Indian, heathen approach'. (Hopefully, it will become clear during this chapter, why this distinction is not merely a 'convenient' one.) The first approach is familiar; the second is not so. I will try to conceptualize the difference between these two ways in terms of how they explain what we see: *our limitless desires, our greed, our needs and our wants.* To complete the task in the space I have, I will drastically simplify my theses. I cannot do what intellectuals love: add nuances, subtleties and qualifications. I will merely paint a rough contrasting picture. I hope the reader will forgive me this trespass.

I

One theory we can use to understand the facts about our limitless desires, greed, needs and wants is a variant of 'humanistic psychology'. Abraham Maslow's formulations are the best known and they have been refined in many ways since then. His basic thesis goes something like this: human beings have different kinds of needs ranging from the biological to the spiritual. His suggestion was that these different kinds of needs form a hierarchy: a pyramid, so to speak. Our needs for food, water, clothing and shelter form the base of the pyramid. Once these physiological needs are satisfied, other next-in-line needs emerge: these are safety needs like the need for security, whether it is security of employment or security of revenues and resources. After these are satisfied, there emerge one set of psychological needs: the belonging and love needs involve emotionally based relationships in general, such as friendship, sexual intimacy, and/or having a family. The subsequent set is also psychological: the esteem needs like the need to be respected, to self-respect and to respect others. All these are deficiency needs: once met and satisfied, they get neutralized; they cease to motivate us any further. Then there is the need at the apex of the pyramid that continually motivates us and cannot be neutralized: the need for self-actualization (Maslow 1943).

There are some reasons why I begin with Maslow's idea. First, it is well-known in many intellectual circles because it helps one develop some or another psychological theory about human motivation. Second, it appears 'secular' in the sense that we observe no evident religious assumptions. Third, its language generates with some clarity the goal of social work, social welfare programmes and social security systems: these should aim at satisfying basic human needs. Fourth, theories about 'social justice' require such a language to get off the ground. Fifth, this idea has a *venerable ancestry*. Sixth, its heraldry stretches not only backwards in time but also horizontally across continents today.

Maslow's proposal has been scrutinized closely and nonchalantly ignored in psychology more than in any other domain. It has been reformulated, criticized, tacitly accepted by theories (that speak about 'drives' instead of 'needs', for example), benignly neglected while working within its framework and so on. People working in other areas of human enquiry, whether in philosophy or on management theories, function within the limits set by this language of needs, even where they are ignorant of Maslow's formulation. Perhaps, a very rough outline of the issue suffices for our purposes.

The 'needs' that Maslow talks about are very fundamental: they are constitutive elements of the human makeup. As human beings, we are creatures of 'need'; we are 'suffering beings', as many have called us, because we are 'needy' creatures. We tend to miss out on the precise nature of 'needs', if we merely focus on requirements like food, shelter and clothing, and ignore the other 'needs' that Maslow talks about: security, love, recognition and so on. The latter alert us to the fact that the aforementioned requirements are present in us as 'needs', which makes human beings into 'needy' creatures. The availability of oxygen is a requirement for fire to catch hold, but fire does not have that 'need'. However, the human requirement of food is present as a 'need'. It is in this sense that 'need' is constitutive of human beings.

If we look at multiple human pasts, we notice the wide presence of many other things as well: violence, war, hate, greed and so on. 'Love' and 'hate' vie with each other for prominence; 'esteem' and 'denial' are as frequent as 'security' and 'strife'. Does their ubiquity indicate that 'hate', 'violence' and 'greed' are also expressions of human needs, much the way their counterparts are? If not, why not? Is there an intrinsic conflict between needs, or are we to assume that intrinsic needs do not and cannot possibly ever be in conflict?

There are two known routes of answering these questions. The first builds a picture of human beings as creatures with conflicting 'needs'. The second relegates 'hate', 'violence' etc. to the 'outside' of human beings, namely, to the environment. Love is an 'intrinsic' need of human beings, whereas hate is 'extrinsic': child abuse, peer groups, ideology, society etc. are responsible for its growth, emergence and manifestation. Thus, the existence of conflicting needs indicates that 'natural' needs are in conflict with 'artificially induced' needs or that there is a conflict between the individual and his or her environment, which is man-made. This 'nature' versus 'nurture' debate is far from being settled, and there are no indications suggesting an early truce.

Far more interesting than this debate is the origin of the notion of 'needs'. When and how did this picture of human beings emerge? The important fragment in the answer is this: *the human being as a 'needy' creature is a millennia old idea and is not the result of any kind of scientific research.* As I shall soon show, there is also an equally old alternative picture that fares at least as well in understanding human beings.

II

The Oxford English Dictionary (OED) notices multiple uses of the word 'need' in English. Of relevance to us are two such. If used as a verb with an object, the OED defines it thus: 'require (something) because it is essential or very important rather than just desirable (used as a verb with an object [ex: "I need some help right now"])'. In such cases, one could make do with the synonym *'require'*. When used as a noun, however, the word means the following: 'Circumstances in which something is necessary; necessity (ex: "the basic human need for food") or as 'the state of requiring help, or of lacking basic necessities such as food ("help us in our hour of need"; "children in need")'.

In the English translations of the Bible (both the Old and the New Testament), 'need' is used often in its noun form. Consider, for instance, the following verses:

> 'For there will never cease to be poor in the land. Therefore I command you, "You shall open wide your hand to your brother, *to the needy and to the poor*, in your land"' (Deuteronomy 15:11[ESV], my italics).

'Not that I am speaking of *being in need*, for I have learned in whatever situation I am to be content' (Philippians 4:11[ESV], my italics).

'I know how to be brought low, and I know how to abound. In any and every circumstance, I have learned the secret of facing plenty and hunger, *abundance and need*' (Philippians 4:12[ESV], my italics).

'Let us then with confidence draw near to the throne of grace, that we may receive mercy and find grace to help *in time of need*' (Hebrews 4:16[ESV], my italics).

'But if anyone has the world's goods and sees his brother *in need*, yet closes his heart against him, how does God's love abide in him' (1 John 3:17[ESV], my italics).

'Do not hold against us the sins of past generations; may your mercy come quickly to meet us, for we are *in desperate need*' (Psalm 79:8 [NIV], my italics).

'Need' translates *chreia* from Greek, which is the language of the *Septuagint*. In the New Testament, it occurs 47 times. (See further: Matthew 3:14, 6:8, 9:12, 14:16, 21:3, 26:65, Mark 2:17, 25, 11:3, 14:63; Luke 5:31, 9:11, 10:42, 15:7, 19:31, 34, 22:71, John 2:25, 13:10, 29, 16:30, Acts 2:45, 4:35, 20:34, 28:10, Romans 12:13, 1 Corinthians 12:21, 24, Ephesians 4:28, Philippians 2:25, **4:16**, 19, 1 Thessalonians 1:8, 4:9, 12, 5:1, Titus 3:14, Hebrews 5:12, 7:11, 10:36, 1 John 2:27, Revelation **3:17**, 21:23, 22:5.) Except in the passages highlighted in bold, the sense in which the word is used tracks echochreian, which can be translated as 'having the need'.

Similar words are also to be found in Aramaic: *chashach* (a primitive root from which both *chashchah* as 'things needed', and *chashchu*, as 'requirement', are derived), for instance. In Hebrew, the word *machsor* does the job 'need' does in English.

If someone has a need or is in need, such a person is 'needy'. He is needy in the sense that he is a creature of needs or that needs are intrinsic to such a being. With this in mind, if we look at English translations of the Bible (I will restrict myself to the English Standard Version), we discover that the word 'needy' occurs 54 times in 53 verses. In the Old Testament, it occurs 50 times in 49 verses, whereas in the New Testament it occurs four times in four verses. The latter is no cause for concern because this translation prefers speaking of 'having the need' in the New Testament rather than use the word 'needy'.

It is important to note that the Bible makes a distinction between 'being poor' and being 'needy'. For example:

> 'Therefore I command you, "You shall open wide your hand to your brother, to *the needy and to the poor*, in your land."' (Deuteronomy 15:11[ESV], my italics)
> 'You shall not oppress a hired worker who is *poor and needy*.' (Deuteronomy 24:14[ESV], my italics)

In other words, *one could be poor but not needy, and one could be needy but not poor.*

I shall simply note in passing here that all European languages, including Latin, have their semantic equivalents for 'need', used as a noun, and thus allow us to speak in terms of 'to be in need', 'needy' and such like.

Abraham Maslow's proposal traces this biblical language of needs. In fact, any and every speech that makes use of the language of 'needs' tracks *this biblical notion of needs*, irrespective of whether the person who speaks thus is aware or ignorant of the Bible. That is the case because this biblical picture of human beings has so completely penetrated European languages and thinking that it has ended up becoming a factual assumption while talking about human beings even in the 21st century.

Speaking about conflicting needs in the previous section, I suggested that one option locates the conflict in the nature of human beings. The strife, violence, etc. that we notice in human societies would then be intrinsic to us. Conflict is written into society because it is constitutive of human nature. Whether these 'conflicts' too express a human 'need' or not has remained an unsettled issue so far. As an illustration, consider the story about the 'excessive greed' of the CEOs. Many believe that although greed is a part of human nature, the economic crisis of 2008 has to be rooted not in human greed but in its 'excess'. However, if greed is a part of human nature, 'greediness' expresses a human need the way 'being hungry' expresses hunger. In that case, there could be no 'excessive' greed any more than there could be 'excessive' hunger. (Gluttony is not excessive hunger; going beyond hunger is required for eating to become gluttony. Greed, by contrast, is already a going 'beyond'.) Many people also think in this fashion: because it is impossible to say when greed is excessive and when it is not, the real problem is about its existence in human beings. Further, because greed is an 'undesirable' part of human nature, human nature is internally in conflict. The distance between the Gospel and economics is now a vanishing point.

In any case, the belief about human needs is not a mere factual assumption alone. In the Bible, it imposes a very deep ethical obligation as well. Modern-day thinkers, whether theist or atheist, hold this stance in the 21st century. What has varied a bit, in its unbroken trajectory over the millennia, is the way this idea is discussed, debated and justified today.

In the Bible, as the cited passages show, God imposes the obligation of responding to 'needy' human beings. Our notions of 'obligation' (whether moral or legal in nature) are its secular translations: *there is no notion of 'obligation' available to us today that does not trace the conceptual structure of the biblical 'obligation'*. Because the obligation that God imposed to respond to the 'needy' *is* the conceptual structure behind all ideas about ethical or legal obligation, responding to the 'needs' of our brethren becomes an unquestionable and inviolable obligation. Consequently, the same difficulties that confront the believer also confront us when we violate obligations.

Some of these difficulties are internal to the notion: *who ought to respond to the 'needy'*? If only those capable of such responses are obliged to do so, who are the capable? Is it an obligation on all of us or only some of us? Old issues are endlessly rehashed as answers to these questions: (a) 'faith organizations' (the Church, for instance) ought to do this; (b) charitable organizations (non-governmental organizations [NGOs], for instance) ought to do this; (c) the State ought to do this; (d) the rich ought to do this; etc. Thus, the nature of these 'needs' leads to interminable debates, also resulting in a proliferation of institutions. After all, which 'needs' are artificial, socially induced and extrinsic, and which are natural, basic and intrinsic? Is setting up psychological shelters and social rest-houses a necessary fulfilment of human 'needs' or not? Is guaranteeing the 'health' of fellow human beings an obligation to help the 'needy' and, if yes, who ought to fulfil it and who pays the bill? When simplified in this fashion, we see the contours and rationale of what is called 'the social security system' in the West. The varieties in such a system (including its diversities and controversies) emerge *only* from a picture that makes 'needs' into constitutive elements of human beings. Such a picture is biblical through and through.

III

In this light, consider the social security systems in Western culture. What should be their goal or finality? All that a social security system does (in fact, this is the only thing it can do) is to take care of some of the 'basic needs' of an individual. These needs, in so far as they are considered biological in nature, can only be defined in terms of material goods. This system leaves it to an individual to decide what goals he or she pursues in life or even whether he or she pursues any goals at all. It is interested only in enabling the biological survival of an individual by providing for basic amenities, even though it is a matter of contention what these are and who should meet them. Food, clothing and shelter might qualify. Does medicine join this list or not?

The disagreements and debates go further. Consider the notion of 'obligation' involved in a sentence that speaks of an obligation that X has towards Y. It is the case that 'obligation' can be defined in terms of 'entitlements' or 'rights'. The sentence that Y is entitled to or has the right to X's performance can translate the statement about the obligation that X has towards Y. Because of this, the question can also be posed in terms of 'entitlements' or 'rights', whether legal or moral, of the beneficiary. The obligation that one human being has towards another *is* the right that the other can demand or claim. Of course, this makes perfect logical and linguistic sense within a framework where God imposes obligations. Because no human being ought to violate God's commandment, each can (should, ought to) demand from the other that he or she obeys God. As a human being, it is one's entitlement or right that the other obeys God.

Consider further that this 'obligation' is also called by another name: *charity*. Thus, the 'dole' that people receive from the State (the 'unemployment dole', for instance) is such an act. The act of 'giving to the needy' is 'charity'. Here, it picks out the giver and the act of giving in terms of a human ethical property: *generosity*. One does not become immoral because one is not generous, even if one is immoral because one is greedy or a penny pincher. In the recipient, charity mostly generates a sense of diminished self-worth. Consequently, in the name of human dignity, one could put very stringent requirements on 'dole', including a reduction in the time span.

Both positions on the nature of obligation are perfectly defensible, even if they conflict, as is often the case. The endless controversies regarding the social security system merely express the extent to which they share the same bed. In any case, such a system, in its neutral and most 'objective' form, can only look at human beings as biological organisms. Thus, it treats human beings as animals in a human form; no more, no less.

Only the State can take such a stance and assume such an obligation. Not only because it has the taxed resources of the community at its disposal, but also because the State is the only organization in society capable of treating human beings as *animal rationale*. It can use dossiers, files, numbers and so on to do so. That is, only the State (through its arms like the police, prison, bureaucracy etc.) can treat human beings as no more than biological organisms. No civil organization, whether a club, an association, an interest-group or a lobby, can treat people as items or objects. Therefore, it falls to the State to set up a social security system that treats human beings as receptacles of material goods.

How is this social security system financed? Quite obviously, it can only be supported by the resources available to the State, and these depend on economic conjunctures. If there is continuous and sustained economic growth, it is possible to sustain the social security system. In periods of wealth creation, sustaining a social safety net is not impossible. However, such a safety net is superfluous, except for a tiny minority, during periods of economic prosperity. In other words, the safety net functions when a minority depends on it, whether for unemployment or for pensions.

What happens when the majority needs to be supported by such a safety net, as is the case in Europe today? When the active population begins to become the minority, the economic crisis deepens and the majority wants a decent pension . . . what happens then? The social security system begins to break down. That is, precisely when the need for a social security system is the greatest, the safety net cannot be sustained. This social security system cannot really help human beings because it breaks down, when most needed. Or, *the Western social security system is affordable if and only if it is not required.*

Of course, to shore up such a system, one could try different economic strategies: Keynesian interventions or plan the safety net not to break down during periods of crises. How plausible are these today?

Regarding the first strategy: not only did Keynesian interventions generate an uncontrolled and uncontrollable inflation in Western economies, but such an intervention would be quasi-suicidal because the locus of economic activities is shifting away from the West today. Unlike the immediate aftermath of the Second World War, the production of the kind of wealth required to finance such a system is not a purely Western phenomenon any more. 'Making America Great Again', under Donald Trump, is aiming to address these two issues: shift the economic focus to the United States and indulge in massive State intervention.

Consider the second strategy. At least a century-long experience suggests that the required kind of economic planning is not a plausibility. Neither the nationalization of industries nor prudent and long-term State investment is an option given the history of their failures. Among other things, the difficulty lies in the fact that neither the nature nor the character nor the onset of economic crises is predictable. While one can suggest that economic crises are endemic to capitalism or speak in terms of periodic or cyclical crises, predicting the intensity, scope and duration of any such crisis has not been possible.

What conclusions can we draw from this situation? Clearly, a social security system that focuses on providing material goods to satisfy the 'basic' needs of human organisms is not a viable option in the long-term. Such a system is going to break down precisely when the need for it is the greatest. When that happens, the very goal of such a safety net is compromised.

One of the reasons for the breakdown is the fact that the State sets up a social security system, while its resources are parasitic on something it cannot control. Legislative powers cannot control economies. Neither the outcome of economies nor their internal dynamics can be controlled either by enacting legislations (this is the lesson we have learnt during the last eighty years in different parts of the world) or by management techniques and strategies (also one of the lessons of the 2008 crisis, which is not yet over). Furthermore, the resources of the State come only from 'civil society'. In that case, only this civil society (with its basic units like family, friends etc.) can hope to set up a viable social security system, if such a thing is possible at all.

Such a social security system cannot then be defined entirely in monetary terms and, as such, will not be susceptible to the vicissitudes of the market. Consequently, it could be a viable and stable social security system that is framed in different terms. Which are those terms? The immediate answer is obvious. Because organizations in civil society are incapable of treating human beings as mere biological organisms, the safety net created by civil society should be very tightly connected to what individual human beings seek.

What do they seek? Answering this question requires understanding the kind of creatures we are. What if our understanding of human beings imparts the knowledge that we are not entities with 'needs'? What if it transpires that we are not 'needy creatures' at all? Indian culture takes this route. Let us see where that takes us.

IV

To change routes, we need a bridge of some kind. Let the issue about what human beings seek play that role here. If we work with the idea of 'needs', it is easy to suggest that human beings seek to satisfy these needs, whether their 'complete' satisfaction is possible or desirable. If we do not work with this language or use this notion, what options are open to us?

Perhaps, it is best to begin by gaining some clarity about what human beings do not seek: *unhappiness*. Even when people seek things that make them unhappy, it is very difficult to maintain that human beings actively aim at being unhappy. Further, when people are unhappy, they mostly seek to move away from their state of unhappiness. Ignorance does not inhibit this striving. Not knowing the why or the how or the what of unhappiness does not prevent the attempt to become less unhappy. This movement is more a move 'away' than a move 'towards': human beings want to leave their state of unhappiness behind.

The move 'towards' could be the next step in a process. That is, one could seek a state qualified as 'peaceful', 'content', 'balanced' or whatever else. Depending on the understanding of the individual in question, one could also seek 'happiness', keeping in mind that it is always an individual affair in two senses of the term. In the first sense, only the individual in question can know whether he or she is happy or unhappy. In the second sense, this knowledge is also partially dependent upon what happiness is (or means) to that specific individual. Even if some unit in civil society (say, a family or club) does not always keep the second sense in mind, the first sense is obvious to it because its focus is always some or another specific person.

If this reasoning is plausible, we could say that a social security system created by society-at-large is oriented towards helping human beings find what they seek, namely to move away from their unhappy state. It is of no consequence whether this move 'away' is also a move 'towards'. It is equally of no consequence how many different notions of happiness prevail in society and what they are. In this sense, this social security system is completely neutral or indifferent with respect to any formulation of the intended goal (i.e. 'towards' happiness), but is extremely sensitive or receptive to a search that seeks to move 'away' (from unhappiness).

Can such a system ever be built? My answer is: yes. Indian culture has done it. It is also the most ideal form that a safety net could ever take. Before exploring this answer further, let me reiterate two conclusions from the previous sections: Western social security systems (a) are founded on a specific conception of human beings as 'needy' creatures and (b) they are unstable, unviable and break down precisely when the requirement is at its greatest.

Now, the challenge is to show that (a) a different conception of the human being that exists elsewhere is both plausible and attractive;

(b) a different social security system can be built using that conception; (c) such a safety net is stable, viable and does not break down when the requirements are at their most acute.

V

If Indian culture does not talk about human beings in terms of 'needs', what other terms does it use? To answer this huge question, I will begin by looking at Sanskrit equivalents for the word 'need'. It would be advisable to use Sanskrit–English dictionaries created by European savants because they would be at home with the multiple meanings of the word 'need'. Monier-Williams' dictionary suits us here because of its impeccable pedigree. (Monier-Williams, 1872 others, earlier or later, do not contradict these findings.

Which Sanskrit words are used to translate the word 'need' from English? The Sanskrit–English dictionary of Monier-Williams suggests three words: *apeksha* (looking for, expectation, hope, need, requirement); *upachchanda* (anything necessary or needful, a requisite); *avashya* (inevitable, indispensable, necessary). The last word knows grammatical forms such as *avashyaka* (necessary, inevitable, indispensable), *avashyakata* (necessity, obligation, certainty) and *avashyam* (necessarily, inevitably; certainly, at all events, by all means, surely, of course).

However, each of these words track the English word 'need', when used as a verb with an object. As is obvious from the meanings he gives, these words mean *requirements or necessities*. These depend on agents, contexts, goals, available means etc. What is necessary for someone in some context may or may not suit another in a similar context. However, the noun form of the word 'need' picks out either some intrinsic things common to all of us or it identifies us as creatures of a specific kind. Vegetation, which needs water to grow, is not 'needy' because of that requirement. The last two Sanskrit words mentioned above, because they can be used in conjunction with any object (animate or inanimate), do not qualify as translation of 'need'; the first word connotes an anticipatory attitude and, as a consequence, could be *presumed* to signify 'needs'. However, this is not a linguistic fact about the Sanskrit word; it indicates the anthropological assumption of the translator.

If the above words in Sanskrit do not do the job, are other options open to us? Monier-Williams further suggests three other words, which, in their compound form, are translated as 'need' in its noun form.

The first is *Samkashta* (distress, trouble, need), which can be compounded in the following way: *samkashtachaturthi katha; samkashta chaturthivratakatha; samkashtaharachaturthi vrata; samkashtaharacaturthivratakaalanirnaya; samkashtaharanastotra; samkashtanaashanaganapatistotra; samkashtanaashanastotra; samkashtanaashanaan vrata; samkashtavrata*. However, these compound words translate differently than the English 'needs', as for instance in 'hymns to defeat distress' (*samkashtaharanastotra*); 'ritual to destroy distress' (*samkashtanaashanaanvrata*); and so on. The language of needs tells us that needs can only be fulfilled or satisfied; they can be neither defeated nor destroyed. Therefore, whatever else *samkashta* is (e.g. distress, trouble), it cannot translate the word need in its noun form.

The second compound word is *vyasanakaala* (time of need). But *vyasana* as a noun, according to Monier-Williams, means 'evil predicament or plight, disaster, accident, evil result, calamity, misfortune'. In its plural form, *vyasanaani* denotes misfortunes: 'ill-luck, distress, destruction, defeat, fall, ruin'. The word *kaala* picks out time: say a period or an epoch, that is the Sanskrit word refers to a time-slice. Therefore, this compound word cannot be translated as 'time of need' either. Again, one must assume an anthropology of 'needs' to understand the time of misfortune or disaster as a 'time of need'. Language alone does not give that licence. In fact, it forbids such a move: *vyasana*, as Monier-Williams himself translates this noun, is not an intrinsic and invariant trait in human beings.

The third combines the word *sahaaya* (help) with either *aapat* or *aaptah*: *aapatsahaaya* and *aaptasahaaya*, respectively. In its first combination, the compound word *aapatsahaaya* has often been rendered as 'help in need'; the second combination is rendered as 'helping a friend in need'. These do not quite work as translations of 'need' because, according to Monier-Williams, *aapat* translates as 'a calamity, misfortune, danger, distress, adversity'. This word is applicable only to events and situations and cannot be used to pick out a trait or a property of an organism or an object. The word *aaptah* (or even *aapta*) means 'intimate, respected, confidential' etc. Consequently, neither of these words could refer to 'need'. Therefore, it is obvious that the Sanskrit word for 'help' must be read as 'help rendered in times of need', in order to use these compound words to translate 'need'. However, 'help' in English does not mean 'help rendered in times of need', any more than the Sanskrit word. In short, these Sanskrit words simply cannot mean what the translators 'think' or assume they do.

The English 'need' is best read as *requirement*, if one wants to use that word. 'Requirement' picks out something that is necessary for performing a task, even if the task itself is contingent in nature. Monier-Williams finds more Sanskrit words to capture this notion of requirement: apart from *apeksha* (which was used by him to translate 'need' in its noun form earlier, see above), *kshudraklripti* ('arrangement of the minor requirements [of a sacrifice]'); *yathaayogam* ('as is fit, according to circumstances, according to requirements') *yathaayogena* ('as is fit, according to circumstances, according to requirements') and *yaavadartha* ('as many as necessary, corresponding to requirement'). However, none of these Sanskrit words could be used to indicate 'need' in its noun form.

This point becomes evident, if we look at the Sanskrit equivalents for the word 'needy'. A search suggests the following: *daridra* ('poor, needy, deprived of, a beggar'); *jasvan* ('needy, hungry'); *nadhita* ('oppressed, needy, suppliant'); *kathera* ('a needy or distressed man, pauper') or *pradraanaka* ('sorely distressed, very needy or poor') *nirdhana* or *adhana* (pauper) and *diina* (afflicted).

However, these words refer to situations that people find themselves in, whether physical, social or psychological. Hence, one often uses them to derivatively talk about states of being. That is, one could use the word 'poor' to indicate the status of a person with respect to something or another and make a derivative claim about that individual's trait: 'he has emotional poverty', 'he is morally bankrupt', 'he is poor in spirit' and so on. The Sanskrit words used above function in this fashion. Precisely this linguistic fact disqualifies their usage as translations of 'needy'.

When we use the word 'needy', we talk about a creature in some state that expresses an inherent or intrinsic trait of that being. Thus, one cannot think of being needy, unless one brings this word into a *semantic connection* with 'need'. Because 'needy' expresses an intrinsic trait, one cannot understand that word if one does not have the notion of need. By contrast, none of the suggestions of Monier-Williams for translating 'needy' requires knowledge (even implicitly) of the words used to translate 'need'. In other words, one can use these Sanskrit words without having a Sanskrit equivalent for 'need'. This is possible only if the words that Monier-Williams suggests for translating *'needy' are semantically independent of the meaning of 'need'*. Such a semantic independence does not exist either in English or in other European languages.

I would submit that what I have said about Sanskrit is applicable to all other Indian languages. If that is the case, *how do Indians talk about such things as 'basic human needs', 'the needy' etc. in their vernacular languages, when words are absent in their languages and the associated concept cannot therefore be expressed in those languages?* Whatever the answer, let us look at two points that arise when this question gets formulated.

The first is rather trivial: very often, one hears that it is not possible to translate many Sanskrit terms into European languages (e.g. *Dharma*) and that any such attempt would distort Indian culture. We must realize that the same argument also goes the other way: it is not possible to translate many English words into Sanskrit either. What follows from this? Surely, Indians must also distort Western culture in their attempts at translation. When maintained so baldly, this thesis is of little interest to serious students of cultures.

If stated less baldly, it generates implications worth pondering about. Most Indians living in India learn English through their native languages. How, then, could they access the meaning of words like 'need' or 'needy' without doing philological and linguistic work of the kind required? They could not. Then, the next question is obvious: *how much of English do they understand?* If we expand the scope of this question to include words like 'rights and obligations', 'moral norms and ethical commandments', 'citizens and State', 'religion and secularism' etc., what can be said about the current Indian discourses on these subjects? How about laws that are designed to help the 'needy' in modern India or legal judgements about their implementation?

Apart from the above, there is a second, more important point to notice. We are not talking about mere linguistic facts and difficulties of translating words across different languages. Instead, it is about *the existence of a profound difference in the conception of human beings between two cultures.* One sees Man as a needy creature, a creature whose nature it is to have needs. The other cannot conceptualize or express this idea in its native languages. If a culture cannot even use words to express these concepts or ideas in its treatises and tracts about human beings, would it not have formulated an entirely different story about human beings, how they stand in the world and how they should relate to other creatures including themselves? If yes, what could be the rough outlines of such a story? Before seeking such an outline, we must become clear about the cognitive conditions that it must satisfy.

VI

I began with the intention of contrasting two cultural ways of talking about human beings. However, a contrast requires a common vocabulary, which seems to be absent in this case. The Indian traditions cannot talk about the 'needy' nature of human beings. The West talks about it at great lengths. To contrast one picture of human beings that holds 'needs' as a fundamental given with another that simply does not do so, and to evaluate which of the two is better, we require a vocabulary that they at least partially share. If both cultures speak about human desires, one could try *the notion of desires* to build such a common vocabulary.

Prima facie, this appears a reasonable suggestion. According to Monier-Williams, Sanskrit has more than 950 words for 'desire' derived from ten root verbs. *Amarakosha*, a famous old Indian treatise on synonyms, provides us with: *abhilaasha, lipsaa, iihaa, icchhaa, kaama, vaanchaa, spruhaa, tarpa, manoratha, trushna, kaankshaa* as synonyms. 'Greed' too has many words in Sanskrit, nearly 73 in total. *Merriam-Webster* provides us with about 30-odd words as synonyms for 'need' and about 17 synonyms for 'desire' (with non-sexual connotations) in English. In the Bible (ESV), one can discern the use of the word 'desire' 170 times in 167 verses. In the New Testament, the word is used 74 times in 71 verses. Even where Sanskrit lacks the equivalent of 'need', it can talk about desire. I do not want to make much of these linguistic indices except to say that a vocabulary of desire might be what we seek. In what follows, I shall make this assumption.

In the rich history of the Western intellectual traditions, we discern ways of talking about 'needs', while bracketing their ontological status. Many have spoken of 'drives', 'motivations' and even 'desires' without explicitly embracing the language of needs. For the moment, it is of no consequence to us whether the way they have thought about desires is beholden to the language of needs or not. Let us simply say that *needs take the form of desires* or that *desires express needs*. Would this be adequate for our purposes?

We all know or assume that desires are geared towards objects. These multiple desires seem to function as motivations for human beings. To satisfy their desires, human beings act. These indefinitely many desires are also (mostly) doubly qualified. The first qualification is this: desire is oriented towards an object, because a desire is mostly a desire for something. This qualification is partially determined by the linguistic role of the word. In its noun form, the OED says, 'desire' does not have to be qualified in this manner, especially when used with sexual connotations: for example, lust, libido, sensuality, sexuality, carnality etc. In its verb form, though, it means 'to want or wish for (something): to feel desire for (something): to want to have sex with (someone): to express a wish for (something)'. The second qualification in desire specifies the object. For instance, you do not merely desire food, but you desire a pizza. You do not merely desire clothes, but you desire Armani clothes, and so on. In this sense, mostly, *desires are qualified by a particular object.*

Thus, we could say that desires emerge in us and such desires are also mostly doubly qualified. How about new desires, or further qualifications to the existing ones? New objects can either create new desires for those objects or qualify the already existing desires. That is, in any given period, human desires are formed socially and culturally. Thus, human beings are creatures with indefinitely many desires for indefinitely many things. New desires emerge as new products come into being and are marketed successfully.

However, it could be sensibly said that one could desire an object (say, a smartwatch) without there being a 'need' for that object. In such cases, one is differentiating between 'need' and 'desire' and refusing to accept that the latter is an expression of 'need'. This objection does not endanger the proposal. Whether all (or only some) desires express human needs can only be determined after we decide about the ontological status of needs. Until such time, we can suspend our judgement. The proposal entails no ontological commitment regarding human needs.

This vocabulary closely tracks the idea that Man has multiple needs by seeing this multiplicity expressed in a multiplicity of desires. Whether we are needy creatures or not, it does not appear possible to deny the empirical fact that human beings appear to have a multiplicity of desires. Consequently, even if India has built a picture of human beings without appealing to the notion of 'human needs', it cannot possibly deny that human beings try to satisfy multiple desires. In that case, how does Indian culture explain this phenomenon? Such an explanation is required because an alternative to the theory of needs must satisfy *adequacy conditions* involving this multiplicity: it can deny neither the expression of multiple desires, nor the existence of a multiplicity of phenomena like greed, violence, hatred etc. that we observe in this world. The theory of needs attempts to explain this multiplicity; any alternative to it, therefore, must do the same. That is, one cannot simply postulate that this multiplicity constitutes the furniture of the world and begin from there, because the theory of needs has transformed this multiplicity into its empirical fact. Any rival to this theory, therefore, must account for this 'fact', if it is to be a serious contender.

The question, therefore, becomes: *how does Indian culture account for this multiplicity*? How can there be a multiplicity of desires, and how do conflicting multiplicities (of emotions, actions, etc.) emerge from the kind of organisms we are? There are many stories that try to answer these questions; here, let me sketch the outline of a story, which, I think, not only highlights the common structure undergirding various Indian traditions, but also meets the adequacy conditions mentioned above.

VII

Human beings do not have *intrinsic and multiple* desires for specific objects, say these Indian traditions. They have *Desire*: in the singular, unqualified and objectless. Consequently, to say, as we do, that we have 'many desires', or that 'we have a desire for something' would be misleading. However, Desire attaches itself to any and every object. When I desire Armani clothes or a pizza, I do not have desires for these specific objects. What I do have is just one 'Desire' that attaches itself now to Armani clothes and then to the pizza. Desiring multiple objects does not show that we have many desires, but shows, instead, that it is merely one and the same Desire attaching itself to different objects. The limitlessness of our desires does not have anything to do with the limitless number and variety of objects in the world but with the fact that Desire has no intrinsic goal or object. That is why Desire cannot be satisfied: *nothing can satisfy it*.

To make this notion of Desire perspicuous, let me use an economic metaphor. The Desire that the Indian traditions talk about is like Money. Money is a singular; there are no plural monies. Money can become wages, savings, profits, financial capital, industrial capital, mercantile capital, money-lending capital, or merely something we exchange for some commodity or another. Money can take the form of various currencies, shares, gold, a hoard or any other commodity. Money can buy anything because it is indifferent to what it is exchanged against. To Indian traditions, Desire is like Money: it is limitless; it has no object as its intrinsic goal; it can be accumulated in any form, quantity or degree and, thus, can attach itself to any object.

Letting this Desire orient our strivings is intrinsically and inherently frustrating. Such an endeavour is also a direct cause of unhappiness because no object can satisfy Desire. I believe that the Buddha was talking about the singular nature of Desire, amongst other things, when he spoke of 'grasping' as the cause of human unhappiness. 'Grasping' refers to the property of Desire clinging or attaching itself to objects. 'Clinging' predicates Desire thus: *Desire clings*. A similar consideration applies to those emotions which are identified as the six enemies of human mind. (A very, very rough translation of these emotions would be: lust, rage, greed, blind attachment, bloated sense of self-accomplishment and jealousy.) Each of these clings, whether they cling to objects, events, entities or whatever else in the world. These are classified as enemies (*ari*) in a group (*varga*). To belong to a group (or a set), the individual members of that group must possess at least one common property. That common property, I would suggest, is Desire: singular, objectless and goalless. Desire for a specific object (say, money) becomes a desire for that object (money). It is important here to recognize the 'clinging' property of Desire: *it can attach itself to any and every object.*

However, Desire is not a trait in human beings that constitutes human nature, the way need supposedly is. Indian traditions make a different claim: Desire has its origin in certain kinds of human activities. Once Desire emerges from this cluster of interactions, it *attaches itself also to the human mind, the way it attaches itself to other objects* in the world. Such a stance coheres with their notion of Desire, of course. If indeed, as Indians claim, Desire is indifferent to what it attaches itself to and can cling to any object whatsoever, why should the human mind be an exception?

VIII

In a world with antagonistic needs (or desires), *conflicts are inevitable*. Such conflicts are many. First, there is an internal struggle within human beings because needs (or desires) conflict internally. Second, as the Good Book says, its consequences are also inevitable: '*What causes quarrels and what causes fights among you? Is it not this, that your passions are at war within you?*' (James 4:1 [ESV], my italics). Indeed. Conflicting needs, when present in individual human beings, cannot remain individualized: this conflict of needs must, *of necessity*, express itself as conflicts between human beings, because a conflict between needs remains a conflict irrespective of whether these needs are localized inside or outside the individual. The presence of one and the same need among different individuals could also generate conflicts between them in situations of 'scarcity'. If human beings form small groups, conflicts between such groups are also inevitable. If these small groups emerge as a nation, that nation will become an arena where conflicts are played out. Of course, if we want a society with less conflicts than more, we must *devise ways for conflict resolution*. In other words, put simply, embracing the Christian conception of Man justifies conflicts both between groups and within individuals. Happiness on earth, as the Bible says, would then be impossible.

If we look at the theories at our disposal, all of them posit conflicts both inside human beings and between human beings. Taking some examples at random, we encounter Hegel who sees the struggle between Master and Slave (each is driven by the need for recognition) as the condition for the emergence of human history itself; we later encounter his student Marx, who sees class struggle (the struggle between social classes, each fighting for the interests that express its needs) as the very motor of history; we also come across Jacques Lacan, who sees the need for recognition in the child as a momentous event in its development. His master, Freud, saw in the conflict between the pleasure principle and the death principle in human beings the cause for the emergence of human civilization itself. Any number of contract theorists who have come and gone, from Locke to Rawls, have told us stories about the origin of the State and civilization as a way of *resolving conflicts between human beings* that are both inevitable and necessary in their hypothetical 'state of Nature'. Thus, we could go on and on citing theories and theorists selling a biblical story *as the truth* about human beings. Believers would have no problems with this, perhaps. But I do, because I am not willing to accept the Bible as the truth only on its say so.

Be that as it may, what happens if we look at the consequences of not embracing Christian theology but instead work with the notion of human beings that Indian culture proposes? In the first place, to reiterate, Desire also latches itself to the individual human mind. Second, this human being cannot struggle against Desire for the simple reason that Desire is not an embodied entity. It does not have a will or an interest of its own. Therefore, Man is not in conflict with Desire and, hence, he does not have the internal conflict that the Apostle says we have. Third, an individual might become unhappy by chasing after the objects that Desire latches on to. But if that individual wants to be happy, he or she must learn how to deal with this Desire. Fourth, all Indian traditions with their extraordinary collection of practical methods (often called 'meditative' techniques) not only teach this as knowledge, but also teach individuals *how to go beyond it*. That is, not only is there no conflict between human beings, and Desire but there also exist ways to transcend Desire. Fifth, the best way of transcending Desire would be to avoid it altogether, if one does not want to be unhappy. Sixth, an individual is not placed in a situation of conflict with himself or herself but is alerted to *the possibility of avoiding* it.

In Western thinking, the nature of the world is used as a pragmatic argument to suggest that we must restrain our desires. Our desires are infinite, but the resources of the world are finite. However, this argument convinces only those who want to be convinced; it cannot convince the sceptic, who might be an optimist ('science and technology will solve the problem') or an ignoramus. Further, this argument makes the 'Other' – whether that other is Nature or fellow human beings – into the enemy: the 'Other' is the source of human unhappiness. Consequently, *the 'Other' is always a threat that the 'self' confronts in its attempts to fulfil its desires.* One could blame human nature here, but it tells us that our nature will make us unhappy and cannot 'deliver us from evil'. In seeking happiness as a goal or in seeking to move away from unhappiness, we are our worst enemies: human nature prevents us from finding what we seek. Gurus, priests or experts are the only ones who can tell us what 'happiness' is and further advise us that we can be (partially) happy or less unhappy if only we learn to be ascetic and restrain our needs and desires. However, because these are constitutive of our nature, we are doomed to be unhappy: after all, when one part in us fights and wins against the other, we end up as the losers.

In the Indian traditions, by contrast, neither the 'self' nor the 'other' has anything to do with the limitless nature of our desires or our inability to satisfy them. Desire cannot be satisfied. Consequently, going-about with Desire is crucial to being happy or less unhappy. One can *learn* to be either. This learning enables the acquisition of the ability to deal with Desire. *Circumventing or avoiding Desire* is a key to this process. Asceticism is of no help as a societal solution, even if some individuals could be happy or less unhappy by living ascetically. The road away from unhappiness involves people learning this truth about Desire. *Truth or knowledge liberates,* and this can be learnt and taught. The Buddha or Shankara, for instance, claims to teach us knowledge about human beings the way scientists teach us about Nature.

IX

As the last two paragraphs suggest, these different conceptions contrast two different ways of being in the world. These ways of being human profoundly influence the pursuit of the end goals, if human beings pursue such goals at all. This contrast deserves a closer look.

Let us assume that most human beings, in all times and places, seek to be happy. (Here, we are working with a very weak notion of happiness, namely, as a state of being less unhappy.) The question, in that case, is simple: if human beings indeed seek happiness, why do they not find it? One possible answer to this question is to transform the human search for happiness into a 'need' or, in the proposed vocabulary, into a desire.

Such a story would then suggest that human beings desire to be happy. One could begin with the idea that human beings are happy, if their desires are satisfied. However, as we proceed further, happiness ends up becoming a desired object. If human beings are seen to desire happiness the way they desire any other object, questions can then be asked about it: what kind of an object is happiness? Is it possible to specify its properties? Is it a psychological feeling, an attitude to life, a quantity of goods, the quality of life? (Most modern studies about happiness are busy with such issues.) When these questions are asked, our task becomes even more complex: satisfying our desires now includes satisfying the desire to be happy. Happiness becomes both an object of desire and something that is dependent on the satisfaction of other desires.

Notice that two things happen in this process of transforming happiness into a desire. First, we can ask whether this desire to be happy is the proper end of humankind, and we can even ask the normative question 'Is it good to be happy?' Second, we can speak of different 'kinds' of happiness: happiness as a desire as against the happiness we seek by satisfying all our other desires. It is now totally unclear what relation, if any, exists between these two kinds of happiness. Hence, we say, as we often do: even though someone has satisfied all his desires, he has not yet found 'happiness' (or 'he is not *truly* happy').

Correspondingly, two aspects to finding happiness become visible. The first aspect seeks happiness directly and the second seeks it indirectly. However, because happiness is so elusive and we do not know what it is, a search for it can only frustrate us. That is, if we seek happiness directly, we will end up becoming unhappy. What if we seek it indirectly? Because our desires are indefinitely many, and they could never be satisfied fully or completely, we will never find happiness. Both aspects carry the same message: *human beings might desire happiness; this desire can never be satisfied.*

The religion which has dominated Western culture suggests: we can never find 'true' happiness on earth by chasing either happiness or by trying to satisfy our desires for material things. Instead, we need to seek God and constrain our desires. Our needs are innate because that is how God created us. Our desires are not merely expressions of these God-given needs. We have cultivated other desires, which owe their existence to human striving. These make us unhappy too.

However, if you want to follow humanistic psychology and do not want to speak of God, you can say the following: even though some of our needs are biological givens, satisfying them is not enough. Human beings cannot be 'truly happy' until spiritual desires are also satisfied and their limitless desires for material objects are curtailed. Humanistic psychology can now live in peace with Christianity. Of course, it would be wrong not to mention that many Christians do not like this marriage. Hence there is also a call for a divorce.

X

Let me now invite you to think along with me and continue to agree that all human beings seek happiness (this time, we even abandon the weak formulation). Then, we cannot assume anything about the relationship between happiness and desire, including whether happiness requires a satisfaction of desires or not. In that case, it appears as though the sentence 'all human beings seek to be happy' itself becomes senseless because we cannot make sense of what 'happiness' means. Not so. The Indian traditions try to make the sentence meaningful by making meta-claims about it. Therefore, let us now imagine the following meta-claim: *each human being can be happy*. There are consequences attached to that statement.

1. There is no special or specific condition for being happy. One could be a man, a woman or a child; one could be rich or poor; one could be intelligent or stupid; one could be young or old. . . . None of these qualifications matters: anyone and everyone can be happy. The only possible condition is that one is a human being and, even here, it is left vague as to what it means to be a human being.
2. The second implication is the answer to the question, 'when can someone become happy?' The answer is obvious: *anytime, anywhere and in any manner*.
3. The third consequence is this: if every human being can be happy, that means there *cannot be a conflict* between the happiness of one person and the happiness of the other.
4. The fourth consequence is this: because each one of us is occupied in different ways in the world, each one of us has a different psychology than the other, no occupation or no individual psychology can prevent us from being happy. That is, 'being happy' is something either so general that it is applicable to all human beings or something so plastic that it can adapt itself to every situation and every person.
5. Because of all these considerations, the next consequence is necessary: every path and every way we traverse in the course of our journey through life can lead us to this goal. That is, it is not

possible to speak of only one way of being happy. There are indefinitely many ways of being happy.

6   What does it mean to claim that there are indefinitely many ways to be happy? Now comes a startling consequence: you can take happiness as a goal and find it in your life; or you can chase after material goods and still find happiness. (I am limiting myself here to just these two possibilities to draw the contrast.) That is, you can chase after happiness either directly or indirectly. From this, it follows: not only can people, be happy but also there is no such thing as 'true' as against 'false' happiness. There is only one thing we all seek and that is to be happy.

If all these consequences are derivable from the meta-claim about the sentence, the question arises: why are people unhappy then? Surely, if it is that simple and so obvious, why is the majority of humankind unhappy? The Indian traditions provide a double answer to this question which is deceptively simple. Its simplicity lies in the content of the answer. Hence it deceives: we are encouraged to think that we understand 'the' simple answer because it is nowhere near to being as complicated as our secular theories and philosophies.

Here is the first element of the double answer: one reason why people are unhappy is because they do not 'really' seek happiness. To be happy, one must merely seek it; 'seek, and ye shall find.' Seek what though? How can we seek in total ignorance? Surely, if we are ignorant of what we seek, we cannot recognize it when we find it.

'Indeed, we cannot,' say the Indian traditions, which constitutes the second aspect of the answer. We cannot seek something until we know what we seek. However, instead of telling us what we 'ought' to be seeking, or imparting knowledge of what we seek, the Indian traditions do something remarkable: they draw attention to our ignorance in this case and ask us to reflect upon its nature.

If, indeed, all of us can be happy in different ways, if there is no 'true' happiness as against multiple illusions about it, and if the meaning of the word depends on what individuals take it to mean, then no theory can tell us what *all of us* 'ought' to be seeking. Nor could we have knowledge about 'happiness' the way we could have knowledge about objects, events and states in the world. If a believer, an atheist and an agnostic (for example) can all be happy, then either happiness has nothing to do with the belief in God or happiness means different things to these different people. Therefore, we cannot even say whether they have sought and found the same thing, even when all three use the same word. The Indian traditions do not prescribe a 'normative end' to all human beings; they merely notice factually that we all seek 'happiness' as an end.

Therefore, instead of 'defining' what the word 'happiness' means or what it 'really' is, Indian traditions *focus on the impediments to achieving* what we think that end is, no matter how we define that end. They tell us that we are prevented from achieving that end, which we call 'happiness', because of ignorance. That is, even though each could 'define' happiness differently from the other, ignorance prevents all of us from reaching the end we seek. Therefore, they say, think about ignorance and understand how it prevents you from reaching the end you seek. Are they saying that we cannot be happy because we lack knowledge of what 'true' happiness is? They are not. What else are they saying? Answering this question requires that we take their suggestion seriously. Let us do so and ask: *what is ignorance?*

XI

To begin with, ignorance signifies an absence: the absence of information or knowledge. This answer is intuitively familiar to us: we are ignorant 'about' some things. At one level, this answer amounts to the claim that we cannot be happy until we gain knowledge about the nature of our desires, wants, greed and such like, about the kind of beings we are and about the nature of happiness. While there is nothing wrong with this notion of ignorance, it is not of much help here.

There is also another notion of ignorance that Indian traditions use: it is that which hinders the emergence of knowledge. That is, they see ignorance not merely as an absence of something else (namely, information or knowledge), but also as something that *functions* as or plays the role of an obstruction. To get a grip on this 'property' of absence, let us agree that if something has to 'do' something else in the world, it must exist first. Something which does not exist cannot have impact on objects that exist. What does not exist does not and cannot play any role in the world nor can it have any 'properties'. So, as an absence, ignorance cannot hinder. In fact, in this sense of 'absence', ignorance is a precondition for knowledge. How to make sense of the idea that ignorance hinders or impedes?

Consider statements of the following sort: 'Knowledge removes ignorance'; 'knowledge cures ignorance'; 'ignorance prevents one from seeing the truth'; 'forgiving people for their ignorance' ('Lord, forgive them, for they know not what they are doing') and so on. How can knowledge 'remove' or 'cure' or 'be prevented by' something that does not exist?

One could make sense of these statements by suggesting that they pick out the situation of having false beliefs. How do false beliefs prevent knowledge? If false or wrong beliefs were to possess properties that prevent us from accessing truth or knowledge, neither science nor scientific progress is possible. False beliefs are not true; but we discover the falsity of a belief even when we do not know the truth. The falsity of geocentric theory did not prevent the emergence of the heliocentric theory. If it could, there would have been no heliocentric theory. Of course, people who hold false beliefs might prevent others from proposing or propagating true beliefs. However, this is a claim about people, their beliefs and what they do with them. It does not appear to be about the relationship between true and false beliefs.

But, consider how one could explain this conflict between people in such situations. Some kinds of false beliefs or some circumstances in which one holds such beliefs (or both) hinder the emergence of knowledge. For instance, the Church held that its belief about the sun and the earth was true and persecuted Galileo because he tried to propagate false beliefs. The Church not only endorsed the geocentric theory (a false belief) as true but it also (falsely) believed that a Pagan thinker, namely Aristotle, was required for knowledge about the world. This is how Darwin's theory of natural selection is treated in many parts of America today. If we look closely at how such incidents are described or explained, we see that their explanations formulate the situation as a conflict between truth and falsity. That is, the explanations do not tell us how or why there could be a conflict between truth and falsity but try to explicate the reasons why it was either seen or presented as such a conflict. The conflict itself is not explained; the conflict between truth and falsity is presented as an empirical fact requiring explanation. Whether at one extreme the appeal is to the notions of 'truth', 'falsity' or 'rationality' of that period, or to the alleged threats to the 'vested interests' of the Church at the other extreme, what does not appear to require any explanation is the fact that *it is a conflict between truth and falsity*. This attitude is expressed in metaphors like 'truth shall prevail', 'truth will triumph', 'only truth will ultimately be victorious', and so on. In other words, Truth (or knowledge) is always (or latently) in conflict with falsity (or ignorance).

Indian traditions take a different route. They see knowledge as an 'emergence', that is they tie knowledge to the states (cognitive, psychological, physiological) of the organism that it emerges from. More generally, our beliefs emerge from the states that an organism is in. What we call ignorance refers to such states from which either false beliefs emerge or to the states from which knowledge does not arise. The state from which knowledge does not arise is an *impediment* in the sense that the transformation of that state is not simple and smooth. Some external input is required before this state (let us call it a state of ignorance) shifts or changes into a state from which knowledge could emerge. If we are willing to call false beliefs as 'ignorance', then we could also say that ignorance itself emerges (because all beliefs emerge from the state an organism is in). Then, we are permitted to say that the state of the organism which allows the emergence of knowledge also *prevents* knowledge *from arising*. In this sense, and only in this sense, both knowledge and ignorance emerge; their origins can be localized in different states of the organism. We cannot 'fight' a state of being; we can, however, *change such states*. Changing the state of an organism takes time, but all of us can learn the 'how' sooner or later. This kind of ignorance is not in conflict with knowledge or truth. *Each human being can allow knowledge to emerge by intelligently transforming the states which generate ignorance.* Thus, one reason given to explain the unhappiness of individuals picks out their states of being because ignorance emerges from such states. Here, there is no intrinsic and inherent conflict between truth and falsity. Therefore, 'ignorance' contains multiple dimensions. 'Truth' and 'falsity' pick out logical or semantic properties of sentences, when these are about the world. Consequently, when one fights battles and wars in the 'name of truth', one must explain what is at stake and why. Seeking truth, which is a semantic property of sets of sentences about the world, does not become a mysterious 'cognitive goal' that justifies itself. ('It is obvious that people seek truth', 'we prefer truth to falsity' etc.) Truth seeking requires a goal; we can ask justificatory questions about it. Even if 'truth-telling' is a virtue (whether cognitive, moral or both), one must explain why it is a virtue, why is it preferable to telling lies, whether in all circumstances it is so and so on. What is sold by the West as a commonplace becomes a problem to understand: why do human beings fight out some conflicts as a conflict between truth and falsity? Why do some human conflicts take this form and why do they engender different effects?

XII

Now, we can move further. Let us imagine that Indian culture has built a social security system. What could the goal of such a system be? Its only goal would be to enable human beings to find happiness. Because there are no qualifications (or requirements) to reach this end-state, in principle, every human being can reach it. However, due to different reasons and a multiplicity of contingent circumstances, human beings might fail in their search. At such moments, which could occur at any stage in an individual life, the system renders support of a kind that enables people to achieve happiness. Such a system would be the most ideal social security system that could ever be built.

At first sight, it looks as though the biggest obstacle facing any attempt at building such a system is variety or diversity. There are enormous individual differences: between psychologies, social positions, attitudes and aptitudes, inclinations and capacities. There are individual differences in conceptualizing the end-state that we have called 'happiness'. Together, these varieties generate multiplicities regarding requirements. If we take these into consideration, the idea that a single system ('the' social security system) could address this diversity appears as a pipe dream.

Not quite. It becomes a pipe dream if one believes that a centralized or standardized organization is the best way to deal with diversities and varieties. Events from the past have continuously shown that this belief is false. Whether one looks at life on this planet or at the structure of human brain, we find neither centralization nor standardization. These two systems are also the most successful organizations that we know. Events from the human past have endlessly reiterated the lesson that all attempts to standardize varieties fail, whether one tries that with economies, political structures or social organizations. A heterarchical organization is the only viable way for dealing with varieties and diversities.

That is also the answer we receive from the Indian social security system, a heterarchical system that deals with variety and diversities. Indian traditions are extraordinarily varied and diverse. Each tradition that appears to sketch out a single route to human happiness turns out, on closer inspection, to be a family consisting of multiple routes and practices. Ideas and practices flow across each of these traditions seamlessly, even though these traditions seem to be diametrically opposed to each other. The 'atheistic' Jain temples are filled with 'Hindu gods'; an *advaitin* has no problems in remaining a Brahmin and devoutly practice *bhakti*; a Buddhist does to a statue of Buddha what a 'Hindu' does to the *Linga* and so on. To the Western savants and to those influenced by them, these express inconsistencies in and contradictions of Indian culture; yet, some 'system' is visible and some 'structure' is discernible even to them.

Because no single route will work for everyone, an indefinite plurality of routes to happiness is the only way to keep the system maximally accessible. None of these traditions defines what happiness is, but each can help you overcome the hindrances you face in your quest for happiness. This is how this safety net helps, whether you are poor or rich, intelligent or dumb, young or old, man or woman. These traditions have built up a great variety of practices too: from visiting temples, through singing *bhajans*, to the arduous task of thinking about abstract issues. Choose whatever suits you the best in your search for happiness. No human being falls outside such a safety net because there are routes from every point and station in life to the sought end-state. It would guarantee each of us that we can be happy by providing us with just that route which we want (and can follow) to become happy.

Like all social security systems, this too requires constant replenishment. It too must draw from the total 'wealth' in society to keep reproducing itself. As society and its environment change, this wealth must be constantly produced to keep the social security system going. For this to happen, people should consistently generate wealth. However, what constitutes 'wealth' to feed such a social security system? The answer is obvious: the only possible wealth that can keep such a social security system going is an increase in the diversity of routes to the end-state. That is, because the variety in individual psychologies continues to increase and the changes in their environments occur constantly, the only possible contribution that can sustain such a security system is something that keeps pace with this increasing variety and change. In other words, as diversity increases, so too do the routes to the end-state of being happy. The continuous production and reproduction of this wealth is the only thing that can keep such a security system solvent. How shall we define such wealth? Because it is not material wealth, let us call it 'spiritual wealth'. 'Spirituality', as a first approximate definition then, is about people's happiness. Indian social security system is such a spiritual system; its diverse routes are spiritual routes.

In fact, were you to look at Indian culture and examine its so-called religions, it is striking that, without exception, all have one central and overriding concern: how can human beings be happy? Each of these traditions, where each tradition is itself an embodiment of great diversity, provides us with routes to that end-state that all human beings seek: happiness. Because of this concern, these traditions can neither be otherworldly nor utopian: they cannot be otherworldly because they are concerned with the happiness of human beings here on earth; they cannot be utopian because the routes they sketch must 'work', if they are to function as routes to happiness at all. However, as we have seen, this multiplicity of routes to happiness has definite ideas about the kind of beings we are. They propose some explanations of such beings and their factually observed limitless desires. These explanations, as we have also seen, are the opposite of what people in the West tend to believe.

We can now appreciate better what kind of wealth is required to keep such a social security system functioning. The wealth consists of indefinitely many routes and knowledge about using them. Such a system is something within which individuals learn, that is such a social security system is also a teaching system. That is why happiness is not a desire or a need of human beings, but something that can be learnt.

Finally, let us turn our attention to a dimension that constitutes the focus of the Western social security system: satisfying the requirements for physical survival. Who needs 'spirituality' when there is no food to eat? The answer to this question is twofold. One: this question makes sense, if and only if you accept the idea that human beings have some basic needs, a picture that Western culture has made a part of our common sense. Second: because society-at-large builds this safety net, people have to be taken care of within the units that belong to civil society, namely, family, friends, charitable organizations, temples and such like. It is not the responsibility of the State to do this but that of the units in civil society. If that is the case, a question about pain and suffering arises: should we, as members of a society, be indifferent to the pain and suffering of our fellow human beings then?

XIII

Of course, Indian traditions do talk about human pain and suffering. The best way to understand their talk is to focus on some examples: an Olympic swimmer has an accident because of which a promising career gets broken in the middle; a Casanova, who made a career of chasing after women, discovers his waning attraction; a beautiful woman, who prided herself on her beauty, begins to grow old; a rich man loses money in a stock-market crash; a young mother discovers that her infant baby has terminal cancer; a young couple breaks up; a loved one dies; so on and so forth. In each of these cases, the resultant pain and suffering are obvious. How does one respond to these situations? The obvious answer is that one tries to comfort these people and provide them with some solace. Yes, but how and why?

Let us first note that the contrast set for pain and suffering is pleasure and enjoyment. Indian traditions suggest that we locate the origin of pain and suffering: the sorrow of the swimmer has its roots in his joy about his physical excellence; the Casanova enjoyed his physical prowess and his capacity to attract women; the beautiful woman enjoyed and took pride in her youth and beauty; the rich man took great pleasure and derived enjoyment from his wealth; the young mother's joy was her baby; the young couple enjoyed their love for each other; the loved one gave pleasure and joy to those who loved her or him; and so on. In short, each was attached to something or another, and appeared to take a great deal of pleasure and enjoyment from that object.

Why do they suffer now? Because, it appears that the object of their attachment goes missing. That is, one could say that their pain and suffering of today is a result of losing the source of their joy yesterday. So, a great deal of human pain and suffering in the world could then be seen the result of loss or an 'absence'. In that case, 'loss' generates suffering. However, 'loss' or 'absence' cannot possibly generate or cause anything in the world; how could any absence be a causal force in the world? Many, many answers are possible, each emphasizing some or another aspect of human psychology and human experience. Let me pick out one well-known answer form Indian culture.

Both the nature of these objects and the kinds of our attachments to them are impermanent and transient: the idiosyncrasies that charmed once now become sources of irritation, when the 'ardour' of love cools; youthful prowess changes into old-age infirmity; the loved child is now the source of distress and discomfort; and so on. Changes occur in the world and temporality is not just a Kantian 'intuition' which structures phenomena. It plays a more active role in human life than it does as an inert referential framework within which we experience. Therefore, if nothing human is permanent and what is present today will be absent tomorrow, either our attachment to objects or the objects themselves (or both) are the only sources of pleasure and enjoyment, pain and suffering. At one time (i.e. in one temporal slice), this source generates joy and pleasure; at another time (i.e. in another time-slice), the very same source generates pain and suffering. Consequently, one and the same source generates both. What, however, is this 'source'? Does the object (or the event) uniquely cause joy in us because of which its loss generates sorrow or is a specific kind of relationship ('attachment') to objects (and events) the cause of both pleasure and pain in different time-slices or something else?

If we identify an object (or an event) as the cause of joy and its loss as the cause of pain or suffering, we are forced to accept that 'absence' is a causal force in the world. Not only that. One is also forced to postulate indefinitely many 'absences': the sorrow caused by the loss of a parent is different from the sorrow that the loss of a child brings, for instance.

But the problem is that it is not possible to differentiate one 'loss' from another because 'absence' does not have properties that allow us to differentiate them. In this sense, there can only be one 'absence': there are no infinite empty sets; the set is unique. The different objects that one loses could be unique, but their absence cannot generate unique feelings. If 'absence', the empty set that it is, could do this, anything and everything in this world could be explained as the result of the causal force exerted by 'absence'. Everything in the world would then be caused by 'absence', the empty set. Attempts to 'explain' the world using this unique set would merely explain the world away.

The answer I am focusing on brings our relationship to the object, calling it 'attachment', into the picture. That the same source, namely our attachment, produces two different sets is understood with respect to the role that temporality plays in human life.

In and of itself, most of us know that temporality plays an active role in life. Of course, we do not see time playing a causal role; but we do know that the difference between an unripe and a ripe banana is time, even though we see organic processes as causal factors. We speak of the curative role of time ('time heals all wounds'), its educative role ('only time will teach'), its predictive role ('time will tell'), its historical role ('the spirit of the time'), its generative role ('now the time is ripe'), its social role ('the time has come'), its indicative role ('it is now the time') and so on. In none of these cases is there any attribution of causality to time or temporality. We merely recognize that time plays an important role in life and that it is not just *anschauung*, that is it is not a mere 'intuition' or merely 'an element in sense perception'. The notions of 'impermanence' and 'transience' that Indian traditions speak about pick out the role(s) of time in human affairs and do not merely make the banal point that organisms that are born also die. Nor does this idea presage the notion of 'entropy' and its increase or decrease in the universe. The idea neither says that time-slices causally generate pleasure and pain, nor does it suggest that non-existent objects produce or cause changes in the world at another time-slice. Even though more requires saying in this context, I will content myself by noting that one cannot understand Indian notions of transience within the framework of a Kantian understanding of time.

Still, it might not be amiss to say a word or two more about the nature of 'attachment'. I have already alluded to the fact that Desire clings or that it attaches itself to objects. It has also been made clear that Desire is the result of human activities and not an innate property or trait of the species. We can temporarily tie them together in a simple fashion thus.

Let us assume that all organisms seek a state of pleasure and avoid a state of pain. We access pleasure or joy through objects and events in this world. In one sense, all objects in the world allow us to access the state we seek; therefore, any and every object is a means of access. As human beings grow up, they begin to believe that the means through which they *access* the state of joy and pleasure is the source or cause of that state. Consequently, human beings begin to focus on such objects and events. This 'focusing' is structured by a cluster formed by beliefs (about the object or event as the cause of joy), experience (the state of pleasure) and actions (that led to the state of joy). This cluster gives birth to Desire. Because any object can be a source of joy and pleasure, Desire can cling to any object whatsoever. Not only that. It also further cements and strengthens the cluster from which it is born. In doing so, it sustains and nurtures the relationship between the elements in this cluster from which it is born. This relationship can be described at different levels: as 'attachment', if described as the way human beings relate to objects and events; as 'grasping', if we described in terms of the nature of action that mistakenly seeks the object as though it is the end-state; and so on.

If we focus on this aspect, we could also say that when an object (or event) ceases to exist, human beings are unable to access the state of joy and pleasure that they could through the specific objects and events they used. This does not mean that they lose their abilities to access the state they seek but merely do not know how to do so without these objects and events.

If absence cannot be a cause, loss cannot generate sorrow. Its source must lie elsewhere. However, if joy and sorrow emerge from the same source, the options are not many: if you want to reduce the one, you need to reduce the other as well. Pain and pleasure, joy and suffering, become two faces of the same coin. You cannot separate them, and they do not occur independently of each other. *This is the human condition*, as this answer looks at the issue.

If this is human condition, how can we respond to pain and suffering? Minimally, we could cultivate the ability to go about with pain. That is what the Indian traditions advocate and Indian culture does: help us deal with pain and suffering by accepting its presence as the inevitable obverse side of the human ability to take pleasure and enjoy.

However, it is important to note that acquiring this ability does not reduce either the pain or the suffering. The Olympic swimmer has lost his abilities in an accident; the young mother lost her baby to cancer. Therefore, in so far as these individuals are in a state of pain, no alleviation of pain or suffering is possible. The only thing that one can teach them is the ability to bear this pain.

From the assumption that all organisms, not merely human ones, try to avoid pain and suffering and seek joy and pleasure, one can pursue two paths. One path wants to reduce pain and suffering, and maximize joy and pleasure; the other advocates learning to go about with them. The one believes that these are relatively independent of each other. The other denies such independence and claims that they are two faces of the same coin.

If you take one path, which is also the path that Christianity stipulates, you can formulate the question: should not our primary concern be one of alleviating human pain and suffering? If you take the other path, the path that the Indian traditions advocate, you formulate the following answer: except seeking and finding happiness on earth, which all of us aim at, there is no other remedy for pain and suffering. In the absence of such an end, merely trying to reduce pain and suffering is to impair human capacities for joy and pleasure. That is, such an attempt would end up making us less human. What appears as a genuinely human concern, when you look at it from the Western point of view, that is, our attempts to reduce pain and suffering of fellow human beings by increasing their joy and pleasure, becomes its opposite when perceived from within the framework of Indian traditions: *it becomes inhuman*. A genuinely human concern for our fellow human beings requires that we create conditions where everyone can seek and find happiness on earth.

XIV

Much more must be said than what I have been able to do. However, let me bring this chapter to its conclusion by picking up two very intimately related questions.

Let me begin with the first: I have suggested that the biblical conception of Man makes needs (and desires) constitutive of human beings. However, many thinkers who talk about needs are non-believers, or come from other traditions and cultures. How to understand their acceptance of this biblical idea?

During the last three decades or more, I have focused on answering the above question in many of its dimensions in most of my writings. It consists of the suggestion that Christianity, in its character as a religion, expands in two ways. One is well-known: *proselytization*. Here, people are converted to or inducted into Christianity. There is, however, a second, more insidious process of expansion of Christianity that most of us misunderstand: *secularization*. Mostly, *secularization* is presented as the process of moving away from Christianity or a religion, a process where people and intellectual domains free themselves from the grip of Christianity (or even religion in general). Nothing is further from truth. Today's 'secular' theories (about Man and society), even when we invest them with the accolade of 'science', are Christian theologies in disguise: I identify this as the process of an expansion of de-Christianized Christianity. Here, biblical theories are presented to us in a secular dress. As I have argued in my writings, we have all become Christians. Hence the reason why a scholar like Abraham Maslow can sell us the biblical image of Man as the beginning of 'humanistic' psychology. That image of human being as a creature of needs is assumed as true by many more.

Consequently, merely switching the terminology from needs to desires will not mean much here. Whether one calls Man a bundle of needs or a bundle of desires, the source is the same: the Christian Bible. This Christian notion of Man has spread far and wide in many secular guises. I am not signalling that such is the case simply because this thought occurs in the Bible. If our scientific understanding of human beings were to confirm or support this idea, one could accept the possibility that the truth of the Bible is also a truth about us, human beings. However, that is not the case. We only use one way of describing human actions: namely, we act out our intrinsic needs or desires. This cannot simply be presented as a fact about human existence. As we have noticed, there are other ways of describing the same situation: the multiplicity of desires indicates that Desire attaches itself to multiple objects.

Therefore, we need to test these competing ideas and proposals as hypotheses about human beings. Such a test would not only mean that we use the best criteria we have today to assess their cognitive worth. It also means that we do more, much more. We must understand how it is cognitively possible that religious ideas become unquestioned empirical, factual and anthropological trivia. Developing hypotheses about this process is only a part of the task facing us today. The other part flows from the realization that these ideas have founded the creation of social, political, economic and cultural institutions as well. That is, the secularization of Christianity does not occur only in the realm of ideas; it also creates and generates a 'secular' world. If our intellectual and social worlds are both 'secularized' religious worlds, what do we do? How do we change the world we are living in so that it does not continue to remain a de-Christianized Christian world?

These questions are urgent. They require answers sooner rather than later because both Christians and non-Christians living in this world are paying a huge price for inhabiting a de-Christianized Christian world. Even though we cannot appreciate this tragedy in depth here, let me indicate its nature by taking up the second question that also requires an answer.

XV

The second question is this: If India has indeed built such a 'wonderful' social security system, what happened to it and where is it now? I will focus on only one thread of an answer.

Indians are children of two colonialisms. One of the effects of these colonialisms is the resulting damage: not so much on Indian culture as on its transmission. There are two things of importance here. One: Indian culture continues to be transmitted from one generation to the other. Second: today, however, making Indian culture one's own requires a conscious effort, that is, one must relearn what has already been learnt. Because what is learnt about a culture is mostly implicit, it is possible to superimpose ways of explicit thinking upon such a process, even when what is superimposed conflicts with what it is imposed upon. This is the case with India.

Christian thinking in its de-Christianized form is superimposed in a deformed way on structures that are its opposite. There is an important double result arising from this act of superimposition: first, the superimposed is itself distorted; second, serious problems arise because of the nature of the distortion. That is, (a) Christian thinking gets deeply deformed in the process of trying to map it onto incompatible thought structures; (b) those who try to imbibe the superimposition fail and suffer because of their inability to perceive a non-existent symmetrical form in the grotesquely deformed.

Consider, for instance, most of the programmes that modern India has instituted. Their central characteristic is this: they are called 'social welfare' programmes. This is where distortion occurs: in trying to imitate the West, the modern Indian State institutes what it believes to be 'similar' programmes, while failing miserably in the process. It makes conceptual sense in Western culture to speak of basic of human needs, which the State tries to satisfy. I have already suggested that this need-talk makes no sense in Indian culture. Consequently, these programmes in India do just the opposite of what the talk (about needs and desires) does. In post-independent India, these 'social welfare' programmes provide the following: free sarees to widows, free bicycles to students from some caste groups, free milk to children, scholarships to a specific set of caste groups, highly subsidized rice for some professions, guaranteed education, promotions and jobs to members of some castes, and so on. These are not 'social welfare' programmes in any sense of the term. In Western culture, *only* private charitable foundations can dispense their largesse *in this fashion*. A State can only pursue the general interests of society and cannot randomly make laws that disburse the resources of the state exchequer only to those groups that take the fancies of a political party or a government. Programmes that embody such arbitrary laws do not qualify as 'social welfare programmes'. Yet, the Indian State doles out charities to groups that a party or government fancies and enacts laws to that effect.

This is called 'statecraft' in India. In that case, a good government is identical to a well-run NGO. The NGOs dole out charities, which is what it means to 'govern' in India today. Perhaps this idea explains why the previous government (under Manmohan Singh) was so directly controlled by a select group of NGOs under the able leadership of Mrs. Sonia Gandhi. This is not 'populism'; it is what 'politics' means in India: each government, each political party prides itself on the particular interests it serves. Being 'pro-farmers', 'pro-women', 'pro-Dalit', 'pro-workers', 'pro-widows', 'pro-poor' etc. are the only available legitimate and legitimizing distinctions. 'Government' and 'governance' mean this in modern India.

One of the most inviolable goals of democratic states in the West is to focus on the general interests of society. The State cannot pursue corporatist or sectional interests, even if a particular group happens to be in the majority. That is, democracy cannot and does not allow the State to pursue particular interests at the cost of general interests. Particular interests are always subordinated to general interests. The Indian state, by contrast, pursues only particular interests: privileging one caste group or another, defending the interests of this or that specific group to the detriment of general interests etc. To understand the *why* of this situation, as it is relevant to the theme of this chapter, we need to appreciate another dimension of Indian 'politics'.

We all know that India is a representative democracy. However, what should be 'represented' in a democratically elected parliament? If we look at the relevant legislations or at the rules that political parties impose on themselves or at the hardly implicit criteria used to field candidates for elections, we observe the following: 'representation' refers to the presence of people from different castes in the parliament. Implicitly, the belief appears to be that the more a parliament represents the differences between people, the better a job it does at being a 'representation' of the people. 'Caste' and 'religion' play a major role here because, as the standard textbook story has it, 'the caste system' and 'religious diversity' structure Indian society. Therefore, electoral constituencies are also 'reserved' for caste groups: contesting democratic elections in such regions is an issue of caste-certificates.

To get a flavour of this notion of representation, assume that laws and rules are legislated in a democracy requiring that the parliament must have representatives from: the 'mentally disabled', 'the physically disabled', at least one from every single 'ethnic group' present in that society, one from every 'minority' group etc. Assume further that these people are the elected representatives, who legislate laws for that society. The laws and rules for their election lay down almost explicitly what these people should do in the parliament: each must 'represent' and 'defend' his or her sectional and group interests and negotiate with the others to get his or her proposal approved by the majority. Is this the notion of 'representation' in a representative democracy, as we have known it over centuries?

If yes, by providing legitimacy to the pursuit of narrow and sectional interests, the answer opens the door to an even more insidious phenomenon, which is psychologically and sociologically actual. The 'narrowest' interest that one could strive for is one's own. Consequently, it becomes very legitimate to further one's individual interests as an 'elected representative' in the parliament. Such a pursuit might require the use of an appropriate language and an ability to collude. But this is a pragmatic issue: in principle, 'representation', here, can only mean representing personal interests. Indian politics incorporates this notion of 'representation'.

If we confine ourselves to the theme of this chapter, the reason for this state of affairs is not far to seek. The notion of 'interests', whether particular or general, is intimately connected to and very dependent on the notion of 'needs'. One can sensibly begin speaking about 'interests', when one links actions to its outcomes and to their contributions to a satisfaction of 'needs'. Aiming to satisfy the 'needs' of all people in society is to pursue general interests; particular interests pick out the pursuit of satisfying the needs of a particular group of people. Consequently, in a culture where the notion of 'needs' makes no sense, neither does the notion of 'interests'. This means that Indian languages do not have words to express the notion 'interests', even if some or another word has been coined for the purposes of 'translation'. In this sense, the public interest litigations in India are not expressions of 'judicial activism', as some have called it. It is probably a phenomenon of an entirely different kind.

Be that as it may, in its functioning, the modern Indian State retraces old Indian stories about kings, instead of resembling a democratic state. These kings of yesteryears endowed gifts: pieces of land to this or that temple or individual; wealth to this or that intellectual or to paupers; money to build public utilities; rice and sarees to the poor and the widows; and so on. That is exactly what the State does in India. A good government here is one which functions like an NGO or a king.

XVI

The Indian notion of Desire also helps us track the effects of these deformations. The results of such State programmes can only be catastrophic in nature. The State would merely strengthen the force of Desire among the beneficiaries of such programmes and increase the intensity with which it latches on to objects. Strengthening the force of Desire in an individual is to encourage greed and feed unhappiness. The policies of the State are creating such multiple social layers in society with its programmes, while feeding them greed, jealousy, hate, covetousness and, thus, unhappiness. The talk of 'needs' flows into the pseudo-language of 'social justice' to justify the strengthening of conflict and hatred between people. Each fights for its 'share' of charity, which, of course, is the scarce resource of the public exchequer. Receiving such 'doles' morphs into a *birth right*: only those with the 'right' birth certificates are entitled to them. However, this occurs in the name of 'social equality'. The language of needs is a mantra now. It has become that, not only because it is chanted without understanding, but also because chanting could never serve as justification.

The psychological profiles of the continuous beneficiaries of the State dole that emerge from an institutionalized language of needs show many invariances across cultures. In these people, hatred of those who are perceived as 'better off' increases almost proportionately with their dependency on the 'good will' (or the taxes) of those others. While they can be beneficiaries only because of the existence of others, these 'others' are identified as the 'real causes' for their present status. The received 'charity' becomes a right; intensified covetousness for material goods breeds resentment towards a society that does not allow them to lay claims to all goods. These psychological properties, in their turn, give birth to other emotions and experiences that end up as a cluster which transforms human beings into a seething cauldron of resentment, discontent and unhappiness. In response to this, perhaps, a generalized contempt towards such continuous beneficiaries begins to emerge in society at large.

In any case, the problem with India is not that it is following the Western path; it cannot. It is trying to imitate the Church without being able to understand her. No imitation is possible, however, if the imitated cannot be very closely tracked. That is where India is today.

The only route forward for Indians, as I see it, is to begin accessing their own culture consciously. This does not mean that one repeats Buddha's *anatta* or Shankara's *atman* instead of 'needs'; or that we need the *Yogasutra* today or that we should speak the language of the *Brahma Sutra*. A formulation of thoughts from Indian culture in the scientific language of the 21st century is the requirement today. It is either the case that God came to the Arabian Desert to impart knowledge about human beings, or it is the case that Indian notions can generate theories about Man and society that could challenge current hypotheses.

Conclusion

There are, of course, many objections that require to be met. I shall leave those for other times and places. However, there is one other point I want to make. I am not taking the position that India does not need science and technology or that we should not aim at improving the health of people or even that we should be indifferent to poverty and suffering. I merely emphasize that (a) we need to be clear about the goals of a social security system; (b) the creation and sustenance of such a system cannot be undertaken by the State. Further, with respect to the Western social security system, I imply that it looks at human beings as animals (in the sense that one treats them the way one treats household pets, giving both exactly the same kind of 'care'), except that the State treats its citizens with more suspicion ('not wanting to work', 'wanting to be on the dole all the time', 'cheating the State', 'being fraudulent' etc.) than how people treat their pets. This background is pervasive in the kind of social security system that the West has generated and sustained over millennia, on the one hand, and in the conception of being human underlying that safety net, on the other. Thus, we begin to see how to think about cultural differences in new and interesting ways.

References

The Holy Bible: English Standard Version (ESV). 2001. Wheaton: Standard Bible Society.
The Holy Bible: The New International Version (NIV). 2011. Grand Rapids, MI: Zondervan.

Maslow, Abraham H. 1943. 'A Theory of Human Motivation', *Psychological Review*, 50 (4): 370–396.
Monier-Williams, Monier. 1872. *A Sanskrit-English Dictionary Etymologically and Philologically Arranged with Special Reference to Greek, Latin, Gothic, German, Anglo-Saxon, and Other Cognate Indo-European Languages.* Oxford: The Clarendon Press.
Oxford English Dictionary. 1989. 2nd edition. Oxford: Oxford University Press.

10
THE POLITICS OF KNOWLEDGE, HERE AND NOW
A conversation with Ashis Nandy

Ashis Nandy and *Ananya Vajpeyi*

This interview was conducted in Professor Ashis Nandy's office at the Centre for the Study of Developing Societies, in one long sitting, on 8th June 2015.

In fact, it was but a stage in an ongoing conversation that we have been having over the past five years or so, most of which is not documented in any systematic way. Ashis da and I often chat about Indian classical music, both Hindustani as well as Carnatic. This is a shared passion for us, although I am invariably the one to learn from him, as he has been listening to this music a lot longer than I have, and has had a personal acquaintance with some of its great exponents as well as its theorists over the past four to five decades. Music has given us a concrete way to talk about questions of tradition, innovation, creativity, inspiration, history, futures, the arts, classical and popular forms, aesthetics, emotions, consciousness, cultural politics, civil liberties, freedom of expression, beauty, religion, caste, spirituality, transcendence ... a broad range of subjects that interest Ashis da and that he has thought and written about over the course of his long and illustrious career.

In this interview, edited extracts from which are published below, we did not set out to speak specifically about music. Rather, I was at that time in the process of editing a journal issue on classics and philology, triggered in part by the 'culture wars' between India's left-liberal intellectual establishment and the ideologues of the Hindu Right, loyal to the BJP-led national government that has been in power in Delhi since mid-2014. Classical arts and ancient texts have now become the most likely targets of reactionary appropriation, making philological scholarship and historical analysis even more difficult than usual, adding political difficulties to the already considerable challenges of institutional crisis and marginalized or worse, endangered epistemologies.

But true to form, Ashis da's response was not that of any of the other classicists, historians, artistes, writers, culture critics and political commentators I had invited to think about India's knowledge systems either in the past or about the past. With his usual dexterity, he was able to steer our discussion in quite an unexpected direction, firmly bringing the focus back from the past to the present, from the classical to the contemporary, from texts to practices, and from cultural memory to cultural life. His insistence on the complex temporalities and the multiple genealogies of cultural forms in the present moved us – or at least me – away from the sense of crisis and the fear of loss to a reconsideration of what it is that we do, whether in music or architecture or theatre or philosophy or literature, what we do *here and now*, which is at once and inevitably a product of and a departure from all that was done in times gone by.

As with all good psychoanalysis, the result was both a better understanding of the situation at hand as well as, in the long run, just the necessary and sufficient degree of hope to continue with the tasks of creativity and criticism even in the face of extreme political provocation.
—Ananya Vajpeyi

* * *

AV *[Ananya Vajpeyi]:*   Let's talk about the politics of knowledge.
AN *[Ashis Nandy]:*   But let us not try to handle the main problem it poses without entering the politics of knowledge.
AV: Which problem?
AN: The problem of colonial dominance and its consequences in the knowledge sector. My feeling is that exactly as you need a knowledge of ancient India, you need a knowledge of the little cultures of India – not an ethnography of one of them but an acquaintance with a number of them – particularly the way many of them came into their own in the medieval period and crossed caste, religious and sect boundaries to set up a new definition of cosmopolitanism. That provides you with some real clues to the way some of the knowledge systems are likely to go in the future. Simply reading ancient texts or the thousands of previously unread manuscripts will not do, and this responsibility is really shunned by many. I have nothing against the classics. Every society loves its classics, but they do not live by them. They live by their vernacular or popular incarnations.

That is one of the reasons I've concentrated mostly on the little cultures, usually the political cultures of communities or of specific knowledge systems, such as law, psychology, environment, modern science, popular cinema or cricket. I've never gone into any elaborate interpretation of ancient texts. If a problem originates in the contemporary politics of knowledge such a problem has to be solved politically, within the contemporary context. My friends sometimes grumble about it: 'You're not going into the texts, why don't you go into the texts?' Why should I go into much-studied, authoritative, ancient texts? Would they give me clues to the contemporary politics of knowledge?

The second point I want to make is this – we should be clear about our vantage point and categories from the beginning. What kind of a great knowledge system is there in India, where you don't have any negotiation or engagement with the living carriers of knowledge, but engage only with ancient texts or ancient commentators? If it is truly a living knowledge system, then you should be able to deal with contemporaries, with people who are living and working here now, and *in whom the ancients survive*, even if in an attenuated form and perhaps unwittingly. If Shudraka, the Sanskrit playwright, exists in contemporary playwrights – surely that is a sign of a living tradition? You might then claim that the tradition of Sanskrit drama is alive and kicking. Many insist that if one digests Abhinavagupta, one will get clues. His categories survive. But even if I get clues, I won't know why or how to use them! For no contemporary has processed Abhinavagupta for me by writing plays or literary criticisms of contemporary playwrights, influenced by Shudraka directly or by a long tradition of Sanskrit drama or by Abhinavagupta himself. What do I do with those clues? Playwrights are playwrights; they write plays not commentaries. They are also not *bhashyakaras*, fortunately. At most they read who they think are the other relevant or 'living' playwrights. A living system survives on living beings.

AV: Yes...
AN: Indian classical music is a good example! It is a living tradition; I'm willing to talk about its culture. I'm willing to talk about its experts, performers, theorists – from Swami Pragyananda and Dilip Kumar Roy to Dhurjati Prasad Mukherjee and Vamanrao Deshpande. I'm willing to engage with all of them. But you cannot tell me to go in to some old text on music to grapple

with contemporary politics of music – that's not my interest. I am interested in meeting some of the *stapathis* of Tamil Nadu because they are still building temples. In that way their skill, their knowledge of temple building is living. But beyond a point I'm not interested in that either, because it's a highly specialized skill that tells you very little about contemporary politics of architecture.

I am more interested in living practitioners who, by using traditional crafts people from different communities in different parts of the country, are co-creating new architectural traditions in contemporary India. In this sense, Laurie Baker for me is a more serious candidate for engagement than many Indian architects – Baker being a contemporary architect who engaged with Indian traditions of architecture in practice. I want to know what made him tick as an *Indian* architect. Does skin colour or blood lines determine the borders of Indian cultures of science or art?

Likewise, if I ever think of writing on Hussain, I shall have to ask why he is not considered one of the greatest iconographers of Hinduism. Is it because of his Muslim name? Geeti Sen, the art critic, tells me that he was a devout Muslim but I am also told that he belonged to the small Sulaymani Bohra community, a Muslim community that has over generations engaged with Hindu gods and goddesses with deep reverence and piety, somewhat like the Patuas of Bengal. Did the illiterate vandals who destroyed so many of his priceless paintings and their political godfathers know of this other intimacy? Did Hussain have the right to decide how to convey the divinity of goddesses Durga and Saraswati, or did that right belong only to the vandals and their political patrons? At what point do the small mafia-like bands begin to think that they protect Hinduism and have the exclusive right to speak on behalf of millions of Hindus who believe that Hinduism protects them?

Recently, I have written a paper on R. L. Kumar, an untrained architect who died at a young age a couple of years ago. He was wonderfully creative in many of his works. I have tried to locate the sources of his creativity, his ability to harness the creativity of local artisans in his ventures, his reactions to contemporary politics, how the city of Bangalore shaped him and the politics of his architecture.

AV: It seems to me that, in all the examples you gave of living traditions, you can find that 'life' – in literature, in the performing arts, in the plastic arts, in crafts (so-called), and maybe in architecture and so on. But I think it would be fair to say that you can't find it in philosophy. You can't find that living tradition in philosophy; in other words, we possibly aren't producing contemporary *mimansakas* or *nayyayikas* or even Buddhists in that discipline or sphere (I mean in philosophy); you are forced to look at old texts because the frontiers of that knowledge have frozen some time ago and they are not evolving. Do you think that's true, or not really?

AN: It is mostly true. Though we should also acknowledge that the issues we confront in philosophy are not absent in the domains of science, social knowledge, fine arts and architecture. Now to come back to our main concern, I have nothing against going back to traditional texts or ancient texts, but that's a different exercise. You cannot take off from a contemporary politics of knowledge and say that by going to ancient texts you will handle that politics. It's like going to Chanakya, and hoping to attack problems of contemporary statecraft and geopolitics. Yes, if Chanakya exists within people, in the hearts of people – is a living reality and a continuous presence and not merely a surviving metaphor – then maybe one should take interest in his texts at some point. Ramachandra Gandhi tried to blow life into Vedanta in *Sita's Kitchen* and Sudhir Kakar into Vatsyayana's gymnastics and cultural geography of sex in *The Ascetic of Desire*. A roughly similar argument can be made about D. Venkat Rao's recent work on mnemonic cultures. I take them seriously. Sudhir and Venkat usually stay out of politics, but *Sita's Kitchen* is a direct intervention in the contemporary politics of knowledge.

The basic argument is simple. Because you have to look at the past while you yourself are living in the present, the past and future meet at *this* point of time. *This* moment is the moment of engagement. You cannot enter past politics, but you have to confront the politics of the past now. When the doctor asks you, 'Did you have stomach aches earlier?' Or, 'Do you have a history of forgetfulness?' there is no expectation that you would give precise, technical answers. For, whatever your answers, the doctor has to interpret it and diagnose what is wrong with you now. Your imprecise, non-technical case history of sickness lives out its life in the diagnosis. After all, the doctor treats a living being suffering from a set of symptoms in the present.

AV: So your fundamental premise is that culture is always living. In as much as we are trying to diagnose culture or diagnose knowledge, we can only do so if we proceed as though these are living things.

AN: Yes and no. Many cultures that demand sustained intensity cannot or did not last very long. The culture of India's freedom movement is now gasping for breath. The culture of revolutionary violence too now looks doomed. The culture of Third Reich is dead. Its slightly comic version, Italian fascism, is more resilient. In different guises, it sometimes raises its head in Latin America, Africa and now in South Asia. On the other hand, the culture centering on virtual reality is a new entrant on the world stage.

The onus is partly on us to make some cultures part of a living tradition. They are not automatically so. I reiterate that I have nothing against the classical tradition. A classical tradition surviving in a university department is not the same as a classical tradition being a part of a living tradition of literature or philosophy. I am saying that if you are interested in the politics of knowledge, you may have to go to the *puranas*, some of which are an integral part of life not merely in India but also in Thailand, Malaysia and Indonesia.

Over the centuries, we have expressed our anxieties, fears, hopes and ambitions through the language of the *puranas*. In the case of the *Ramayana*, for instance, a diverse lot of people – ranging all the way from Kamban, Krittibas Ojha and Tulsidas to Michael Madhusudan Dutt, Rabindranath Tagore and Mohammad Iqbal – have kept the epic alive. Valmiki's *Ramayana* enters the picture only if you are comparing it with, say, the *Ramcharitmanas* to show how and why Tulsidas has entered public consciousness more deeply than Valmiki has in our times or to examine how *Ramcharitmanas* is different from the other vernacular *Ramayanas* and what does that difference tell us about the changing contours of our cultural life. It is no accident that Iqbal, the great poet and one of the founding fathers of Pakistan, too wrote a brilliant *prashasti* of Ram. Similarly, the *Mahabharata* is part of our living culture because of its various vernacular versions and because of the creativity in our times of a whole series of gifted persons such as Rabindranath Tagore, Irawati Karve, Shivaji Sawant, Buddhadev Bose, Shyam Benegal and even theatre persons like Dharmaveer Bharati and Heisnam Kanhailal.

AV: Okay, I was going to ask you that. When people, even our colleagues or even in your work, say that the *Mahabharata* and the *Ramayana* are relevant to us and epic themes and forms are a part of us . . . or let us say, Asoka, or Kautilya, or *Manusmriti*, when people say, or you say, let's read these because they are already in our heads somehow, then would you say that there is a distinction in reading philologically versus doing that organically? Do we have any organic relationship to these texts? Are we differently motivated and prepared in approaching different texts – do some texts come more naturally to us than others? Is Chanakya easier than Kalidasa?

AN: That is an important and suggestive question. We perhaps don't have in all cases the organic relationship that you have in mind. We do distinguish between different kinds of texts. Chanakya may be easier than Kalidasa, but I doubt if any one reads Chanakya except specialist-scholars. Kalidasa is loved, though probably not read that much. But you can read vernacular versions of the *Mahabharata* and the *Ramayana* and read or see novels, plays and films inspired by them; that is more relevant. The organic relationship ensures that you do not have to brainwash people to read texts in the name of nationalism. Sometimes people live with a text without knowing or reading it. It is mnemonically there in us. When Delhi University purged A.K. Ramanujan's essay on 300 Ramayanas, it exiled a part of the Indic civilization and Hinduism, too, from the campus.

AV: By 'organic' I mean – can we or do we make them our own, or are they already in us, in some sense?

AN: In the sense that they are already in us. We recover or access that – but from their cultural presence, not from Sanskrit. The Sanskrit text is not in us; it is in a small section of the population. In this sense, it's a bogus claim that Sanskrit is the mother of all languages. Many tribal languages, perhaps even some of the Dravidian languages have led parallel lives. Yet, we can recover our sense of organic bonds with these texts – a sense of owning them, as you call it. That 'organic belonging' happens; you do not have to ensure it through the coercive apparatus of the state. Nor do you have to go to Sanskrit to enforce it.

AV: I guess, I am just trying to understand to what extent we might have a relationship to certain texts, or might not. . .

AN: I think it is our definitions and starting points. That is why nothing much is coming out of it.

AV: Is it our definition?

AN: Yes, our definition of what is important. Look, if you want to talk about dialectical thinking in India before Hegel, theory of evolution before Darwin, and differential equations before Newton, you read one kind of texts. If Nagarjuna or Lokayata is organically in you, and therefore you reach out for Hegel, it becomes another story. Hegel then becomes a very useful critique of our tradition. You are then not willing to wait eternally for all Indians to turn Hegelians for your political project. You yourself are not awed by him; you cannot then miss the presence of racism in Hegel and in many left Hegelians like Marx and Engels.

The ancients might have been very wise, but they did not know of organized genocides, famines used as a genocidal device, concentration camps and gas chambers. They did not know of a four-continent slave trade justified by Social Darwinism, nuclear weapons used to wipe out entire cities of non-combatants, carpet and napalm bombings of civilians, and global warming threatening the survival of the earth itself. They worked with a more innocent concept of evil.

Nor did they know the story of our freedom struggle. That story tells us more about what Indian traditions – living Indian traditions – are capable of than any ancient text can do. At the cost of repetition, I shall insist that even if you want to map the presence of epic heroes in Indian society or the location of women and femininity in public life, you may have to go to vernacular, more accessible versions of the *Ramayana* and *Mahabharata* that have been touched by contemporary life – and to the changing social sensitivities and the profiles of creativity of our contemporaries – self-consciously or unwittingly searching for new *yugadharmas*. Rabindranath Tagore's *Kavye Upekshita* and *Karna-Kunti Sambad*, Irawati Karve's *Yuganta*, Shivaji Sawant's *Mrityunjaya*, and Dharamveer Bharati's *Andha Yug* are random examples. Even the popular cinema of Manmohan Desai, who once claimed that all his successful films had plots inspired by the *Mahabharata*, and the more serious efforts of Shyam Benegal's *Kalyug* or Heisnam Kanhailal's *Karna* help to keep alive a tradition.

AV: So, in other words what you are saying is, what is proximate or recent is always going to take precedence over what is very distant and ancient?

AN: No, but the proximate is likely to give a better clue to the politics of it, because the politics you are talking about is proximate.

AV: But then that is just the nature of time, isn't it? That is, anything which was a longtime ago cannot know about whatever came later – the relationship of X reflecting on Y is going to be a one-way relationship, from Y to X and not vice versa. You can look back on the past, but the past cannot look to the future. . . . We can look back, but the ancients cannot look. . .

AN: Forward. . .

AV: . . . Say anything to us, because. . .

AN: They say many things to us, in works of literature, social knowledge and philosophy, but if you are thinking of a contemporary politics of dominance in the knowledge sector you have to come back to the question of how that ancient knowledge system has survived till today, if it has survived at all. Or, you can take the position of Max Mueller who made his students promise that they would never visit India. For, contemporary India didn't reflect or tell anything about ancient India and vice versa.

AV: Really?

AN: Yes. He himself didn't visit India ever.

AV: Oh, I didn't know he made his students take a vow!

AN: Even today, there are many enthusiastic Indians who can be called born-again Max Muellers; they don't want to look at their contemporaries. Because if you move out of the classical frame, they feel, you will go down the global hierarchy – to the humbler communities of artisans and musicians or to low-brow artists or to non-modern healers, for instance, who will compromise your status and mess up your categories. If you are an architect, you will move closer to Laurie Baker and R.L. Kumar; if a musician, you might have to take more seriously your semi-literate guru and his memory-intensive, highly personalized teaching style and lose contact with the heavyweight historians and theorists of Indian music and their learned treatises.

AV: Because they don't recognize the improvizational nature of music?

AN: Yes. The first thing you have to recognize is that Indian music is mnemonic and improvizational. Venkat talks about mnemonic cultures, but there are, along with them, mnemonic disciplines and mnemonic parts of our own self. Ravi Shankar was a well-educated, modern man well-exposed to the world. Then he went to learn from Alauddin Khan in semi-rural Maihar, a town in central India unknown to most Indians and had to learn to live with a mnemonic discipline. While learning Indian classical music you internalize your guru in the long run, but on your own terms. The gurus are like walking 'universities' and walking 'encyclopedias', and when they die, this university closes and this encyclopedia goes out of print. But if you are a worthy student, you become a new university and a new encyclopedia that carry with them the memory traces of older ones. That is what a living knowledge system is.

And I would focus on that kind of resistance to the dominant knowledge system than on the curiosity that takes one to Chanakya on statecraft or strategic studies and Abhinavagupta on aesthetics.

AV: Why?

AN: Well, read some ancient texts on *natyasastra*, *shilpasastra* or whatever but also please read Ananda Coomaraswamy, the 20th century art historian and philosopher, who tried to bring some of these texts to life for us. Without such mediations classics live only for the classicists. Nothing wrong with that. But then, we are at the moment discussing the politics of knowledge, not the fate of classical studies.

AV: I'm getting your point. I'd say this state of affairs gives rise to two problems. One is that you are not able to ever come up with a satisfactory rebuttal or response or you're not able to fight back. This is the attitude of many people in the field of theory, or postcolonial theory or people trying to discover: What is South Asian theory? Such people are invested in equalizing the power imbalance that exists in the discourse of theory. There is colonial domination, but somehow you cannot crawl out from under it and assert your equality because a playing-field is never even, you know you are doing it in English, you are working out of the colonial university, you have a philological relationship to your text, you have forgotten your own languages, and there are all these problems, right? So what you are saying is that we have to shift the battleground, we have to engage with contemporary living traditions, extant cultures and contemporary forms and take them seriously rather than harping on about the greatness of the ancients.

AN: Some bridge between the ancients and today's thinking and practice is a must. Like Dhrupad, which links *Samaveda* and Vedic chants and today's *Khayals* and *Thumris*. The dominance of English literature is not exercised in the name of Chaucer or Shakespeare; it's mostly about modern and contemporary literature in English and its capabilities as a carrier of knowledge.

AV: So you think we seem to have a problem in managing the genealogy of our own knowledge?

AN: *Now* you are talking about the actual work that needs to be done.

AV: We have a problem with that. We haven't solved that problem; we can't deal with that genealogy. We can't even construct it properly because...

AN: It's too diverse and there are very few intermediaries between our presumed ancestors and us. It is like knowing the founders of our families and not knowing our parents and grandparents, not even siblings. We are totally at loss, disoriented and probably going schizoid. But look at music. Look at architecture. These are improvisational forms. They preserve, but they also improvise on tradition to address contemporary concerns, even contemporary tastes. Probably the social sciences in the Southern world should experiment with an improvisational style.

AV: So you're saying whatever is worthy of survival will survive or has survived?

AN: No, I'm not saying that. I am saying that if you don't grant dignity to your contemporaries who have often lived out their creative lives under extreme situations – poverty, absence of recognition and indignity – if you cannot converse with them or deal with that, you have no right to talk on the global politics of dominance because that reactive classicism, that return to the Indian classics, it's only a way of affirming a new hierarchy.

AV: So let me offer a counterexample, just to see what happens. Have you seen the Akshardhaam temple?

AN: Yes.

AV: The one on the bank of Yamuna on the way to NOIDA, built by the Swaminarayan sect?

AN: It's a bloody eye-sore.

AV: So, supposing you say this is contemporary religiosity, and we must grant it dignity.

AN: I see it as a failed modern attempt to connect to the classic unmediated by living traditions of temple building substituting piety with grandeur and size. Compare it with the Lotus Temple of the Bahais, which also is not perfect, but being more modest and not seeking grandeur, is still attractive in its own way. Why does the Lotus Temple work better, as opposed to the monstrosity on the riverbank? That's your responsibility to find out. Only then can you grasp the problem we are posing.

AV: But what I'm saying is, if in the name of contemporary temple building, I'm faced with an Akshardhaam temple, and I hate it, even though it has all the classical references – then what do I do?

AN: Frankly, our criteria are not clear. This is neither coming from ancient texts nor from *sthapatis* still working today nor from places of worship and great temples that have contemporary references and standards of construction. This is pseudo-classicism, an ersatz version of the ancient Indian temple.

AV: In China too you find this. And you always think that it is a 'Chinese' version of something if it's fake or cheap, or nouveau, or kitsch.

AN: Yes. They made an exact replica of the Forbidden City in some other city, so that the Chinese people wouldn't have to go to Beijing to see the Forbidden City. They also have an exact replica of the White House at some distant corner of China.

AV: No, but this is the question, are we to judge this, or are we to be respectful . . . because there is a market place, after all.

AN: You should engage with it, you should be able to say point blank that this is authentic, inauthentic, good, bad, beautiful, ugly, whatever. And I think this is our responsibility. Only then it becomes a part of a living culture. It becomes a living culture by that very exercise of some people rejecting it and some people debating it, and that debate being shared or transmitted and having an effect in the long run in a living culture.

AV: Right, so I guess that brings me to another problem which I see: Why do we fail to do anything useful by way of intervening in the politics of knowledge?

AN: Some people have done it, so we cannot really say it is totally a bleak scene. Even in restoration and conservation, some things are very beautifully done, like Humayun's Tomb in Nizamuddin near which we both stay. When I first came to Delhi 50 years ago, there were ugly constructions around it – temporary baths, toilets and ugly electrical and sanitary fittings, dilapidated mosques, graves, etc. That was understandable because refugees were staying there at the time of Partition. Today the Archaeological Survey of India and the Agha Khan Trust have been doing a nice job.

But there is also Akshardhaam. They threw money at it and tried to make a worthwhile tourist destination out of it, to derive as a by-product some political clout, too. Akshardhaam *is* a statement of power. If you don't handle it just because it is contemporary or ersatz, if you don't grant that this is what Indian 'tradition' has become, then you cannot fight the dominance of a destination like Akshardhaam and you are shirking your responsibility as an intellectual. Otherwise, I don't have any objections against traditions, ancient texts, the recognized classics – I have great fondness for many of them.

People in the West can go and watch contemporary productions of Shakespeare's plays; they can go and hear different contemporary orchestras perform Beethoven or Bach. It's not the same thing; this is not the problem we have. We are talking of the politics of knowledge. And when you talk of politics of knowledge systems, if we are unwilling to converse with our contemporaries, the loss is ours. Take D. Venkat Rao; despite the story of a modern-day pundit he has told in *The Last Brahmin*, despite his marvellous translation, nobody has taken that account seriously!

AV: I took it seriously.

AN: You took it seriously, because you may be an exception. Let there be no illusion about it. Neither Sanskritists have taken it seriously, nor Indologists, nor even those who talk loudly of traditions. Madhu Khanna would not write a review essay on it, nor would Makarand Paranjape – Why? Arindam Chakrabarti might not even have read it. That is dominance, when we are blinded about living tradition. Those who have brought that to our attention – let's engage with them. If you are seriously interested in tradition, that's what we have to do.

AV: So, I guess I was wrong to say that with a few exceptions like, let's say the restoration of Humayun's Tomb which is well done, or interventions like those made by Venkat Rao or S. N. Balagangadhara or others, most of the time there is a divorce...

AN: In D. R. Nagaraj, there was no divorce. I had immense hopes, emotional and intellectual investments in that man, because I thought he carried the future of this kind of sensitivity instinctively. Not so many do so these days; there are not many people who are aware of the politics of the classical and are willing to engage with it at every level.

AV: So, while there is paucity of such efforts and of such individuals, the discourse gets hijacked by the political right wing because there is a vacuum.

AN: And we were taught in our childhood that nature abhors a vacuum. The political right wing never cared for D. R. Nagaraj.

AV: No, they have not cared for D. R. Nagaraj, but they have tried to appropriate various aspects of the study of the past, various artefacts, and various texts.

AN: They're doing it because we are giving them the handle; we are treating the knowledge of ancient texts like apolitical or depoliticized neophytes – that is why the so-called right finds it so easy to get away with their colonial version of Hinduism. By the way, the Left has not cared for Nagaraj either, outside a relatively small geographical region, nor do most Dalit intellectuals outside South India.

That's why I'm saying I don't want to study Abhinavagupta. Enough is enough! Everybody, everywhere I go, discusses Abhinavagupta. Why not look at the direct or indirect impact of Abhinavagupta on, say, Girish Karnad? Have the Vacanakaras or the tradition of Yakshagana influenced Karnad more? What are the sources of his creativity? Did Karnad have to grapple with the classical and modern simultaneously? How has he done so? I am waiting for someone to work on those kinds of issues. There is a living tradition of theatre after all.

AV: Okay, let's say for example when you see these discussions on ancient science, which are now again gathering some momentum, you see completely bogus arguments made by votaries of the Hindu Right. Many of them say: 'I'm an engineer, I'm a scientist, I'm telling you that such-and-such traditional practice or folk theory is scientific.' What are we supposed to do with this?

AN: I should clarify at this point that I have stopped classifying people in terms of the Right–Left dichotomy. I consider those you call the Hindu Right as a left-handed sect, a somewhat perverted *baam-panthi* sect promoting a rather comical version of, what my friend activist-intellectual Arun Kumar alias Panibaba calls, toady Hinduism. It was a loving gift of European colonialism to South Asia, as was the blood-thirsty version of positivist Marxism that for a long while dominated our intellectual scene. Some of our modern scientists are giving them the scope to get away with their hare-brained ideas because they too, along with the Hindu nationalists, suffer from the same feelings of inferiority.

AV: Okay. This is a question you engaged with for 30 years, at least?

AN: Perhaps longer.

AV: In this time, in dealing with alternative sciences and with the history and politics of science in India, have you seen that there has been some change or some improvement in the discourse, some advances in the argument?

AN: Yes.

AV: Then why are we *still* in a situation where people are saying 'We had airplanes, we had plastic surgery, we had surrogate births, we had genetic engineering, in 5000 BC we had atomic warfare, etc., etc.?'

AN: They have to say that. Why is the American Right saying that God created the world 4,000 years ago?

AV: Then what are you saying, that these arguments cannot be won?! That the right wing anywhere will always hold on to stupid, irrational claims?

AN: No, I do not think so. Rightist parties are not as foolish as they may seem. They have brought down mighty leftist empires, not always by the use of arms. China turned to capitalism without being coerced by external forces. They also have won crucial electoral battles not always by buying their votes or through false propaganda or media gimmicks. Nixon and Kissinger between them sealed America's relationship with China. Vajpayee and Nawaz Sharif, both rightists, came very close to doing something similar in the case of India and Pakistan. But they have to play to their constituency, even when they know they are saying something stupid. Never underestimate your enemies.

In any case, even if the Rightists are irrational and stupid, they do not have a monopoly in the matter of stupidity. Since the middle of the 19th the so-called Left, while fighting class-based inequalities, has consistently collaborated with new hierarchies based on race, culture and ideologies like progressivism. Do you think Frederick Engels was being very intelligent and rational when he wrote after the French conquest of Algeria that was a good thing to happen because Algeria would join civilization? What about the famous radical economist Joan Robinson's favourite formulation that the only thing worse than being colonized was not being colonized?

The arguments emerging from the intellectual riffraff of the 'Right' cannot be defeated if you try to cope with their emotions cognitively; you are reading symptoms as the illness, because ultimately you have nothing to offer as an alternative to them. Gandhi had; they had to kill him to keep him away from the nascent Indian state and then resurrect him in a safer form in their morning prayers.

AV: So would you say that through the various arguments that you had here, at the Centre for the Study of Developing Societies, in the 1980s and 1990s – do you feel that you were successful in creating a school of thought?

AN: No, perhaps not. But we sometimes came close to it. It was difficult to sustain a conversation with so many participants, over so many years.

But we did have certain common values and shared concerns. For instance, even those who were not involved in studies of alternatives and futures knew these were a crucial part of the Centre's research agenda. Similarly, serious quantitative empirical studies of political and social processes were valued by even those who did not do such studies.

AV: I'm thinking of PPST (Patriotic People's Science and Technology Group), Lokayan (a forum created by the Centre for the Study of Developing Societies activists, scholars and activist-scholars), Sunil Sahasrabudhey (an activist-scholar engaged peasant studies and peasant movements) and the Loka Vidya Abhiyaan (a movement concerned with the study and recovery of people's knowledge). . . . All of these movements were/are within the ambit of what you would call 'the politics of knowledge', movements around science and technology studies, around arts and handicrafts, artisan communities, tribal knowledge, local knowledge, what D.R. Nagaraj called 'technological communities', little traditions and so on – even these have died a terrible death with globalization. . . . No? And this has occurred within our lifetime. So, is there a place in the academy which can preserve some of those radical energies, or is it that capitalism is making it impossible anywhere?

AN: Society has a way of throwing up new forms of human ingenuity which can sustain dissent. Capitalism did try to break the trade union movement – look at what Margaret Thatcher did in England. In India, the same task was begun by Indira Gandhi and the Shiv Sena when they crushed the railway strike and Datta Samant's textile mill workers' strike at Bombay. Bombay was famous for its trade unions, so was Calcutta. They are now shadows of their old selves. But now so many NGOs have come forward to fill that vacuum. It used to be said during the colonial times that wherever colonialism went, syphilis went with it. Now my activist friend Fred Chiu (also known as Ah Fei) claims that nowadays wherever capital goes, NGOs go with it. It is not that easy to suppress dissent. Nature abhors a vacuum, physicists say...

AV: Venkat [Rao] has a very interesting theory that basically until we completely change our understating of what caste is, what *jatis* are, we can't proceed in our knowledge.

AN: He has a point. Everybody confuses caste with the caste system and then fixates on the hierarchical nature of that system. But many communities are also castes – look at the Manganiyars. They are a community, they are a caste, they are Muslims, they follow their traditional vocation, and they live by their music. They used to live in poverty, but they have been 'discovered', so to speak, and now they have a huge international fan following. They too are a 'caste', at least they themselves claim so.

AV: Venkat Rao says that the *jati* is a repository of memory; it's a mnemonic entity of some sort...

AN: That probably is true.

AV: He says *jatis* are 'lively archives', they are bodily embodiments of knowledge traditions and individual members of the *jatis* make, preserve and transmit knowledge.

According to Venkat [Rao], until you completely discard the idea of the caste system as being about social hierarchy, and replace it with an understanding of *jati* as the carrier of cultural memory – which is a completely different model – you can't make sense of Indian society.

AN: Maybe, but that point has to be pushed harder research-wise.

AV: He says: How you are going to record anything if your culture is 'alithic'? – It is basically not a culture of writing, so it's all recorded in the body itself, in the memory and the mind.

AN: In the mind, yes, people don't forget these things. A different black history of America has come down to us through the memories of the black people. That history is not as hilariously funny as the Hindu nationalist history. Hence it is taken more seriously. That is why I have tried my hand in a serious critique of the political status of history as a discipline in the Southern hemisphere.

AV: That's what Venkat is saying; let's displace the text from the centre of our culture...

AN: We should be grateful to him for that. That's not so easy in a predominantly Brahmanical culture, which values text, writing and literacy so highly. I have an essay called Memory Work which has been inspired by Venkat's work. Freud introduced the concept of 'dream work'; 'Memory Work' argues for an extension of the scope of the idea to shared memories.

GLOSSARY

Aaapatasahaaya   Help in need
Aadhyatma   Concerning human happiness; a 'spiritual' tradition; experiential search for enduring happiness
Aapat   A calamity, misfortune, danger, distress, adversity
Aapatsahaaya   Help in need
Aaptah (or *aapta*)   Intimate, respected, confidential
Aaptasahaaya   Helping a friend in need
Aavashyaka   Necessity, inevitable, indispensable
Aavashyakata   Necessity, obligation, certainty
Abhilaasha   Desire
Adhana   Pauper
Adhyasa   When experience is covered over and misidentified with what it is not
Aadhyatma   Concerning human happiness; a 'spiritual' tradition; experiential search for enduring happiness
Advaita   Non-dualism (of Vedanta)
Apeksha   Looking for, expectation, hope, need, requirement
Altertumswissenschaft   The science of antiquity, particularly with reference to the systematic study of ancient Greek and Rome
Ananda   The 'eternal happiness' – the goal of *aadhyatma*
Anubhaava   Experience of eternal happiness; literally it means in accord with what is/happens.
Ari   Enemy, hostile
Atman   Traditionally (and misleadingly) translated as self or soul. The concept designates the real (contrasted with what exists).
Avashya   Inevitable, indispensable, necessary
Avashyam   Surely, of course
Avidya   Ignorance
Baamapanthi/vaamapanthi   Left-wing
Bhakta   Seeker on the path of *aadhyatma*

GLOSSARY

Bhakti   A path for seeking *aadhyatma*
Bhasha   Language
Bhashyakara   Commentator, interpreter, writer of a commentary of a root text
*Bhuta*s   Phenomenal-perceptual resources
Bildung   Education, self- formation
Chashach   Need
Chashchah   Things needed
Chaschu   Requirement
Chreia   Need
Daridra   Poor, needy, deprived of, a beggar
Dharma   The ethical order that sustains all activities
Dina   Afflicted
Echochreian   Having the need
Episteme   Scientific knowledge
Eudaimonia   Happiness, well-being or flourishing
Gamaka   A reflective-performative tradition from Karnataka involving a combination of singing, storytelling, reconstruction and interpretation. The poems sung are generally drawn from old Kannada epics.
Icchaa   Desire
Iihaa   Desire
Itihasa   Used as an Indian term for history, it means 'thus indeed it was'.
Jan-jatis   Biocultural formations called 'tribes'
Jasvan   Needy, hungry
Jati   Indian word for 'caste'
Kaala   A period or an epoch; a time-slice
Kaama   Desire
Kaanksha   Desire
Kala   Patterns of visual, graphic and performative articulations
Karma sanchita   Actional endowments
Kathera   A needy or distressed man, pauper
Kshudraklripti   Arrangement of the minor requirements (of a sacrifice)
Kula   A synonym for a caste or a tribal community
Lipsaa   Desire
Maya   Refers to a structure that conceals the nature of the real
Machsor   Need
Maibi   Female guardian figure of ritual and memory of Meetei community of Manipur
Manana   Silent/meditative recall
Manoratha   Desire
Mimansakas   Philosopher in the Mimamsa school of philosophy (Vedic hermeneutics)

GLOSSARY

Mukti   Freedom from the self and subjective ends
Nadhita   Oppressed, needy, suppliant
Natyasastra   Foundational text on Dramaturgy attributed to Bharata, taken as the basis of the performing arts, especially dance and theatre, in the Sanskrit tradition
Nayee Talim   New Education (Training)
Nayyaayika   Philosopher in the Nyaya school of philosophy (logic/analytic philosophy)
Nirdhana   Pauper
Oikos   Household economy
Paddana   A song-performing tradition of Tulu region of Karnataka
Para   That other that inhabits inside and outside the body
Phawar   A song-performing tradition of the Khasis of Meghalaya
Phronesis   Practical wisdom or the knowledge of how to perform the right action in specific situations
Praani koti   Lively millions
Pradraanaka   Sorely distressed, very needy or poor
Prashasti   Eulogy, praise-poem; a poem in praise of a king
Purana   A genre of sacred text, with stories of deities, demons, kings and mythical beings
Raaga   Melodic mode in Indian music
Riyaz   Practice
Sahaaya   Help
Samkashta   Distress, trouble, need
Samkashta Chaturthi   Fourth day after the full moon of the Hindu lunar calendar when ritual to destroy distress is held
Samkashta Chaturthi Katha   Story told during *Samkashta Chaturthi (see above)*
Samkashtahara Caturthi vrata   Ritual to destroy distress
Samkashta naashana ganapatistotra   Hymns of Ganapati to defeat distress
Samkashtanaashana stotra   Hymn to defeat distress
Satyagraha   The act of firm grasping of truth and dwelling in it
Satyagrahi   The one who practices Satyagraha
Shravana   Listening
Sastra-vangmaya   Compositions of the verbal universe
Shantam, Shivam, Advaitam   Peace, 'that which is not', Oneness
Shat-sthala   Six distinct progressive levels/states in the search for happiness
Shilpasastra   The science of building
Shunya   Experience of eternal happiness; synonym for 'ananda'
Sthapati   Temple-builder; a caste of temple builders and architects
Swaraj   Self-rule/self-governance

GLOSSARY

Talamaddale A traditional form of recitation/debate using stories from the Kavyas and *Puranas*; a reflective-performative art form involving Taala (cymbal) and Maddale (drums). It combines storytelling, music, discourse, discussion and debate. It is found in the coastal regions of Karnataka.

Tattva Verbal visual inquiry into that other that inhabits the body

Techne The knowledge of how to make

Teyyam A ritual-performance tradition of north Malabar region of Kerala

Upachchanda Anything necessary or needful, a requisite

Upadhi Translated variously as 'limitation', 'adjunct' or 'imposition'; support

Upanishads The last parts of the *Vedas*, embodying their highest purpose

Vaasana Latent tendencies/desires that the senses get drawn into

Vachana Pithy reflective-imaginative compositions/utterances associated with the 'saint-poets' of Karnataka from 11th to late 19th centuries

Varga Group

Vaasana Latent tendencies/desires that the senses get drawn into

Vidya Forms of verbal-acoustic learning

Virashaiva Also known as Lingayat(a) is a 'caste community' found mainly in today's Karnataka.

Vivarta Internal mutation

Vyasana Evil predicament or plight, disaster, accident, evil result, calamity, misfortune

Vyasanaani Ill-luck, distress, destruction, defeat, fall, ruin

Vyasanakaala Time of need

Wissenschaft Any form of systematic study (Science), including the natural sciences, humanities, arts, religion and philosophy

Yaavadartha As many as necessary, corresponding to requirement

Yakshagaana A traditional art form similar to *Taalamaddale* but with costumes, dance and stage conventions. The theatrical form is found mainly in the coastal regions of Karnataka and involves a unique form of storytelling (often episodes from ancient epics) and their interpretation.

Yathaa yogam As is fit, according to circumstances, according to requirements

Yathaa yogena As is fit, according to circumstances, according to requirements

Yugadharma The *dharma* that is proper to an age; the salient normative order in a particular age or era

INDEX

Note: Italic numbers indicate figures.

adhyatma: happiness and 149, 163; reflection on 87, 90; relation to jati 165–166, 168, 170; relation to past 81–82
Achilles 179–181, 183, 185
action: actional frame 92n10, 93n16; contextual action 87–89; Gandhian action 41–46, 58, 60, 62, 66, 68, 75; right action 44; reflection on action 42; theoretical, practical action 31–38
action-theoretic 89, 93n18
Alexander III of Macedon 19, 189, 197–198, 201
Ambedkar, B.R. 123, 125, 128, 130, 141, 144n12, 145n31
anubhaava 163, 172n17
Appadurai, Arjun 57–58, 69, 70n1
Arendt, Hannah 134
Aristotle 183, 191, 197
attachment 251, 263–265
Avebury, Eric, Lord 122, 126, 143n4, 144n15

background 1, 6–8, 10, 24
Balagangadhara, S.N. 10, 13; on colonial consciousness 128–129; on cultural difference 20–22, 95, 118, 124; on happiness 163–165, 170, 172n18, 172n19; on Orientalism 131–132, 135, 138, 140–141, 144n27, 144n28, 149–150, 154, 157, 159

Bayly, Susan 129, 136–137, 139, 142, 145n29
beliefs 33, 36–37, 43
Bernier, Francois 104–106
Bhakti 150–151, 152, 157–158, 167, 169
Bhatt, Chetan 130–131
Bible, the 236–239, 248, 251–252, 267
Bildung 27, 31–34, 40, 46, 48n10
biocultural 207–208, 211–212, 214, 219, 221–225
Brahmanism 128–130, 132, 135–138, 141
Brahmin 131; anti- 141–142, 150; 'ideology' 211–212, 21; polemics 158–159, 162, 168, 171, 173, 208; as priests 136–138

CARE 121
caste 14, 16–18, 108, 111–112; debates on 63–66, 69–70; groups 268–270; as 'system' 117–173; *see also* cultural formations, jati
categorical imperative 32
category habit 31, 47, 48n9
Catholics 145n29
Census 122, 139
Christian 13, 15; caste reservations in India 119–120; theology 16–17, 21, 251–252, 255, 267–268; tradition 155–157; 122–124; tribals 122; *see also* caste, Dalits

INDEX

Christianity 16, 155, 157, 234, 255, 266–267; Aryan invasion and 128–129; as Aryan religion 138; conversion to 128, 136; converts to 136; Indian religion and 120, 128–129, 136–137, 142, 145n29; Orientalism and 135–136, 142–143; *see also* proselytism
civilizing mission 62–63
Claerhout, Sarah 137
classical music 274–276, 283
classical tradition 279, 282, 286–287
cluster 210, 214–216, 219–226, 228n19
colonial consciousness 118, 128–132, 140, 145n31
colonial discourse 95–97, 104–105, 114n5
colonialism 129, 138–140, 149, 205, 207–208, 226
colonial scholarship 96–97
communalism 95–98; Manshardt and 100–102; McPherson and 98–100; Hindu communalism 107–108, 111; Muslim communalism 107, 110–111; as a problem of religious antagonism 96–97, 102, 104, 106
concept of education 27, 31
conscience 31, 34, 36
constellation 209–210, 212–213, 215–216, 219, 221–226, 228n19
Corbyn, Jeremy, MP 123
creaming off 74, 75
critical humanities 8, 10–12, 20, 23–24, 69, 206, 216–219, 220–226
cultural difference 38, 49n26
cultural formations 207–209, 211–214, 216–219, 221–225, 228n19; *see also* jati
cultural forms 205, 207–210, 216, 218–219, 222, 224–225, 228n19
cultural learning 72–73, 75–77, 79–80, 86–87, 89–91

Dalits 120, 122–123, 141, 143n7, 144n26

Davis, Donald R. 133–135, 137–138, 142, 144n24
De Roover, Jakob 137, 144n22
Deben, Lord 122–124, 128, 143n8, 144n14
Derde, Willem 130, 141
Derrida, Jacques: on humanities 9–10; 14, 18, 22, 24, 47n2, 92n11, 205, 211, 231n25; on justice 6–7; on legacy 2–4
Desire 248, 250–253 264–265, 267, 271
desires 234, 248–255, 257, 262, 264–268
dharmashastra 134, 141–142, 144n25
Dholakia, Navnit, Lord 126
Dilthey, Wilhelm 61
Dirks, Nicholas 117, 129, 136, 139–142, 145n29
disciplinarity 57–59, 67
discipline 57–58, 61, 66–67, 69
diversity 57–59, 66, 69
Dow, Alexander 105

education 13–16, 205–207, 212, 215–216, 218–219, 225–226, 230n23
endogamy 125
enlightenment 166, 172n17
Equality Act 2010 (UK) 117, 118–128, 135, 143n10
Equality and Human Rights Commission (UK) 119
erotics 89
ethical 27, 38, 41, 43–46, 51n33
eudaimonia 32
Europe 1, 3–4, 8–9, 16, 34–35, 38, 46, 62, 85, 96–97, 99–100, 102–103, 107, 113, 135–137, 205, 208, 212, 215, 241
European accounts 77, 84–85, 138–139, 141, 155, 159, 162, 211–212; categories 28–29; encounter 34–35, 37; episteme 8–9, 15–17, 62–63; experience 102–104, 130, 133, 135–136, 217–218; legacy 1–5, 11–13, 19–24, 221

INDEX

European Union Race Directive 121, 143n2
experience 2, 4, 10–11, 15; affective-praxial- 2; colonial/Western 102–103, 110, 113, 129–130, 132, 136, 156, 166, 184, 187, 205, 241, 263, 265, 271; distortion of 28–30, 72–76, 90, 72–76, 80–91, 93n15, 95, 97; human 21–23; learning and 15, 29, 75; lived 28; reflection on 15, 38, 45, 82–84, 86–87, 90, 130; of the South (non-European) 10–11

Flather, Shreela, Baroness 127
form of life 32, 42, 50n28
freedom 32, 34, 37, 45

Gadamer, Hans-Georg 69
Gandhi, Mohandas K. 65, 69, 129–130, 140–141
Ganga 19, 177, 198, 201
Ganges 19, 197–201; *199*
Gelders, Raf 129–130, 135, 141, 144n28
genos 8–9; hetero- 20
greed 233–235, 238, 248–249, 251, 257, 271
Greek culture 2, 4, 179–181, 187
Green, Kate, MP 125–126
group solidarity 107–108

Habermas, Jürgen 61
Hamilton, Alexander 104, 106
happiness 109, 114n16, 251, 253–257, 259–262, 266; (un-) 243, 250, 252–254, 256, 259, 271
Harries, Richard, Lord 121–123, 126, 143n3, 143n4, 143n8, 144n15
Hegel, G.W.F. 61
Herodotus 184, 189
Hindu Forum of Britain 121–122
Hindu law 133–134, 137
Hinduism: caste and 127, 140–141; as Brahmanism 150–151; as false religion 35–36, 129, 134; Orientalist account of 82–85, 88, 92n12; Protestant accounts of 135–137, 141, 145n29; as (tribal) religion 108–113, 129, 133–137
Hindu–Muslim antagonism 98, 104–106, 114n8
Hindu–Muslim relations 101, 112, 114n7
Hindus 98, 101–102, 104–105, 111, 113, 128, 132–134, 138; 150, 151, 171n13, 274; caste and 132, 134, 145n29
history 2, 10–11, 15; discourse of 33–35, 44, 64, 73, 99, 102, 106, 113, 117, 121, 132, 135, 139–140, 142, 177, 187, 190, 197, 205, 208, 214–215, 227, 230n23, 241, 248, 252, 274, 278, 288, 290; philosophy and 15, 73, 76, 90–91; reflection on 64; in relation to past 76–82, 90–91, 92n4, 92n5
Holy See 120
home 73–74, 90–91
Homer 179–180, 183–84, 191, 202n1
human: conception of 21–22, 243, 247; cultivation of 32–34, 44–45, 48n14; discourse of 65, 67, 72–73, 84, 88, 91, 119, 126, 128, 130; experience 21, 134, 263, 267; happiness 259–268, 271–272, 289; idea of 3–4, 6, 9–15, 18–22, 132–134, 162–165, 177–78; nature 22, 32, 233, 238, 251, 253; non- 11, 177; possibilities 14, 32; psychology 233–236, 238–257
humanities: concept of 29, 33; critical 8–15, 20, 22–24, 95, 206, 215–226; discipline of 66–67, 69–70, 72, 76, 95, 149, 207, 210–212; education 57, 59, 61, 205–207; European 1–4; new 69
Humboldt, Wilhelm von 59–60
hypothesis 157–165, 169

ideology 211–212
ignorance 243, 256–259
improvisation 213–214
Inden, Ronald 129, 133, 137, 139–140, 144n21

INDEX

Indian context 12–13, 15, 17, 19–22, 34, 58–59, 64, 66, 68, 106–108, 143, 171n9, 206, 209, 215–217, 224, 62–68, 72–76; culture 117–123, 126–133, 155–161, 162–165, 169–173, 206–209, 212–217, 223–224, 233–234, 242–244, 246–253, 255–261, 263–268, 270–272, 274, 276–277, 281–282, 284–286, 289–290; past 78–87, 89–90; problem 95–104, 111–113; students 36–40, 45–46, 50, 57–59; thought 16, 73, 81–82, 85–87, 89–90; traditions 15, 21, 40, 45, 72–73, 82–83, 85–87, 89, 92n10, 92n11, 131, 135–143, 149–150, 156–160, 163–165, 169, 247, 250–253, 255–258, 260, 262, 264–266, 277, 281, 285; universities 14, 57, 59, 63–64, 67, 142
Indian culture 242–244, 247, 249, 252, 259–261, 263, 265, 268, 272
Indian legal system Constitution (Scheduled Castes) Order 1950 119–120
Indian traditions 149–150, 156–160, 163–165, 159, 247, 250–253, 255–258, 260, 262, 264–266; *see also* Lingayat tradition
in-discipline 57, 66–70
Indology 208, 211, 218
interest group 113
interests 102, 108–113
International Dalit Solidarity Network (IDSN) 122

jan-jatis 210, 213–216, 218, 221, 225–226, 227n3, 228n19; *see also* cultural formations
jati: *aadhyatma* and 165–169; as cultural formations 209–223; difference 157–159, 206, 207–208; a minor issue 162–169, 171n11; *see also* caste, cultural formations
Jews 122, 137, 145n30
Judaism 129

kala 213, 216, 218–219, 229n21, 229n22, 230n24
Kannada 152–153, 155, 159, 165
Kant, Immanuel 60–61
kavyas 77, 83, 89
Keane, David 142
Keppens, Marianne 138
Kothari, D.S. 63, 65
kshatriyas 138
kula 154, 164–167, 169

legacy 1–2, 12–13, 15, 20, 24
Lester, Anthony, Lord 121, 126
liberal education 26–27, 35–36, 41
liberty 64, 68
Lingayat tradition 150–152, 154–160, 162–163, 165–170, 172n18, 172n22; Vachana 150, 165
lively archive 209–210, 213–215, 219, 221, 223, 225
living tradition 276–279, 283–287
Lubin, Timothy 134, 137, 144n24, 144n28
Luther, Martin 137

Manshardt, Clifford 100–103, 105, 112
marriage 119, 125, 128, 144n12
Marx, Karl 137
maya 82, 86–87, 89–90
McPherson, Hugh 98–103, 105
memory: accents of 208–212; articulations of 208–210; loss of 3–4; repository 290–291; work of 282–283
Menski, Werner F. 143n8, 144n25, 145n32
Mill, James 132–135, 142
mnemocultures 208–212, 219, 221, 223, 228; mnemoscapes 2; mnemopraxial 8–9; *see also* jati, kala, lively archives, memory, vidya
moral agent 27, 33, 48n14
Muslims 121, 123–124

Nagaraj, D.R. 286–287, 289
Nayee Talim 41, 43, 45–46; as nai Talim 65

INDEX

Nandy, Ashis 13, 22–23, 28
National Council for Hindu Temples (UK) 143n7
National Secular Society (UK) 120
needs: in the Bible 236–239, 248, 266–267; deficiency 234; desire and 248–249, 251–254, 262, 266, 271; Indian culture and 244–247; 249, 271–272; Maslow and 234–236, 238; social security system and 241–243, 262
Nepal 120, 123–125
new politics of truth 68–69
normative 27, 29, 32, 34, 36, 41–43, 50n31
normative ethics 127–128, 144n22

Oceanus 179, *181*, 183–184, *185*, *186*, 195, 202n1
Oddie, Geoffrey 125, 136
Orientalism 118, 128, 131–133, 135–136, 140, 142–143, 144n28, 149, 157; Area Studies as 133

pain 262–266
parasitism 73–76, 79, 86–89
past 73, 76–81, 87, 89–91, 92n4, 92n5
pedagogy 206
performative 210–211, 213, 216, 219–221, 225, 228n19, 229n22
Periyar 141, 145n31
phantasy 88–89
philosophy 73, 76, 78–79, 81–84, 86–87, 90–91, 92n11
Plato 4, 191
polemics 159–162, 169, 171n13
politics of knowledge 275–276, 278–279, 283, 285–286, 289
postcolonial approach 26, 28–30; condition 62–63; destitution 130, 217–218
practical knowledge 42, 50n28
practice 31–36, 38, 41–47, 49n22, 51n32
practitional matrix 87–90, 93n18
proselytism 118, 120, 122, 124, 136, 142
proselytization 108–109, 113

Protestants 129, 137
puranas 77, 165, 198, 213, 219, 279

Radhakrishnan, Sarvepalli 63, 65, 129, 140
rain terrain 19, 178, 195–197, 201
real estate 73–75, 88, 90
reason 27, 29–30, 32–36, 39, 42, 44–45, 48n14
reform 101, 106–107, 109
religion: eradication of 16, 106; false 35–36, 109, 120, 129, 134, 137, 139; form of 151, 156; history of 35, 135; idea of 5–7, 10, 14, 16–17, 33–38, 82–85, 92, 105–113, 119–124, 128–129, 132–139, 141–142, 144n27, 151, 155–156, 161, 171n6, 228n19, 234, 247, 254, 261, 266–267, 269, 274, 295
religious antagonism 96–97, 99, 103
Risley, Herbert 139
river literacy 201
Roy, Arundhati 128, 141

Said, Edward 118, 133
salvation 109, 114n15, 114n16
Sanskrit: 'ideology' 211–212; knowledge 207–209; as sacred language 138–139; translation 244–248; writing 214–215, 217–218
satyagraha 89
secularism 16, 62, 106–107, 247
secularization 32–33, 48, 118, 266
self: autonomy of 48n13, 48n14, 50n30, 51n32; cultivation of 27–28, 31–34, 36, 40, 43; as practice 45–46
Sen, Ronojoy 120
Sharma, Alok, MP 144n16, 144n17
Shils, Edward 63–64
Shourie, Arun 120, 141
shunya 163, 172n17
Singh, Indarjit, Lord 127
sites of learning 89, 91, 93n17
Smith, W.C. 98, 106–107, 109–113
social justice 65–66, 227n3, 235, 271

300

INDEX

social security system 235; of India 259–262, 268, 272; of the West 239–244

State 2, 21–23, 28, 35, 58, 60, 64, 66, 75, 82, 88, 99, 102–103, 107, 114n16, 123, 141, 154, 206, 217, 221, 224, 231n26, 233, 239–243, 246, 247, 252, 262, 268–272, 280

structures of ethical formation 27

suffering 22, 25, 235, 262–263, 265–266, 272, 278

techne 44
techno-scientific paradigm 59
temporality 263–264
Testaments, the Old and New 236–237, 248; *see also* Bible
textualization 36
theological model 31, 33, 36
theology 77, 80–84, 91
time 245, 263–264
toleration 97–98, 103–107
tradition of activity 44
translation 73, 82–86, 89–90
truth 31, 33–37, 39, 41, 45, 47, 49n27

United Nations 122; Conference Against Racism 120
United States 117–118, 121, 129

university: disciplines of 217–221, 224; as European 1–4; humanistic 8–11; idea of 37, 39–40; indiscipline of 14–15, 22; outside of 46–47; postcolonial 57–71, 211, 214–215, 279–280, 283
untouchables 138, 143n3
upadhi 73, 82, 86, 89, 91

Vachana: jati and 150, 154, 157–159, 161–169; modern interpretation of 151–157
values 32
varna 127, 138, 145n29
Venkat Rao, D. 128, 130, 143, 145n31
vidya 213, 216, 218–219, 229n21, 229n22
Virashaiva movement 152–153

Waughray, Annapurna 117, 121, 125, 128, 144n23, 145n32
West 234, 239, 241, 243, 248, 252; savants of the 259–260, 262, 266, 268, 269, 271, 272
Western culture 239, 247, 254, 262, 268–269
will 31–34, 45, 48n14
wissenschaft 46
Wolpert, Stanley 142
world religion 107–111

Young, Robert 61